LEARNING ONE'S NATIVE TONGUE

LEARNING ONE'S NATIVE TONGUE

Citizenship, Contestation, and Conflict in America

TRACY B. STRONG

THE UNIVERSITY OF CHICAGO PRESS | CHICAGO AND LONDON

The University of Chicago Press, Chicago 60637
The University of Chicago Press, Ltd., London
© 2019 by The University of Chicago
Published 2019
Printed in the United States of America

28 27 26 25 24 23 22 21 20 19   1 2 3 4 5

ISBN-13: 978-0-226-62319-1 (cloth)
ISBN-13: 978-0-226-62322-1 (paper)
ISBN-13: 978-0-226-62336-8 (e-book)
DOI: https://doi.org/10.7208/chicago/9780226623368.001.0001

Library of Congress Cataloging-in-Publication Data

Names: Strong, Tracy B., author.
Title: Learning one's native tongue : citizenship, contestation, and conflict in America /
    Tracy B. Strong.
Description: Chicago : The University of Chicago Press, 2019. | Includes index.
Identifiers: LCCN 2019016598 | ISBN 9780226623221 (paperback) | ISBN 9780226623191
    (cloth) | ISBN 9780226623368 (ebook)
Subjects: LCSH: Citizenship—United States—History. | Citizenship—Political aspects—
    United States.
Classification: LCC JK1759 .S87 2019 | DDC 323.60973—dc23
LC record available at https://lccn.loc.gov/2019016598

♾ This paper meets the requirements of ANSI/NISO Z39.48-1992
(Permanence of Paper).

In memoriam, Charles E. Nathanson,
American great spirit and good friend

For, dear me, why abandon a belief
Merely because it ceases to be true.
Cling to it long enough, and not a doubt
It will turn true again, for so it goes.
Most of the change we think we see in life
Is due to truths being in and out of favor.
... Oftentimes, I wish ...
I could devote and dedicate forever
To the truths we keep coming back and back to.
ROBERT FROST, "THE BLACK COTTAGE"

CONTENTS

ACKNOWLEDGMENTS

This book has been long in the making. I come to it as an American who spent most of his childhood and adolescence in other countries—first the Far East, then Europe. But I also come to it as a white Anglo-Saxon whose family was always quietly though never ostentatiously conscious of an American ancestry extending back to the early seventeenth century and before that to minor and major English aristocracy (or so some of my ancestors liked to believe). I have thus sought to come to grips with my country without ever actually having "grown up" in it. I am thus perhaps differently conscious of its promises and its failures than someone whose formative years were concretely in this land. I write this book in the period following the election of Donald Trump as president—and do so with a sense of the dangers of loss.

Over the years, I have taught versions of this book. Its origins come from a sudden decision between Steven Hahn, Charles Nathanson, and myself, all of us then in different departments at the University of California, San Diego. Fueled no doubt by a little too much spirit, we agreed that the university needed a course on this topic and eight weeks later found ourselves teaching it. What follows in this book owes much to those friends and that original course, as well as to the contributions in a subsequent year of Professor Rachel Klein. Subsequently, I have taught the entire material by myself. Steven is now at the University of Pennsylvania; Chuck passed away in 2003—I mourn him and dedicate this book to his memory.

Most of my debts will appear in the footnotes to this book. Aside from those mentioned above, I might note in particular the work of Alex Gourevitch, Alexander Keyssar, Maurice Isserman, Leon Fink, Rogers Smith, Peter Irons, Todd Gitlin, Michael Schudson, Sherry Turkle, and James Miller. Wilson Carey McWilliams's *The Idea of Fraternity in America* has informed me since before it was written. I should also acknowledge the presence of two voices who have helped me up several stairs: Stanley Cavell and George Kateb.

An earlier version of a portion of chapter 9 has appeared in "The Social and Political Construction of the Cold War," in *American Foreign Policy: Studies in Intellectual History*, ed. Jean-François Drolet and James Dunkerley (Manchester: Manchester University Press, 2017).

I am grateful to the librarians at the Houghton Library (Harvard University), the John Carter Brown Library (Brown University), the Suzzallo Library (University of Washington), and the Butler Library (Columbia University) for permission to consult and use archival material deposited there. I thank Lori Meek Schuldt for her careful and intelligent assistance during the production process.

I am also in particular debt to the Leverhulme Trust of Great Britain for awarding me a fellowship in 2016 that permitted me to take a year from teaching duties and write this book.

I thank my students in the courses where this material has been taught. I began teaching these themes at the University of California, San Diego, an extraordinary institution still at that time in the process of making and finding itself. I teach now at the University of Southampton in the United Kingdom—a new and receptive dwelling place. My thanks in England go especially to David Owen.

INTRODUCTION

In America, men are born equal so they do not have to become so.

ALEXIS DE TOCQUEVILLE, *DEMOCRACY IN AMERICA*

In Plato's account, Socrates opens his defense at his trial for corrupting the youth and not believing in the gods of the polity in the following manner:

> How you, men of Athens, have been affected by my accusers, I do not know; but I, for my part, almost forgot my own identity, so persuasively did they talk; and yet there is hardly a word of truth in what they have said. But I was most amazed by one of the many lies that they told—when they said that you must be on your guard not to be deceived by me.

I begin with this citation because the questions I raise in this book are as old as our sense of the issues raised by membership in a polity. Socrates starts his defense by expressing his distress that a false understanding of his membership as an Athenian has almost made him lose his own sense of his identity as an Athenian.[1] Who or what he is, as he reasserts through the *Apology* and, wondrously, even after his condemnation, in the *Crito*, *is* a citizen of Athens. What it means to be an actual citizen of Athens has, however, apparently been

---

1. Plato, *Apology* 17a, in *Euthyphro, Apology, Crito, Phaedo*, trans. Harold F. North (Cambridge, MA: Harvard University Press, 1966). The original Greek reads: ὅτι μὲν ὑμεῖς, ὦ ἄνδρες Ἀθηναῖοι, πεπόνθατε ὑπὸ τῶν ἐμῶν κατηγόρων, οὐκ οἶδα: ἐγὼ δ᾽ οὖν καὶαὐτὸς ὑπ᾽ αὐτῶν ὀλίγου ἐμαυτοῦ ἐπελαθόμην, οὕτω πιθανῶς ἔλεγον. καίτοι ἀληθές γε ὡς ἔποςεἰπεῖν οὐδὲν εἰρήκασιν. μάλιστα δὲ αὐτῶν ἓν ἐθαύμασα τῶν πολλῶν ὧν ἐψεύσαντο, τοῦτο ἐν ᾧἔλεγον ὡς χρῆν ὑμᾶς εὐλαβεῖσθαι μὴ ὑπ᾽ ἐμοῦ ἐξαπατηθῆτε.

lost by a substantial number of Athenians—though not by all, as he assures them and us that were only thirty to have voted differently, he would have been acquitted and that had he had more than the allotted hour, he very likely would have convinced them to do so. The question of what being a true/authentic/actual citizen is, is constantly up for dispute and negotiation. Being a citizen is a *political* matter, Socrates teaches us—hence always the subject of controversy and dispute. If it is a political matter, it is also an individual one: for one to be a citizen, in the strongest sense of the term, the criteria of citizenry (whatever they may be) must be incarnate—part of what or who one is: the more substantive they are, the more they will be manifest in each of one's actions. The more abstract they are (and we shall see a growing process of becoming abstract over the course of this book), then the demands of citizenship shrink to lesser significance.[2]

Our situation—as it appears to me—is not that different from that of Socrates. The underlying claim in this book is that one should or can cast the question of citizenship of Americans not as a "right" (though it is that) but politically. This means that I understand the question of being or becoming a citizen as requiring that individuals can successfully and publicly claim to meet certain criteria that are taken to define (at that time, at that place, for this particular set of reasons) what "being a citizen" entails and requires, and that they have that claim acknowledged. Being a citizen thus entails more than simply suffrage, although it most often does entail that. Obviously, then, these criteria change over time in and as response to historical developments; as important, they are thus always the subject matter for political controversy and conflict. (One has only to think of voting rights for women or for blacks in America). I examine these conflicts and the ensuing changes in the conception of citizenship and perforce pay attention to what difference each change makes and what each particular "winning" conception entails socially and politically. As the criteria change, some qualities are lost, others are gained. The nature and value of these losses and gains are the subject of this book.

Being a citizen thus involves or has involved over time multiple criteria: some are civil, some are legal, some, like voting, are more narrowly political. There are two broad kinds of criteria: *natural* and *acquired*. The first set, one might say, are deemed simply "natural" at a particular time and do not de-

---

2. For two differing views on the relation of such thoughts to Hobbes, see George Kateb, "Hobbes and the Irrationality of Politics," *Political Theory* 17, no. 3 (August 1989): 355–91, and Paul Downes, *Hobbes, Sovereignty and Early American Literature* (Cambridge: Cambridge University Press, 2015), chap. 3.

pend on individual action but are perforce collective in that they characterize a group. Thus, in America, to be a voting citizen until 1920 generally required that one be male. To have the civil rights of citizenship, whether or not this included suffrage, was in most of the country not possible for blacks—because they were blacks—until sometime in the late 1860s and in much of the country not until one hundred years later. A second set of criteria is rather consequent to the *manifestation of "acquired"* qualities. These "acquired" qualities require individual effort and will. They are the stuff of choice and action. Thus, as we shall see, in Puritan New England, becoming a church member was a prerequisite for suffrage and most civil rights.

The relevance of the natural criteria changes only with considerable difficulty and of a necessity collectively—America fought a civil war in relation to one such change. Acquired qualities, however, are or can be the result of individual choice and action. One can choose to behave in such a manner that one passes the test for church membership or economic independence, being "one's own man." The desired acquired qualities are also modified in relation to changes in the economic, social, and political climate. Thus, when the population comes to include a large number of self-sufficient but nonlandowning artisans, a powerful argument can be and was made to expand the criteria beyond ownership of property. It thus turns out, of course, that no criteria are permanently "natural"—all are subject to contestation and change.

Most of these considerations are not part of usual understandings. This book is written against, or rather in counterpoint to, a number of standard interpretations of American history. I want briefly to set them out here; each of them should receive much more explicit attention, as each has been the subject of extensive analysis and discussion. I do not here provide more than a touchstone sketch.

SOME STANDARD UNDERSTANDINGS

A still dominant understanding of American citizenship is that broadly associated with the "liberal tradition" and the work of Louis Hartz.[3] According to this view, American conceptions of citizenship were centrally shaped by the fact that the country was founded by a "social and political fragment"—a middle class, more or less of the gentry, who did not, in the new country, have to deal on the one hand with aristocrats and on the other with peasants. (That

3. Louis Hartz, *The Liberal Tradition in America* (New York: Harcourt Brace, 1955).

this view remains powerful can be seen from the fact that it is pretty much repeated unchanged in Henry Kissinger's recent *On China*). Hence, this argument goes, liberty was always central to the American experience, and class conflict was supposedly not an integral part of that experience. It followed that these origins were the reason that there had apparently not been an important socialist or working-class movement in the country. This last question was in fact explicitly raised at the beginning of the twentieth century by the great German sociologist Werner Sombart: "Why is there no socialism in America?"[4] For those holding this understanding of American history, the American conception of citizenship is seen as resting on the principle of individual liberty sharpened by a great distress for any unrepresented dependency. It is, one might say, a core-periphery model, where the core is a version of Lockean liberalism and the peripheries are the locus of all that which is not "really" American.[5] In this model, the Revolutionary War is essentially a war to be rid of the supposed tyranny of George III. Furthermore, this model ties painlessly into the emergence of industrial capitalism in the latter part of the nineteenth century: capitalism tends easily, or can be seen, to become the combination of a preexisting liberty and the marketplace.

There is truth to this. The view, however, has always had initial difficulties: it cannot deal adequately with the South, nor the legacy of Puritanism. Freedom and equality tend to be seen as substantially overlapping. It is not an accident that Tocqueville,[6] often incorrectly taken to be a forerunner of the Hartz thesis, starts *Democracy in America* with a discussion of the Puritans, nor that Nathaniel Hawthorne spends the entirety of *The Scarlet Letter* exploring the consequences of the legacy of Puritanism for nineteenth-century America. Tellingly, the first edition of Hartz's *The Liberal Tradition in America* has as epigraph a quote supposedly from Tocqueville—"In America, men were born free and did not have to become so"—which is corrected with an erratum slip in the second edition to what Tocqueville actually wrote: "In America, men were born *equal* and did not have to become so." Equality—at least for an important range of those in America—was presumed from the start—freedom was what had to be obtained and retained.

4. Werner Sombart, *Why Is There No Socialism in America?* (London: Palgrave Mac-Millan, 1976), esp. 15-24.

5. The work of Richard Hofstadter, *The Paranoid Style in American Politics* (1965; repr., New York: Random House, 2008), and Seymour Martin Lipset, *Political Man: The Social Bases of Politics* (New York: Doubleday, 1960), are only two prominent examples.

6. Alexis de Tocqueville, *Democracy in America*, trans. Arthur Goldhammer (New York: Library of America, 2016).

Furthermore, the approach has trouble accounting for the fact that especially the post–Civil War period in the United States was one of great turmoil, resistance, and utopian movements. As even so mainstream a scholar as Robert Dahl once wrote (albeit in a tone of surprise) that American history is among the most violent of Western histories.[7] After all, before 1912, three times as many American presidents (Lincoln, Garfield, and McKinley) were assassinated than were czars in Russia, and barely failing attempts were made on three others (Jackson, Taft, and Theodore Roosevelt). Over the post-1912 period, one counts at least twelve attempts and one success: Kennedy). I share with Rogers Smith's book on "civic ideals" the sense of the limits of the Hartz thesis; I focus more on the contestation of the criteria for citizenship than does he, thereby seeing similarities between models he sees as opposed.[8]

A second model, less in favor now especially after America's post–World War II foreign adventures but not incompatible with the Hartz thesis, is that of American exceptionalism.[9] The doctrine was popularized in the nineteenth century (in *Democracy in America*, Tocqueville referred to America as "exceptional"). It has strong links to the notion of America having a "Manifest Destiny," a term popularized by John J. O'Sullivan in 1845.[10] The claim is that America is "the first new nation," as the political scientist Seymour Martin Lipset put it,[11] with a particular mission (for many observers, perceived as God-given) to establish a just society on earth and to spread that condition widely. One sees some of this already in the Founders. Here is Alexander Hamilton in the First Federalist Paper:

> It has been frequently remarked that it seems to have been reserved to the people of this country, by their conduct and example, to decide the important question, whether societies of men are really capable or not of establishing good government from reflection and choice, or whether they are

7. Robert Dahl, *Pluralist Democracy in the United States: Conflict and Consent* (Chicago: Rand McNally, 1968).

8. Rogers Smith, *Civic Ideals: Conflicting Visions of Citizenship in US History* (New Haven, CT: Yale University Press, 1999).

9. For a "realist" critique see Stephen Walt, "The Myth of American Exceptionalism," *Foreign Policy*, October 11, 2011, http://foreignpolicy.com/2011/10/11/the-myth-of-american-exceptionalism/.

10. There is an extensive literature. See, for example, Thomas R. Hietala, *Manifest Design: American Exceptionalism and Empire* (Ithaca, NY: Cornell University Press, 2003). See also in particular Adam Gomez, "An Almost Chosen People" (PhD diss., University of California, San Diego, 2010).

11. Seymour Martin Lipset, *The First New Nation* (New York: Basic Books, 1963).

forever destined to depend for their political constitutions on accident and force. If there be any truth in the remark, the crisis at which we are arrived may with propriety be regarded as the era in which that decision is to be made; and a wrong election of the part we shall act may, in this view, deserve to be considered as the general misfortune of mankind.[12]

Note in particular the implied danger should the country fail to live up to its mission—we shall see more of this when we look at the Puritans.

A third model, again not incompatible with the first two, is the so-called frontier thesis put forth by Frederick Jackson Turner in 1893. Turner attributed American dynamism and democratic ideals to the progressive movements westward into new territory, a "succession of terminal moraines" leading to "a steady growth of independence" from Europe.[13] This was the America of rugged individuals, necessarily of a certain amount of violence. With the settling of California, Turner foresaw the end of a central quality of being an American: the "territories" to which Huck Finn would "lite out" were gone, erased by the ever-growing iron tracks of the railroads. However, if one sought new frontiers, one found no problem in continuing beyond the Pacific shore. When William Jennings Bryan complained to Theodore Roosevelt about the occupation of the Philippines in 1898, Roosevelt apparently replied that if Bryan had not objected to the taking of California, he should not object to that of the Philippines.[14]

Both the exceptionalism model and the frontier thesis are in fact compatible with the liberal model, or a version thereof. They are in partial contrast with two other approaches I shall now describe.

A fourth model, associated in different ways with, among others, the work of J. G. A. Pocock, Quentin Skinner, and Bernard Bailyn holds that American practice developed not so much from Lockean liberalism as from Renaissance

12. Alexander Hamilton, *The Federalist Papers* in *The Debate on the Constitution*, ed. Bernard Bailyn (New York: Library of America, 1995), 219.

13. Frederick Jackson Turner, "The Significance of the Frontier in American History (1893)," American Historical Association, https://www.historians.org/about-aha-and-membership/aha-history-and-archives/historical-archives/the-significance-of-the-frontier-in-american-history. The literature is again extensive. For a good summary analysis, see Gerald D. Nash, "The Frontier Thesis: An Historical Perspective," *Journal of the West* 34, no. 4 (October 1995): 7–15.

14. The historian William Appleton Williams has argued that the "frontier thesis" encouraged expansion overseas. See William Appleton Williams, "The Frontier Thesis and American Foreign Policy," *Pacific Historical Review* 24, no. 4 (1955): 379–95.

republicanism, itself a reworking of Aristotelianism.[15] The emphasis here was on the achievement of, and the difficulties in achieving, citizenly virtue. I share some of this approach, but I think that it tends to retain a single model of virtue whereas, as I hope to make clear in this book, *what counts as virtue* is itself the subject of contestation.

A fifth model is the communitarian critique of liberalism found in the works of such writers as Michael Sandel and Alasdair MacIntyre.[16] Here I do agree with much of their critique of liberalism as overly atomistic and privatized, but I contend that from the earliest days, America was a polity, that critique has been part of American practice, albeit in a different form from that posited by Sandel or MacIntyre. There was a communitarian strand, but these communitarians were also individualists.

None of these models is simply false. The founders *were not* aristocrats but mainly well-to-do middle class. They *did* think that they were doing something unprecedented in the history they knew. Rome *was* a constantly invoked model. If reformers sought a "cooperative commonwealth," then individualism, at least by the end of the nineteenth century, enjoyed a certain standing as a national ideology. A problem, however, with these models is that they allow one to locate successfully those elements that do not threaten the model: such are relegated to the fringe. Thus the eminent historian Richard Hofstadter could write about the "paranoid style" in American politics such that McCarthyism was deemed an "exaggerated" response to changing international conditions.[17] In general, these models are core-periphery: the center was fundamentally sound, and one had only to make sure that fringe elements were kept at the fringe. Their "agitators" were tellingly "outside," whereas mine are inside. If many of the aforementioned models relegate all that is not central for them to the periphery of the political realm, the difficulty comes from

15. J. G. A. Pocock, *The Machiavellian Moment* (Princeton, NJ: Princeton University Press, 2016); Quentin Skinner, *Liberty before Liberalism* (Cambridge: Cambridge University Press, 1997); Bernard Bailyn, *The Ideological Origins of the American Republic* (Cambridge, MA: Harvard University Press, 2017).

16. Michael Sandel, *Liberalism and the Limits of Justice* (Cambridge: Cambridge University Press, 2010); Alasdair MacIntyre, *Whose Justice? Which Rationality?*, 2nd ed. (London: Bloomsbury Academic, 2013); Alasdair MacIntyre, *After Virtue* (London: Bloomsbury Academic, 2013).

17. Hofstadter, *Paranoid Style*, esp. 3–40. See also Richard Hofstadter, *Anti-Intellectualism in American Life* (New York: Vintage, 1966), and Richard Hofstadter, *The Age of Reform* (New York: Random House, 1988). See the excellent critical analysis in Michael P. Rogin, *The Intellectuals and McCarthy: The Radical Specter* (1967; repr., Cambridge, MA: MIT Press, 1975).

the fact that there were, for most of American history, ongoing and conflictual American traditions—certainly up until the Cold War. There has been a continuing and consistent struggle, one might say, to define the American soul, and one must understand American citizenship in terms of this variegated struggle. As we shall see, the great nineteenth-century authors (Ralph Waldo Emerson, Mark Twain, Nathaniel Hawthorne, Herman Melville, Walt Whitman) worked from another model.

There is one additional, minimalist, model that I must mention. Judith N. Shklar, professor of political science at Harvard (and not incidentally my dissertation advisor), argued in her *American Citizenship* that it was necessary to maintain a clear-cut distinction between loyalty and obligation for a safe or viable notion of citizenship.[18] A fusion of the two would produce nationalism and often ethnocentrism. One should not—one did not—owe *loyalty* to the state, she argued; one had only *obligations*. All that is required to be a citizen of the state is that one have the right to vote and the right to work: beyond that, nothing more. Shklar's is a powerful notion. It derives to some great extent from the fact that she was herself was a refugee from both fascism and Stalinism, thus, that in America, she was always, and was consciously, an exile. She was an American *citizen*, one might say, without being an *American*.

Hers is purposively a minimalist conception of citizenship; as such, it does no harm. Appealing as one might find it, it has severely limited historical actuality. Most important, it is not clear to me that it can deal adequately with the fact that most of us are not exiles and that therefore we do not and cannot keep our loyalties separate from our obligations. Moreover, the awful and perhaps unintended message of George Orwell's *1984* is that even those who wish to forgo loyalty to the state can be made to come around—which is what happens to Winston Smith. And that means that the propensity to do so is already with most of us—hence one must pay attention to it. It is what one comes around *to* that is the question.

What might one say about a broader vision of citizenship? In the early days, citizenship was considered as entailing participation in decisions affecting the collectivity. Over time, the expectation of participation remained as a desirable activity but was increasingly not seen as necessary. Citizenship remained, however, the "right to have rights," as Hannah Arendt put it.[19] Ad-

18. Judith N. Shklar, *American Citizenship* (Cambridge, MA: Harvard University Press, 1995).

19. Hannah Arendt, *The Origins of Totalitarianism* (London: Andre Deutsch, 1986), 277.

ditionally, since the adoption of the Fourteenth Amendment in 1868, anyone who was born in the territory of the United States—jus soli—whether of
American parents or not, was by that fact a citizen (assuming that the person
met the other criteria in force at the time, such as being male, adult, and so
forth).[20] As Herman Melville suggested in *Redburn*, it was as if the territory
itself was mother and father.[21]

Even after the Fourteenth Amendment, however, America has never been
a country where citizenship was understood as dependent only on being the
child of American citizens—though of course it was also that. America was
also the country where one could choose to become a citizen—to some degree
in the manner that one might choose to join a particular church—and where
a successful choice required the meeting of certain criteria that changed over
time. (It should be pointed out, however, that with rare exceptions, this choice
was for 245 years not available to blacks. They were then, collectively, *given*
citizenship.) The meeting of these criteria—whatever they were at the time—
was a public act: it had to be evident to others, themselves citizens, that one
met the designated qualifications. That Americans are repeatedly called on to
pledge allegiance displays a certain anxiety.

America is, and always has been, a project. As we will see in chapter 1,
those who initiated it came to the new shores with the intention of founding a
society that did not at that time exist. In this sense, "America" has always lain
in the future as an idea and could not easily find a past on which to rest. It is
thus the case that the project of America—of citizenship—was always fraught
with anxiety. Was one actually becoming what one was? And anxiety always
opens the temptation toward complacency. It is thus in the instances of social and political and cultural developments that one must look to find the resources for being an American citizen in an attempt to recover the American
project. For it is in those developments that one will also find the basis for the
critique of that for which the country repeatedly settled. Thus claims made
in the name of the American citizen—the "People" in multiple parlances—
always are claims about something that is yet not fully realized. There are
claims that have the power and elusiveness of mythos, of the stories necessary
to find what calls to be found. And there will thus be controversy and quarrel:

20. The practice derives from a case in English law. See Polly J. Price, "Natural Law and
Birthright Citizenship in Calvin's Case (1608)," *Yale Journal of Law and the Humanities* 9
(1997): 73.

21. Herman Melville, *Redburn* (New York: Anchor Books, 1967), 162–63.

countries make mistakes about themselves and need to be called back to what they may become.[22]

I thus contend four things in this book: (1) that there are multiple, more or less parallel, traditions, in constant interaction and often conflict, at times violent, with one another—call these varieties of a particularly complex American republican tradition; and (2) that by examining these traditions we can be led to call into question the supposed centrality of the standard understandings and in particular of the liberal tradition; and (3) that this exploration gives us a more comprehensive understanding and opportunity to recall what is and has been involved in being an American citizen (and of some of the distresses associated with that in our times); and (4) that although these parallel traditions were in constant struggle or conflict with the liberal/exceptionalist one, with the advent of the Cold War (and the myriad complexities that accompany it and make it possible), alternatives tended to fade away. It is possible that one sees something of those alternatives still in the enthusiasm for Bernie Sanders that marked the 2016 Democratic primary contests and, even in a debased way, in some of the following of Donald Trump.

In 1962 Robert Frost published his last collection of poems, *In The Clearing*. In several of them he returned to one of his constant themes—the particular nature of his own country. Most centrally, in "A Cabin in the Clearing," he set up a dialogue between two veils that interfere with the clarity of our vision: "Smoke" and "Mist." "Smoke" wonders why Americans have yet to learn their "native tongue," to which "Mist" replies that they have continually asked about it: "Learning has been a part of their religion."[23] Frost shared the sense of America as a project. He also understood that not only was the project in his time unrealized but that it might continue to be so. For all their questioning, Americans are "none the wiser for it."[24]

HOW DOES THIS ISSUE CHANGE OVER TIME?

Let me now briefly outline the discussion that follows. I trace this story from its Puritan origins through the seventeenth, eighteenth, and nineteenth cen-

22. See Stanley Cavell, "Finding as Founding," in *This New Yet Unapproachable America* (Albuquerque, NM: Living Batch Press, 1989). See also Jason Frank, *Constituent Moments: Enacting the People in Postrevolutionary America* (Durham, NC: Duke University Press, 2010).

23. Robert Frost, "A Cabin in the Clearing," in *In the Clearing*, in *Collected Poems, Prose and Plays* (New York: Library of America), 423.

24. Frost, "Cabin in the Clearing," 424.

turies, into the twentieth and down to the Cold War. What it means *to be* a citizen changes, of necessity mainly in response to three major developments that require and produce important modifications. The first was expansion of the population, thus of political territory, and thus the development of a commercial economy, centered in particular in the rapidly growing cities. The second was the rise of industrial capitalism and of great concentrations of wealth after the Civil War. Here the emancipation of slaves introduced an understanding of a need for a *collective* conception to those seeking to revise the understanding of citizenship. (We see some of this in the Knights of Labor, Grange, Greenbackers, Populists, and Debsian socialists. Women, not having suffrage as a collectivity, present a similar issue.) he third development, beginning after the First World War, occurred when the United States had to deal with the consequences of becoming of necessity a permanent player in the international realm and in particular of the confrontation with another country also claiming universal and exportable values (the USSR). And, with the abolition of slavery, blacks raised as a group a set of new and different demands on citizenship due to the preceding two and a half centuries of servitude and oppression (since 1865, the racial divide had acquired new voices, posed new questions, and moved in new directions). After a consideration of the Cold War and the 1960s, I turn in a more speculative vein to contemporary developments.

This book can be viewed as dividing into three parts. The first part concerns the establishment of the domestic criteria for citizenship—that is, minimally, for electing and being elected but also of the individual's relation to governance. The second part examines how those criteria change when the country is confronted with problems that are inherently collective, including the concentrations of private wealth that characterize the post-Civil War period—what Twain called "the Gilded Age"—as well as the question of the status of groups: women, immigrants, and in particular newly freed African Americans. The third part deals with the issues and problems raised when America's conceptions of itself confront and are actively engaged in the international world—this period begins with the First World War and continues to the present day. Relations with the Soviet Union and the apparent threat of Communism (why was *this* a threat?) in the twentieth century are central. A key point here is that it is precisely the involvement of the United States in the international sphere that leads to new developments in the matters of race in America.

Finally, the book closes with a speculative consideration of the importance of two matters. One is what influence the development of social media (from national television to cable to Facebook, Twitter, and so forth) has for our conception of, and the possibilities for, citizenship. In particular, I am concerned to raise the question of how the increasing prevalence, not to say dominance, of social media has changed the notion of citizenship. As Jane Mansbridge has pointed out, something has changed when I can, as (then) a resident of California, be asked and be expected to support a congressional candidate in Wisconsin and find myself contributing.[25] Some observers have hailed the development of social media as permitting a vast expansion of democracy—I find myself less sure. These questions, however, are still developing and may very likely take unpredicted turns.

The second matter of importance is the effect of the "war on terrorism" on the possibilities for, and vision of, citizenship. Recent years have seen a continuation of the expansion of executive power, a progressive delegitimation of most political institutions, in particular Congress, and a growth of single-issue-oriented groups.

I suspect that these two developments are partially related. One senses that a great disturbance affects many Americans.

A *POLITICAL* THEORY OF AMERICAN CITIZENSHIP?

Overall, I argue and try to show that much of what the more standard models argue in effect relegates what is in fact of great and continuing importance to the political periphery. Thus, although this is a book *that deals with* American history, *it is not an historian's book, nor a book of history*. Nor is this an attempt to write "A People's History of the United States"—besides, Howard Zinn has already done that. I am trying to trace the contestations over a particular concept—that of citizenship—through the course of American history. It is affine to what is called *Begriffsgeschichte*—the history of a concept or conceptual history: it is, one might say, *about* concepts in and over their historical development. Thus I differ from the somewhat polemical stance taken by Samuel Huntington in *Who Are We? The Challenges to American National Identity*.[26] Huntington correctly sees the initial understanding of citizenship as

25. Jane Mansbridge, *Beyond Adversary Democracy* (New York: Basic Books, 1980); Jane Mansbridge, "Clarifying Political Representation," *American Political Science Review* 105, no. 3 (2011): 621–30.

26. Samuel Huntington, *Who Are We? The Challenges to American National Identity* (New York: Simon and Schuster, 2005).

deriving from dissenting English Protestantism. But for him this understanding remains more or less constant until it begins to be eroded in the 1960s by a myriad of factors, national, international, and cultural. His fears and concerns are in the end mostly cultural—my concerns are political. I see the question of citizenship as open to contestations and changes from the start—note the plural. That development is not so much an erosion as productive in and of itself of several substantial changes, with the two most important coming after the Civil War and after the Second World War.

I share much with and have learned a great deal from Rogers Smith, *Civic Ideals*, to which work mine is the closest. His book is more about exclusion and inegalitarianism than is mine, but those themes are related to my concerns. I am less concerned to debunk what he calls "colorful civic myths" than I am to see how they are transformed by historical developments.[27] Indeed, some myths can call one back to oneself. I share with Smith a sense of the promise and of the danger of loss of what we find best about our country.

I rely almost exclusively on primary documents—what a range of people said about what at which time—although I have naturally also been informed by the work of historians and trace those influences in the footnotes. With some exceptions (mostly about the middle nineteenth century, the American Communist Party, and the Seattle strike), all of the material here has been in the public domain: what I hope is fresh is the reading of it.

Where are the sources of an authentically American conception of citizenship? After being condemned, Socrates is offered by his friend Crito the chance to escape from Athens. As Socrates explores whether and why or why not he should escape, he imagines being confronted by the "laws and commonalty" of Athens, by, that is, that which makes the citizens of Athens what they are. They speak to him: "He who has experience of the manner in which we order justice and administer our polity, and still remains, has entered into an implied contract that he will do as we command him. And he who disobeys us is, as we maintain, thrice wrong: first, because in disobeying us he is disobeying his parents; secondly, because we are the authors of his education; thirdly, because he has made an agreement with us that he will duly obey our commands; and he neither obeys them nor convinces us that our commands are wrong; and we do not rudely impose them, but give him the alternative of obeying or convincing us; that is what we offer, and he does neither."[28]

27. Smith, *Civic Ideals*, 33.

28. Plato, *Crito* 51e–52a, in *Euthyphro, Apology, Crito, Phaedo*. In the original Greek: ἂν βούληται, ἔχοντα τὰ αὑτοῦ. ὃς δ᾽ ἂν ὑμῶν παραμείνῃ, ὁρῶν ὃν τρόπον ἡμεῖςτάς τε δίκας

Socrates's point is this, as it is also mine: *one can only learn what it is to be an authentic citizen of own's polity from that polity*, even when or if others (how many others?) of that polity have forgotten or repressed or denied it. This understanding is what informs this book. I hope here to recover some of the lessons from this country that have become increasingly hidden from us. Whence the American idea of citizenship? One can do worse than to cite here the encomium from Pindar's *Second Pythian Ode*, a phrase from which Nietzsche took his touchstone: "γένοι᾽ οἷος ἐσσὶ μαθών—génoi hoios èssì mathón" (having learned, become what you are).[29]

δικάζομεν καὶ τἄλλα τὴν πόλιν διοικοῦμεν, ἤδη φαμὲν τοῦτονὡμολογηκέναι ἔργῳ ἡμῖν ἃ ἂν ἡμεῖς κελεύωμεν ποιήσειν ταῦτα, καὶ τὸν μὴπειθόμενον τριχῇ φαμεν ἀδικεῖν, ὅτι τε γεννηταῖς οὖσιν ἡμῖν οὐ πείθεται, καὶ ὅτιτροφεῦσι, καὶ ὅτι ὁμολογήσας ἡμῖν πείσεσθαι οὔτε πείθεται οὔτε πείθει ἡμᾶς, εἰ μήκαλῶς τι ποιοῦμεν, προτιθέντων ἡμῶν καὶ οὐκ ἀγρίως ἐπιταττόντων ποιεῖν ἃ ἂν κελεύωμεν, ἀλλὰἀφιέντων δυοῖν θάτερα, ἢ πείθειν ἡμᾶς ἢ ποιεῖν, τούτων οὐδέτερα ποιεῖ.

29. Pindar, *Second Pythian Ode*, line 131, in *Pindari Carmina cum fragmentis; Carmina*, ed. C. M. Bowra (Oxford: Clarendon, 1951). My translation after a consultation with Alexander Nehamas.

1

FOR WHAT AMERICA?
TWO VISIONS

The land was ours before we were the land's.
ROBERT FROST, "THE GIFT OUTRIGHT"

Where do we find ourselves?
RALPH WALDO EMERSON, "EXPERIENCE"

It was not precisely a myth that the Europeans who in the seventeenth century came in increasing numbers to the New World encountered "virgin land," land held to be not widely settled, and importantly not to have been improved by labor. Certainly they thought so. As John Locke wrote in the 1680s in his *Second Treatise on Government*:

> I think it will be but a very modest computation to say, that of the products of the earth useful to the life of man nine tenths are the effects of labour: nay, if we will rightly estimate things as they come to our use, and cast up the several expences about them, what in them is purely owing to nature, and what to labour, we shall find, that in most of them ninety-nine hundredths are wholly to be put on the account of labour.
> ... There cannot be a clearer demonstration of any thing, than several nations of the Americans are of this, who are rich in land, and poor in all the comforts of life; whom nature having furnished as liberally as any other people, with the materials of plenty, i.e. a fruitful soil, apt to produce in abundance, what might serve for food, raiment, and delight; yet for want of improving it by labour, have not one hundredth part of the conve-

niencies we enjoy: and a king of a large and fruitful territory there, feeds, lodges, and is clad worse than a day-labourer in England.[1]

According to Locke, value—he moves from estimating it at 9 percent to 99 percent to 999 percent (!)—comes from labor. To the degree that the natives occupying those lands appeared to need much more land than they might have needed had they but settled down and cultivated, they appeared to Europeans to lack all Protestant industriousness. (In point of fact, most tribes in the Northeast cultivated land for periods of several years, and their apparent nomadism was in most cases due to their displacement by whites). Nor was the sense of an empty land, there for the cultivating, entirely without basis: in many areas, the Europeans had (through expulsion, war, and disease) managed in the one hundred years after 1500 to eliminate close to 90 percent of the native population.[2] The diseases brought by the invaders often raced ahead of the actual European incursions. To many Europeans, it could have seemed as if God had prepared the land for their taking. Cotton Mather spoke favorably of the epidemic of 1616 that cleared the land "of those pernicious creatures, to make room for better growth."[3] Locke in fact argued explicitly that while God had given the world to men in common (which appeared to be still the case in the New World), "it would not be supposed that He intended to remain it so." To plow the fields, scatter seed on the land, and husband it to harvest was in fact to do God's work, and any natives present were simply interfering with a God-given task. Nor did Locke, whose thought was so influential on the generation of those who made the American Revolution, have any trouble with the existence of slavery.[4]

The New World appeared not only there for Godly taking but also raised a complex set of questions about the human relation to the world. Thomas Hobbes was merely the culmination of a set of intellectual developments

1. John Locke, *Second Treatise on Government* (Cambridge, MA: Hackett, 1980), 25 (paragraphs 40–41).

2. See Noble David Cook, *Born to Die: Disease and New World Conquest, 1492–1650* (Cambridge: Cambridge University Press, 1998), chaps. 3 and 4. A more popular but excellent book is Charles C. Mann, *1491: New Revelations of the Americas before Columbus* (New York: Vintage, 2011).

3. Cotton Mather, *Magnalia Christi Americana*, cited from Cook, *Born to Die*, 171. See references in Mark Laskey, *Illuminating Shadows*, http://illuminating-shadows.blogspot .com.

4. On Locke, see Robert Bernasconi, "Will the Real Kant Please Stand Up?" *Radical Philosophy* 117 (January–February 2003): 13–14.

that called into question the rational ordering of the world supposedly dating from the days of Adam and the Garden of Eden.[5] Indeed, Bishop Bramhall had found that Hobbes had "removed all ancient landmarks" of authority. Montaigne in "On Cannibals" had suggested that the inhabitants of the New World had essentially none of the qualities of what was known as civilization. This meant that the New World was different from what was known of places like China: Chinese were civilized and awaited only the coming of Christ's word. In the somewhat blinkered minds of the Europeans, the inhabitants of the New World had apparently no development at all. There apparently was (still) such a thing as the "state of nature." And initially (we are, after all, one to several generations before Hobbes's *Leviathan*), the new settlers thought the inhabitants of the New World apparently gentle, peaceful—just the sort one would expect in Eden. And the land was there to be used—there seemed to be no rules or sense of owned property. Columbus's first descriptions are of "naked . . . very well made, very handsome bodies, and very good countenance." And indeed, initially, there was not much conflict: it was to come shortly.[6]

The initial settlers arrived with little sense of hostility from the natives and a general sense that there was lots of land. Who were these people? It is the case that soon a large percentage—some estimates run as high as 75 percent by the time of the Revolutionary War—were indentured servants, imported (that is the only right word) for their labor. They were bound for a period of five to seven years, after which they could try to make it on their own. Some of them were criminals who had been offered deportation as an alternative to the gallows.[7] These, however, were *not* the people who set the terms of citizenship. I am inevitably concerned at this beginning with those who were in positions of power—who were in effect the dominant groups in the New World.

5. Richard Allestree, for instance, accused Hobbes of "demolishing the whole frame of virtue," in *A Sermon Preached before the King*, cited in R. Ashcraft, "Hobbes' Natural Man," *Journal of Politics* 33, no. 4 (1971), 1081.

6. See the excellent discussion in Ashcraft, "Hobbes' Natural Man."

7. See David W. Galson, *White Servitude in Colonial America: An Economic Analysis* (Cambridge: Cambridge University Press, 1981). See Deanna Barker, "Indentured Servitude in Colonial America," National Association for Interpretation, Cultural Interpretation and Living History Section, March 10, 2004, http://mertsahinoglu.com/research/indentured-servitude-colonial-america/. Most comprehensive is the recent Wendy Warren, *New England Bound: Slavery and Colonization in Early America* (New York: Liveright, 2016), albeit with a certain enthusiasm for exposing the dark side of New England. (In 1680, the eighty-year-old Governor Bradstreet states that there are not more than 120 slaves in Massachusetts, although he may have been underestimating.)

And the first place to look for the sense of what criteria had to be met for one to call oneself a citizen is in New England.

When the Protestant Reformation swept over Europe, it took a different form when it reached England. As is well known, King Henry VIII broke, somewhat reluctantly, with the Roman Catholic Church and founded the Church of England, of which he was the head (and the English monarch remains the head of that church to this day). There were several reasons for this Caesaro-papism. The most notorious was Henry's desire for a male heir and his expectation that Anne Boleyn would, if his wife, provide him with a legitimate one. Another reason, more materially salient because of the tendency of people to leave land and other donations to the (Roman Catholic) Church, was to help with England's finances. From the use of such gifts for the purchase of indulgences and such matters, approximately one-third of the English territory (there were 850 "religious houses") belonged to the Catholic Church—and paid no or only voluntary taxes. It did not take much to see the economic benefits to be gained from putting into political reality Luther's excoriation of the practice of indulgences.

If, however, the church could be established by human ordering—as it had just been in England—then the question of what it meant to be a member became salient in a way that it was not under universal Catholicism. How does one recognize a church member? How does one recognize *oneself* as a member? How should that person behave? And as this was a matter of one's eternal soul, the question was significant. Among those who sought to be pure (hence "Puritans"), a focus on the forms of external behavior as the outward and physical manifestation of an inward and spiritual grace became essential. We find this idea parodied already in Shakespeare's *Twelfth Night* (1601-2) in the character of Malvolio, who is so "best persuaded of himself, so cramm'ed (as he thinks) with excellences, that it is his grounds of faith that all that look on him love him."[8] When, under the reign of Charles I (who had a Catholic wife), Archbishop Laud sought to enforce universally on Protestants the king- and episcopacy-centric strictures of the Anglican church, he gave rise to more or less open rebellion on the part of those who were concerned for the purity of their behavior.[9]

Some separated themselves from the English church. These were commu-

8. William Shakespeare, *Twelfth Night*, in *The Complete Shakespeare* (New York: Pelican, 1968), 2.3.137-39. References are to act, scene, and line.

9. See Hugh Trevor-Roper, *Archbishop Laud, 1573-1645* (1940; repr., London: Palgrave, 1988), 42.

nitarians. They called themselves Pilgrims and often held all things in common, with collective decisions made by voting. They crossed the Atlantic on the *Mayflower* and, upon arrival in what is now Provincetown, Massachusetts, collectively signed the Mayflower Compact to form a "civill body politic." While symbolically significant in what becomes American history, the Pilgrims in fact engaged in conflict with Native Americans, many died of disease, and, although eventually the remaining few founded a colony at Plymouth (of the "Rock" fame), they were over time absorbed into broader developments.[10]

Pilgrims had wanted to separate themselves from the English state church. Puritans, on the other hand, wanted only to purify it. In England, the decrees and persecutions of Archbishop Laud were of such severity that the Puritans, like the Pilgrims, thought that moving to a new, and apparently empty, land was necessary. Accordingly, a group of eleven ships, led by John Winthrop aboard the *Arbella*, carried about seven hundred Puritans to New England during the summer of 1630. From the pressure of a wealthy group of fellow Puritans and sympathizers, they had obtained a royal charter to establish a colony in Massachusetts Bay—and it is likely that Charles I was happy to get rid of them. The charter gave them remarkable latitude. The Governor and other officials were to be "constituted, elected and chosen out of the Freemen of the saide Company, for the tyme being, in such Manner and Forme as hereafter in their Presents is expressed, which said Officers shall applie themselves to take Care for the best disposeing and ordering of the generall buysines and Affaires of, for, and concerning the said Landes and Premisses."[11] The company elected Winthrop to be their governor. These Puritans did not think of themselves as breaking off from the English church, merely going to where they could do it better. They did, however, have unusual latitude in the question of self-governance.

As did Alexis de Tocqueville, it is to the Puritans that I look for a first picture of the requirements of citizenship in the New World, for much of what one finds in Puritan thought continues to inform American conceptions—note the plural—of citizenship to this day. Central to their understanding was that political authority was not established by social status or birth but by contract or covenant. Such a conception was important to Protestantism from early on,

10. See Nathaniel Philbrick, *Mayflower: A Story of Courage, Community, and War* (New York: Penguin, 2006).

11. "The Charter of Massachusetts Bay: 1629," Avalon Project, Yale Law School, http://avalon.law.yale.edu/17th_century/mass03.asp. "Freemen" were at least small landowners not bound to a lord.

drawing on sources found as far back as Saint Augustine and more recently in John Calvin.[12] Protestants held that there had been a covenant between Adam (Locke included Eve) and God—and it is because Adam and Eve broke that covenant that humans no longer live in Eden and now, knowing sin and mo- rality, are mortal. Of importance and not so incidentally, for Puritans it is our knowledge of sin (from the eating of the fruit of the tree of the knowledge of good and evil) that makes us mortal. (Hence God must keep Adam and Eve from eating of the Tree of Eternal Life, less they become like God and have no use for him). Mortality is acquired, not originally given. Its source is, how- ever, a defining human trait ("In Adam's Fall, sinned we all"[13]), and those who deny it deny their humanity. It follows that, for the Puritan, sin is a human fault and that being moral is what is required by our mortality. And, if our lot is consequent to the breaking of the original covenant with God, it is now meet and right to attempt a new covenant in order to, as far as possible, make up for the breaking of the first one.

There is a profound implication here for the conception of authority. As God was to Man so are men (the status of women remains ambiguous) to the Ruler. Politically speaking, humans (as citizens, not rulers) are analogous to God. From this, it would follow that if a ruler breaks the covenant by which he was bound, he should be punished by men, just as God had punished Adam and through him the human race. Charles I, who in the 1649 Articles of Im- peachment was held by Parliament to be "trusted with a limited power to gov- ern by and according to the laws of the land, and not otherwise," was to find this out shortly, less than twenty-five years after the arrival of the Puritans in the New World. The model of the political covenant is thus taken from that of the religious covenant, and it notably attributes potentially total author- ity to the covenanter who has *not* broken faith. As John Winthrop argued in a "Speech to the General Court," "It is yourselves [the people] who have called us to this office and being called by you we have our authority from God."[14]

12. Augustine, *The City of God*, trans. R. W. Dyson (Cambridge. Cambridge University Press, 1998), 16.27; John Calvin, *Institutes of the Christian Religion*, trans. Ford Lesis Mc- Neill (Battles, MI: Westminster Publishing, 1960), 4.14.18.

13. This was a well-known medieval adaption of 1 Cor. 15:22 (AV). It can be found in *The New-England Primer: A Reprint of the Earliest Known Edition, with Many Facsimiles and Reproductions, and an Historical Introduction*, ed. Paul Leicester Ford (New York: Dodd, Mead, 1899), 14.

14. John Winthrop, "Speech to the General Court," in *The American Puritans*, ed. Perry Miller (New York: Anchor Books, 1956), 91. See the excellent discussion of Winthrop in John H. Schaar, "Liberty/Authority/Community in the Political Thought of John Win- throp," *Political Theory* 19, no. 4 (1991): 493–518.

The expression of the people transmits the will of God. (It is no accident that some people have proclaimed the 2016 election of Donald Trump to be "the will of God"—not necessarily because God directly chose him but because, in their view, the people did).

If sin is a human fault, then the cure for sin could involve the collectivity. Others are with us to help us on the path the righteousness and remind us when we stray. The Puritans were thus very careful to distinguish two types of liberty. Tocqueville cites this passage from Winthrop's "Speech to the General Court" as a "beautiful definition of liberty." Winthrop is laying out an understanding of "independence," Tocqueville cites him:

> There is in fact a corrupt sort of liberty . . . which consists in doing whatever [men] like. This liberty is the enemy of all authority; it is impatient with all rules. With it, we become inferior to ourselves. . . . But there is a civil and moral liberty that finds its strength in union and which it is the mission of power itself to protect: this is the liberty to do what is just and good without fear. This sacred liberty we must defend in all circumstances and if necessary risk our life for it.[15]

That when following the corrupt sort of liberty, we "become inferior to ourselves," entails that each of us has a higher nature to which we should aspire. This higher nature is of such importance that we should be willing to die for it. Thus the willingness to risk mortality is a sign of our ability to keep our covenant with God. There is a kind of individual perfectionism in Puritanism, albeit within the confines of its church. In this view, "civil and moral" liberty consist in freely doing what is right; it is the role of the authorities to help each person on his or her way to such righteous action. As with all forms of perfectionism, this is both positive *and* negative liberty, to recall and overcome the distinction made famous by Isaiah Berlin. We are not constrained by anything, hence it is negative; but we are required to freely do what is right for our self, which is positive. (That our freedom carries a categorical imperative—thus a compulsion—will be established philosophically by Immanuel Kant, one hundred years later). The role of government was to enable people to choose freely what is right. It was not that government was itself the source of what was morally right but that it made possible the pursuit of that right, something that could only be achieved in concert one with the other.

Highly individualistic, Puritanism was also highly communal. Anyone

---

15. Quoted in Tocqueville, *Democracy in America*, 47–48.

holding these views will of necessity spend a great deal of time figuring out what is right. We know, for instance, that it was a common practice for families to come together to discuss the Sunday sermon at some length. Alan Heimert caught this concept well. The conflict between the first version of liberty and the second, he writes, "was not as generally assumed simply a token of the unwillingness of the latter to confess itself an anachronism in an age of reason and science." Rather, Puritanism "embodied a radical and ever democratic challenge to the standing order of colonial America."[16] And in many parts of that America, it was originally *the* standing order.

Central to the Puritans' sense of government was that they were on a God-given mission, in the way of which no one had the right to stand. America was, so to speak, the new Israel, and all the efforts of government were to be directed toward empowering this task. John Cotton, who had fled from Lincolnshire to Boston in 1633 and was promptly chosen the leader of the Boston church, set out the "limitations of government": magistrates should never "affect more liberty and authority than will do them good, and the people good.... Power should therefore be limited."[17] But the reason that government should be limited is so that citizens make use of that limitation for themselves, and, *by themselves, do what is right*. It was not up to the government to coerce people into doing what is right but to make it possible or likely that they should to do it. The role of the government was, should they err, to remind them of the right way and, should they continue in their faulty ways, to punish them. Cotton remarked that the basic truths are so small in number that if they be well expounded, no one could fail to believe them. Only if a person persisted in error after being admonished twice can he or she be punished, Cotton explained, as now this person is "sinning against his [or her] conscience."[18] The role of government is to get the citizen to live up to what being a citizen means.

One response to this Puritan view, and not a totally incorrect one (genealogies include all sorts), is to see it as the ideological ancestor of the House Committee on Un-American Affairs, which, after World War II, sought to make clear a particular conception of what it meant to be an American and to punish those who did not adhere to that understanding. There is, however, another side to the Puritan stance, and we can get some idea of it by looking carefully at the famous sermon preached by Winthrop on board the 350-ton *Arbella* as

16. Alan Heimert, *Religion and the American Mind* (Cambridge, MA: Harvard University Press, 1966), 12. See the related discussion in Downes, *Hobbes, Sovereignty*, chap. 4.

17. John Cotton, "Limitation of Government," in Miller, *American Puritans*, 86.

18. Cotton, "Limitation of Government." Hence sinning against oneself.

it approached the shores of New England in June 1630.[19] In this sermon, "A Modell of Christiane Charitie," Winthrop sets out the vision of citizenship and political society that he expected to establish in the colony. He argued that the very existence of society is a sign that we are all in the world together and that when our fellow human is in need, we are to aid him or her so as not to "tempt God in putting him upon help by miraculous or extraordinary means."[20] The Fall of Adam—the original broken covenant—not only divided man from God but also man from man. Against this we have two "rules whereby we are to walk": justice and love, which come together in the commandment to love one's neighbor as oneself.

The vision is thus of the body politic as a whole but composed of individuals. As Winthrop explains, "There is no body that but consists of parts . . . that which knits them together gives the body its perfection. . . . Thus it is between the members of Christ, each discerns by the work of the spirit his own image and resemblance in another and therefore cannot but love him as he loves himself. . . . The soul is of a sociable nature." It followed from this argument that "the care of the public must oversway all private respects by which not only conscience but mere civil policy doth bind us; for it is a true rule that particular estates cannot subsist in the ruin of the public." And Winthrop continues with a set of exhortations or commandments. We must "do justice"; be "knit together as one person"; "entertain each other in brotherly affection"; "abridge ourself of superfluities for the supply of other's necessities"; "delight in each other, make others' conditions our own, rejoice together, mourn together, labor and suffer together."[21] The list is quite extraordinary from a contemporary point of view: we are *required* to "delight in each other" as well as to give of what we do not need to help those who do not have enough. President Clinton once told a man suffering from AIDS that "I feel your pain"—he was only echoing these thoughts, albeit abstractly.

Much was at stake. Winthrop closes his sermon with a famous promise and a less well-known worry.

Now the onely way to avoyde this shipwracke, and to provide for our posterity, is to followe the counsell of Micah, *to doe justly, to love mercy, to*

19. Records show that the ships carried ten thousand gallons of wine, three times the amount they did of water. The wine had been almost totally consumed by the time that the ships arrived.

20. John Winthrop, "A Modell of Christiane Charitie," in Miller, *American Puritans*, 81.

21. Winthrop, "Modell of Christiane Charitie," 83.

walk humbly with our God. For this end, wee must be knitt together, in this worke, as one man. Wee must entertaine each other in brotherly affection. Wee must be willing to abridge ourselves of our superfluities, for the supply of other's necessities. Wee must uphold a familiar commerce together in all meekeness, gentlenes, patience and liberality. Wee must delight in eache other; make other's conditions our oune; rejoice together, mourne together, labour and suffer together, allwayes haueving before our eyes our commission and community in the worke, as members of the same body. Soe shall wee *keepe the unitie of the spirit in the bond of peace.* The Lord will be our God, and delight to dwell among us, as his oune people, and will command a blessing upon us in all our wayes. Soe that wee shall see much more of his wisdome, power, goodness and truthe, than formerly wee haue been acquainted with. Wee shall finde that the God of Israell is among us, when ten of us shall be able to resist a thousand of our enemies; when hee shall make us a prayse and glory that men shall say of succeeding plantations, "the Lord make it likely that of *New England.*" For wee must consider that wee shall be as a citty upon a hill. The eies of all people are uppon us. Soe that if wee shall deale falsely with our God in this worke wee haue undertaken, and soe cause him to withdrawe his present help from us, wee shall be made a story and a by-word through the world. Wee shall open the mouthes of enemies to speake evill of the wayes of God, and all professors for God's sake. Wee shall shame the faces of many of God's worthy servants, and cause theire prayers to be turned into curses upon us till wee be consumed out of the good land whither wee are a goeing.[22]

Winthrop closed with a citation from the book of Deuteronomy, 30:19–20, a passage having to do with the Lord's warnings to the Israelites as to what they must do to merit passing over into the land that he had promised them:

> Therefore lett us choose life
> that wee, and our seede
> may liue, by obeyeing His
> voyce and cleaveing to Him,
> for Hee is our life and
>   our prosperity.[23]

22. Winthrop, "Modell of Christiane Charitie," 83.
23. Full text can be found at Hanover Historical Texts Collection, August 1996, https://history.hanover.edu/texts/winthmod.html; and an excerpted one in Miller, *American Puritans,* 79–83.

The image of a "city on a hill" is an example is drawn from the Sermon on the Mount (Matthew 5:14). And the image recurs frequently in American political rhetoric, most famously in the speeches of Presidents Kennedy and Reagan. Notably, what is *not* cited in those speeches is the high level of anxiety that Winthrop displays. "If we fail" in this task, the results will be world shattering. There is thus in this founding document—for that is what it is—not only the sense of what America and Americans should achieve but of a general disaster for all should America fail.[24] President Carter did catch some of this anxiety:

> We are at a turning point in our history. There are two paths to choose. One is a path I've warned about tonight, the path that leads to fragmentation and self-interest. Down that road lies a mistaken idea of freedom, the right to grasp for ourselves some advantage over others. That path would be one of constant conflict between narrow interests ending in chaos and immobility. It is a certain route to failure.
>
> All the traditions of our past, all the lessons of our heritage, all the promises of our future point to another path, the path of common purpose and the restoration of American values. That path leads to true freedom for our nation and ourselves.[25]

He practically echoes Winthrop. The picture of citizenship is this: the basis of the consent that men give is such that government exists not for individual advantage per se but to seek a just form of government for each and all. The presumption underlying such citizenship is that it refers to the life of people in a given place—the metaphor of a "city on the hill" was not just a metaphor; it was a life lived together. This is not an abstract notion of freedom: it is freedom as it pertains to life in *this* place in *these* times. As Harry Stout has written:

> By locating power in the particular towns and defining institutions in terms of local covenants and mutual commitments, the dangers of mobility and atomism—the chief threats to stability in the New World—were

24. See the discussion of this "whimpering," as Perry Miller called it, as well as his excellent discussion of the Winthrop sermon, in his "Errand into the Wilderness," *The William and Mary Quarterly* 10, no. 1 (January 1953): 2–32, especially the discussion of "errand" on p. 4.

25. Jimmy Carter, "July 15, 1979: 'Crisis of Confidence Speech,'" Miller Center, University of Virginia, https://millercenter.org/the-presidency/presidential-speeches/july-15-1979-crisis-confidence-speech.

minimized. . . . As churches came into being only by means of a local covenant, so individual members could be released from their sacred oath only
with the concurrence of the local body. . . . Persons leaving without the
consent of the body sacrificed not only church membership but also property title, which was contingent on local residence. Through measures like
these, which combined economic and spiritual restraints, New England
towns achieved extraordinarily high levels of persistence and social cohesion.[26]

What was it like, then, to be an "American" in the first half of the seventeenth century? It was from the beginning a project to be realized. On the one
hand, the land appeared to be an exceptional place and a God-given opportunity. It was initially fairly peaceful: there are only two major wars, only one of
which was in New England, between the English colonists and Native Americans during the first half of the seventeenth century. (There were, however,
other substantial wars between the Dutch or the French with Native Americans.) Along with this opportunity, there was the high expectation that one
might establish God's colony, as it were, and at least attempt to remedy the
broken covenant between humans and the divine: a righteous government
founded by righteous men and women who think that they can come to agree
on what righteousness meant. And central to this project was the expectation,
even the necessity, that the eyes of all the world should be on New England,
both to find there an exemplar and to keep it from falling away from its project. With the advent of the English civil wars in the 1640s, European Protestantism turned away from New England. Indeed, the English military leader
Oliver Cromwell was indifferent as to the religious affiliation of the soldiers in
his New Model Army.[27] This mounting indifference not only changes the energy available for the original project but also places a demand on the New En-
glanders (and then Americans) to make sure somehow that they are *noticed*.

Still, the question of what righteousness meant was to be worked out. But
can all accomplish the task of citizenship? It involved a partnership between
government and the church, although the church was autonomous and not
a state church. Each church, in fact, was to a considerable degree under the
authority of its congregation, which itself chose its minister. Government,
also, was by election (important sermons were famously preached on election

26. Harry Stout, *The New England Soul: Preaching and Religious Culture in Colonial New
England* (New York: Oxford University Press, 2011), 23.
27. See Miller, *American Puritans*, 15–18.

days), and voters had to be church members to be eligible to vote. The reason for this was not so much a privileging of the faithful (although it was that in practice) but the recognition that a church member, to have become a church member, had to have manifested some quality of responsibility and seriousness. *Church membership was a criterion for voting because it showed that one would or could vote responsibly for a public good and that one would conceive of the public good as one's own good.* Church membership also meant that one was known to one's fellows as one was to oneself. Membership was the outward and visible sign of one's internal membership in the community. The result was or could be individual fulfillment, political stability, and participation.

If civil magistrates were elected by the righteous, there would therefore be a much greater chance that those magistrates would be righteous. Righteous civil magistrates were essential for a number of reasons. First, there was always a danger of zealots and factions. Second, as noted earlier, a fairly large number of ungodly types resided in the colonies. Third, the distance from England meant that one could not rely on the motherland for any succor. Fourth, the problem of scarcity loomed large and affected everyone. Finally, because the colonists lacked a common enemy, there was no external threat that would bind the nation together. It is important to note here that the criteria for church membership were not rigorous. No matter how much a man like Michael Wigglesworth might have tormented himself as to his internal worth,[28] becoming a member of the church was relatively simple and involved merely a certain mild conformity of behavior and practice of the rituals.

WHAT AND WHERE IS A CITY?

The picture of citizenship politics outlined in the opening section of this chapter has a certain coherence to it except for one important lack: it fails to establish whether there are necessary limits, if any, to membership. If some are in, then some are out—but what precisely is the dividing line between them? Is it a natural (that is, given in the nature of the differences between humans) or a contingent division? And this was the issue raised precisely by Roger Williams and somewhat later Anne Hutchinson.

Williams arrived in New England in 1632 at around the age of twenty-nine. He had first been ordained in the Anglican church but had converted to Puri-

28. See Edmund S. Morgan, ed., *The Diary of Michael Wigglesworth, 1653–1657: The Conscience of a Puritan* (1946; repr., New York: Harper and Row, 1965).

tanism sometime in the latter 1620s. As with other Puritans, the persecutions of Archbishop Laud had led him to flee to America. By the time he arrived in New England, he had become a Separatist, thinking that the Church of England was corrupt. He was young, newly married, charming, sweet-tempered, courageous—and God-intoxicated, saintly, and stubborn. Turning down an offer at the Boston church on the grounds that it had not separated from the English church, he moved to Plymouth as an assistant minister. (Previously he had been offered a pastorship in Salem—a church more inclined toward Separatism—but the offer had been withdrawn after protests from Boston were accompanied by a quiet intervention from Winthrop). As Williams's theology developed, it contained several elements. God's truth was held to be difficult to arrive at (in contrast to the relatively relaxed criteria for membership in the Boston church). But precisely this difficulty meant that there was a need for free exploration and for free ideas—all external authorities are therefore problematic in that they get in the way of the search for God's truth. If, as Oscar Wilde once quipped, the problem with socialism is that "it takes too many evenings," there is a sense in which one might have the same feeling about Williams, for he promoted constant and unending discussion over that which was to be considered holy.

Religious practice was, however, to be kept separate from the secular world. Williams argued that the civil magistrates had no authority in religion, not even authority to uphold the Sabbath laws. Furthermore, he insisted on a kind of hyper or separate purity. It frequently happened that New England Puritans returned for a period to England, often to see or fetch a relative: if they had attended the Church of England while they were there, their continuing membership in the New England church on return, Williams held, was not to be tolerated. (Remember that the Puritans had not originally sought to separate from the Church of England, merely to purify it).

While at Plymouth, he also came into extensive contact with local Native Americans. This interaction led him to raise serious questions about the validity of the charter establishing the Bay Colony, as the charter made no reference to those already inhabiting that land.[29] Rather, he advocated that the land now be purchased from the Native American tribe that lived or had lived on it. (The Dutch had "purchased" Manhattan from the Lenape tribe in 1626 for sixty guilders). In 1633, Salem thought better of its previous refusal and invited Williams back as assistant pastor. He promptly raised the question as

29. In 1632, Williams wrote a treatise questioning the validity of the patent. No copies appear to have survived, no doubt because the Puritans sought to destroy it.

to the right of whites to own that land, arguing that the patent was stolen and given by a king he deemed corrupt.

With this argument, Williams is calling the very legitimacy of the Puritan experiment into question. He had during his time in the New World become friends with John Winthrop. Winthrop, who had always respected Williams's intelligence, honesty, and zeal, apparently sought to mitigate Williams's pronouncements. This attempt proved to be of no avail—Williams publicly called the king a liar. In 1635, Williams was elected minister at Salem and immediately summoned to the General Court in Boston, where he was accused of holding that civil power can have no power over conscience. Williams replied that congregations are independent of civil power. The court then threatened to revoke Salem's claim to its land if Williams were not removed. The Salem church circulated a letter to other churches to the effect that they are being attacked by Boston. Williams and Winthrop exchanged letters in which the following appeared: Winthrop asked Williams, "What has your purity gotten you?" to which Williams replied that Winthrop (and presumably others) was to "abstract thyself with a holy violence from the dungheap of this earth." Eventually, in 1636, the court banished Williams, and he became the founder of Providence in Rhode Island.[30]

Williams and the Puritans agreed on the fact that the power of magistrates was derived from the people. They also agreed that such delegation of authority had to take place within God's dictates.[31] But that said, Williams did not think that God had invested in *any* civil body the right to determine or even affect religious matters. And that being so, no such power could pertain to civil authority. In other words, civil authority should have nothing to say about morality (if we understand that in religious terms) or human excellence. Today we might think him a libertarian. It would follow, incidentally, from Williams's position that a court (civil authority) cannot require that child receive a transfusion if the parents of the child hold that the transfusion is contrary to their sincerely held religious beliefs.[32] Such a position is, by and large, the

30. See Perry Miller, *An Errand into the Wilderness* (Cambridge, MA: Harvard University Press, 1956).

31. See Timothy Hall, *Separating Church and State: Roger Williams and Religious Liberty* (Champaign: University of Illinois Press, 1998), 77f.

32. The law is complex and finally less than clear, as one might expect. In *Commonwealth v. Twitchell*, 416 Mass. 114 (1993), the doctors were authorized to administer a transfusion. The law, however, seems to depend on the case. On the requiring of pledging allegiance, *West Virginia State Board of Education v. Barnette* (1943) overturned an earlier case, *Minersville School District v. Gobitis* (1940). In 2014, the US Supreme Court refused to hear

present legal situation in the United States, though much less the case in the United Kingdom. In effect, thought like that of Williams opens a gap between the public and the private, even if it conceives of the private in religious terms.

In 1644, then back in London, Williams set down the most comprehensive statement of his views in a chaotic but brilliant treatise entitled *The Bloody Tenent, of Persecution, for cause of Conscience, discussed, in a Conference betweene Truth and Peace*. The instigation was his desire to refute John Cotton's "Answer" to an Anabaptist tract. What drew the brunt of William's ire was Cotton's claim about punishment due when a congregant had repeatedly refused to follow proper church doctrine. Williams was outraged that Cotton could claim that the meaning of Scripture was clear. Cotton had explained the parable in the Gospel according to Matthew (13:24–43) where a master tells his servants not to pull up the weeds in a field for fear of also pulling up the wheat. Weeds and wheat are to be allowed to grow together, and the weeds then can be separately burned at harvest. Cotton's reading of this passage was that one had to tolerate less-than-perfect church members while in this world: they would get any punishment due them at the Last Judgment. On our earth, one should not aim for an impossible perfection. Civil government could take care of civil crimes, but a range of toleration inside the church was acceptable and necessary.

Williams would have none of it. In the 1644 tract, he argued that the difference between those inside and those outside the church was not as great as might be thought, and that this principle applied even to non-Christians such as Native Americans. Everyone is lost in the wilderness and there is no city and no hill. Indeed, as the persecutor always believes that his cause is just, there are no preferable earthly institutions—something that accounts for the fact that the Bible contains no model of government or even church organization. Those who are righteous cannot be gathered into an institution.

The political consequences were important. There can obviously be no holy war, but there is also no real concern for a more moral politics or even for more than an order-maintaining role for government. All that is necessary is for civil authority to keep the peace, and this can be done without reference to the Bible. Hence there is no covenant, past, present, or future. Civil authorities do not have the right to punish people for crimes that might have to do with

---

an appeal of a lower court judgment that the estate of a deceased Jehovah's Witness could not sue the doctor for negligence as they had not insisted on a transfusion. We find the same argument about the right of the Amish to remove their children from schooling. See Amy Gutmann, *Democratic Education* (Princeton, NJ: Princeton University Press, 1987) for a strong defense of state intervention.

religion. In effect, government should stay out of moral questions and matters of public virtue.

We can see some of the consequences of Williams's stance by a short examination of one of the other major crises of the period, the case of Anne Hutchinson. Hutchinson was born in England in 1591. She received a much more extensive education that was normal for girls at the time and, with her family, was a follower of the local minister, John Cotton. When Cotton emigrated to Massachusetts in 1633, the large Hutchinson family followed a year later. They joined the Boston church, the most important in the town, the one, in Winthrop's words, that was "the most publick, where Seamen and all Strangers came."[33] In Boston, she worked as a midwife and assembled a circle of women to whom she would comment on the Sunday sermon and lead Bible study. Her basic stance was for the primacy of the "covenant of grace" as opposed to the "covenant of works." The covenant of grace in effect made eternal life purely the consequence of faith in Christ, a faith that of necessity had to be intense. A covenant of works, on the other hand, made eternal life dependent on complete obedience to God's commands. Hutchinson was led to condemn most ministers as espousing the latter covenant rather than the former.

Word of her views soon got out, and Hutchinson was put on trial in 1637; she was convicted and banished and, a year later, excommunicated. Initially, the trial did not go well for the prosecution until when, on the second day, Hutchinson gave them, to a great degree without direct provocation, adequate reason to condemn her. The court had queried her on what grounds she knew her position to be true.[34] Her response was troubling:

> You have no power over my body, neither can you do me any harm—for I am in the hands of the eternal Jehovah, my Saviour, I am at his appointment, the bounds of my habitation are cast in heaven, no further do I esteem of any mortal man than creatures in his hand, I fear none but the great Jehovah, which hath foretold me of these things, and I do verily believe that he will deliver me out of your hands. Therefore take heed how you proceed against me—for I know that, for this you go about to do to me, God will ruin you and your posterity and this whole state.[35]

33. Cited in Michael Paul Winship, *The Times and Trials of Anne Hutchinson: Puritans Divided* (Lawrence: University Press of Kansas, 2005), 35.

34. Richard B. Morris, "Jezebel before the Judges," in *Anne Hutchinson: Troubler of the Puritan Zion*, ed. Francis J. Bremer (Huntington, NY: Robert E. Krieger, 1981), 62.

35. Charles F. Adams, *Antinomianism in the Colony of Massachusetts Bay, 1636–1638* (Boston: Prince Society, 1894), 175.

In essence Hutchinson was claiming to know what God wanted. She threatened with the consequences of a perfectionism that was essentially the flip side of Williams's doctrines. If she knew what God wanted, then neither church nor civil authority could question or contradict her understanding. And she defended it well against her principal interrogator, Governor Winthrop. The following exchange occurred:

> MR. NOWEL [assistant to the court]: How do you know that was the spirit?
> MRS. H.: How did Abraham know that it was God that bid him offer his son, being a breach of the sixth commandment?
> DEP. GOV. (MR. DUDLEY): By an immediate voice.
> MRS. H.: So to me by an immediate revelation.
> DEP. GOV.: How! an immediate revelation.
> MRS. H.: By the voice of his own spirit to my soul.[36]

While her point about Abraham was telling, it put her in the position of claiming that she had had direct access to what God wanted. Such a claim could not possibly be proven wrong, but, more important, it was in itself destructive of the political realm and civil government. If someone can claim such absolute justification, then whatever they do in God's name must be in their eyes legitimate—a problem not unfamiliar to America at present. In effect, Hutchinson made the idea of civil membership, thus citizenship, irrelevant or at best of second- or third-place importance. If citizenship is necessarily a collective matter, the claim by a single individual to be in possession of *the* truth necessarily stands in complete contradiction to the possibility of citizenship being anything other than a merely formal category.

With Hutchinson, Williams is often thought to be the founder of the liberty of conscience as it develops in American politics. This characterization, however, is misleading. Williams always claimed in fact that his doctrines made people the best civil subjects. The vision of a government we find in Williams and Hutchinson is close to entirely divorced from moral values—which meant that one could not invoke moral values against a governmental policy. In a paradoxical way, it is the mild intermixing of morality and politics that we find in Winthrop and Cotton that will, or can, in the end make for a more just polity.

36. "Trial and Interrogation of Anne Hutchinson (1637)," Swarthmore College, http://www.swarthmore.edu/SocSci/bdorsey1/41docs/30-hut.html.

AMERICA'S TWO SOULS

These arguments set a stage that in one way or another will continue for much of American history. The Puritan/Winthrop challenge is to find the best form of government that, with all their flaws, human beings can construct. Tocqueville again:

> In their hands, political principles, laws, and human institutions seem to be malleable things, capable of being shaped and combined at will. The walls that imprisoned the society into which they were born fall before them. . . . The human spirit . . . sets out in every conceivable direction. When it reaches the limits of the political world, however, it stops of its own accord. In trepidation, it foregoes the use of its most redoubtable faculties. It forswears doubt. It renounces the need to innovate. It refrains from even lifting the veil of the sanctuary. It bows respectfully before truths it accepts without argument. Thus in the moral world everything is arranged, . . . decided in advance. In the political world, everything is agitated, contested, uncertain. On the one hand, passive albeit voluntary obedience; on the other, independence, contempt for experience, and jealousy of all authority.[37]

This is the basis of what will come to be called American exceptionalism. But the Puritan claim to exceptionalism did not carry with it a claim to a final truth. It involved placing the good of the whole as consonant with the good of the individual and the sense of a common goal, for the attainment of which, however, no one could claim special abilities or privilege. Within limits, it was tolerant of human fallibility, at least in those who were of the community. It deemed itself superior, however, to those who were not of the community, who were not on a shared pilgrimage. It shared the sense of the political found in Calvin:

> But as we lately taught that that kind of government is distinct from the spiritual and internal kingdom of Christ, so we ought to know that they are not adverse to each other. The former, in some measure, begins the heavenly kingdom in us, even now upon earth, and in this mortal and evanescent life commences immortal and incorruptible blessedness, while to

37. Tocqueville, *Democracy in America*, 48–49.

the latter it is assigned, so long as we live among men, to foster and maintain the external worship of God, to defend sound doctrine and the condition of the Church, to adapt our conduct to human society, to form our
manners to civil justice, to conciliate us to each other, to cherish common
peace and tranquility. All these I confess to be superfluous, if the kingdom
of God, as it now exists within us, extinguishes the present life. But if it is
the will of God that while we aspire to true piety we are pilgrims upon *the
earth, and if such pilgrimage stands in need of such aids, those who take them
away from man rob him of his humanity*. As to their allegation, that there
ought to be such perfection in the Church of God that her guidance should
suffice for law, they stupidly imagine her to be such as she never can he
found in the community of men. For while the insolence of the wicked is so
great, and their iniquity so stubborn, that it can scarcely be curbed by any
severity of laws, what do we expect would be done by those whom force
can scarcely repress from doing ill, were they to see perfect impunity for
their wickedness?[38]

Against this particular Puritan claim to a self-questioning exceptionalism,
there was from early on also an insistence that one should give up the claim
that the citizens of this country be exceptional. This rejection of exceptionalism could take the form found in Williams, of reducing the claims of the
political realm merely to the keeping of order, or that found in Hutchinson,
of the related claim of solely *individual* perfectibility. On the side of Winthrop
and his friends, there was the sense that a polity was more than simple rights
and freedoms but was contained in a vision that government could be made
moral and *was* necessary to helping its citizens be moral. On the side of Williams and his cohort, there is a sense that the government does not respond
to moral categories and that there is nothing to say about it, morally speaking.
Government can and should therefore be, in this second view, limited in scope
and quality. The question posed by both sides concerns the degree to which
participation in the polity is part of what being a member entails and what
one must have demonstrated as certain qualities of character to be entitled to
such participation.

The validation of their project, however, depended on it being an exemplar
to the world. And America was thus always somewhat conscious of the need
for an audience. Perry Miller caught it nicely: "If an actor, playing the leading role in the greatest dramatic spectacle of the century, were to attire him-

---

38. Calvin, *Institutes of Christian Religion*, 4.20.2 (emphasis mine).

self and put on his make-up, rehearse his lines, take a deep breath, and stride onto the stage, only to find the theatre dark and empty, no spotlight working, and himself entirely alone, he would feel as did New England around 1650 or 1660."[39] Nor does the feeling go away with time. Robert Frost found two roads in his yellow wood; I find a question for each path and for others too. But which one that one takes does make a difference.

39. Miller, *Errand*, 16.

2

TO WHAT DOES ONE AWAKEN?

These are the times that try men's souls: The summer soldier and the sunshine patriot will, in this crisis, shrink from the service of their country; but he that stands it now, deserves the love and thanks of man and woman. Tyranny, like Hell, is not easily conquered; yet we have this consolation with us, that the harder the conflict, the more glorious the triumph. What we obtain too cheap, we esteem too lightly: it is dearness only that gives every thing its value. Heaven knows how to put a proper price upon its goods; and it would be strange indeed if so celestial an article as freedom should not be highly rated.

THOMAS PAINE, *THE AMERICAN CRISIS* (1776), READ BY
ORDERS OF GENERAL GEORGE WASHINGTON TO HIS TROOPS

What happens to this vision of the Puritans, to the city that stands on a hill as exemplar to the world? Origins are, as they always are, centrally important. As noted, in *Democracy in America*, Alexis de Tocqueville takes pain to detail the importance of America's Puritan origins. It was not only foreigners who saw this. In *The Scarlet Letter*, Nathaniel Hawthorne similarly investigates the complex legacy of those origins for the American polity. In doing so, Hawthorne takes the sins of his forefathers on his head in a real sense—and as an author therefore on our heads—and acknowledges and reformulates them. As the sense of sin was central to the Puritan sense of community, the writing of his book is itself a political act of renewal or creation.[1]

1. See David Stouck, "The Surveyor of 'The Custom-House': A Narrator for 'The Scarlet Letter,'" *Centennial Review* 15 (1971): 309-29. See also Tracy B. Strong, "Hawthorne, the

It is important to note that Hawthorne does so by presenting the various elements of society in such a manner that it is up to the reader consciously to take upon him- or herself each of them without trying to resolve them to one—something Hawthorne refuses to do. Just one example: Hester Prynne has conceived and given birth to a child from an unmarried relationship. After jail time, she has been required to wear a large scarlet letter *A* (for *adulteress*) on her breast. In chapter 7, "The Governor's Hall," she has been called before Governor Bellingham because a move has been made to take her child away from her. During the course of the interview, not to say trial, the city minister Arthur Dimmesdale, in fact the unrevealed father, will urge successfully that they not do so. The following scene occurs just as proceedings are about to start. There is in the hall a suit of armor, of recent making, "so highly burnished as to glow with white radiance." Pearl, Hester's daughter, who has accompanied her mother, spends some time looking at the "polished mirror of the breastplate. "'Mother,' she cried, 'I see you here. Look! Look!' Hester looked . . . and she saw that, owing to the peculiar effect of this convex mirror, the scarlet letter was represented in exaggerated and gigantic proportions, so as to be greatly the most prominent feature of her appearance. In truth she seemed absolutely hidden behind it." Adultery, if reflected in an older worldview, is greatly magnified. Pearl, however, we are now told, takes a "naughty merriment" in the reflection. As readers, we simultaneously observe the scene from, first, the perspective of Pearl, who sees an object of amusement; from, second, that of Hester, who sees how she will be seen by the authorities; and, third, from that of the governing body (the armor standing in for the about-to-arrive governor), which sees her as an adulteress and sinner. In the same time and by the same words, the importance of the symbol and its multiple significances is made manifest. Sin has many faces, and Hawthorne was concerned to explore them all: they are all bound together in the polity we call America. The retention of a multiplicity of perspectives is necessary if one is to deal with the complexities that form America.

Hawthorne is here, as all through his writing, concerned with the foundations of American citizenship—of what it means to claim to be an American. The multiple perspectives that he adduces manifest the complexity of that citizenship. Much as we saw in the analysis of the Winthrop-Williams encounter, Hawthorne finds all of them in his analysis of the Puritans because he is clear that a deep-seated ambivalence lies at the foundation of American member-

Politics of Sin, and Puritanism," *Telos* 2017, no. 8 (Spring 2017): 121–42, https://doi.org/10.3817/0317178121.

ship. On the one hand, there is a responsibility, both self-assumed and somehow thrust upon Americans, to establish a just society. On the other hand,
there is a desire to remain free from the demands of any external authority,
often accompanied by doubts about any internal one. Hawthorne's convey-
ance of this ambivalence has led to the various interpretations of Hawthorne's
novel, interpretations that correspond to the different perspectives noted by
Hawthorne. For some observers, Hester sinned, and while her sin is less than
that of Dimmesdale (who hides his sin) or Chillingworth (who seeks to destroy), it is still sin: she has denied the attempt to build collective justice and
order. For others, Hester appears as a romantic heroine, lawless to the point of
being "Nietzschean" (a comparison made by Regis Michaud already in 1928[2]),
and there is no real sin except in the eyes of the oppressive community (here
of Puritans, but not only theirs). For still others, Hester manifests a conflict of
values that only a change in her life can resolve—a sort of Hegelian *Aufhebung*
imperative.

Each of these readings is by itself misleading: my point is that the ambivalence is the point. (Indeed, the range of interpretations of this novel and its
characters is as extensive as the range of interpretations of any great political
theorist—Plato, Rousseau, Nietzsche only for a start). To permit this range, it
is important that Hawthorne not write a didactic novel (like, say, *Uncle Tom's
Cabin*). Hawthorne is not instructing us—he is showing us what we are confronted with. The "decapitated Surveyor" who narrates the novel may try to
give us lessons but can have no lasting success. Perhaps, as Joel Porte has
written, "Hawthorne's purpose . . . [was] . . . to illustrate the process by which
past pain and secret suffering flower into moral truth."[3] What is clear is that
Hawthorne does not wish to re-create the moralistic didacticism of his ancestors. James Baldwin will, a century later in relation to the situation of blacks
in America, make the same complaints about the moralism he finds in *Uncle
Tom's Cabin* and Richard Wright's *Native Son*.[4] But the central question of
Hawthorne's novel remains: what can/should Americans do with the actuality of sin in a country founded on the hope that the consequences of sin might
be overcome?

I shall return to Hawthorne's novel. He was correct, however, to foreground

2. Regis Michaud, *The American Novel Today* (Boston: Little, Brown, 1928).

3. Joel Porte, *The Romance in America* (Middletown, CT: Wesleyan University Press,
1969), 98.

4. James Baldwin, *Notes of a Native Son*, in *Collected Essays*, edited by Toni Morrison
(New York: Library of America, 1998), 11–18.

the importance of the sense of sin for the developing American polity. Here, as a preliminary look, it is useful to consider the figure of Jonathan Edwards and the First Great Awakening (1730–55).[5] Edwards understood that something was going to be needed to keep the citizens of the American colonies virtuous—that is, behaving as good citizens. The intensity of the experience of founding a new society and the responsibilities thereunto appertaining (those, the importance of which, Winthrop had tried to enforce on his flock) could not be maintained. Much as Hawthorne was to see, as each generation succeeded the previous, the touchstone memory of that sense of calling and mission would necessarily erode.

What to do when the historical memory of that to which one is called weakens? Trained in science and theology at Yale, Edwards was minister of the church in Northampton, Massachusetts. As his theology developed, he argued that God had absolute sovereignty over human affairs and that God's granting of grace or his refusal to do so was entirely within the purview of divinity. Edwards's sermons of the early 1730s were an important impetus to a revivalist movement—the "Great Awakening"—that spread widely throughout New England churches. The key to this regrounding of Americanness was the "awakening." It was from our emotional experience that we could awaken to a knowledge of what Christianity required. He notes, as much to himself as to any reader, "Though sin has dominion in the heart, yet . . . the Spirit of God, when It convinces and awakens a sinner . . . frees [the conscience] in a measure from its clog and hindrance by sin."[6] Perhaps paradoxically, sin was almost a good and certainly a necessary thing, as it made possible the experience of awakening—an experience necessary to the change of life that was required. Edwards, in fact, wrote that God must have a "higher purpose" in allowing humans to sin. (Thus Roman Catholic doctrine proclaims the sin of Adam to be a "happy sin"—*felix culpa*—in that it permits redemption by Christ). Edwards's fame spread such that, after difficulties with the Northampton church, he eventually accepted the presidency of the College of New Jersey, now Princeton.

His most famous sermon was "Sinners in the Hand of an Angry God"

---

5. The secondary material is extensive. See, e.g., George M. Marsden, *Jonathan Edwards: A Life* (New Haven, CT: Yale University Press, 2004), and especially Perry Miller, *Jonathan Edwards* (New York: Praeger, 1973).

6. Jonathan Edwards, "Miscellanies, 471," in *A Jonathan Edwards Reader*, ed. John E. Smith, Harry S. Stout, and Kenneth P. Minkema (New Haven, CT: Yale University Press, 2003), 47. See also Jonathan Edwards, "A Faithful Narrative," in *Jonathan Edwards Reader*, 73–75.

(1741). Preaching on a passage from Deuteronomy 32:35 ("Their feet shall slide in due time"), he asserted that whether one—in particular, someone who has not accepted Christ as his or her savior—*at any moment* goes to hell or not is simply the "mere pleasure of God."[7] As with most of his sermons, this one was printed and widely distributed. Much of it consists of "considerations" that can be summarized as follows:

- At any moment God may cast wicked persons into hell, which they deserve.
- Divine justice will not prevent this.
- Those who were wicked suffer in hell at this moment, and even if they were still on this earth, they must not think that God is not angry with them.
- God may permit Satan, at any moment, to seize the wicked.
- It is only God's restraint that keeps the hellish principles in wicked men from precipitating them into hellfire.
- No one should feel secure. All one might do to save oneself from hell is to no avail if one continues to reject Christ and is not of the Covenant of Grace.

Edwards sought to awaken a sense of despair among his congregation with the sense that it could be overcome if the congregant were to "awaken" to the power of Christ. This awakening would then carry over into everyday life—and rekindle the enthusiasm that propelled the early settlers. In the most famous passage, he compares his congregants to a spider held over a fire. (It is of note that Edwards published scientific papers on spiders.)

> The God that holds you over the pit of hell, much as one holds a spider, or some loathsome insect, over the fire, abhors you, and is dreadfully provoked; his wrath burns you like fire; he looks upon you as worthy of nothing else, but to be cast into the fire; he is of purer eyes that to bear to have you in his sight; you are ten thousand times so abominable in his eyes as the most hateful venomous serpent is in ours. . . .
>
> Now undoubtedly it is as it was in the days of John the Baptist, the ax is in an extraordinary manner laid at the root of the trees, that every tree that brings not forth good fruit, may be hewn down, and cast into the fire.

7. Jonathan Edwards, "Sinners in the Hand of an Angry God," in *Jonathan Edwards Reader*, 90.

Therefore let everyone that is not of Christ, now awake and fly from the wrath to come. The wrath of almighty God is now undoubtedly hanging over great part of this congregation: let everyone fly out of Sodom.[8]

He concludes by citing Genesis 19:17, the story of Lot fleeing Sodom: "And it came to pass, when they had brought them forth abroad, that he said, 'Escape for thy life; look not behind thee, neither stay thou in all the plain; escape to the mountain, lest thou be consumed.'"[9]

Tellingly, this is an Old Testament–centered sermon. What Edwards has done is to seek to replace the sense of calling on which Winthrop had relied as a basis for good citizenship with an appeal to emotion and fear that is to lead to an "awakened" knowledge of one's self as a sinner. The knowledge of oneself as a sinner meant that one would or could or should find oneself in communion with the other sinners around one. It was a dangerous move: his rhetoric was overwhelming, and several parishioners, convinced of their damnation, took their own lives. And, as opposed to the individual-based acceptance of Christ characteristic of the Congregationalism of the previous century, these revivals were collective events.

I must stress that Edwards did not find reason to be an adequate basis for virtuous behavior. Such would have to rest on something else and that was emotion. Many critics, in fact, saw in Edwards the perils of an appeal to emotion over reason and liberality. Enlightenment-oriented clergymen, such as Charles Chauncy, the minister of the First Church, Boston, spoke vigorously against the Awakening. In his *Seasonable Thoughts on the State of Religion in New England* (1743), Chauncy asserted, "Their main Design in preaching, seems not so much to inform Men's Judgments, as to *terrify* and *affright* their Imagination; by *awful Words* and *frightful Representations*, to set the Congregation into hideous Shrieks and Out-cries."[10] Edwards was his great opponent. Elsewhere he wrote, "Edwards mistakes the fire in men's bowels for the light in their minds."[11]

---

8. Jonathan Edwards, *Sermons and Discourses, 1739-1742*, vol. 22, 411, 418, Jonathan Edwards Center at Yale University, http://edwards.yale.edu/archive. Also in Edwards, *Jonathan Edwards Reader*, 103.

9. Edwards, *Sermons and Discourses*, 418.

10. Charles Chauncy, *Seasonable Thoughts on the State of Religion in New England*, 96, Evans Early American Imprint Collection, https://quod.lib.umich.edu/e/evans/N04182 .0001.001/1:6?rgn=div1;view=fulltext.

11. Chauncy, cited in Wilson Carey McWilliams, *The Idea of Fraternity in America* (Berkeley: University of California Press, 1973), 167.

In his preaching, Edwards urged the constant proximity of damnation. In consequence, a life should be lived in response to this constant proximity: each of us is to live thoroughly and completely in each examined moment, thus in the present only. We are not to live in anticipation of future redemption, nor in examination of past behavior—none of that matters. As he writes wonderfully, "It is certain within me that the world exists anew every moment: that the existence of things every moment ceases and is every moment renewed." He goes on to claim that this means that "we every moment see the same proof of a God as we should have seen if we had seen Him create the world at first."[12] Virtue requires doing the right thing in the present and not for any instrumental reason. The present was constant, a timeless moment. An awakened person was not subject to the erosions of time and history. Edwards prayed for God to "stamp eternity on [his] eyeballs."[13]

This was a tough doctrine, so tough that in 1751 his congregation dismissed him from the pulpit. It was, however, also in effect strongly antiauthoritarian and democratizing. We are *all* sinners; *each* of us can awaken to the grace of God. It was also strongly individualistic: all (true) knowledge rested on experiences (what Edwards called the "gracious affections"), and these experiences were necessarily awakened on an individual basis, a "new birth of the soul."[14] The doctrine proved too tough for those rationally and commercially oriented, those whose lives were constantly being lived not in the moment but toward the future. And even for those who held to it, it was hard to maintain in an unalloyed form. There was little, almost nothing, about collective *political* life. At most, as Edwards found America to be a "new land," it was less encumbered by inherited sinful practices and might therefore be the land where, in a paraphrase of *Revelation*, "all things are made new." In general, though, the focus on individual experience—Edwards was much influenced by the sensationalism of John Locke—meant that collective and political things were left pretty much to themselves. In *The Scarlet Letter*, Hawthorne foresaw the developments to which it might give rise. He writes that "Pearl [Hester's child] saw the children of the settlement, on the grassy margin of the street, or at domestic thresholds, disporting themselves in such grim fashion as the Puritanic nature would permit; playing at going to Church, perchance; or scourging

12. Quoted in Harvey G. Townsend, ed., *The Philosophy of Jonathan Edwards* (Eugene, OR: WIPF and Stock, n.d.), 76.

13. This is from a prayer of Edwards's that I have not been able to track down. It is, however, a favorite quote among religious internet entries. See, e.g., "Jonathan Edwards Quotes," Goodreads, https://www.goodreads.com/author/quotes/75887.Jonathan_Edwards.

14. Edwards, *Jonathan Edwards Reader*, 42.

Quakers; or taking scalps in a sham-fight with Indians; or scaring one another with freaks of imitative witchcraft."

The problem Edwards confronted is one that will reappear multiply: when the initial energy underlying a conception of a virtuous polity decays because of time, what will replace it? If the full weight of Edwards's urgings was too much for most people to bear, at least for very long, and if inevitably the virtuous excellence of the origins faded over time, there remained nonetheless the sense that the settlers lived in *American* land and that one should be master over it. The status of the colonies was, as noted in chapter 1, one of considerable independence from the British Crown. By the middle of the eighteenth century, the thirteen colonies controlled the land from what is now Maine to Georgia and from the Atlantic to the Appalachians. The territory beyond the Appalachians consisted of Crown lands reserved to the Native Americans by a treaty of 1763 but nonetheless claimed by the colonies. Much of the land surrounding the Great Lakes, north of the Ohio River and west to the Mississippi River, was Native American territory mainly under the control of the Iroquois confederacy.[15]

What did it mean to be an American under these circumstances? Despite increasing tensions with Native Americans, relations of the colonies to the motherland appeared to be going along reasonably well. In fact, as late as May 1775—after, that is, the battles of Lexington and Concord, and while the Second Continental Congress was preparing for the military defense of the colonies—Thomas Jefferson still could argue that "we mean not to dissolve that union which has so long and happily existed between us" and "we have not raised armies with ambitious designs of separating from Great Britain, and establishing independent states."[16] In the early 1760s, Benjamin Rush, an Enlightenment-oriented scientist from Philadelphia, recalled that when he visited the Houses of Parliament and saw the king's throne, he

---

15. There is an ongoing controversy over the possible influence of the Iroquois confederacy (already two hundred years old in the eighteenth century) on the shape taken by the early American polity. Drawing mainly on a letter by Benjamin Franklin in 1754 that suggested that if the Iroquois could work out a confederacy, so also might the colonists, Donald Grinde and Bruce Johansen in *Exemplar of Liberty: Native America and the Evolution of Democracy* (Los Angeles: American Indian Studies Center, 1991) present the case for a strong influence. Whatever the reality, it seems that Grinde and Johansen push well beyond what the evidence allows. See Elizabeth Tooker, "The United States Constitution and the Iroquois League," *Ethnohistory* 35, no. 4 (Autumn 1988): 305-38.

16. Jefferson quoted in Barry A. Shain, ed., *The Declaration of Independence in Historical Context* (New Haven, CT: Yale University Press, 2014), 177.

"felt as if he walked on sacred ground" with "emotions I cannot describe."[17]
So why does someone who says what Jefferson said in May 1775 become a
leader in a widespread revolt the next year?

A standard picture, often thought to have been taken from the language of
the Declaration of Independence, is that of a tyrannical King George. But in
fact, this is at most a half or quarter truth. In 1765, there had occurred the so-
called Stamp Act crisis. The British had imposed a tax on all legal documents
to pay for the expenses of the French and Indian War (1754–63). In that war,
after a shaky couple of years of defeat or stalemate, and consequent to extensive reinforcements, the British forces had triumphed, acquiring Canada, the
French lands between the Appalachians and the Mississippi. The British also,
in a trade with Spain for Cuba, had taken possession of Florida. Although the
war was in defense of the colonies and to their benefit, the imposition of the
tax and various provisions of the Stamp Act (in particular, the requirement
that violations were to be tried by military and not civilian court) provoked
great resistance. Pamphlets of a death's-head threatened retribution on those
who paid the tax. Thanks to the eloquent intervention of Benjamin Franklin at
Parliament, the act was repealed;[18] a new one, however, was promulgated by
the Townshend Acts in 1767 on all imports.[19] In 1768, troops were sent to quiet
Boston, and all taxes except those on tea were repealed. The importation of
tea, however, was given over in 1773 to the East India Company as a monopoly,
and the company did not tarry in raising prices. The tea tax was to be collected
at each port. Benjamin Rush, now no longer in awe of the Crown, declared
that the ships carrying tea brought "the seeds of slavery."[20] Notices such as
this one were posted promising violence against those who paid the tea tax.

PRO PATRIA,
The first Man that either
distributes or makes use of Stampt

17. Benjamin Rush to Ebenezer Hazard, October 22, 1768, in *Letters of Benjamin Rush*,
ed. L. H. Butterfield, 2 vols. (Princeton, NJ: Princeton University Press, 1951), 1:68.

18. On this act of Franklin and in general, see Alan Houston, *Benjamin Franklin and the
Politics of Improvement* (New Haven, CT: Yale University Press, 2009).

19. Parliament appears to have been under the impression that the colonists objected
only to internal taxes. See the two books by Peter D. G. Thomas, *The Townshend Duties
Crisis: The Second Phase of the American Revolution, 1767-1773* (Oxford: Oxford University
Press, 1987), and *Tea Party to Independence: The Third Phase of the American Revolution,
1773-1776* (Oxford: Clarendon Press, 1991).

20. Cited in Benjamin W. Labaree, *The Boston Tea Party* (Boston: Northeastern University Press, 1979), 100.

Paper, let him take care of
his House, Person, & Effects.
Vox Populi;
We dare.[21]

The colonists found the tax on tea unsupportable. And in 1774, a group of Bostonian members of the Sons of Liberty, some disguised as Mohawk Indians, carried off what has come to be known as the Boston Tea Party, dumping 340 chests of tea into the harbor.[22] England responded harshly, canceling the self-government of the state and shutting the Boston Harbor to commerce. On the face of it, it must be said, the tax seems a perfectly legitimate response to the costs incurred in the French and Indian War. Why, then, the opposition? It came not so much as a resistance to being taxed as to the *procedures* by which the "internal taxes" were levied. The opposition derived from a sense of what being a citizen entailed: the tax was imposed on the colonies by the English Parliament in which the colonies were neither represented nor had any say—in effect, a form of slavery.[23] What was wanted was representation— that the colonies should impose the tax on themselves, or at least be participants in the process by which it was imposed. (It is not clear what the response would have been had the colonies had members in the British House of Commons and still lost the vote.) In other words, the imposition of the tax was understood as a threat to the independence and autonomy of the colonists and to their self-conception as citizens. The problem was conceptual and political— and not financial.

21. Benjamin Rush, *An Address to the Inhabitants of the British Settlements in America, upon Slave-Keeping* (Philadelphia, Dunlap, 1773), 19, Evans Early American Imprint Collection, https://quod.lib.umich.edu/e/evans/N10229.0001.001/1:2?rgn=div1;view=fulltext. For the Tea Party, see image from a Twitter post, https://pbs.twimg.com/media/Btm5 M84IMAA4MCY.png:large. The tea weighed more than ninety-two thousand pounds and was valued in today's dollars at $1.7 million.

22. See Benjamin H. Irvin, "Tar, Feathers, and the Enemies of American Liberties, 1768–1776," *New England Quarterly* 76, no. 2 (June 2003): 197–238. A comprehensive account that brings in the issue of slavery is Benjamin L. Carp, *Defiance of the Patriots: The Boston Tea Party and the Making of America* (New Haven, CT: Yale University Press, 2010),esp. 204–17.

23. The extension of the fear of being enslaved to questioning the existence of black chattel slavery as an institution gathered some strength over the course of the years leading to the Boston Tea Party but was only slowly accepted. Massachusetts did effectively put an end to slavery by case law late in the century. The census of 1790 shows no slaves. As an institution, however, slavery was not officially abolished until 1865. See Carp, *Defiance of the Patriots*, 216–17. The 1787 Northwest Ordinance forbade slavery in the territories bounded by the Ohio and the Mississippi Rivers.

The event became a touchstone of a vision of independence. John Adams wrote in his diary on the following day, December 17, 1773, "This is the most magnificent Movement of all. There is a Dignity, a Majesty, a Sublimity, in this last Effort of the Patriots, that I greatly admire. The people should never rise, without doing something to be remembered—something notable And striking. This Destruction of the Tea is so bold, so daring, so firm, intrepid and inflexible, and it must have so important Consequences, and so lasting, that I cant but consider it as an Epocha in History." He followed up his reflection with a letter to James Warren, the president of the Provincial Congress of Massachusetts, in which he stated, "The Dye is cast . . . The Sublimity of it, charms me."[24] This single event served as an examplar of what a free people was.

A cartoon of the time portrays America as a bare-breasted woman being held down by lecherous Englishmen, one of them peering up her skirts and another pouring tea forcibly down her throat. In the background, Boston is being cannonaded, and to the right, an English solider stands ready to enforce the proceedings. The figure of Justice covers her eyes so as not to witness the scene.[25] Two things are of note here. The first is the fear of enslavement. Rush clearly did not mean that England was going to reduce the colonists to chattel slavery. His fear was that the colonists were going to be reduced to mere and only subjects, to being, as it were, defenseless women, held down for English pleasures. Collectively, the individuality of "being one's own man" was essential to the vision of citizenship that the colonists held and which they felt threated by the imposition of a (perfectly reasonable) tax over which they had no control.

The second important issue is the sense expressed by Adams of a decisive moment: the Boston Tea Party, in his reading, transformed everything—it is or can become an act of founding. Important here is his exaltation in the sense that one can, by a single "sublime" act, break away from the past and start anew. The American sense of itself found in the Boston Tea Party was a new version of the possibility of beginning afresh. Symbolically, the Boston Tea Party is the equivalent of the voyage on the *Arbella*. It serves as a memory touchstone for future action, an event the recalling of which is a constant

24. John Adams, *John Adams: Revolutionary Writings 1755-1775*, ed. L. H. Butterfield (New York: Library of America, 2011), 280, 288. See Bernard Bailyn, *The Ordeal of Thomas Hutchinson* (Cambridge, MA: Harvard University Press, 1976), for a sympathetic portrayal of the Loyalist side.

25. Most of the elements of the cartoon recurred in the controversy surrounding the nomination of Brett Kavanaugh to the Supreme Court in 2018.

present. Having such moments available publicly is, as Hannah Arendt was to point out, essential to any substantive conception of citizenship.[26] It is also the case, as we shall see, that the memory of such events needs constant renewal or it will necessarily fade over time in strength and salience. It is no accident that an insurgent movement in our times has appropriated the name of the Tea Party. The need for an appeal to a defining moment or event will reappear over the course of American history: it is, as we shall see, what Lincoln called a "living history."

This sense was centrally important to the growing American sense of itself—and it marked a new but continuous step beyond the calling to which the Puritans had felt themselves responding. A few decades later, in the first of the *Federalist* papers, Alexander Hamilton wrote:

> It has been frequently remarked that it seems to have been reserved to the people of this country, by their conduct and example, to decide the important question, whether societies of men are really capable or not of establishing good government from reflection and choice, or whether they are forever destined to depend for their political constitutions on accident and force. If there be any truth in the remark, the crisis at which we are arrived may with propriety be regarded as the era in which that decision is to be made; and a wrong election of the part we shall act may, in this view, deserve to be considered as the general misfortune of mankind.[27]

Puritans had a calling and were anxious about being able to live up to it. Hamilton and his Federalist fellows do not find themselves called by God: they have the mission inside them as human beings. And the stakes are no longer just American, nor only those of one's soul. What America is doing is to be an example for the world and a founding memory for itself. Should it fail, all, not only Americans will be worse off: it will be "the general misfortune of mankind." The city on the hill has become world-historical. The intention, the anxiety, and the sense of having one's destiny in one's hands are much the same as they were in Winthrop, albeit without the religious underpinning. Other countries might have lived off of an inherited deeply engrained history—not so America. However, what was a local enterprise for Winthrop

---

26. See Hannah Arendt, *On Revolution* (New York: Penguin, 2006). See also Aristide Zolberg, "Moments of Madness," *Politics and Society* 2, no. 2 (March 1972): 183–207.

27. Hamilton, *Federalist Papers*, no. 1.

and his cohort—at most an exemplar—is now of importance to all humankind. It raises, and potentially enforces on everyone, the question of whether human beings are capable of what is being attempted in America.

What vision of politics and citizenship comes with the growth of actual political independence? Two elements seem important. The first, partly derived from the Scottish Enlightenment writers, is a belief in and a pursuit of the knowledge given by science. Good politics will come from good knowledge. Franklin was renowned as a scientist and member of multiple scientific societies.[28] Jefferson, to take another example among many, had a famous library; he owned scientific instruments and a telescope, and he even installed three (likely flush) privies at Monticello. But this science did not give one just knowledge of the external world: it was of *political* importance. In his last letter he wrote, Jefferson assumed that if "all eyes are opened . . . to the rights of man," it is *because* of "the general spread of the light of science [that] has already laid open to every view the palpable truth that the mass of mankind has not been born with a saddle on their backs."[29] Knowledge would now enable, or could enable, the building of a just society.

The second and related element is a concern with virtuous politics, or that politics be virtuous. J. G. A. Pocock has established that much of the intellectual source for this development lies in the Renaissance reworking of Roman republicanism.[30] If politics should be the realm of virtuous actors, then the greatest threat will be that of corruption. Hence, insofar as possible, institutional setups should be so constructed as to mitigate the potential for corruption. We shall have opportunity to consider the relation of science and citizenly virtue.

If you considered yourself politically virtuous and had a concern for the public good, how did the world look to you? The first and most obvious consideration was that most human beings were necessarily imperfect. Imperfection could characterize the strong as well as the weak and hence one of the central tasks of government was to protect the weak, perfect or not, from the imperfect strong. The consequence of such imperfections, however, was that any individual or like-minded group would naturally tend to want more and more.

28. See Houston, *Benjamin Franklin*; and Joyce Chaplin, *The First Scientific American: Benjamin Franklin and the Pursuit of Genius* (New York: Basic Books, 2007); and I. Bernard Cohen, *Benjamin Franklin's Science* (Cambridge, MA: Harvard University Press, 1990).

29. Thomas Jefferson, *Writings* (New York: Library of America, 1984), 1517.

30. Pocock, *Machiavellian Moment*.

This greed could be remedied by various institutional means: officials should be selected by election and subject to recall. The question of who should do the electing is thus centrally important. In all cases, those who impose taxes should have also to pay them.

Democracy, in the sense of the rule by the majority, was seen as likely to be a dangerous form of government as it would enable the poor to dictate policy. The perceived problem here is that the poor, lacking independence, seemed much more likely to be seduced by power. Being needy, they are more open to corruption and the acceptance of bribes and so forth. Such succumbing would mean that they would not be acting as their own person but as the *subject* of someone else. In effect, the fear in relation to Parliament expressed by someone like Rush found itself reborn in day-to-day politics. It followed from this line of thinking that representation had to be virtuous and by virtuous men, and so inevitably it would be from the more well-to-do sectors of society, or at least from those who were financially independent.

How might one know who these men are? Despite Roger Williams's earlier efforts, the question of the status of Native Americans was hardly raised at all. Additionally, two other kinds of beings, women and blacks, are mostly overlooked: The question of women and their participation of lack of it in the polity simmers alongside other considerations from the time of the American Revolution, begins to gather strength in the 1840s, and eventually results in the passage of the Nineteenth Amendment in 1920. The question of blacks eventually divides the country into a war. By 1850, twenty-five out of thirty-one states required that one be white (and male) to vote.[31] Being white and male—both "natural" qualities—was seen as at least a bedrock minimal sign of the capacity for responsible and independent voting. Those who were excluded were excluded because they were deemed incapable "by nature" of exercising the necessary qualities of citizenship. Sexism held that women were beholden to their husbands and incapable of independent responsible political choice; racism held that blacks were essentially children and even more incompetent.

For the Puritans, the answer to the question of who should be an elector

---

31. There were some exceptions at various times. Free blacks could vote in Connecticut until 1818, in Delaware until 1792, and in a handful of other states, most of which abolished black voting by 1815. Massachusetts and Vermont never restricted it. See Alexander Keyssar, *The Right to Vote* (New York: Basic Books, 2000), table A 4. A number of states permitted women to vote in presidential elections for a few years before the Nineteenth Amendment passed. See A. Keyssar, *Right to Vote*, table A 19.

required that one be able to put the common interests about the private. The criterion for this ability had been that one be a church member. Being a church member required that one manifest certain forms of behavior and that one be willing to pledge one's soul to a concept of virtue. As noted in chapter 1, the actual requirements were not high and there was great suspicion of those who claimed supererogatory qualities, such as Anne Hutchinson. It is a mistake here to think of this as a narrow form of restriction of citizenship to like-minded folk. The concern is that electors manifest at least a minimal amount of virtue and that it be recognizable in external signs. I do not deny, of course, that this notion can become tyrannous—witness the President Trump's musing that those who burn the flag should be stripped of their citizenship. In general, though, in Puritan New England, as John Cotton had proclaimed, the insisted-on criteria were quite relaxed. It does not follow from steps taken too far that no step should be taken at all.

By the time we reach the men of the Revolutionary period, the reliance on religious faith had weakened, to some degree in response to what was seen as the exaggerations of the Great Awakening, many of the so-called Founding Fathers being Deists. Religious tests for holding office remained in some states, including Delaware, Georgia, and South Carolina, until this requirement was repealed by Article VI of the US Constitution in 1787. The major criterion of virtuous citizenship become the possession of property. By the end of the eighteenth century, property qualifications of a greater or lesser extent were standard in most states. Some estimates show that at least 40 percent of white men were without the franchise.[32] In several states, however, free blacks who met the property test could vote.

Why property? Those who lacked property were thought to be easily manipulated. The fear was of the formation of factions on the part of individuals who were corruptible: factions had concern only for themselves and no concern for the public good. If, however, one owned property, in particular land, then one had of necessity a stake in the common good and would resist the imposition of tyrannical demands. One would not succumb to the temptations of corruption. Not to own property was understood as a form of enslavement: one's existence depended on others. It is worth noting that in 1792 Madison spends three pages defining *property*, insisting that it is the role of government to protect property (which includes liberty and opinions) without mentioning

32. See A. Keyssar, *Right to Vote*, 7. Keyssar notes regional variations. See also Michael Schudson, *The Good Citizen: A History of American Civic Life* (Cambridge, MA: Harvard University Press, 2009), 11–89.

the question of right to vote.[33] In fact, anything that infringed on property was thought to be the source of slavery.

In 1787 at the Constitutional Convention, Madison said the following (by "freeholders" he means landowners): "Viewing the subject in its merits alone, the freeholders of the country would be the safest depositories of republican liberty. In future times the great majority of the people will not only be without land but any other sort of property. These will either combine under the influence of their common situation, in which case the rights of property and the public liberty will not be secure in their hands; or, which is more probable, they will become the tools of opulence and ambition, in which case there will be equal danger on another side."[34] The metaphor of slavery was present in many more concerns than simple chattel slavery: the fear of enslavement was overwhelming. The Declaration of Independence details a relentless list of twenty-eight crimes of King George III to conclude that "a Prince, whose character is thus marked by every act that may define a Tyrant, is unfit to be the ruler of a free People." What is of note here is that the definition of tyranny is adduced from the accumulation of specific actions. It is because of those actions that the king is a tyrant, and it is those actions that threaten American independence, requiring thus that such independence be declared. The truths to which the Declaration committed itself were "self-evident"—in a semi-Edwardsian mode, they required no argument but only acknowledgement.[35] Not only were the actions of the king dangerous in themselves, but they also could blind men to that which should be self-evident. To counter such danger, a virtuous citizenry was necessary, and that could only be obtained by virtuous electors, electors who had a stake in the public common good. And such, claimed not only Madison but almost all of the Founding Fathers, required that one be self-sufficient, which meant that one owned property.

Again: as with church membership, the primary concern is that citizens behave as (good) citizens should and not give in to the temptations of corruption. The ownership of land constitutes a criterion by which to judge whether a given individual can in fact be expected to act in the common good and not

33. See William T. Hutchinson et al., eds., *The Papers of James Madison*, vol. 14 (Charlottesville: University of Virginia Press, 1983), 266–68. See also the volume on Madison edited by Samuel Kernell, *James Madison: The Theory and Practice of Republican Government* (Stanford, CA: Stanford University Press, 2003).

34. Max Ferrand, ed., *Records of the Federal Convention*, 3 vols. (New Haven, CT: Yale University Press, 1937), 2:203–4.

35. See the detailed analysis in Danielle Allen, *Our Declaration—A Reading of the Declaration of Independence in Defense of Equality* (London: Liveright, 2015), esp. chap. 2.

in his narrow individual interest. It is of course the case that this criterion effectively empowered the wealthy. But it did so at least nominally in the name of the general good. It is always a mistake to think that these Founding Fathers were simply self-interested gentry. It was in the name of a vision of the public good that they placed restrictive criteria on the right to vote. In 1821, Madison was still worrying through the relation between suffrage, property holding, and those without property and trying to work out a more detailed analysis of that which had moved him at the Constitutional Convention. After working through the possibilities, he gave in to demographic realities and argued that the best solution would be to have a property requirement for one house of Congress but not for both.

> Under every view of the subject, it seems indispensable that the mass of citizens should not be without a voice, in making the laws which they are to obey, & in choosing the magistrates, who are to administer them, and if the only alternative be between an equal & universal right of suffrage for each branch of the Govt. and a confinement of the *entire* right to a part of the citizens, it is better that those having the greater interest at stake namely that of property & persons both, should be deprived of half their share in the Govt.; than, that those having the lesser interest, that of personal rights only, should be deprived of the whole.[36]

The forces empowered by this understanding of citizenship are those who, in 1787, sought to replace the Articles of Confederation with the US Constitution that we possess today. The contrast between the tone of and substance of the two documents is striking. The Articles of Confederation, ratified after the American Revolution over a period of four years by the thirteen states, had established a decentralized polity. Each state was to retain its sovereignty in all matters not explicitly delegated to the nation. The states were to enter into "a firm league of friendship with each other, for their common defense, and their mutual and general welfare." Each state was to have one vote in Congress, and congressmen were to be appointed by the state legislature. Whereas war could only by declared by the nation, military appointments at the rank of colonel

36. James Madison, "Note to His Speech in the Constitutional Convention on the Right of Suffrage," in *The Founders' Constitution*, vol. 1, chap. 16, document 26, University of Chicago Press, http://press-pubs.uchicago.edu/founders/documents/v1ch16s26.html. For his note at the convention, see James Madison, "Note on Suffrage, [7 August?] 1787," Founders Online, National Archives, https://founders.archives.gov/documents/Madison/01-10-02-0086.

and below were to be made by the states. A president was to serve for no more than one year of each three-year congressional term.[37]

The Articles of Confederation were quite obviously a set of institutions designed highlight the confederated, and one might say fraternal, quality of the now ex-colonies. As Norman Jacobson has written:

> To the Revolutionary generation in America it was axiomatic that in all times and circumstances government is a necessary evil. Society, produced by the wants of mankind, encourages felicity through uniting our affections. . . . Society is a blessing in every state. . . . Government, even in its best state, is a punisher. . . .
>
> But the men who drafted the Constitution proceeded on a different theory. While they agreed the government is a punisher, they were fearful that this unpleasant duty might be shirked, and they knew that in the absence of coercion the passion in men would neither relent nor be contained. . . . For sustained somberness of mood, the Constitution of the United States is extraordinary. Its authors anticipated little good, but mainly evil: war, universal corruption, public insolence and insubordination. . . . The Articles . . . read like the work of a band of hopeful amateurs. But the Constitution is the product of a group of sophisticated professionals.[38]

The Constitution establishes a strong central government, or at least makes it possible. (Adams, in fact, wanted the president to be called "Your Highness.") Yet it also gave rise to a high degree of political anxiety among the nonelites. In 1782, there was a tax revolt in Connecticut, and in early 1783, there were several organized resistances to foreclosure in Massachusetts. By August 1786, these and other revolts had taken the form of direct action in what has come to be called Shays's Rebellion. Its leaders were indicted as "disorderly, riotous and seditious persons."[39] The rebellion had sought mainly to

37. For the Articles of Confederation and related documents, see "Primary Documents in American History," Library of Congress, April 25, 2017, http://www.loc.gov/rr/program /bib/ourdocs/articles.html. See also John D. Lewis, *Anti-Federalists versus Federalists* (New York: Chandler, 1967). There is extensive secondary literature on the quarrel.

38. Norman Jacobson, "Political Science and Political Education," *American Political Science Review* 57 (1963): 561–69.

39. From the indictment of the leaders of the rebellion by the Massachusetts Supreme Court on September 19, 1780, cited in Howard Zinn, *A People's History of the United States* (New York: Harper, 2015), 93. In general, sere David P. Szatmary, *Shays's Rebellion:*

counter the power of the courts and the central administrative apparatus. The passage of the Constitution, undertaken in great part in response to the fear of popular movements such as these, only exacerbated the anxieties among those who saw in it the seed of centralized tyranny. In 1787, the Constitution was buried in a mock funeral in South Carolina.[40]

The important point for our purposes is that there existed a counterideology to the Constitutionalists, with a large portion of the populace more or less aligned with it. The ideology of this group has its origin as far back as the sixteenth century in England and was located mostly among both artisans who owned their tools and small farmers with limited land. Most accepted the notion that ownership led to virtue and thus to independence. Some groups in England in the seventeenth century—the Levellers and the Diggers, for example—had gone further and wanted to redistribute property. Both groups were a nightmare for the rich gentry.

These groups, or rather their descendants, also crossed the Atlantic and tended to congregate in the growing cities—Philadelphia, New York, Boston, Charlestown. These were commercial rather than manufacturing cities. By the middle of the seventeenth century, it is estimated that 50 percent of the male inhabitants of these cities were artisans. The male literacy rate was high, overall about 85 percent in the cities and rising to nearly 100 percent in Boston. Similarly located women were not far behind.[41] Local newspapers were legion, and the knowledge of public affairs was strong.

At the time of the American Revolution, the colonies all still had property requirements for office.[42] The artisan population of the cities, however, would occasionally develop into what became known as "the crowd."[43] And such were not chary of publicizing themselves. An extensive set of tracts detailing the conditions of this class circulated. In one from New York, an election pamphlet urged New York voters to join "Shuttle" the weaver, "Plane" the joiner,

The Making of an Agrarian Insurrection. (Amherst: University of Massachusetts Press, 1980); and Leonard L. Richards, Shays's Rebellion: The American Revolution's Final Battle (Philadelphia: University of Pennsylvania Press, 2002).

40. See Pauline Maier, Ratification: The People Debate the Constitution, 1787-1788 (New York: Simon and Schuster, 2011).

41. See Kevin Lockridge, Literacy in Colonial New England (New York: Norton, 1975). See also E. Jennifer Monaghan, "Literacy Instruction and Gender in Colonial New England," American Quarterly 40, no. 1 (March 1988): 18–41.

42. See the tables in A. Keyssar, Right to Vote, 306-7.

43. One counts at least twenty riots or insurrections on the part of colonists against their institutions over the fifty-year period preceding the American Revolution.

"Drive" the carter, "Mortar" the mason, "Tar" the mariner, "Snip" the tailor, "Smallrent" the fair-minded landlord, and "John Poor" the tenant and stand against "Gripe the Merchant, Squeeze the Shopkeeper, Spintext and Quible the Lawyer." The electorate was urged to vote out of office "people in Exalted Stations" who scorned "those they call the Vulgar, the Mob, the herd of Mechanicks." Direct action was taken again and again against landowners, the police, governors. According to a pamphlet from Massachusetts, "Poverty and Discontent appear in every Face (except the Countenances of the Rich) and dwell upon every Tongue." The author spoke of a few men, fed by "Lust of Power, Lust of Fame, Lust of Money," who got rich during the war. "No Wonder such Men can build Ships, Houses, buy Farms, set up their Coaches, Chariots, live very splendidly, purchase Fame, Posts of Honour," and called them "Birds of prey . . . Enemies to all Communities—wherever they live."[44]

A number of forces brought these elements to the fore. One factor was the rapid expansion of the population. In 1730, the colonies had fewer than 300,000 inhabitants. By the time of the American Revolution, they had 2.5 million. Additionally, the average life span extended. If one lived past childhood, the chances were that one would live to at least age seventy.

Craftspeople formed their own societies—an early example of what Jürgen Habermas calls the "public sphere." For those volunteering to the militia, military service became the site of political debating societies. In many of the troops, soldiers sought to elect their own officers, carrying over the practices of religious Congregationalism to the secular realm. As one conservative viewer put it, "The crowd began to think and act."[45]

It is into this complex and occasionally violent world that Thomas Paine came in 1774. Born in 1737 to a Quaker family and trained as a corset maker but a journalist by profession, Paine in London had made the acquaintance of Benjamin Franklin, who had urged him to emigrate to America. Paine became editor of the *Pennsylvania Magazine* in Philadelphia. In January 1776, he published *Common Sense*. It was an instant best seller and sold more than one hundred thousand copies in the first three months. What was unusual about it? First, and centrally important, was the style. Paine indulged in no literary fancies; there were very few classical allusions. The language was clear, simple, and direct: the king "was a royal brute." The development of cheap printing meant that his work was quickly and easily read throughout society.

44. Cited from Zinn, *People's History*, 51.

45. Steven Hahn, personal communication with the author. See also Jürgen Habermas, *The Structural Transformation of the Public Sphere* (Cambridge: Polity, 1989).

Bernard Bailyn estimates that more than four hundred of Paine's pamphlets were published in the early 1770s and as much as four times that number by 1783. They sold for a few pennies, at most a shilling.[46]

For Paine, the excellence of a polity was held to rest on "the constitution of the people and not the constitution of the government."[47] More important, being an American was consequent to living in America and not to one's national origin. Paine pointed out that "not one third of the inhabitants, even of this province, is of English origin."[48] The vision of citizenship in *Common Sense* was one of friendship and mutuality, of residence in a common space. He concludes as follows:

> In short, Independence is the only BOND that can tye and keep us together. We shall then see our object, and our ears will be legally shut against the schemes of an intriguing, as well, as a cruel enemy. . . .
>
> On these grounds I rest the matter. . . . WHEREFORE, instead of gazing at each other with suspicious or doubtful curiosity, let each of us, hold out to his neighbour the hearty hand of friendship, and unite in drawing a line, which, like an act of oblivion, shall bury in forgetfulness every former dissention. Let the names of Whig and Tory be extinct; and let none other be heard among us, than those of A GOOD CITIZEN, AN OPEN AND RESOLUTE FRIEND, AND A VIRTUOUS SUPPORTER OF THE RIGHTS OF MANKIND AND OF THE FREE AND INDEPENDANT [*sic*] STATES OF AMERICA.[49]

What were the criteria for citizenship? Paine shared an essentially Lockean vision of membership. Those who were self-sufficient were to be voting citizens. In Locke's England, this meant that heads of household were citizens, whereas servants, as they were dependent on the household, were not. Famously, Locke had argued in the *Second Treatise on Government* (paragraph 28) that "the turfs my servant has cut, the grass my horse has eaten, are mine."[50] They are "mine" because I am the head of household, whereas my horse and my servants work *for* me, are of my household. Richard Ashcraft has shown

46. See Bernard Bailyn, *Pamphlets of the American Revolution, 1750–1765* (Cambridge, MA: Harvard University Press, 1965), 3.

47. Thomas Paine, "Common Sense," in *The Works of Thomas Paine* (National Historical Association, 1925), 106.

48. Paine, "Common Sense," 128.

49. Paine, "Common Sense," 181–82. See G. Stedman Jones, *An End to Poverty? A Historical Debate* (London: 2004).

50. Locke, *Second Treatise*, 19 (see chap. 1, n. 1).

that this criterion of independence included approximately 80 percent of the adult male population by the 1680s.[51] Contrary to Madison and the then dominant thought in the colonies, however, Paine did not think that self-sufficiency was consequent only to the possession of landed property. In the *Letter Addressed to the Addressers* (1792), he argued that every man over the age of twenty-one who pays taxes in some form had the right to vote. To pay taxes, you had to be able to earn your living by your own hands. In practice, this meant that the tool-owning artisans of the cities were to be entitled to participate fully in the polity—to elect and be elected.

Like the Puritans, but on a secular basis, Paine thought that humans had it in their power to begin the world over again and, this time, to do it right. In *Common Sense*, he contended that "our great tale is American; our inferior one varies from place to place." It is America's mission: "a new creation is entrusted to our hands . . . ; we may begin the world anew . . . [and] exhibit a character hitherto unknown." As his writing evolved over time, it manifested an increasing drive toward universalism and the brotherhood of all (men). In the 1770s, in America, the criterion is independence. By 1795, under the impact of the French Revolution, he had moved much closer to universal criterion-less suffrage.[52] Paramount in his vision of citizenship throughout, however, is the unity of the country.

The impact of his writing was widespread—as noted in the epigraph to this chapter, Washington had *The American Crisis* read to the troops—such that, combined with the sociological realities of the cities, it converted his friend Jefferson and pushed Madison to accept an enlarged definition of citizenship. Jefferson, in fact, responding in 1813 to a request that the correspondence between him and Paine be published, refused but said the following: "I thank you for your polite attention on the subject of my letters to the late mr Paine, while he lived, I thought it a duty, as well as a test of my own political principles to support him against the persecutions of an unprincipled faction. My letters to him therefore expressed the sincere effusions of my heart, old now, and retired from the world, and anxious for tranquility, it is my wish that they should not be published during my life, as they might draw on me renewed molestations from the irreconcilable enemies of republican government."[53]

51. Richard Ashcraft, *Revolutionary Politics and Locke's Two Treatises of Government* (Princeton, NJ: Princeton University Press, 1986).

52. See the discussion in Eric Foner, *Tom Paine and Revolutionary America* (Oxford: Oxford University Press, 2004), 142–44.

53. Thomas Jefferson to Margaret B. Bonneville, 3 April 1813, Founders Online, National Archive, http://founders.archives.gov/documents/Jefferson/03-06-02-0044.

Jefferson had, for instance, written to Paine on June 19, 1792, "Go on then in doing with your pen what in other times was done with the sword: shew that reformation is more practicable by operating on the mind than on the body of man, and be assured that it has not a more sincere votary nor you a more ardent well-wisher than Yrs. &c."[54] Jefferson had in fact commissioned a portrait of Paine when the two had met in Paris in 1787.[55]

The facts of artisan life are incorporated into the practices of citizenship and thus change the property qualification. Owning a skill and the ability to make something and sell it—Paine envisages a commercial republic—are now sufficient grounds for being a citizen. This view has a number of important consequences. It is most centrally the grounds for giving up the supposed necessity of a small state—a central argument in the *Federalist Papers*. Before that work, it had always been assumed that a virtuous polity would of necessity be small. Madison and the others now understood that if the basis for future was simply self-sufficiency, then, contrary to previous republican theorists, large size was not a drawback; indeed, it was a positive good. Paine knew this also, and indeed urged the then President Jefferson in 1802 that the United States purchase the Louisiana territories that Spain had ceded to France. He was not alone in this policy: the need to acquire that territory and especially control over the port of New Orleans, through which three-eighths of US exports passed, was already a matter of concern to Jefferson. In any case, the purchase was accomplished the following year. The extension of the franchise expanded the boundaries of what counted as a citizen and also changed its character. Self-sufficiency was now the criterion that had to be met and became the basis of virtue. And this expansion also meant that the polity was safer from the scruffiness of the "crowd." The effect of Madison's argument was to legitimate any and all expansion of the American polity: political virtue was no longer understood as requiring a limit on size. There was, after all, a whole continent to the West.

Making something or the ability to make something is now important as a, or even *the*, basis of citizenship—and with it comes a valuation of science and technical skill. Self-sufficiency and "independence" are increasingly conceived of in individual terms. The great threat always remains that of

54. Thomas Jefferson to Thomas Paine, 19 June 1792, American History from Revolution to Reconstruction and Beyond, University of Groningen, http://www.let.rug.nl/usa/presidents/thomas-jefferson/letters-of-thomas-jefferson/jefl99.php.

55. Simon P. Newman and Peter Onuf, *Paine and Jefferson in the Age of Revolution* (Charlottesville, NC: University of Virginia Press, 2013), 229.

enslavement—dependency on others for one's livelihood and thus openness to the lure of corrupting promises.

The fear was, on the one hand, of loss of independence and, on the other, of those who were dependent. The expansion of the criteria for citizenship dealt with some of the sociopolitical changes that corresponded to the growth of the now new nation. There remained, however, an elephant in the room. By 1770, the overall black population of the thirteen colonies was more than 20 percent; in the South, it was close to 40 percent, and in the North, less than 5 percent (and less than 1 percent in New England). And free blacks were overwhelmingly concentrated in the North, with many of the free being refugees from the revolt in Saint Domingue. By 1790, the year of the first US census, blacks numbered about 760,000, of which 93 percent were slaves.[56]

When the question of slavery was confronted at the Constitutional Convention, it was approached with extreme caution. The word *slavery* was not used. There were references to "other persons" and "persons in service or labor." "Slavery" was after all what the colonists had rebelled against. What to do about this apparently glaring contradiction? As is well known, various compromises were worked out between the Northern and Southern states to ratify the Constitution. It is possible that those in the North opposed to slavery could comfort themselves with the sense that time would eventually deal with the question. After all, slavery was being or had been abolished in the North. Private manumission was made legal in the South, the law in Virginia having already been eased in 1782. In response to the Fugitive Slave Act of 1793 that permitted owners to cross state lines to recapture escaped slaves, several Northern states passed laws guaranteeing black persons liberties. The importation of new slaves was declared to be illegal after 1808.[57]

Jefferson, in his personal notes at the debate around the drafting of the Declaration of Independence, remarked that "the clause too, reprobating the enslaving the inhabitants of Africa, was struck out in complaisance to South Carolina & Georgia, who had never attempted to restrain the importation of slaves, and who on the contrary still wished to continue it. Our Northern brethren also I believe felt a little tender under those censures; for tho' their people have very few slaves themselves yet they had been pretty considerable

56. Peter Kolchin, *American Slavery 1619-1877* (New York: Hill and Wang, 1993), 81, 241-42. See Sean Wilentz, *No Property in Man: Slavery and Antislavery at the Nation's Founding* (Cambridge, MA: Harvard University Press, 2018), for the "slavery a small factor" argument.

57. I draw on Kolchin, *American Slavery*, chap. 3. See R. J. M. Blackett, *The Captive's Quest for Freedom: Fugitive Slaves, the 1850 Fugitive Slave Law, and the Politics of Slavery* (Cambridge: Cambridge University Press, 2017).

carriers of them to others."[58] This omission results eventually in the notorious clause I.2 of the Constitution to the effect that for census purposes, and thus for determining the number of representatives to which each state was entitled, Native Americans should not count at all and "other persons" (i.e., blacks) should count as three-fifths of a person. Jefferson's notes also make it clear—and we know this from other documents—that, already in 1776, he saw that the existence of slavery posed a contradiction. And it was equally clear to him and most others at the Constitutional Convention that the political prudential requirements for establishing a new society required covering over that contradiction. The ruling understanding of citizenship was for most of the Constitution's framers not flexible enough to include blacks, nor women.

There were other additional reasons for this obfuscation than the desire for political union. One was economic, which became dramatically more important after the end of the eighteenth century. Cotton production in the South was only three thousand bales a year in 1790. Consequent to the invention in the same year of the cotton gin, however, production increased rapidly and by the time of the Civil War was in excess of four million bales, three-quarters of which were exported, mainly to England. Much of the rest provided the foundation for the industrialization of the North. By permitting mechanical extraction of the seeds, the gin also allowed the much wider and more extensive planting of short-staple cotton. The seeds of the short-staple variety were harder to extract manually than those of the long-staple: the gin solved that problem. Additionally, whereas long-staple cotton required a semitropical climate, short-staple cotton could be planted all across the South.

A final reason for avoiding the chattel slavery question was political fear. Up until the end of the eighteenth century, manumissions were fairly common. In 1800, however, Gabriel Prosser, a Virginia slave (and literate blacksmith), planned a rebellion in which he hoped to lead one thousand slaves into Richmond, take the armory, and hold Governor James Monroe hostage until their demands were met. He was betrayed for a reward by another slave (to whom the reward was only partially paid) and eventually apprehended and hanged with twenty-five coconspirators. The possibility of widespread rebellion, especially following the successful slave revolt on Saint Domingue, sent a wave of fear through the South. Additionally, in 1793 in the aftermath of the French Revolution, the French had freed all slaves in territories over which

---

58. "Notes of Proceedings in the Continental Congress, 7 June–1 August 1776," Founders Online, National Archives, https://founders.archives.gov/documents/Jefferson/01-01 -02-0160. See the discussion in Shain, *Declaration in Historical Context*, 500–501.

they had dominion. White reaction to the potential rebellion, coupled with fears over the number of free African Americans, led to a severe tightening of control over slaves in America. Freedom of travel and the possibility of education were greatly restricted. Overall, historians have identified hundreds of slave revolts in the 150 years preceding the Civil War.[59]

Jefferson's ambivalence about slavery is well known. On the one hand, he thought slavery to have lifted the "Negro out of savagery"; on the other hand, he owned close to six hundred human beings and freed only seven of them; and on yet a mysterious third hand, when confronted with the issue, he remarked that "if God is just, I tremble for my country." In 1774, in "A Summary View of the Rights of British Americans," he had argued that "the abolition of domestic slavery is the great object of desire in those countries where it was unhappily introduced." In the *Notes on the State of Virginia*, he remarks that "the whole commerce between master and slave is a continual exercise in the most boisterous passions, the most unremitting despotism on the one part, and degrading submissions on the other." Slavery was an "unhappy influence" as it taught domination and subordination to children.[60] (One cannot refrain from thinking ironically of his relations with Sally Hemmings, his slave-mistress.) However, he never supported any antislavery society and expected after the 1803 Louisiana Purchase that slavery would move into those territories. In an 1814 exchange, Edward Coles, who had been governor of Illinois, approached Jefferson to obtain his support for the emancipation effort. Jefferson replied that the public climate was not conducive. He noted that whether from nature or nurture, those who have been kept in bondage are "as incapable as children of taking care of themselves" (even those he had referred to earlier as having successfully rebelled in Saint Domingue). The cause, he assured Coles, "shall have all my prayers, and these are the only weapons of an old man."[61]

Jefferson was sure that, whether from nature or nurture, blacks were at least at present inferior to whites. And he, like many others, was worried about

59. See here Herbert Aptheker, *American Negro Slave Revolts* (New York. International Publishers, 1993), though he tends to exaggerate the number of revolts; and more popularly, the six-episode PBS television series by Henry Louis Gates and Donald Yacavone, *The African Americans: Many Rivers to Cross* (available in a boxed set of DVDs or on YouTube). See the bibliography in Kolchin, *American Slavery*, 276-79.

60. Jefferson, "Query XVIII—Manners," *Notes on the State of Virginia*, in *Writings*, 288.

61. Thomas Jefferson, *Writings*, 1345-46. See *Slavery at Jefferson's Monticello: "After Monticello,"* Smithsonian NMAAHC/Monticello. The literature of Jefferson and slavery is extensive.

the nondocile behavior of slaves. With the slave uprisings, firmly in mind and fearful of others, Jefferson and other rich slave owners came to the conclusion that the only possible solution was colonization—the repatriation (on the assumption that there was a patria) of African Americans to Africa. Accordingly, in 1817, the American Colonization Society was founded and over fifty years managed to send about six thousand free blacks to Liberia. The movement was doomed on two grounds: the expense of repatriation and the economic importance of slavery.[62] Here the thought was that since blacks cannot (for whatever supposed reason) be citizens, the only solution was to get rid of them. Additionally, as we shall see, for a wide range of Southerners, slavery began to be thought of as a positive and even moral good.

In point of fact, for the first part of the nineteenth century most white Americans, in both North and South, tended simply to live with the contradiction and the unspoken hope that it would somehow go away. With considerable success, they more or less unconsciously took unawareness upon themselves. In 1851, Herman Melville made the point forcibly in his novella *Benito Cereno*. Drawn and fictionalized from an actual occurrence, the story involves two ships. In Melville's account, the *Bachelor's Delight*, captained by Amasa Delano, encounters a Spanish ship, the *San Dominick* (so renamed by Melville to recall the successful slave revolt), off the coast of southern Chile. The Spanish vessel is in seriously bad repair. Delano goes over to it to offer help and finds a ship whose personnel consists mainly of blacks, albeit with a white captain, Don Benito Cereno, and very few other white sailors. Cereno tells a tale of disaster and death from storms, fever, and scurvy to account for the condition of the boat. He is assisted in all things by the African Babo, a small and physically unprepossessing man, who appears to be his body servant and never leaves his side, even when Delano asks for a private conversation with Cereno. As things develop, the reader and Delano learn very slowly and only at the end that the Spanish ship is a slave ship, that the slaves have revolted and taken it over, killing most of the white crew. During the whole development, Delano remains completely unaware of the possibility that something is out of the normal order on the *San Dominick*—he cannot imagine blacks capable of accomplishing anything. This blindness is despite the fact that he is a New Englander (indeed, the historical Delano was an ancestor of Franklin Delano Roosevelt) and a citizen of one of the most antislavery states. Melville's point is that the actuality of slavery makes little or no impact, even and

62. See Kolchin, *American Slavery*, 164–65.

perhaps especially on those Americans whom one might have expected to be most aware of it.[63]

For most whites, in both North and South, it was hard to find the right thing to say. Again, Melville caught this inner struggle succinctly. After the situation on the *San Dominick* has become clear and after the blacks are captured, Delano comforts Cereno. To Delano's insistence that the "mild trades [winds] that now fan your check, do they not come with a human-like healing to you?" Cereno replies, however, that "their steadfastness but waft[s] me to my tomb." It is at this point that the central teaching of the novella appears.

> "You are saved," cried Captain Delano, more and more astonished and pained; "you are saved; what has cast such a shadow upon you?"
> "The negro."
> There was silence.

Cereno's answer—explicitly—puts an end to all further conversation. There is not another word of direct speech in the novella, as if with this response, nothing more could be said, as if words had failed. At the outset of the story, we were warned at the end of the third paragraph that there were "shadows present, foreshadowing deeper shadows to come."[64] Melville sets his story in 1799, thus in close temporal proximity to the revolt on Saint Domingue, while the actual events on which it is based are from 1805: there were indeed deeper shadows to come. Slavery was an issue that for many people was simply not to be part of the conversation of most whites.

63. See Tracy B. Strong, "A Tale of Two Ships," in *Melville and Political Theory*, ed. Jason Frank (Lexington: University of Kentucky Press, 2012).

64. Herman Melville, "Benito Cereno," in *The Piazza Tales* (New York: Library of America, 1984), 784, 673.

3

DEFINING BOUNDARIES

Whatever else the Civil War was for
It wasn't just to keep the States together,
Nor just to free the slaves, though it did both.
She wouldn't have believed those ends enough
To have given outright for them all she gave.
Her giving somehow touched the principle
That all men are created free and equal.
And to hear her quaint phrases, so removed
From the world's view to-day of all those things.
That's a hard mystery of Jefferson's.
What did he mean?

ROBERT FROST, "THE BLACK COTTAGE"

In 1935, the great black poet Langston Hughes wrote a poem he entitled "Let America Be America Again." It recalled for its readers that the polity that wished to call itself "America had never yet been" *and* that it was those who had been over time pushed aside (the farmer, the worker, the Negro, the poor white, the young) who "dreamt our basic dream."[1] In this chapter I take up various attempts—some successful, some not—to dream that dream. In his 1962 poem "A Cabin in the Clearing," Robert Frost wondered whether Americans— "the sleepers in this house"—would ever know where and what they are: "I begin to fear they never will."

---

1. Langston Hughes, "Let America Be America Again," Academy of American Poets, https://www.poets.org/poetsorg/poem/let-america-be-america-again.

During the period from the 1820s through the 1850s, six interrelated developments attempted to come to grips with the contradictions between the fear of enslavement, the fear of slaves, and the achievement of independence, collectively and individually: (1) another religious revival, this one called the Second Great Awakening; (2) a temperance movement; (3) a reasoned defense of the institutions of chattel slavery; (4) an abolitionist movement; (5) a diverse feminist movement; and (6) experiments in communitarianism. All of these developments took place in the context of profound sociological and economic change; all of them fed into and against one another. In turn, what it meant to be a citizen changed. The person who grasped the interrelation of these changes most profoundly and attempted to formulate a conception of citizenship adequate to them was Abraham Lincoln, who will be the subject of chapter 4.

THE SECOND GREAT AWAKENING

In the First Great Awakening, Jonathan Edwards and the others had sought to bring citizens back to the fundamental values of Puritanism through a direct apprehension of the emotion and fear of damnation. The movement had taken place mainly in the context of the original states. By 1845, however, statehood extended as far as the Mississippi River (and with Texas even beyond it, despite the fact that Mexico had never recognized Texas's independence). West of the Appalachians, most of the population was rural or in small towns. Only four cities west of the mountains ranked in the one hundred largest: Saint Louis (number 24), Cleveland (67), Dayton (68), and Chicago (92).[2] A religious revival swept through the country, centered mostly around large camp meetings and with very little institutional reference, positive or negative.

The theology, however, was different from that of the preceding century. Whereas Edwards had emphasized man's originally sinful nature and hence one's fateful dependency on God's grace and the fear consequent to that, thus one's *lack* of choice, these preachers argued that sin and salvation were determined by personal choice. One can—and one should—choose to be holy: after all, had not Jesus urged: "Be perfect even as your Father in heaven is perfect" (Matt. 5:48). The responsibility was all on one's self, but if one perfected oneself, one would be saved. Whereas the First Great Awakening had focused to a

2. "Biggest Cities by Population—Year 1840," Biggest US Cities (website), updated July 2, 2018, https://www.biggestuscities.com/1840.

great extent on the middle and upper classes—Edwards's theology was of great sophistication—the Second targeted the lower classes and the less educated.

In contrast to the earlier awakening, revival meetings were now spread by itinerant ministers—ministers who were, that is, not attached to a particular church, which meant that the revival took place in the absence of a regular congregation and of an institutional structure. In an established church, desirable pews were most often reserved for the elite of the congregation. At these meetings there were, perforce, no pews, only communal benches. Preachers—sometimes several at the same time—spoke from raised platforms.

Such revival meetings were thus quite naturally often strongly antiauthority, especially against that of the established church. As the return of Christ at the millennium was expected, converts were expected to purify society in preparation for his return. The movement reached back into the eighteenth century. James Davenport, Yale educated and from an old Puritan family, became an itinerant preacher. He denounced the clergy of the established churches as "dead husks" and "deceivers." He accused Joseph Noyes, the pastor of New Haven, of being a "wolf in sheep's clothing."[3] He is the originator of the "bonfire of the vanities," the organized burning of jewelry, wigs, books by ministers, and such. (Indeed, at one such conflagration, overcome with enthusiasm, he took off his own pants and threw them into the fire.) Present at these meetings were slaves and women: they were mass events. In Cane Ridge, Kentucky, in 1801, a revival meeting led by more than eighteen ministers had drawn an attendance of twenty thousand.[4] The appeal was greatly to the poor and marginalized: distinctions among worshippers were pretty much obliterated. Women apparently outnumbered men three to two, and the appeal to the young was particularly strong. The revivals were thus democratizing and antiauthoritarian: they shaped groups that had been only marginal participants in the mainstream of society.

Rapture was its basis and it ran high. A report from the young James Finley, who had attended a camp meeting in 1802 of twenty thousand people tells us:

> The noise was like the roar of Niagara. The vast sea of human beings seemed to be agitated as if by a storm. I counted seven ministers, all preaching at one time, some on stumps, others on wagons. . . . Some of

3. See Thomas S. Kidd, *The Great Awakening: A Brief History with Documents* (New York: Bedford/St. Martin's, 2008). He mentions the pants episode on page 1.
4. See Paul Keith Conklin, *Cane Ridge: America's Pentecost* (Madison: University of Wisconsin Press, 1990).

the people were singing, others praying, some crying for mercy. A peculiarly strange sensation came over me. My heart beat tumultuously, my knees trembled, my lips quivered, and I felt as though I must fall to the ground. A strange supernatural power seemed to pervade the entire mass of mind there collected. I became so weak and powerless that I found it necessary to sit down. Soon after I left and went into the woods and there I strove to rally and man up my courage. I tried to philosophize in regard to these wonderful exhibitions, resolving them into mere sympathetic excitement—a kind of religious enthusiasm, inspired by songs and eloquent harangues. My pride was wounded, for I had supposed that my mental and physical strength and vigor could most successfully resist these influences. After some time I returned to the scene of excitement the waves of which, if possible, had risen still higher. The same awfulness of feeling came over me. . . . Then it was that I saw clearly through the thin vail [*sic*] of Universalism, and this refuge of lies was swept away by the Spirit of God. Then fell the scales from my sin-blinded eyes, and I realized, in all its force and power, the awful truth, that if I died in my sins I was a lost man forever.[5]

This is a revolutionary set of ideas for it locates sin and virtue in character and, more important, in individual choice. And in doing so, it modifies the understanding of slavery: slavery now means capitulation (either enforced or from weakness of will) to passions, artifice, and excess. As even the Unitarian William Ellery Channing wrote, "little is gained against outward despotism if the soul is in thrall."[6] It locates the capacity for virtuous behavior inside each individual and not simply in the performance of what John Calvin had called "posterior signs." To commit oneself to Christ meant, however, that one had to eschew all that which might turn one away from that commitment. Especially during the first stages of the Second Great Awakening, there was a strong sense of millenarianism—the Second Coming of Christ was felt to be at hand, and it behooved one to get one's soul in order as rapidly as possible. While it proved hard to maintain for long a strong saliency of the imminent end of time, it is important that the movement was connected directly to the achievement of a perfect social situation.[7] All that stood in its way had to be

5. James Finley, "A Testimony from the Cane Ridge Revival, 1801," cited from Finley's autobiography of 1853, SermonIndex.net, http://www.sermonindex.net/modules/newbb /viewtopic.php?topic_id=30740&forum=40.

6. William Ellery Channing, *Slavery* (Boston: Monroe, 1835).

7. The Greek for "perfect" is τέλειοι, which carries the connotation of a final state to be attained.

refused. The Awakening lay the most weight on the individual—what he (or she) did as an individual determined whether or not that person was virtuous. There is almost no *collective* sense of what counted as virtue: with the Second Great Awakening, a more exclusively individual sense of virtue takes increasing hold.

TEMPERANCE

The emphasis on individual self-development means that it is not therefore surprising that along with the revival movement came a second movement: a drive for temperance. Whereas beer, wine, and liquor had been an important part of Puritan life, a temperance movement seems to have first started with resistance to the growth of the distillation of whiskey (as opposed to wine and beer)[8] but soon spread to total abstinence. Mark Lender refers to this change as consequent to the "stewardship tradition," by which a moral elite would set the standards for the rest of society.[9] The American Temperance Society was formed in 1826 and developed rapidly, merging in another group in 1831 to become the American Temperance Union. Women were especially attracted to the movement, in part no doubt because drinking was expensive and took men away from the home.[10]

It is thus a mistake to think, as did Richard Hofstadter, that the temperance movement was simply a cramped offshoot of a lamentably Puritanical America. The movement was widespread, was politically salient, and cut across class divisions. It corresponded to a rise in the concern for the role of women in society, and if it saw women as mostly providing for a good home life, it also held that a good home life was essential for political virtue, a further pri-

8. The literature is extensive. See, e.g., Norman H. Clark, *Deliver Us From Evil: An Interpretation of American Prohibition* (New York: Norton, 1976); Mark E. Lender, *Drinking in America: A History* (Chicago: Free Press, 1987), 1–86. Older work includes Ernest Cherrington, *The Evolution of Prohibition in the United States of America* (Westerville: Ohio American Press, 1920); Peter Odegaard, *Pressure Politics: The Story of the Anti-Saloon League* (1928; repr., Octagon Books, 1966).

9. Lender, *Drinking in America*, 65.

10. See the review essay by Paul A. Carter, "Temperance, Intemperance and the American Character; Or, Dr. Jekyll and Mr. Hyde," *Journal of Social History* 14, no. 3 (Spring 1981): 481–84. And that by Jed Dannenbaum, "The Crusade against Drink," *Reviews in American History* 9, no. 4 (December 1981): 497–502. See also Jed Dannenbaum, "The Origins of Temperance Activism and Militancy among American Women," *Journal of Social History* 15, no. 2 (December 1981): 235–52.

vatization of the prerequisites of citizenship. The all-male delegation to the 1833 Ohio State Temperance Convention passed a resolution urging "that it is a matter of high importance to the cause of temperance that the united influence and energies of females should be enlisted actively in its support: *Resolved, therefore*, that a committee of five be appointed to prepare an address to the ladies of this State on that subject."[11] Some women soon formed themselves into bands and took direct action breaking up saloons and destroying liquor supplies.

The temperance movement blossomed into a considerable political force, especially on the state and local levels. It is estimated that over the next quarter century, the consumption of alcohol in the United States fell by 50 percent.[12] Three things are important about these events. First, as with the revival movement, the possibility of virtue became increasingly individual. Second, virtue was increasingly sited in nonpolitical arenas, in particular the family. And third, to some degree in tension with the previous point, although women did not vote or hold office, they were important in the movement and, on many occasions, empowered themselves to take the law into their own hands. Ranges of women, though unable to vote, became increasingly involved in public affairs, albeit public affairs that related to domesticity. This means that there grew up a cadre of women accustomed to leadership and to acting autonomously. I shall return to this development when considering the various feminist movements later in this chapter.

DEFENSE OF CHATTEL SLAVERY

A third development has the same origins in individualization but is ultimately different in effect. It now appears more and more clearly that one of the things that is wrong with chattel slavery is that the condition of slavery, being one of dependence, *prevents the slaves from being able to choose the path of individual righteousness*. Christianity entailed a monogenetic understanding of the races—that all are descended from a common ancestor.[13] Hence,

11. Cited in Dannenbaum, "Origins of Temperance," 236.

12. See John Niven, *The Coming of the Civil War, 1837–1861* (Arlington Heights, IL: Harlan Davidson, 1990).

13. See R. Allen Bolar, "There's Power in the Blood: Religion, White Supremacy, and the Politics of Darwinism in America" (PhD diss., University of California, San Diego, 2010). The debate continues. See Kenneth W. Kemp, "Science, Theology and Monogenesis," *American Catholic Philosophical Quarterly* 85, no. 2 (2011): 217–36.

blacks are just as much children of God as are the other races, and to deny them the possibility of self-perfection was to go against God's law. Slaves were at the mercy of their masters—and this was especially troubling in relation to female slaves. Especially prominent in the North was an increasingly strong conviction that the South was an "erotic society" where the owners were filled with a "lust for power" as well as a lust "for pagan pleasures." According to a newspaper in upstate New York, the South was "one great Sodom" and "compared to the South a Turkish harem is a cradle of virgin purity."[14] Lust made achieving perfection impossible.

Such accusations were to some great degree exaggerations, but they were increasingly widely believed in the North. In response, the South was not long in developing a defense of slavery to overcome the apparent contradiction between the American fear of dependency and the actuality of chattel slavery. It should be noted here that this defense was *not* the contemporary one that might possibly have been drawn from the work of some years back by present-day economists. In *Time on the Cross*, Robert Fogel and Stanley Engerman argued that far from being particularly sadistic or exploitative, Southern slave owners were in fact good businessmen who ran an efficient enterprise—more efficient, they argued, by 35 percent than farm labor in the North. Slaves were, in their analysis, generally well treated, rarely punished: the South was a set of normally happy households and generally unified families, both slave and white. If the Marxist historian Eugene Genovese had earlier presented a picture of a white and noncapitalist South that was not without its attractive cultural features, in effect what Fogel and Engerman did was to present a picture of the white South as a sustainable, economically successful capitalism that was not particularly oppressive.[15]

While the argument was a part of the Southern defense, the contention that slaves were supposedly not (generally) harshly treated was, however, not its

14. "Politics and the Pulpit," *North Star* (Rochester, NY), June 13, 1850, 1, http://www .libraryweb.org/~digitized/newspapers/north_star/vol.III,page1.pdf. See also Robert Fogel, *Without Consent or Contract: The Rise and Fall of American Slavery* (New York: Norton, 1989); and C. Vann Woodward, review of *Without Consent or Contract*, by Robert Fogel, *New York Times Book Review*, November 5, 1989.

15. Eugene H. Genovese, *The Political Economy of Slavery* (New York: Vintage, 1965); Robert Fogel and Stanley Engerman, *Time on the Cross: The Economics of American Negro Slavery* (New York: Norton, 1974). The Fogel and Engerman book produced a storm of controversy and considerable dissent, both scientific and moral. See, e.g., Kolchin, *American Slavery*, chap. 4; Herbert Gutman, *Slavery and the Numbers Game: A Critique of "Time on the Cross"* (1975; repr., Champaign: University of Illinois Press, 2003). For an extended symposium on the book, see *Explorations in Economic History* 12, no. 4 (October 1975).

core. To understand that defense, we need to look at the context. In the first part of the nineteenth century, suffrage had been generally stripped of its property requirement and was by and large available to all self-possessed white male individuals.[16] Note that young people, prisoners, those deemed insane, felons, those not meeting a residence requirement, most nonwhites, women, and even (until 1984) the homeless were still not permitted to vote. And various age requirements existed for holding federal and many other offices. The extension of suffrage took place in a society that was not economically capitalist—that is, in a society where the contractual relationship between labor and ownership was not basically a matter of wages. Most goods were not produced by wage labor but by slavery, by craft production, or by family farmers (69 percent of the labor force). And, whereas in the late eighteenth century it was possible for a right-thinking white Northerner and some Southerners to expect that slavery would simply fade away, for reasons that we will see, this was no longer the case by the first third of the next century. Slavery became increasingly well entrenched and an important part of the national economy.

Nor was there a strong anti-chattel slavery movement. Although property qualifications for voting had mostly disappeared, the sense that property could not be taken away by state force remained strong. I am not concerned here, then, with the profitability of slave economies but with the political consequences of that economic form. In any case, there is debate about the matter: if Fogel and Engerman argued that it was profitable, Genovese argued that it was not intended to be as profitable as possible. Their respective conclusions are not incompatible: slavery could still be profitable and correspond to a less-than-capitalistic entrepreneurial way of life.[17] The point is that slavery was viable, a conclusion perhaps first arrived at in an article by A. H. Conrad and J. R. Meyer. Whether or not their economic analysis holds up, and it has been critiqued, the *political* conclusions one can draw from it seem to me telling.[18]

I summarize here their article as well as provide some background. In 1790, slavery was concentrated mainly in Virginia and in the Carolinas. By 1819, it spread extensively to Louisiana and Kentucky, and was making in-

16. Rhode Island was the last state to do away with property requirements—amid considerable conflict and controversy. See material from Brown University, John Carter Library, on Rhode Island and property requirement in the 1840s.

17. One could explore this point by looking at the first sections of Anna Firor Scott, *The Southern Lady: From Pedestal to Politics, 1830-1930* (Charlottesville: University of Virginia Press, 1995).

18. Alfred H. Conrad and John R. Meyer, "The Economics of Slavery in the Ante Bellum South," *Journal of Political Economy* 66, no. 2 (1958): 95-130.

roads across the Mississippi. By 1830, it is prevalent across most of the country south of the Ohio River, a trend that intensifies for the next twenty years; it soon moves West to Texas and Arkansas.[19] As the white Americans (and their slaves) spread westward, driving out or killing the Native Americans who lived there, the question naturally arose of whether or not those new territories and eventually new states would allow slaveholding. By 1820, there were no recorded slaves in New England, nor in Pennsylvania, Ohio, Indiana, and most of Illinois, and only a small number in New York and New Jersey. In 1820, the Missouri Compromise, brokered by Speaker of the House Henry Clay, admitted Maine as a free state, allowed for slavery in the new state of Missouri, but nowhere else north of the 36°30′ N latitude (thus all states north of the Ohio River). This left the American land south of that latitude potentially open for slave states, but not the Northwest Territories, and had no effect on the Southwest and the West Coast, which were mostly controlled by Spain.

For the next twenty years, the Missouri Compromise covered over the question of slavery. Slavery was an institution south of 36°30′ N, and for citizens of New England, it pretty much could be kept out of mind as it was out of sight. In *Adventures of Huckleberry Finn* (set in 1844), Mark Twain quietly presents an example of how the compromise permitted a kind of willed blindness. In chapter 16, the raft carrying Jim and Huck down the Mississippi is run over at night by a riverboat. In the fog and dark, they have missed the turn-off to the Ohio River and the free state of Illinois. Huck thinks Jim dead and the raft gone. Swimming ashore, he is taken in by the Grangerford family. After they determine he is not related to the Shepherdsons, with whom they are in perpetual feud, they take him in as a family member—and give him a slave. In chapter 18, Huck remarks, "Each person had their own nigger to wait on them—Buck [the young Grangerford son] too. My nigger had a monstrous easy time, because I warn't used to having anybody do anything for me, but Buck's was on the jump most of the time."[20] Although it might seem strange for a family to bestow a slave on a young boy whom they found after a riverboat accident, Twain makes nothing more of this in the story. It is possible, however, from his detailed description of the accident to locate (Google

19. Data drawn from Jason G. Gauthier et al., *Measuring America: The Decennial Censuses from 1790 to 2000*, Report No. POL/02-MA(RV) (Washington, DC: US Census Bureau, September 2002), updated April 6, 2017, https://www.census.gov/library/publications/2002/dec/pol_02-ma.html. The census likely underestimates the prevalence and presence of slavery, listing none in Vermont, for example, which is incorrect.

20. Mark Twain, *Adventures of Huckleberry Finn* in *Mississippi Writings* (New York: Library of America, 1982), 729.

Earth!) the precise place of the riverboat crash—Twain was, after all, a licensed riverboat pilot and knew the river intimately. If one does so, one finds that the crash occurs just *after* the raft crosses latitude 36°30′ N. Once south of the Missouri Compromise line, apparently the most natural thing in the world is for a white person, even Huck, to acquire a slave.[21] The point of Twain's not calling attention to this is that very few *were* paying attention.

But things were slowly to change. After 1808, the importation of new slaves from Africa had been forbidden. As noted in chapter 2, the invention of the cotton gin had permitted the rapid expansion of cotton culture in the "New South" (what we might today call the Deep South: Alabama, Mississippi, and Louisiana) and in particular the planting of short-staple cotton that would grow well in that climate. The effect of long-term cotton monoculture in the North was to deplete the soil and promote various soil-borne diseases.[22] Over time, cotton production in the Old South—Virginia, Maryland, North Carolina, South Carolina, and Georgia—tended therefore to be replaced by the development of a slave market to the New South, by tobacco crops, and by some rice production along the coast of Georgia and South Carolina. The main crop of the New South was now cotton—it was profitable, rarely subject to recession, and, as the investment in slaves and land had already been made, the gin allowed for easier and more lucrative production. The Old South shift to mostly tobacco, was, however, to a product with an unstable market.[23] As noted, Old South slave owners often rented out their skilled slaves.

Thus the New South depended economically on cotton production—we will see those arguments shortly—and an important part of the economy of the Old South became a market for slaves. It was also clear that over time the soil depletion problems that had affected the Old South would affect the New South. The movement of slaves was already from the Northeast to the Southwest: the question of the slave-or-no status of the potential territories west of Texas became important.

In 1846, President James K. Polk and his extensive allies in Congress provoked a war with Mexico over the Southwest territories. Polk coveted Califor-

21. For further detail, see Tracy B. Strong, "'Glad to Find Out Who I Was': What Can Be Learned on a Raft," *Journal of Law, Culture and Philosophy* (2010).

22. See Rui Li et al., "Chemical, Organic, and Bio-Fertilizer Management Practices Effect on Soil Physicochemical Property and Antagonistic Bacteria Abundance of a Cotton Field: Implications for Soil Biological Quality," *Soil and Tillage Research* 167 (April 2017): 30–38, https://doi.org/10.1016/j.still.2016.11.001.

23. The relevant work is well summarized in Alan Brinkley, "Cotton, Slavery and the Old South," chap. 11 in *American History: A Survey*.

nia and wanted to keep it from the British, who also had their eyes on it. Mexico refused an initial US offer (which was an insulting one) and, after military defeat, lost or had to give up for a very reduced sum the lands that stretched from Texas to California, including what are now Utah, Nevada, and part of Colorado, a territory larger than Western Europe.

John O'Sullivan, a Jacksonian Reformer Democrat and newspaper man, had written in 1839:

> The American people . . . have, in reality, but little connection with the past history of any [other nation], and still less with all antiquity, its glories, or its crimes. On the contrary, our national birth was the beginning of a new history, the formation and progress of an untried political system, which separates us from the past and connects us with the future only; and so far as regards the entire development of the natural rights of man, in moral, political, and national life, we may confidently assume that our country is destined to be the great nation of futurity.[24]

Six years later—when he is urging the annexation of Texas—he famously writes, "It is our manifest destiny to overspread the continent allotted by Providence for the free development of our yearly multiplying millions."[25] And O'Sullivan was not alone: while Herman Melville also had strong anxieties about the integrity of his nation, he could write (albeit with a warning) in *White-Jacket*: "We Americans are the peculiar, chosen people—the Israel of our time . . . the political messiah . . . has come in us, if we would but give utterance to his promptings."[26] The importance of the claim to "manifest destiny" is that it simply extends in space the creed as to where it was the lot and duty of America to build a godly and virtuous society. John Winthrop had pretty much restricted such efforts to the territory at hand. With O'Sullivan and many others, there were to be no obstacles before the shores of the Pacific. Where did "America" stop? In 1845, a proposal for a transcontinental railroad was presented to Congress; construction started before the Civil War. Before actual

24. John O'Sullivan, "The Great Nation of Futurity," *United States Democratic Review* 6, no. 23 (November 1839): 426. See also Hietala, *Manifest Design* (see intro., n. 9). O'Sullivan forms the subject of one of the chapters of the PhD thesis of one of my students; see Gomez, "An Almost Chosen People" (see intro., n. 9).

25. John O'Sullivan, "Annexation," *United States Magazine and Democratic Review* 17, no. 1 (July-August 1845): 5-10, at 7.

26. Herman Melville, *White-Jacket*, in *Redburn, White-Jacket, Moby Dick* (New York: Library of America, 1983), 506.

construction could begin, however, a choice between two proposed routes had to be resolved—a southern one from New Orleans through the land acquired from Mexico and a northern one from Chicago through the territories.

The annexation after the war with Mexico of this land was greeted with enthusiasm by Jacksonians like O'Sullivan (though not by Ralph Waldo Emerson or Lincoln or others). But the question still remained as to their status as territories vis-à-vis slavery. Were blacks citizens? Under the control (at least supposedly) of their masters, thus not independent, slaves manifestly were not. The Missouri Compromise had forbidden slavery north of latitude 36°30′ N. In the railroad debate, slave states preferred the southern route, for obvious reasons. In 1854, however, due in great part to the efforts of Senator Stephen Douglas, who had heavy railroad interests, the Kansas-Nebraska Act was passed: the railroad would take the northern route. Douglas above all wanted the new territories open for settling by whites and stood to profit greatly from the northern route. Slave or not was of secondary interest to him, though he certainly was never a supporter of abolition.

With the 1854 act, all the land from the Mississippi to the Rockies was available for white settlement and potentially open for slavery. (The impact on Native Americans hardly needs repeating here).[27] According to the Kansas-Nebraska Act, the new territories were to decide by vote on which economy they were to develop. In actuality, vote totals tended to depend on who counted them. This provision gave rise to extensive violent conflicts between the factions: settlers rushed to claim parcels and then to keep out those with a different orientation. Kansas became known as "Bleeding Kansas." *Bleeding* here referred to whites killing one another and not to the genocide also committed against the Native Americans who occupied these lands. Native Americans were generally compelled to cede land in exchange for small reservations farther and farther west, undesirable lands in the territories of New Mexico, Arizona, and Utah—all of which made for more land for whites over which to contest with one another.[28]

27. See Michael Rogin, *Fathers and Children: Andrew Jackson and the Subjugation of the American Indian* (New York: Random House, 1988), for an account of the "trail of tears." For more detail, see Brenda Wineapple, *Ecstatic Nation: Confidence, Crisis, and Compromise, 1848–1877* (New York: Harper Collins, 2013).

28. A reading of the reports of the commissioner for the Bureau of Indian Affairs shows that the bureau superintendents thought of Native Americas as their "wards," that they tried to keep the treaties observed, and that they generally failed. See US Office of Indian Affairs, *Annual Report of the Commissioner of Indian Affairs, for the Year 1856*, 65–131, http://digicoll.library.wisc.edu/cgi-bin/History/History-idx?type=turn&entity=History.Ann Rep56.p0066&id=History.AnnRep56&isize=M. Commissioner George Manypenny, who

This is the *political* lesson that one can draw from Conrad and Meyer: the logic of the economics of slave-based cotton production generated an ecological movement toward the Southwest.[29] Already Arizona and New Mexico, having not been part of the Missouri Compromise, were open to slavery. That territory was rich in minerals: Spaniards had used slaves successfully in mines in various countries in South America.[30] With the opening of those territories, the possibility of economic gain and the maintenance of a slave-based society were an ongoing reality: there was little chance that slavery would perish from inefficiency. Coupled with this reality, the passage in 1850 of the Fugitive Slave Act, whereby citizens in *all* states, free or slave, were required to apprehend and return escaped slaves, generated an impossible tension: chattel slavery could no longer be ignored by people of the North. In Boston, broadsheets warning "Colored People" that they might be kidnapped were widely distributed. To the degree that slavery was permitted in the new territories, it threatened free (Northern) white labor and thus the economic health of the North.

Frederick Douglass, an escaped slave associated with the abolitionist cause, understood the implications as well as any white person and much better than most, including white abolitionists. Addressing his audience as "fellow citizens" but referring repeatedly to "your" Fourth of July ("I am glad, fellow citizens, that your nation is so young"), he delivered his famous oration "What Is the Slave to the Fourth of July?" to an abolitionist audience in Rochester, New York, on the day after Independence Day in 1852. He spoke of the Fugitive Slave Act as standing

> alone in the annals of tyrannical legislation. . . . The right of the hunter to his prey stands superior to the right of marriage, and to all rights in this republic, the rights of God included! For black men there are neither law, justice, humanity, nor religion. The Fugitive Slave Law makes MERCY TO THEM, A CRIME; and bribes the judge who tries them. An American JUDGE GETS TEN DOLLARS FOR EVERY VICTIM HE CONSIGNS to slavery, and five,

had been bureau director, later wrote the book *Our Indian Wards* (Cincinnati: R. Clarke, 1880).

29. Whether correct or not, there is criticism of Conrad and Meyer's economics, but I do not think this criticism affects the validity of the political conclusions one can draw from their article. See Michael Greenberg, "The New Economic History and the Understanding of Slavery: A Methodological Critique," *Dialectical Anthropology* 2, no. 131 (January 1977).

30. Chile abolished slavery in 1823, Mexico in 1829, Uruguay in 1830, and Bolivia in 1831. Other Latin American countries followed. Peru, where the mines were staffed with slaves, waited until 1854.

when he fails to do so. The oath of any two villains is sufficient, under this hell-black enactment, to send the most pious and exemplary black man into the remorseless jaws of slavery![31]

Douglass sees that slavery stands in fatal contradiction to the promise of the Declaration of Independence: "The existence of slavery in this country brands your republicanism as a sham, your humanity as a base pretence, and your Christianity as a lie. It destroys your moral power abroad; it corrupts your politicians at home. It saps the foundation of religion; it makes your name a hissing, and a by word to a mocking earth. It is the antagonistic force in your government, the only thing that seriously disturbs and endangers your Union." He concludes by noting that America now could no longer maintain a self-centered distance from other developments in the world: "Intelligence is penetrating the darkest corners of the globe. . . . Oceans no longer divide, but link nations together."[32] America will eventually have to respond to itself.

Two matters are of importance in the politics of the rhetoric of this speech. First, his differentiation between "fellow-citizens" and "your" Fourth of July marks the fact that, as a citizen *and* a black man, Douglass necessarily spoke from outside the dominant (white) culture of the country, even to this group of abolitionists. He spoke, in other words, in the voice of an as yet unrealized citizenship. In another address, he said that "notwithstanding the impositions and deprivations which have fettered on us—not withstanding the cunning, cruel and scandalous efforts to blot out that right, we declare that we are, and of right ought to be, American *citizens*."[33] That we *are* and yet *ought to be* means that citizenship remains a project.

Second, Douglass, in the Rochester speech, catches a matter of great importance to the achieving of citizenship. In the introduction, I noted that Socrates's sense of his citizenship derived in part from the fact that in Athens he had almost "forgotten who [he] was." In effect, Douglass he is claiming the same: that it is precisely as an outsider to "your" Fourth of July that he can in fact speak more accurately as a true American citizen than do those who have

---

31. The full speech is presented in Dave Zirin, "What Is the Slave to the Fourth of July? by Frederick Douglass," *Nation*, July 4, 2012, https://www.thenation.com/article/what -slave-fourth-july-frederick-douglass/.

32. Quoted in Zirin, "What Is the Slave."

33. Frederick Douglass, "The Claims of Our Common Cause," *Selected Speeches and Writings* (Chicago: Lawrence Hill, 1999), 264, cited in Frank, *Constituent Moments*, 219 (see intro., n. 21). I have learned much from Frank's brilliant book, here especially on Douglass, 211–36.

internalized the increasingly conventional understanding of the country. (He notes in the Fourth of July oration that the dominant [white] understanding of the American project has "never lacked for a tongue. . . . [It] is as familiar to you as household words.") This speech occurs after the Fugitive Slave Act: he speaks therefore from the position of one who better understands America than do those assembled in that hall, than the United States Congress, than the US Supreme Court.[34] One hundred years later, James Baldwin will still have to make the same claim: "If we—and now I mean the relatively conscious whites and the relatively conscious blacks, who must, like lovers, insist on, or create, the consciousness of the others—do not falter in one duty now, we may be able, handful that we are, to end the racial nightmare, *and achieve our country*, and change this history of the world." And like a latter-day Winthrop, Baldwin concludes by warning that if we do not, there will be "the fire next time."[35] The hope expressed in "achieve our country" and the anxiety and the temporality reflected in Langston Hughes's use of "yet" in his "America" poem condense this thought into a single mantra.

For whites, the times thus required a reasoned defense of slavery to preserve their vision of the Union. Such a defense, however, had to be compatible with the vision of citizenship prevalent at the time. The Southern defense of slavery took several forms, with the most striking being those developed by John J. Calhoun and George Fitzhugh. To the question whether blacks could be members of the polity, their answer was a reasoned and uncompromising no. Their argument went like this. The claim in the Declaration that "all men are created equal" was manifestly and empirically untrue. As Calhoun wrote, "These great and dangerous errors have their origin in the prevailing opinion that all men are born free and equal—than which nothing can be more unfounded and false."[36] His approach was sociological: there are natural divisions between humans, something reflected in the very structure of any society. The existence of the division of labor makes this clear. Race is one of these divisions and is a special case of the division of labor. Liberty furthers the development of the race; protection ensures its continuity. If protection is in question, liberty must yield.[37]

34. There are similar remarks in Frank, *Constituent Moments*, 220.

35. James Baldwin, *The Fire Next Time*, in *Collected Essays*, edited by Toni Morrison (New York: Library of America, 1998), 346–47, my emphasis. Frank cites the "achieve our country" segment in *Constituent Moments*, 234.

36. John C. Calhoun, "Disquisition on Government," *The Works of John C. Calhoun*, vol. 1 (New York: Appleton, 1854), 56.

37. Calhoun, "Disquisition on Government," 55.

What, however, should society do about the consequences of this division? There are and always will be those who are poor, landless—had not Jesus in fact said that "the poor are with you always"? What was to be done? Sounding like, but *only* sounding like, a remodeled Winthrop, Calhoun argued that those who are rich, who have land, are responsible for those who are poor and those who have no land. The landed are not to cast out the landless to rely on their own resources—as, he pointed out sharply, happens in the North. Rather, they are to take responsibility for them. Contrariwise, the North is an irresponsible, immoral society that does not take into account the social realities of inequality. The Northern system leads to strife and misery. As George Fitzhugh wrote, "Liberty and equality throw the whole weight of society on its weakest members; they combine all men in oppressing precisely that part of mankind who most need sympathy, aid and protection."[38]

Slavery was thus in fact, as Calhoun writes, "a good—a positive good."[39] Indeed, he argued, it is the source of prosperity and greatness: "The relation that now exists between the two races . . . had grown with our growth, and strengthened with our strength."[40] Protection is to be preferred over liberty, which, "when forced on a people unfit for it," will lead to "anarchy, the greatest of all curses."[41] To this, he opposed "Christian benevolence" as the most humane and human form of government. Thus the strong will protect the weak; labor and capital will be united. The vision of the free and independent basis for citizenship is not given up: it is just that blacks are not capable of independence—hence they are the most susceptible to corruption and to succumbing to tyranny and to giving rise to anarchy. (The various slave uprisings were taken to have confirmed this notion for most white Southerners).

What is important here is that Calhoun has in effect taken a prevalent and widespread theory of citizenship and used it to justify chattel slavery. If being a citizen requires free and independent men, able to resist the temptations of corruption and possessed of the means to do so, then, in his eyes, clearly slaves and blacks in general do not have those qualities. From which it follows that they cannot be citizens, as they cannot meet the necessary criteria. In fact, since they lack these qualities, their bondage is a benefit to them. Cal-

38. George Fitzhugh, *Sociology for the South: or the Failure of a Free Society* (Richmond, VA: Morris, 1854), 232.

39. John C. Calhoun, "Speech on the Reception of the Abolition Petitions," in *Speeches of John C. Calhoun*, vol. 2, ed. Richard Challe (New York: Appleton, 1860), 631.

40. Calhoun, "On Abolition Petitions, March 9, 1836," in *Speeches of John C. Calhoun*, 488.

41. Calhoun, "Disquisition on Government," in *Speeches of John C. Calhoun*, 55.

houn and his compatriots have moved from considering slavery a necessary evil—which is how Thomas Jefferson saw it—to arguing that it was a positive good. They retain, however, the notion that citizenship is dependent on the manifestation of certain qualities of self, which, they assume, blacks cannot have—blacks are children.

There were, however, free states and slave states, and people, *including slave owners*, moved between them, often with their slaves. What were relations with such states and those who moved between them to be? In the 1857 case of *Dred Scott v. Sanford*, Chief Justice Taney attempted to resolve two issues. The first has to do with the relation of the state constitution to the federal Constitution; the second has to do with the status of blacks as pertains to citizenship and thus to the idea of citizenship itself. Dred Scott was a slave who, over a period of four years, had been moved with his family by his master from the slave state of Missouri to the free state of Illinois and then the free territory of Wisconsin. They had then returned to Missouri, where Scott had attempted to purchase his freedom but had been refused. He sued on the grounds that, having lived in a free state, he was free and that his daughter, born on free territory, was also free. An initial court case held for Scott, but his owner appealed. The Missouri Supreme Court ruled against Scott, who then sued in federal court. Eventually the case made it up to the US Supreme Court, where, on a 7-2 decision, the ruling went against Scott.

Let us look at the two principal issues that Taney addressed. First was the relation of the state constitution to the federal—for which a little background is necessary. The Founding makes manifest tensions in the American notion of citizenship applied to the country as a whole, tensions that recur in each of the forms that it assumed from the revolutionary period on. A new notion of citizenship is consequent to America becoming a national state. In Puritan New England, the active element of one's citizenship was clearly local, something to which Tocqueville had called attention in *Democracy in America* even if, in the 1830s, he was well aware that it was rapidly fading. But the victory in the Revolutionary War raised a whole new set of problems.[42] There is now something like a *nation*.

The problem was Congress. What *was* the Congress and what was its role? It was, after all, an institution that had to a great degree been cobbled together to pursue independence from England, but now that that independence had

---

42. I am influenced here and draw generally upon Arthur Jacobson and Bernhard Schlink, introduction to *Weimar Jurisprudence* (Los Angeles: University of California Press, 2002).

been achieved, what was its role, in particular in relation to the states? The 1778 Articles of Confederation made explicit reference to the sovereignty *of the states*. Article II: "Each state retains its sovereignty, freedom, and independence, and every Power, Jurisdiction, and right, which is not by this confederation expressly delegated to the United States, in Congress assembled." So: is one primarily a citizen of the United States, or is one a citizen primarily of (e.g.) Virginia? Prior to the adoption of the Articles of Confederation and even to the Revolutionary War, most of the states had revised their constitutions, attributing to themselves ultimate authority. This was thus the self-understanding of the states that was agreed to through the articles. All republican theory, from that of Jean Bodin (sixteenth century) to Jean-Jacques Rousseau (eighteenth century), however, had held that sovereignty was unitary. What, then, was one to conclude about the pieces of the union? By the 1780s, under the influence of events and of forceful arguments (by James Madison and Alexander Hamilton, among others) as to the inadequacy of the Articles of Confederation for national defense, trade, economic problems[43]—for anything collective—the new Americans began to formulate a federal version of sovereignty. Sovereignty was conceived of as dual, and the Constitution sought to institutionalize that concept as best as might be achieved. A lot, however, was left unresolved, in particular the question of the right of states to nullify laws passed by Congress as they might pertain to their particular state.[44] (As we shall see, this tension will eventually lead to the Civil War, but even that only partially resolved it: ironically, whereas under President Obama, conservative-dominated states claimed a version of the nullification right, under Trump, progressive states such as California come close to doing the same.)

Most specific questions of nullification could be pragmatically resolved and were. However, the question of whether a state could secede from the union was not so resolved, nor was that of where the ultimate loyalty of a citizen should lie: in the state or in the nation. The Articles of Confederation had held that the union was "perpetual" (Article 13). The US Constitution, however, says nothing about secession, and little about citizenship. There is no discussion of sovereignty: one could thus argue that the authority of the Con-

43. I draw here from Richard B. Morris, *The Forging of the Union* (New York: Harper and Row, 1987) and owe the reference to Jacobson and Schlink.

44. The first clear assertion of the lack of such right was famously made by Justice John Marshall in Marbury v. Madison, 5 U.S. 137 (1803). See, among others in a wide literature, Peter Irons, *A People's History of the Supreme Court* (New York: Penguin Books, 1999), 104–7.

stitution rested on the states. Such were the issues that Justice Taney sought to address in his decision in *Dred Scott*. The Constitution had left this relation to sovereignty ambiguous, and this ambiguity was, Taney recognized, at the source of the firestorm of controversy that was sweeping the country after the Kansas-Nebraska Act. Taney's resolution, in favor of the states' privilege, is not incoherent given the ambiguities of the federal Constitution in relation to sovereignty and thus to an issue such as slavery.[45]

Then there was the question of entitlement to citizenship. Invoking both the powers of Congress and his sociological sense of blacks, Justice Taney wrote for the Supreme Court. Blacks were "beings of an inferior order, and altogether unfit to associate with the white race, either in social or political relations, and so far inferior that they had no rights which the white man was bound to respect." He further argued that if the court were to find in the favor of Scott, it "would give to persons of the negro race, . . . the right to enter every other State whenever they pleased, . . . to sojourn there as long as they pleased, to go where they pleased . . . the full liberty of speech in public and in private upon all subjects upon which its own citizens might speak; to hold public meetings upon political affairs, and to keep and carry arms wherever they went."[46] They would, in other words, then be fully citizens. Note the anxiety about armed rebellion in the last clause. In effect, the case declared that blacks had and could have no rights as citizens anywhere in the United States.

Taney's argument thus carried three incendiary political consequences. First, he dismissed the idea that there was any distinction between human rights, political rights, and civil rights—something that would become important later in arguments that blacks were citizens but were not necessarily entitled to the vote; second, he asserted a federal court authority to determine the extension of slavery; and third, he made law the claim that one could own human beings as property. Paradoxically, Taney was asserting the power of the federal government over the states, though he framed it as asserting the primary power of the states: after all, a *state* could give blacks the rights of citizenship in that state but it could not make them *American* citizens.[47] For Taney, the Declaration of Independence could not be understood to have included blacks as persons with "inalienable rights." Taney asserted that

45. See Jack M. Balkin and Sanford Levinson, "13 Ways of Looking at Dred Scott," Yale Faculty Scholarship Series, Paper 229, http://digitalcommons.law.yale.edu/fss_papers/229. Originally published in *Chicago/Kent Law Review* 82 (2007): 54.

46. "The Dred Scott Decision: Opinion of Chief Justice Taney," Library of Congress, https://www.loc.gov/item/17001543/.

47. Balkin and Levinson, "Looking at Dred Scott," 57.

the men who framed this declaration were great men—high in literary acquirements—high in their sense of honor, and incapable of asserting principles inconsistent with those on which they were acting. They perfectly understood the meaning of the language they used, and how it would be understood by others; and they knew that it would not in any part of the civilized world be supposed to embrace the negro race, which, by common consent, had been excluded from civilized Governments and the family of nations, and doomed to slavery. They spoke and acted according to the then established doctrines and principles, and in the ordinary language of the day, and no one misunderstood them. The unhappy black race were separated from the white by indelible marks, and laws long before established, and were never thought of or spoken of except as property, and when the claims of the owner or the profit of the trader were supposed to need protection.[48]

And he goes on to note that public opinion was still the same as it had been in 1776. As Balkin and Levinson point out, Taney's position is not so outrageous as it might seem. Until the 6–3 decision in *Romer v. Evans* (1996), it was, for instance, not at all clear that citizens were "bound to respect" gays and lesbians; indeed, polygamous Mormons were stripped of their citizenship in the late nineteenth century.[49]

Taney's was not an isolated voice. Other writers developed the Taney/Calhoun/Fitzhugh arguments. In 1854, Henry Hughes argued that the Southern economic system was not properly slavery but what he called "Warrantism." Influenced by the positivistic sociology of Auguste Comte, he argued that there were two forms of production: the "free sovereign" and the "warranted" or "ordered sovereign." In the former, the relations between capitalist and laborer are antagonistic and random. They are exploitative for it is to the advantage of the capitalist to have a surplus of workers. Jobs, and thus income, and thus the means to provide for oneself and one's family, are not "warranted." Contrariwise, in a "warranted" economy, there is no unemployment, and all who work are guaranteed at least enough to keep body and soul together.[50] He

48. Dred Scott v. Sanford, 60 U.S. 393 (1856) at 410, Justia Legal Resources, https://supreme.justia.com/cases/federal/us/60/393/case.html.

49. Balkin and Levinson, "Looking at Dred Scott," 60. The same applies to the reversal of *Bowers v. Hardwick* (which had criminalized oral and anal sex between consenting adults) in *Lawrence v. Texas*.

50. Henry Hughes, *A Treatise on Sociology: Theoretical and Practical* (Philadelphia: Lippincott, 1854), esp. 285–86.

closes with a reference (again!) to the perfection of society: "When these and more than these shall be the fulfillment of Warrantism; than shall this Federation and world praise the power, wisdom and goodness of a system which may well be deemed divine; than shall Experience aid Philosophy and VINDICATE THE WAYS OF GOD TO MAN."[51] Hughes intended this as a defense of slavery, but his argument went much further: in effect, it was a provision for a form of what we might today call socialism, of a guaranteed income and a right to work, but viewed, as with Calhoun, from the point of view of the elite. In doing so, however, slavery raised the question of the legitimacy of a wage-labor economy and was understood by its defenders to do that.

It is worth noting here that many people took these debates very seriously. Thomas Skidmore, sounding like Marx, started his "A Plan for Equalizing Property" (1831) by proclaiming that "the world is divided into two classes: proprietors and non-proprietors." He proposed a new Constitution under the terms of which all property would be divided equally, including that of the present slave states: "He who commands the property of the State, or even an inordinate portion of it, has the liberty and the happiness of its citizens in his own keeping. . . . He who can feed me, or starve me, give me employment, or bid me wander about in idleness; is my master; and it is the utmost folly for me to boast of being anything but a slave."[52] Skidmore tried to solve the question of the qualification for citizenship by making all equal in terms of property. He did not, however, deal with the fact that an increasing portion of the population worked for wages.

In an 1858 speech discussing the admission of Kansas, Senator James Henry Hammond of South Carolina used the labor argument in direct terms against such radical positions. Hammond is best known for this oration, his "mudsill" speech, in which he pointed out that all societies required a group of people to do the labor that others were unwilling to do. If, as he proclaimed, "Cotton was King," then a society dependent on cotton production required cotton pickers. These workers were the "mudsill." Hammond also returned, however, to the argument made by Hughes and the others. Addressing himself to the North, he said that "in short, your whole hiring class of manual laborers and 'operatives,' as you call them, are essentially slaves. The difference between us is that our slaves are hired for life and are well compensated; there

---

51. H. Hughes, *Treatise on Sociology*, 292.

52. Thomas Skidmore, "A Plan for Equalizing Property" (New York, 1829), 125, 388. Skidmore went on to found the Working Man's Association.

is no starvation. No begging, no want of employment among our people and not too much employment [read "exploitation"] either. Yours are hired by the day and not cared for."[53]

There are two important consequences to the Southern defense. First, it opened itself up to a kind of demonstrative refutation. Douglass caught this tellingly in the Fourth of July address. He worked his way through a litany of all the activities in which the "Negro race" engages, from plowing to metal working to professional work, to family life, to worshipping the "Christian's God," and concluded that it is incredible that one is nevertheless "called upon to prove that we are men." This was not so much a call for recognition on the part of whites as a remarking that the very performance of these activities on the part of blacks in American society reveals a deep inner contradiction on the white dominant culture. The same tactic—it is not really an argument but a demonstration, a *showing*—will be used in the early days of the civil rights movement and the sit-ins.[54]

Second, the Southern defense called the whole economic institution of the North into question, a critique that could not then and would not later go unnoticed in the North, both before and especially after the Civil War. When coupled with the political developments in the 1850s, the reasoned defense of slavery thus had the effect of identifying and exacerbating differences between the North and the South. It became increasingly difficult for the North simply to allow the South to go its own way, for the South was not only defending slavery, it was also proclaiming the superiority of its economic system *on moral grounds*. The matter became unavoidable as the differences were leading to increasingly violent conflicts in the new territories.[55] At one point the struggles in "Bleeding Kansas" saw pitched battles between one thousand proslavery forces and four hundred men led by the abolitionist John Brown.

53. James Henry Hammond, "Speech on the Admission of Kansas," US Senate, March 4, 1858, in *Selections from the Letters and Speeches of the Hon. James Henry Hammond of South Carolina* (New York: Trow, 1866), 318, 319.

54. Douglass quoted in Zirin, "What Is the Slave." This understanding is spelled out brilliantly in Patchen Markell, *Bound by Recognition* (Princeton, NJ: Princeton University Press, 2009). Chapter 10 of the present volume will explore further the tactic as used during the civil rights movement.

55. There is an interesting Congressional report from 1856 on the Kansas situation: *Report of the Special Committee Appointed to Investigate the Troubles in Kansas, with the Views of the Minority of Said Committee*, Making of America Books, at http://quod.lib.umich.edu/m/moa/afk4445.0001.001/11?page=root;rgn=full+text;size=100;view=image.

ABOLITIONISM

Abolitionism is a fourth development in response to the contradictions that were becoming increasingly prominent due to the existence of chattel slavery. Despite its surface radicalism, abolitionism did not provide a thought-through alternative to other visions of citizenship. It took both simple, not to say simplistic, and more complex forms. Let us examine the simpler first.

The most prominent voice in the abolitionist movement was that of William Lloyd Garrison. Garrison was the proponent of "Immediateism," which he contrasted with "Gradualism." For Garrison, slavery was such a moral sin such that there was and could be no reason not to put an end to it right away. Garrison's position rested on the presumption that the only reason slavery continued to exist was that people were not doing anything to put a stop to it. In this respect, Garrison shows himself to be in line with the orientation of the Second Great Awakening: the problems lie in *us*. External authority can have no claim; coercion cannot be a means to order. Though focused on a political problem, Garrison's stance is fundamentally nonpolitical. Garrison believed that the most important thing was not to be controlled by anyone: to be self-possessed, which literally means to be the owner of yourself. The abolitionists, and not least of all Garrison, were possessed by a moral self-confidence and righteousness that held that the mere existence of slavery meant that one tolerated evil. The abolitionists thus shared much of the sense of the perfectibility of men that characterized the revivalists of the Second Great Awakening. They had no problem demanding the dissolution of the Union. A consequence would be, as Fredrick Douglass remarked, that while they "started to free the slave: [they end] by leaving the slave to free himself."[56] In fact, Douglass came to see the necessity of breaking with Garrisonism and, not without pain, did so.[57]

The effect of the abolitionist position was to remove the Constitution from its position as law of the land. While it is true that in the North there was no slavery, the North was subject to a Constitution that allowed for slavery. The arguments of people like Hammond as to the economic importance of slavery and the dependency of the North on Southern cotton for its mills, the fact that slaves were understood to be private property—none of that mattered to

56. Cited from Wilson Carey McWilliams, *The Idea of Fraternity in America* (Berkeley: University of California Press, 1973), 274.

57. See the discussion in Frank, *Constituent Moments*, 230.

the abolitionists in face of the wrong that was slavery. Garrison and the other abolitionists thus wanted to disrupt the Union, violate the Constitution, produce economic chaos, and call private property into question, all in the name of a moral good. The Anti-Slavery Society sent out organizers with detailed instructions as to how to carry the message of immediatism. Yet what could be the American concept of citizenship if the Constitution were irrelevant?

It is not surprising that in the North also there were diverse resistances to the extremist elements of those holding the abolitionist position. Charles Grandison Finney, an evangelical pastor and president of Oberlin College (not incidentally, the first "white" college to admit blacks, in 1835, and to become coeducational, in 1837), worried "that we are in our present course going fast into a civil war." He was alarmed (as he put it) by the fact "that the absorbing abolitionism has drunk up the spirit of some of our most efficient moral men and is fast doing so to the rest." His desire and the thrust of his preaching and work was to make abolitionism "an appendage of . . . the revival"—in other words, to temper a policy (the abolition of slavery) by making it consequent and derived from a commitment to moral virtue. This approach, he claimed, had worked with temperance. He noted that "many of the Abolitionists are good men but few of them are wise men."[58]

Other resistances were more categorical. Abolitionism was widely resisted not only in movements often led by the old commercial elites threatened by industrialization but also by the nascent labor movement. Artisans, concerned with their own prosperity, were distressed at the exclusive focus of the abolitionists on chattel slavery—far more important to them were the conditions of wage labor in the North. A cartoon from the period shows blacks with the prestigious jobs on a construction site scaffold while whites toil at the hard labor on the ground. A fat-cat capitalist encourages the blacks. The whole thing is titled "The Results of Abolitionism." A broadsheet called for a meeting to protest the "Outrage of the Abolitionist." The prospect of a sudden increase in the available workforce (should slavery be abolished) could not promise much for higher wages. William Weld, engaging in a debate published in Garrison's paper the *Liberator*, not only favorably compared chattel slavery to wage slav-

58. Charles Grandison Finney to Theodore Weld, 21 July 1836, Weld-Grimké Papers, William L. Clements Library, University of Michigan, http://www.gospeltruth.net/Finney letters/finlets/finlet%201830-1839%20done/finlet1836-07_21.htm. Finney may have been responding to a worry that Weld had expressed to Lewis Tappan, on November 17, 1835, that Finney might have been backtracking on abolition. See Gilbert H. Barnes and Dwight L. Dumont, eds., *Letters of Theodore Dwight Weld, Angela Grimké Weld and Sarah Grimké, 1822–1844*, vol. 1 (London: Appleton, 1934), 242–43.

ery but, turning an argument on its head, held that wage slavery *worsened* immorality. "Wherever wage slavery is substituted for chattel slavery, universal prostitution, both legal and illegal, must ultimately take the place of partial concubinage."[59] Again of note here is that the question of slavery raises the question of the place of women as somewhat parallel to that of chattel slaves.

Abolitionism thus helps consolidate a trend that we have already seen taking form. For the abolitionists, citizenship consisted simply in self-determination and self-control. The problem with slavery was simply that slaves were not individually free: freedom was conceived of on purely an individual basis. While abolitionists were not concerned with wage labor per se, their vision of human independence and freedom is one that fits easily into a marketplace-based society—all you own is yourself, and what you do with it is supposedly your own affair. A famous abolitionist broadsheet shows two blacks, male and female, chains on their hands and clad only in a kind of loincloth, imploring, "Am I not a man and a brother (sister)?" Nothing was demanded beyond this simplest of recognitions.

There was, however, a more complex, and in the end, more political, vision of the need for abolition. Thoreau famously refused to pay a tax and went to prison for a night until his aunt bailed him out. The episode is well known: Thoreau did not want to pay taxes to "a State that buys and sells men, women, and children, like cattle at the door of its senate-house."[60] The episode is directly related to Thoreau's complex understanding of citizenship. In *Civil Disobedience*, he says the following:

Some years ago, the State met me in behalf of the Church, and commanded me to pay a certain sum toward the support of a clergyman whose preaching my father attended, but never I myself. "Pay," it said, "or be locked up in the jail." I declined to pay. But, unfortunately, another man saw fit to pay it. I did not see why the schoolmaster should be taxed to support the priest, and not the priest the schoolmaster: for I was not the State's schoolmaster, but I supported myself by voluntary subscription. I did not see why the lyceum should not present its tax-bill, and have the State to back its demand, as well as the Church. However, at the request of the selectmen,

59. William West, "Wage Slavery and Chattel Slavery," *Liberator*, April 21, 1847. It is worth noting that Garrison issued his paper weekly for thirty-one years.

60. Henry David Thoreau, *Walden*, "The Village," para. 3. in *A Week on the Concord and Merrimack Rivers / Walden* (New York: Library of America, 1985).

I condescended to make some such statement as this in writing:—"Know all men by these presents, that I, Henry Thoreau, do not wish to be regarded as a member of any incorporated society which I have not joined." This I gave to the town clerk; and he has it. The State, having thus learned that I did not wish to be regarded as a member of that church, has never made a like demand on me since; though it said that it must adhere to its original presumption that time.[61]

The complexity comes from the next sentence: "If I had known how to name them, I should then have signed off in detail from all the societies which I never signed on to; but I did not know where to find a complete list."[62] Thoreau cannot call a slave government *his* government, but he is clear that, willy-nilly, it is *our* government insofar as he is an American. And that poses the problem for him as a citizen. He is both of and not of the country: what to be done about this double status? And that was a problem that would become ever sharper.

In 1855, Ralph Waldo Emerson proposed that the United States take the course that Britain had followed in 1833 and compensate slave owners for the manumission of their slaves. He estimated the total cost at about two billion dollars, many times what it had cost in England because there were many more slaves in the United States.[63] The proposal went nowhere, perhaps because of the cost and that Emerson then spent some time detailing the sacrifices that would have to be made ("We will give up our coaches, wine and watches").[64] Emerson was to become a strong proponent of a more sophisticated abolitionism, even entertaining John Brown in his house.[65] Emerson found slavery an impediment to the vision of America that he held up as exemplary and spoke of "the growth of the abolition party, the true successor of that austere Church, which made nature and history sacred to us in our youth. I often ask myself, what is to take the place, to the young people, of those re-

61. Henry David Thoreau, *Civil Disobedience*, in *Collected Essays* (New York: Library of America, 2014), para. 12.

62. Thoreau, *Civil Disobedience*, para. 12.

63. English costs, however, were not trivial. Twenty million pounds sterling was allocated, about 5 percent of the UK gross domestic product.

64. Ralph Waldo Emerson, "American Slavery," *The Later Lectures of Ralph Waldo Emerson, 1843–1871*, vol. 2, ed. Joel Myerson and Ronald Bosco (Atlanta: University of Georgia Press, 2001), 13.

65. See Lawrence Buell, *Emerson* (Cambridge, MA: Belknap Press of Harvard University Press, 2003), 269–70, for a discussion of the growth of Emerson's sentiments.

straining [for "restaining"] influences which the old Calvinism, or Puritanism, exerted on the youth of such are as old, or almost as old, as I am."[66] In the great essay "Politics," he notes, "Society is an illusion to the young citizen."[67] If that is so, then again the question is as to what will take the place of that which provided the political coherence of virtue as the old fades away.

As we shall see in more detail in chapter 4 with Lincoln, Emerson shares here, with writers like his friend Hawthorne, the sense that something has to be found to replace that which held America to its original vision. Doing so was all the more difficult as the society itself was undergoing continuous change. This is a classic problem in political theory: how does one change to deal adequately with the historically new and yet remain true to that which one is? As Nietzsche, a profound reader of Emerson, was to put it, how does one "become what you are"? Indeed, in "The Man of Letters," Emerson actually cites the Pythian Ode of Pindar from which Nietzsche's encomium is drawn.[68]

FEMINISMS

We have already seen the involvement of women in the temperance movement. As such, it soon gave rise to a broader development. As Sojourner Truth, an unlettered free slave, exclaimed, "If the first woman God ever made was strong enough to turn the world upside down all alone, these women together ought to be able to turn it back, and get it right side up again! And now they is asking to do it, the men better let them."[69] In July 1848, a group of about three hundred people, mostly women, gathered in Seneca Falls, New York. The gathering was organized by a group of female Quakers, the most prominent of whom was Lucretia Mott, a well-known orator, along with Elizabeth Cady Stanton, a seminary-educated follower of Finney. The group formulated a "Declaration of Sentiments" modeled—as many such American declarations are modeled—on the Declaration of Independence. The participant women were almost all Garrisonian abolitionists and followers of the temperance movement.

66. Cited from the complete text of his lecture as reproduced in Louis Ruchames, "Two Forgotten Addresses by Ralph Waldo Emerson," *American Literature* 28, no. 4 (January 1957): 428–29.
67. Ralph Waldo Emerson, "Politics," in *Essays and Lectures* (New York: Library of America, 1983), 559.
68. Ralph Waldo Emerson, "The Man of Letters," in *Essays and Lectures*.
69. Sojourner Truth, "Ain't I a Woman?" Sojourner Truth.com, http://www.sojourner truth.com/p/aint-i-woman.html.

Where did these women come from and what motivated them? The question of women's suffrage had been quietly brewing since the American Revolution. Famously, Abigail Adams had urged her husband to "remember the ladies" as "we are determined to instigate a rebellion." In the eighteenth century, women had been able to vote in New Jersey who were "otherwise qualified"—that is, property owners. New Jersey was, however, alone among the states in allowing some women to vote, and the right of female suffrage was removed in 1808.[70]

The vision of women in the culture at large was complex. Literature of the first part of the nineteenth century tends to show that "spinsterhood" was often seen as somewhat desirable—such women were independent. This image went side by side, however, with a cult of domesticity, and indeed, popular magazines often carried articles suggesting that there was something "unfeminine" about independence.[71] Thus one reads in the *Young Lady's Own Book* of 1833 that "a woman may make a man's home delightful and may thus increase his motives for virtuous exertion" because "domestic life is a woman's sphere, and it is there that she is the most usefully as well as most appropriately employed." In fact, "her weakness is an attraction, not a blemish."[72] That said, ten years later, the editor of the Universalist journal *Rose of Sharon*, Sarah Edgarton, urges that a wife share her husband's "mind as well as his heart." She goes on to say that "woman is not necessarily born for marriage. She has the birthright of independent existence; and to this birthright she owes reverence as a holy gift. . . . Though it may be expedient for her to marry, it is her privilege to remain single."[73]

What was a white, upper-middle-class, literate, educated woman to do? On the one hand, she could engage in charity work—women were, after all, understood to be the guardians of domestic virtue and moderation. It is thus the case that those women who sought to break away from the prison of domesticity had to determine for themselves what their roles might be. As Lisa Pace Vetter has written, "By rejecting common law, the main source of wom-

70. A. Keyssar, *Right to Vote*, 43–44.

71. The classic text here is Ann Douglas, *The Feminization of American Culture* (New York: Farrar, Straus and Giroux, 1998), esp. 17–120. See her interesting discussion of Melville's reaction to the cult of domesticity, 294.

72. Anonymous, *Young Lady's Own Book* (Philadelphia: Kiel, Milke and Bidle, 1833), 13, 15.

73. Sarah C. Edgarton, "Female Culture," *Mother's Assistant*, vol. 3 (1843), 94–95. Her writing was collected in Sarah C. Edgarton, *Selections from the Writings of Mrs. Sarah C. Edgarton Mayo: With a Memoir, by Her Husband* (facsimile ed., Los Angeles: HardPress Publishing, 2012).

an's identity for centuries and embracing liberalism, early woman's rights advocates including [Sarah] Grimké were left without norms to help determine their new roles in society."[74] In this sense, involvement in the temperance and abolitionist movements was simply an extension of a socially sanctioned role. However, given the fact that participation in these movements was segregated by sex, someone among these female activists had to learn how to organize a meeting, lead, come to a decision, and take action. Thus, over time, participation in these movements generated women with political skills and experience, a female leadership group. And these developments naturally raised the question of the political status of women, in particular as to their citizenship.

The slavery that the women opposed as abolitionists lent itself easily to a parallel use in relation to the political and social situation of women. Sarah Grimké was the daughter of a wealthy South Carolina slaveholding family. As an adolescent, she had secretly taught her slave to read and write—a breaking of the state law. Her father was furious. In apparent response, she moved to Philadelphia in her early twenties and, joined by her sister Angelina, began to speak to abolitionist gatherings that included both men and women—such were termed "promiscuous gatherings." Sarah deplored that women were trained to become "butterflies of the fashionable world" and that even when they did work, they were paid less than were men for the same job. A set of Sarah's *Letters on the Equality of the Sexes* (1837), nominally addressed to Mary Parker, the president of the Boston Female Anti-Slavery Society, and signed "thine in the bonds of womanhood," covered not only the United States but the rest of the world. An original and God-given equality, she argued, had been perverted by social arrangements that favor men: "I shall not find it difficult to show, that in all ages and countries, not even excepting enlightened republican America, woman has more or less been made a *means* to promote the welfare of man, without due regard to her own happiness, and the glory of God as the end of her creation."[75] After spending a dozen pages showing that there were no biblical precedents for American slavery, Sarah foresaw the eruption of violence if the South would not mend its ways. In her *Appeal to Christian Women of the South*, her Angelina supported her sister's view, contending that

74. Lisa Pace Vetter, *The Political Thought of America's Founding Feminists* (New York: New York University Press, 2017), 126. See her chap. 4 for an extended discussion of Sarah Grimké. Other chapters deal with Lucretia Mott, Elizabeth Cady Stanton, and Sojourner Truth.

75. Sarah Grimké to Mary Parker, 17 July 1837, "Letter II: Woman Subject Only to God," in *Letters on the Equality of the Sexes*, National Humanities Center, http://national humanitiescenter.org/ows/seminarsflvs/Grimke%20Letters.pdf.

"slavery always has, and always will produce insurrections wherever it exists, because it is a violation of the natural order of things, and no human power can much longer perpetuate it. The opposers of abolitionists fully believe this; one of them remarked to me not long since, there is no doubt there will be a most terrible overturning at the South in a few years, such cruelty and wrong, must be visited with Divine vengeance soon. Abolitionists believe, too, that this must inevitably be the case if you do not repent."[76]

In June 1840, the World Anti-Slavery Convention was convened in London. After a day of somewhat acrimonious debate, the female delegates (including Mott, Stanton, and Lady Byron, divorced from Lord Byron) were allowed to attend but required to remain in the gallery.[77] In 1848—a year of revolution all across Europe—the gathering at Seneca Falls had concluded with the Declaration of Sentiments, which identified tyranny not in the personage of the political ruler but in the male in general. Sixteen "He has" bullets detail the crimes of the male gender, starting with the refusal to permit "her inalienable right to the elective franchise" and concluding with "He has endeavored, in every way that he could, to destroy her confidence in her own powers, to lessen her self-respect, and to make her willing to lead a dependent and abject life." It was accompanied by a set of "Resolutions" concluding with the following four:

> *Resolved*, That woman has too long rested satisfied in the circumscribed limits which corrupt customs and a perverted application of the Scriptures have marked out for her, and that it is time she should move in the enlarged sphere which her great Creator has assigned her.

> *Resolved*, That it is the duty of the women of this country to secure to themselves their sacred right to the elective franchise.

> *Resolved*, That the equality of human rights results necessarily from the fact of the identity of the race in capabilities and responsibilities.

> *Resolved*, therefore, That, being invested by the Creator with the same capabilities, and the same consciousness of responsibility for their exercise,

---

76. Angelina Grimké, *Appeal to Christian Women of the South* (1836), 25, University of Virginia, http://utc.iath.virginia.edu/abolitn/abesaegat.html.

77. See Kathryn Kish Sklar, "'Women Who Speak for an Entire Nation': American and British Women Compared at the World Anti-Slavery Convention, London, 1840," *Pacific Historical Review* 55, no. 4, (November 1990): 453–99.

it is demonstrably the right and duty of woman, equally with man, to promote every righteous cause, by every righteous means; and especially in
regard to the great subjects of morals and religion, it is self-evidently her
right to participate with her brother in teaching them, both in private and
in public, by writing and by speaking, by any instrumentalities proper to
be used, and in any assemblies proper to be held; and this being a self-
evident truth, growing out of the divinely implanted principles of human
nature, any custom or authority adverse to it, whether modern or wearing
the hoary sanction of antiquity, is to be regarded as self-evident falsehood,
and at war with the interests of mankind.[78]

In the same year, Karl Marx and Friedrich Engels issued *The Communist
Manifesto*. Among the qualities they pointed out as characterizing capitalism
was the famous claim that "all that is solid has melted into thin air," by which
they meant that capitalism tended to eradicate all natural differences between
persons and reduce their relations to that of exchange. The "Seneca Falls Declaration" was in many ways an admirable setting out of the oppressed status
of women in the America of the time (and not just that time). There are, however, two not-unrelated aspects to it. On the one hand, the male claims that
women were incapable of being responsible citizens in that they were deemed
dependent, less intelligent, and beholden to their spouse's opinions were resisted on precisely the grounds that none of these supposed lacks was real.
Women, it was claimed, met all established (male) criteria for being citizens.
On the other hand, it in effect also attacked all those institutions (for many,
marriage) that stood in the way of capitalism and a wage/market economy.
In effect, though not in purpose, the declaration helped prepare the way for
a new capitalist economy where each was in possession of oneself and could
do with it as was possible and one saw fit or necessary. A modern parallel can
be found in the debate in the 1960s and 1970s as to whether women (wives)
should be paid for housework. One understands that equality demands a positive answer, yet this sort of remuneration simply extends the cash nexus even
further into people's lives.[79]

78. The "Declaration" and "Resolutions" have been widely reprinted and posted. See,
e.g., "Declaration of Sentiments and Resolutions: Woman's Rights Convention, Held at
Seneca Falls, 19–20 July 1848," Elizabeth Cady Stanton and Susan B. Anthony Papers Project, Rutgers University, http://ecssba.rutgers.edu/docs/seneca.html.

79. See Pat Mainardi, *The Politics of Housework* (1970) at *cwluherstory.com* and the feminist group known as Redstockings—https://en.wikipedia.org/wiki/Redstockings.

Not all women held to this position, but, in the end, many contributed to it in one way or another. Louisa Susannah McCord, daughter of a plantation owner in South Carolina, restless, educated, multilingual, and widely read, defended both the intellectual freedom of women and the central importance of their femininity. One might think of it as a vision of a progressive Southern lady. She was opposed to the "Yankee" vision of female emancipation, holding it to be "but of a piece with negro emancipation," which indeed it was. Rather, she argued, "Let woman make herself free, in the true sense of the word, by the working out of her mission. . . . Woman is freest when she is the truest woman: when she finds the fewest difficulties in the way of conforming herself to her nature."[80]

The left flank, as it were, of the Seneca Falls meeting was held by apparently more radical voices. Amelia Bloomer, writing in the *Lily*, the journal she edited, approvingly printed a letter arguing that "marriage is the slavery of woman" and "does not differ in any of its essential features from chattel slavery."[81] Ernestine Potowsky Rose called for a more extensive divorce law in order to make "true marriages" possible (a position, incidentally, already held by John Milton in the seventeenth century).[82]

These and other texts—Elizabeth Cady Stanton's and subsequent others' 1920 edition of the documents of the American movement comprises five huge volumes—in effect call for a transformation of what had traditionally been thought to be the basis of a stable polity. Domesticity itself was increasingly devalued to be replaced by a vision of self-possessed and self-controlled human beings. Even Louisa McCord's defense of "true womanhood" is framed inside a struggle for her own self. "Is not all intellect suffering?" she writes at one point. A key point here is that the vision shared by the temperance and abolitionist movements is also that present in the Southern defense of slavery: the South simply adds to it by excluding the black as incapable of independence.

80. Louisa S. McCord, "Enfranchisement of Woman," in *Political and Social Essays*, ed. Richard C. Lounsbury (Charlottesville: University Press of Virginia, 1995), 105–24. See the discussion in Cindy A. McCleod, "Louisa S. McCord and the 'Feminist' Debate" (PhD diss., Program for Interdisciplinary Humanities, Florida State University, 2011).

81. Letter on "The Marriage Institution," *Lily* 7 (July 15, 1855).

82. Speech by Ernestine Potowsky Rose at the National Woman Rights convention, New York, May 10–11, 1860, in *History of Woman Suffrage*, 3 vols., ed. Elizabeth Cady Stanton, Susan B. Anthony, and Matilda Joslyn Gage (Rochester, NY: Charles Mann, 1887), 1:731, https://ia801409.us.archive.org/22/items/historyofwomansu01stanuoft/historyof womansu01stanuoft_bw.pdf.

COMMUNITARIANISM

The shared direction of these trends did not go unnoticed. The economic cri-sis that started in 1837 lasted for seven years, with unemployment running as high as 25 percent. Forty percent of American banks closed. "Young men have no hope," wrote Emerson in his journals. "Adults stand like day laborers idle in the streets. None calleth us to labor."[83] It is therefore not surprising that especially across much of the northeastern quadrant of the country there de-veloped communitarian movements that sought to counter the rising forms of individualism. Emerson took note and wrote, "I have hardly met a thinking man without a draft of a new community in his waistcoat pocket."[84] Various freethinkers around Boston sought to form a perfect community. Indeed, in 1841, Nathaniel Hawthorne resigned his position as weigher and gauger in the Boston Customs House and joined that utopian socialist community at Brook Farm in Roxbury, Massachusetts. The community had been established by the Unitarian minister George Ripley: its full name was the Brook Farm Insti-tute of Agriculture and Education.[85] Members did whatever work appealed to them, and all were paid equally. Although the community was almost never solvent, the intention was to survive on profits made from selling agricultural products and clothing and from the fees for the education that they provided.

Brook Farm was not the only such adventure. A reasonable estimation is that more than one hundred such communities were founded and lasted for a varying amount of time. The Oneida Community endured for eighty-nine years, succumbing only to the Great Depression that began in 1929. We still can buy the silverware that was one of that community's revenue-producing products. For Oneida, as for most of the other communities, the central ques-tion was one of property and individual ownership. Thus in Oneida, founded by John Humphrey Noyes, members held all property in common; practiced a rotating marriage scheme (hence no "*my* wife"); initiated their children to sex; and insisted on planned procreation, thus requiring nonejaculatory intercourse from men. They also practiced regular criticism sessions where

83. Cited in Andrew Kopec, "Emerson, Labor and Ages of Turbulence," *ESQ* 60, no. 2 (2014): 251–84, at 251; see also Philip F. Gura, *Man's Better Angels: Romantic Reformers and the Coming of the Civil War* (Cambridge, MA: Belknap Press of Harvard University Press, 2016).

84. Cited from Akash Kapur, "The Return of the Utopians," *New Yorker*, October 3, 2016.

85. The best account is probably Sterling F. Delano, *Brook Farm: The Dark Side of Utopia* (Cambridge, MA: Harvard University Press, 2004).

those who had not behaved properly were brought before the community and required to rectify their behavior.[86] In Iowa, the Amana Colonies were founded by German Pietists and also functioned communally. They frowned on marriage and childbearing but still survived until the Great Depression. They prospered economically from their skills in manufacture—we still can purchase Amana appliances. The colonies also remain, albeit now organized as traditional towns, and local artisans there still produce furniture, textiles, wine, and foodstuffs for those who are willing to take a short drive off Interstate 80 to find them.

If the Oneidaers practiced novel forms of sexual relations, the Shakers, an ecstatic sect originating in England in the eighteenth century, went the opposite direction: whereas they also believed in the equality of men and women and were communal, they were celibate. For both groups, the problem lay in the pronouns *mine* and *thine*. By the middle of the nineteenth century, there were an estimated six thousand Shakers—they "shook" from ecstasy whereas their lesser brethren, the Quakers, merely "quaked." The celibacy requirement, however, made perpetuation of the community dependent on new members and the occasional abandoned foundling: groups often quickly died out.

* * *

All of these movements—and there are many others—are concerned with the issues raised by the general question of slavery both in its chattel and wage forms—of dependence and independence. They are responding to inequality, to the exploitation of the wage labor system, to the increasingly apparent accumulation of large fortunes and thus of power and the repeated economic crises. The achievement of equality in external goods is seen as the necessary prerequisite to the achievement of individual internal equality. And as exciting and often daring as these experiments were, the stark reality of chattel slavery continued to call the adequacy of these efforts into question. As Calhoun and Fitzhugh had emphasized, chattel slavery was an *institution* that brought white owners real benefits and against which even a multitude of individual efforts would be fruitless. The advent of the Civil War put an end to many of these experiments (at least until the 1960s) for it made manifest the fact that some social problems were of such a scale that they were not to be

86. See Lawrence Foster, *Women, Family, and Utopia: Communal Experiments of the Shakers, the Oneida Community, and the Mormons* (Syracuse, NY: Syracuse University Press, 1991).

solved by sets of right-thinking individuals.[87] As Hawthorne wrote, on leaving Brook Farm, "I can best attain the higher ends of my life by retaining the ordinary relation to society."[88]

Hawthorne's resolution is telling—it reflects the sense that the various enterprises that have been examined in this chapter did not constitute an "ordinary" relation to society. The question was, however, would might be an ordinary relation given the issues that divided the country? Chattel slavery was one of these issues—but it only posed most strongly, at this period, the ongoing question of what citizenship was and thus of who could be a citizen. The most thoughtful and complex answer to this question was given by Abraham Lincoln, the subject of chapter 4.

---

87. See Gura, *Man's Better Angels*.

88. Nathaniel Hawthorne to David Mack, 25 May1842, in Nathaniel Hawthorne, *Selected Letters of Nathaniel Hawthorne*, ed. Joel Myerson (Columbia: Ohio State University Press), 103.

4

ABRAHAM LINCOLN

A plain man of the people, an extraordinary fortune attended him. He offered no shining qualities at the first encounter; he did not offend by superiority. He had a face and manner which disarmed suspicion, which inspired confidence, which confirmed good-will. He was a man without vices. He had a strong sense of duty, which it was very easy for him to obey. Then, he had what farmers call a long head; was excellent in working out the sum for himself; in arguing his case and convincing you fairly and firmly. Then, it turned out that he was a great worker; had prodigious faculty of performance; worked easily. A good worker is so rare.

RALPH WALDO EMERSON, REMARKS AT FUNERAL SERVICE[1]

Happily for me, there was no vain pomp and ceremony about him. I was never more quickly or more completely put at ease in the presence of a great man, than in that of Abraham Lincoln.

FREDERICK DOUGLASS, 1863

From his earliest public pronouncements, Abraham Lincoln was concerned with the question of the grounding of a virtuous polity. As soon as anyone else, and sooner than most, he realized that neither the energies of the revolutionary generation—even given how long those men had lived: Jefferson and Adams did not die until 1826—nor the memory of those Founders were going to be sufficient to preserve a vision of virtuous citizenship. Memory of

---

1. Ralph Waldo Emerson, "Remarks at the Funeral Services Held in Concord, April 19, 1865," Bartleby.com, http://www.bartleby.com/90/1115.html.

the enthusiasms that kindled and sustained the revolutionary torch faded, both of themselves and as the country expanded in geographic area, in population, and, more important, in experiences. Such matters are the concerns that form the center of one of Lincoln's earliest public speeches, the "Address to the Washington Temperance Society of Springfield, Illinois" of February 1842. A largely self-taught lawyer of progressive politics, Lincoln had been elected to the Illinois House of Representatives in 1834 at the age of twenty-five. He had gained and continued to enhance a strong reputation as a highly effective lawyer; in 1836, he had voted to extend suffrage to all white males, regardless of property. It was on this reputation that he was invited to deliver an address to the Temperance Society. The occasion was the 110th anniversary of the birth of George Washington; the gathering was held in the Second Presbyterian Church of Springfield, Illinois, and most members of the sponsoring association were apparently reformed drunkards.

TEMPERANCE AND CITIZENSHIP

The argument of the 1842 address is subtler than it might appear. Lincoln asks himself first why the temperance cause has had such recent success—some products of that success, after all, make up his audience—and indicates that it is the figure of the redeemed drinker that has been most effective. To make the temperance case, however, he notes that it is centrally important to have "sympathy of feeling" with those one is trying to convince and opposes this to the condemning of the drinker and the liquor salesperson. In other words, it is the making available of examplars and not the argument that will be the most effective convincer—an anticipation of the grounds of his future political skills (and for his well-known habit of invoking a story of which he was "reminded"). Where one cannot persuade, one can still convince. "In my judgment," he explains, "it is to the battles of this new class of champions that our late success is really, perhaps chiefly, owning.... Make the one you wish to convince your friend and you will have much greater success than if you exhort him." After all, drinking, he continues, has been with mankind since the beginning and has been "everywhere a respectable article of manufacture and merchandise." Nor can one justify abstinence based on future benefits: "There is something so ludicrous in promises of good, or *threats* of evil a great way off, as to render the whole subject with which they are connected turned into ridicule." To make the matter vivid, in a manner that will become his trademark, he tells a little Irish story: "Better to lay down the spade you're

stealing, Paddy.—if you don't you'll pay for it at the day of judgment,"—"By
the powers, if ye'll credit me so long, I'll take another, jist."[2] And he reaches
his conclusion about temperance on the *political* grounds that if one were a
slave to liquor, one could not be in possession of oneself, which, he avers, is
the basic prerequisite for being a good citizen.

The picture of the moral basis of citizenship here is self-control, self-
ownership, a quality potentially available to all men (that women apparently
have it, as it were naturally, is not discussed). It is the basis of a virtuous public and must be widely shared. Recall here Lincoln's argument sixteen years
later in the debates with Stephen Douglas: "In this and like communities, public sentiment is everything. With public sentiment, nothing can fail; without
it nothing can succeed. Consequently, he who molds public sentiment, goes
deeper than he who enacts statutes or pronounces decisions. He makes statutes and decisions possible or impossible to be executed."[3] Lincoln understood that laws were only effective if the public realm was strong, which could
only be achieved by the molding of public sentiment. While he is not precisely
preaching, he has adopted an approach similar to Charles Grandison Finney,
who, as we saw in chapter 3, was one of the preeminent reformers of the Second Great Awakening: the *shared word* is the weapon for moral and political
reform. Denunciation will not work as "it is not in the nature of man to be
driven to anything." Lincoln in fact some years later spent an entire speech
extolling the importance of speech, of writing, and of the media that convey
meaning as essential to the human project.[4]

The vision of what temperance is to achieve for the citizen—it is the objective correlative of responsible citizenship—means for Lincoln that he must
seek a revolution equivalent or even superior to that of 1776. Speaking of the
"relative grandeur" of revolutions, he writes, "Of our political revolution of
'76, we all are justly proud. It has given us a degree of freedom, far exceeding
that of any other of the nations of the earth, . . . But with these glorious results,
past, present and to come, it has had its evils too. It breathed forth famine,
swam in blood and rode on fire. . . . These were the price, the inevitable price,
paid for the blessings it brought." Without condemning the violence necessary
to the 1776 revolution, he continues by privileging the "present" revolution:

2. Abraham Lincoln, "Address to the Washington Temperance Society of Springfield,
Illinois," in *The Collected Works of Abraham Lincoln*, ed. Roy P. Blaser, 9 vols. (New Bruns-
wick, NJ: Rutgers University Press, 1955), 1:271–79, at 276 (hereafter cited as *CW*).

3. Abraham Lincoln, "First Debate with Douglas," *CW*, 3:27.

4. Abraham Lincoln, "Second Lecture on Discoveries and Inventions, February 11,
1859," *CW*, 3:356–63.

Turn now, to the temperance revolution. In *it*, we shall find a stronger bondage broken; a viler slavery, manumitted; a greater tyrant, deposed. In it, more of want supplied, more disease healed, more sorrow assuaged.... And what a noble ally this, to the cause of political freedom. With such an aid, its march cannot fail to be on and on till every son of earth drink in its rich fruition, the sorrow quenching draughts of perfect liberty. Happy day, when, all appetites controlled, all passions subdued, all matters subjected, *mind*, all conquering mind, shall live and move the monarch of the world. Glorious consummation! Hail, fall of Fury! Reign of Reason, all hail! ... How nobly distinguished that People, who shall have planted, and nurtured to maturity, both the political and moral freedom of their species.[5]

In other words, the shared but individually instantiated vision of citizenship as self-possession and self-control will replace the revolutionary energies of the Founders and henceforth serve as the basis of citizenship. It will require "nurture"—it is, that is, a project to be realized. Behind this claim lies the question of what the conditions for individual independence are that must be realized and why they are necessary.

The Temperance Society speech and the appeal to "Reason" must be read in the context of a call he had made four years before, to the Young Man's Lyceum, again in Springfield. That lecture was entitled "The Perpetuation of Our Political Institutions" and was given on the occasion of the murder of an abolitionist editor by a proslavery mob. Lincoln addressed the danger he thought confronted the country:

We hope all dangers may be overcome; but to conclude that no danger may ever arise, would itself be extremely dangerous. There are now, and will hereafter be, many causes, dangerous in their tendency, which have not existed heretofore; and which are not too insignificant to merit attention. That our government should have been maintained in its original form from its establishment until now, is not much to be wondered at.... Then, all that sought celebrity and fame ... aspired to display before an admiring world, a practical demonstration of the truth of a proposition, which had hitherto been considered, at best no better, than problematical; namely, *the capability of a people to govern themselves....* They succeeded. The experiment is successful; and thousands have won their deathless names in making it so. But the game is caught; and I believe it is true, that with the

5. Lincoln, "Address to Washington Temperance Society," *CW*, 1:272, 278, 279.

catching, end the pleasures of the chase. This field of glory is harvested, and the crop is already appropriated. But new reapers will arise, and *they*, too, will seek a field. It is to deny, what the history of the world tells us is true, to suppose that men of ambition and talents will not continue to spring up amongst us. And, when they do, they will as naturally seek the gratification of their ruling passion, as others have so done before them. The question then, is, can that gratification be found in supporting and maintaining an edifice that has been erected by others? Most certainly it cannot.[6]

The danger came from the existence of slavery (understood in its narrow but also its broad sense) and the possibility that it could easily lead to tyranny. The danger was especially strong in that the memory of past virtue was fading. Lincoln continued:

I do not mean to say, that the scenes of the revolution *are now* or *ever will* be entirely forgotten; but that like every thing else, they must fade upon the memory of the world, and grow more and more dim by the lapse of time. In history, we hope, they will be read of, and recounted, so long as the bible shall be read;—but even granting that they will, their influence *cannot be* what it heretofore has been. Even then, they *cannot be* so universally known, nor so vividly felt, as they were by the generation just gone to rest. At the close of that struggle, nearly every adult male had been a participator in some of its scenes. The consequence was, that of those scenes, in the form of a husband, a father, a son or brother, *a living history was to be found in every family—a history bearing the indubitable testimonies of its own authenticity, in the limbs mangled, in the scars of wounds received, in the midst of the very scenes related—a history, too, that could be read and understood alike by all, the wise and the ignorant, the learned and the unlearned.*— But *those* histories are gone. They *can* be read no more forever. They *were* a fortress of strength; but, what invading foeman could *never do*, the silent artillery of time *has done*; the leveling of its walls. They are gone.—They *were* a forest of giant oaks; but the all-resistless hurricane has swept over them, and left only, here and there, a lonely trunk, despoiled of its verdure, shorn of its foliage; unshading and unshaded, to murmur in a few gentle

6. Abraham Lincoln, "The Perpetuation of Our Political Institutions," *CW*, 1:113. My emphasis.

breezes, and to combat with its mutilated limbs, a few more ruder storms, then to sink, and be no more.

They *were* the pillars of the temple of liberty; and now, that they have crumbled away, that temple must fall, unless we, their descendants, supply their places with other pillars, hewn from the solid quarry of sober reason. Passion has helped us; but can do so no more. It will in future be our enemy. Reason, cold, calculating, unimpassioned reason, must furnish all the materials for our future support and defence.—Let those materials be moulded into *general intelligence, sound morality*, and in particular, *a reverence for the constitution and laws*: and, that we improved to the last; that we remained free to the last; that we revered his name to the last; that, during his long sleep, we permitted no hostile foot to pass over or desecrate his resting place; shall be that which to learn the last trump shall awaken our WASHINGTON.[7]

Our past no longer shapes our life. What was a "living history" has faded. All that we have now from that past is a document—the Constitution—that is what must provide the basis of life in common. We need to replace the "living history" that informed the revolutionary generation: Can it now be replaced with a reverence for a document? Will that be enough? This is at this time a key concept in his thought: if the "living history" of the American Revolution is eroding and fading, then a new "living history" must be found and made available. The political leader must, in effect, conquer time. The self-consciousness of this speech is astounding, and, as we shall see, Lincoln later sought by the Civil War to make available a different "living history," as the Constitution by itself had proved inadequate.

Lincoln was twenty-nine years old and here set out a political project and strategy he hoped would be adequate to reground citizenship. It is to rest on "reason." "Reason," however, as Lincoln uses it here, follows classic rhetorical tropes: he starts with premises that are asserted to be self-evident; adduces conditions, gives tellingly convincing exemplars, and concludes logically but by an exhortation.[8] Lincoln's speeches are models of forensic acuity—he brings his audience along step by step, establishing an initial shared sense, punctuating his argument with a story or two, presenting a set of apparently incontrovertible facts, and engaging his audience with something to which

7. Lincoln, "Perpetuation of Our Political Institutions," *CW*, 1:115. My emphasis.
8. On Lincoln and reason, see David Herbert Donald, *Lincoln* (New York: Simon and Schuster, 1993), 66–67, 80–83, 118.

they cannot but help agree. The Declaration of Independence had in its rhetorical structure followed the same structure.[9] As Ralph Waldo Emerson once remarked, "eloquence consists in speaking the truth in a manner that those to whom one speaks will understand it."[10]

Yet, one senses, reason may not by itself adequate to the task. As with Max Weber, eighty years later in his great lecture of 1921, *Politics as a Vocation*, when glory or charisma has disappeared and tradition no longer suffices, polities tend to rely on the rational-legal. There is, I think, a touch of distress in Lincoln's speech, much as there will be in Weber's lecture—Weber was to hope for a recurrence of true charisma. Lincoln was brought up during the period of the Second Great Awakening and must have shared some sense that reason alone would not be enough. But even that awakening would not be enough: God himself, before whom Thomas Jefferson had trembled, would now not suffice for America. For Justice Taney, penning his decision in the *Dred Scott* case, God endorsed slavery; for many in the North, however, God did just the opposite. From what will Americans learn unity? It will shortly appear that the answer will be only in war.[11]

LINCOLN ON SLAVERY AND EQUALITY

From the beginning, Lincoln had a deep-seated opposition to slavery. His conviction rested on what he had *seen*. In 1860, he wrote to the Southern Congressman Alexander Hamilton Stephens about the still strong memory of his visit to New Orleans thirty years before, in 1831: "You say that slavery is the corner stone of the south and that if separated, would be that of a new Republic; God forbid. When a boy I went to New Orleans on a flat boat and there I saw slavery and slave markets as I have never seen them in Kentucky, and

9. See the following interesting if somewhat single-minded book: David Hirsch and Dan Van Haften, *Abraham Lincoln and the Structure of Reason* (New York: SavasBeatie, 2010). These authors argue that the speeches are all structured along the lines of Euclid's geometry: Start with a small set of self-evident axioms; derive a number of propositions; work those into a coherent system. Thomas Hobbes had done the same. For a different approach, see the analysis in Allen, *Our Declaration*.

10. Ralph Waldo Emerson, "Eloquence," in *The Complete Works of Ralph Waldo Emerson*, 12 vols. (Boston: Houghton Mifflin, 1904), vol. 8, https://www.bartleby.com/90/0803 .html.

11. I find, after writing this, that there are similar thoughts in my teacher's work: see McWilliams, *Idea of Fraternity in America*, 278.

I heard worse of the Red River plantations. I hoped and prayed that the gradual emancipation plan . . . or the Liberian colonization might lead to its extinction in the United States."[12] Five years previously, he recalled the same experience in a letter about slavery to his friend Joshua Speed:

> You know I dislike slavery; and you fully admit the abstract wrong of it. . . .
> I also acknowledge your rights and my obligations, under the Constitution,
> in regard to your slaves. I confess I hate to see the poor creatures hunted
> down, and caught, and carried back to their stripes, and unrewarded toils;
> but I bite my lip and keep quiet. In 1841, you and I had together a tedious
> low-water trip, on a Steam Boat from Louisville to St. Louis. You may re-
> member, as I well do, that from Louisville to the mouth of the Ohio, there
> were, on board, ten or a dozen slaves, shackled together with irons. *That
> sight was a continued torment to me*; and I see something like it every time I
> touch the Ohio, or any other slave-border. It is hardly fair for you to assume,
> that I have no interest in a thing which has, and continually exercises, the
> power of making me miserable. You ought rather to appreciate how much
> the great body of the Northern people do crucify their feelings, in order to
> maintain their loyalty to the Constitution and the Union. . . . How can any
> one who abhors the oppression of negroes, be in favor of degrading classes
> of white people? Our progress in degeneracy appears to me to be pretty
> rapid. As a nation, we began by declaring that "all men are created equal."
> We now practically read it "all men are created equal, except negroes."
> When the Know-Nothings get control, it will read "all men are created
> equal, except negroes, and foreigners, and catholics." When it comes to this
> I should prefer emigrating to some country where they make no pretence of
> loving liberty—to Russia, for instance, where despotism can be taken pure,
> and without the base alloy of hypocrisy. (*CW*, 2:320–21; my emphasis)

More than anything, it was the visually tangible picture of the enchained blacks that stayed with Lincoln. And more than anything else, he saw that most Northerners, like Captain Amasa Delano in Melville's novella, simply

---

12. See Richard Campanella, *Lincoln in New Orleans: The 1828–1831 Flatboat Voyages and Their Place in History* (Lafayette: University of Louisiana at Lafayette Press, 2010). The letter is not in *CW* but is recognized as authentic. It is cited by Campanella in the "Conclusion," footnote 23 (taken from a Kindle version—location 5157). Whether or not Lincoln actually ever said that he intended to "hit [slavery] hard" should he get the chance, as he is famously reported as having done, Campanella has a strong argument that he must have said something like that to friends.

"crucif[ied] their own feelings" on the matter. And all this stayed with him as a *political* threat to what it meant to be an American: the enslavement of blacks can/will lead to the virtual enslavement of many others. Lincoln may have hated slavery morally: but he also opposed it politically. This is what seared his conscience with and from a commitment to equality of all—it was stronger than any argument, and so we are reminded of the importance of exemplars as a tool for political education and political change that he had advanced in the Temperance Society address. Exemplars are the presentation of incidents in a manner so striking that they become part of your appreciation of world. They change your mind.

Up until 1854, however, Lincoln and most of the North (except for the abolitionists) were willing to let slavery continue as long as it remained confined to the South. They were convinced that it was an inefficient system that would gradually fade away. In his best-selling 1857 book *The Impending Crisis of the South*, Hilton Rowan Helper argued that the South was a failing and failed economic system.[13] In this belief, however, he and the others were mistaken, as my discussion in chapter 3 of the Conrad and Meyer article and the Fogel and Engerman book has established. It will be the case with Lincoln that, as Emerson noted in his funeral oration, "this man grew according to the need."[14]

When Stephen Douglas put through the Kansas-Nebraska bill in 1854, economic issues suddenly leapt to center stage. The moral questions that most of the North was willing to bracket, as discussed in chapter 3, were now conjoined with a serious politico-economic question. Much of the support of the short-lived Free-Soil Party and the new Republican Party came from white artisans and shopkeepers who had suffered from serious recessions in 1847–48 and 1853–54. A panic and a contraction of business activity by almost 25 percent occurred in 1857. Both parties held that free men cultivating their own homesteads formed the basis of a superior economic system to slavery. The possibility that the new territories could become slave economies thus directly threatened this group, a group that was politically all-important as potential home to the new Free-Soil and Republican Parties.

By 1850, there were fifteen slave states and seventeen free ones. Furthermore, the victory in the Mexican-American War of 1846–48 had opened land from Texas to California and north through Utah and Nevada to American

13. Hinton Rowan Helper, *The Impending Crisis of the South* (New York: Burdick Brothers, 1857), electronic ed., Documenting the American South, University of North Carolina at Chapel Hill, http://docsouth.unc.edu/nc/helper/helper.html.

14. Emerson, "Remarks at Funeral Services."

settlers. While California was admitted as a free state in 1850, most of the rest of the area remained territories (with present-day Oklahoma, Arizona, and New Mexico still in that status until the twentieth century). What are now Oklahoma, New Mexico, Arizona, Nevada, and Utah were slave territories. In effect, slavery pretty much split the country North-South at around what had been the lines of the Missouri Compromise and the Ohio River. The opening of the territories to slavery called into question the vision of citizenship that Lincoln and other Free-Soilers held.

The anxiety of the Northerners was only exacerbated by the *Dred Scott* decisions and the Fugitive Slave Act, which required North to do as the South: arrest and return any escaped slaves. From early on, Lincoln opposed Justice Taney's reasoning, noting that in five of the first thirteen states, free blacks had held the franchise (although in three of those it had subsequently been taken away or restricted). William Eustis, the Massachusetts doctor who had served in the Revolutionary War and was later secretary of war under President James Madison, had argued that the blacks who had served in the Revolutionary War were deserving of citizenship.[15] And in making this argument, in a Springfield address, Lincoln's attention turned somewhat from the Constitution to the Declaration of Independence: "In those days, our Declaration of Independence was held sacred by all, and thought to include all . . . but now it is assailed and sneered at. . . . I appeal to all . . . are you really willing that the Declaration be thus frittered away?"[16] It is in this context that Lincoln's understanding of the basis of citizenship acquired fuller purchase. While Lincoln's attitude toward blacks evolved over time, what is also clear, and generally overlooked, is that the basis of his final conclusion and eventually of his policies, remained the same. What changed were the circumstances—and Lincoln responded to them.

In the Springfield address, Lincoln argued that the Declaration of Independence includes all men, *but not in all respects*. He cites Jefferson, who had at one point written that the slaves of Virginia were "one half of the citizens" of the state. Lincoln seems to be making a difference between a vision of human beings as, first, having human rights; and second, having civic rights, these last being in particular the right to enjoy the unalienated fruits of one's labor; and third, having the right to suffrage.[17] No single category necessarily

15. See Alan Gilbert, *Black Patriots and Loyalists: Fighting for Emancipation in the War for Independence* (Chicago: University of Chicago Press, 2012).

16. Abraham Lincoln, "June 26, 1857—Speech at Springfield," *CW*, 2:407.

17. This is certainly the source of Judith N. Shklar's second criterion of citizenship: the right to work. See Shklar, *American Citizenship*, and the discussion in my introduction.

entailed another. Some of this separation is, perhaps, made possible from the difference between citizenship in England and that of the new America. In England, citizenship derived (officially) from being "subject to the Crown." To this, Americans had in the Declaration substituted a pledge to the rights of "Life, Liberty and the pursuit of Happiness" by a people. The Constitution, notably, carried no definition of national citizenship. The important point here is that it was possible to conceive of citizenship without that entailing a right to the suffrage: voting still required certain qualities, which it was assumed that blacks did not generally have. It is worth noting that this matter was highly debated. In 1834, for instance, in a court case in Connecticut, *Crandall v. State*, the court decided that blacks were citizens but did not have suffrage. I cite the case:

> The right of voting is not the criterion of citizenship: the one has no natural or necessary connexion with the other. Cases may exist where persons vote who are not citizens, and where persons are citizens and do not vote. The right of suffrage is nowhere universal and absolute. It is founded in notions of internal police, varying frequently, even in the same government.... No female can vote, nor any minor; but are not females and minors citizens?
>
> If voting makes a citizen, what confusion! The same man in one state, is a full citizen; in another, half a citizen; in another a non-descript; in another, an alien. How absurd to create such a distinction in these states![18]

To approach this matter, let us examine the standard chestnut question about Lincoln: did Lincoln abolish slavery in order to preserve the Union, or did he preserve the Union in order to abolish slavery? In a recent book, George Kateb has approached this matter with a consideration of what he refers to as Lincoln's "single greatest sentence"[19]—the penultimate phrase of the Second Inaugural Address from March 4, 1865: "Yet, if God wills that it [the war] continue until all the wealth piled by the bondsman's two hundred and fifty years of unrequited toil shall be sunk, and until every drop of blood drawn

---

18. Crandall v. State, 10 Conn. 339 (1834), http://press-pubs.uchicago.edu/founders /documents/a4_2_1s21.html. I owe this reference to a citation in Joseph Fornieri, "Lincoln on Black Citizenship," chap. 2 in *Constitutionalism in the Approach and Aftermath of the Civil War*, ed. Paul Moreno and Joseph Fornieri (New York: Fordham University Press, 2013).

19. George Kateb, *Lincoln's Political Thought* (New Haven, CT: Yale University Press, 2015), 208–9. Much of the following several pages draws upon my review of Kateb in *Contemporary Political Thought* 15, no. 1 (May 2016): 33–37.

with the lash shall be paid by another drawn with the sword, as was said three thousand years ago, so still it must be said 'the judgments of the Lord are true and righteous altogether.'" The citation is from Psalms 19:9; the psalmist continues with the assertion that such judgments are "more . . . desired than gold [and] sweeter . . . than honey."[20] Lincoln here asserts that ending slavery, *and the war that it costs*, is "true and righteous" and greatly to be desired, even given the war.

It is clear that, from his earliest days, Lincoln hated slavery. He is explicit about it,[21] but, contrary to most if not all other readings that take this perspective as either less than true (he sometimes seemed willing to allow slavery in the South) or obvious (no one wants to be a slave), we must ask, as does Kateb, the key question: *why* did Lincoln hate slavery?

WHAT IS WRONG WITH SLAVERY?

The answer has several parts. One has been partially given—he thought it would lead to a general despotism in which, little by little, most people would agree to the curtailing of their rights: Lincoln thought that if one became familiar with the "chains of bondage," one was "preparing [one's own] limbs to wear them." "Are you quite sure," he asks, that "the demon which you have roused *will not turn and rend you?* . . . Accustomed to trample on the rights of those around you, you have lost the genius of your own independence, and become the fit subjects of the first cunning tyrant who rises."[22] Enslavement of blacks entails, one might say, Jean-Jacques Rousseau's claim in the first chapter of his *On the Social Contract* that "he who believes himself the master of others is all as much a slave as they."[23] Yet this potential assimilation of a habituation with chattel slavery to the existence of a broad political tyrannical slavery is by itself insufficient, for chattel slavery was in itself for Lincoln also a "monstrous injustice."

Why? The second reason for his hatred of slavery is that Lincoln is committed first and foremost to the equality of individual rights, a commitment that rests on three tenets: nontyranny, self-government, and self-ownership.

20. Abraham Lincoln, "Second Inaugural Address," *CW*, 8:333.
21. Lincoln, "Speech of 10 July 1858," *CW*, 2:492. See Kateb, *Lincoln's Political Thought*, 97.
22. Lincoln, "Speech at Edwardsville, 11 September 1858," *CW*, 3:95.
23. Jean-Jacques Rousseau, *On the Social Contract*, my translation from *Du contrat social* (Paris: Gallimard, 1976), bk. 1, chap. 1.

More specifically, nontyranny: government is not to use people for its own ambitions; self-government: rule is to be consented to, consent being manifest in the exercise of one's rights; and self-ownership: one should not be dispossessed of the fruits of one's labor. Slavery, as Kateb notes, is "an extreme violation of all these."[24] They are the basis of Lincoln's vision of the citizen. But it is not clear to him that it should follow that the suffrage was a *right*—and so I argued in the introduction.

Yet the matter is not yet resolved. What follows from his commitment to equality? Lincoln is quite clear in his prewar writings and speeches that he (or the Republican Party) will observe the existing "constitutional guards." But it is also striking that even as he mentions this, he also invokes the Declaration of Independence. For instance, in the reconstructed transcript of a speech given in Lewistown, Illinois, on April 17, 1858, he claims to be "actuated in this contest by something higher than an anxiety for office"—namely, the Declaration, which he holds asserts the equality of *all* (not "none but rich men or none but white men")—and furthermore that the Founders, Jefferson in particular, shared that opinion despite the fact that they continued to hold slaves (*CW*, 2:546–47). Lincoln's public justification of his commitment to equality rests, in other words, on his assertion—practically a pretense—that Jefferson, if not by his actions, then by his ideas and his sentiments, was opposed to slavery. Lincoln claims historical legitimacy for what was in fact a radical claim. The words of the Declaration were to have priority over the enacted reality.

What, then, about the Constitution, which notoriously enshrines slavery (more accurately: as "other Persons") and thereby privileges white freedom? It was a Constitution that had led Henry David Thoreau to declare in 1848, "How does it become a man to behave toward this American government today? I answer, that he cannot without disgrace be associated with it. I cannot for an instant recognize that political organization as *my* government which is the *slave's* government also."[25] And yet Lincoln did not take Thoreau's position. He revered the Constitution and urged others to do so.

What were Lincoln's hopes for the Constitution? Lincoln appears to have had originally the hope—present in several of the Founders and several of the original states—that slavery would gradually fade away. But, with the repeal of the Missouri Compromise by the (Stephen Douglas–authored and –sponsored) Kansas-Nebraska Act of 1854, Lincoln despairingly realized in a private letter that "no peaceful extinction of slavery [is] in prospect for us." He continued,

24. Kateb, *Lincoln's Political Thought*, 99.
25. Thoreau, *Civil Disobedience*, para. 7.

"We have grown fat and lost all dread of being slaves ourselves, we have become so greedy to be *masters* that we call the same maxim ["that all men are created equal"] a 'self-evident lie.' The fourth of July has not quite dwindled away; it is still a great day—*for burning fire-crackers.*"[26] Lincoln clearly took the quote about a lie from John C. Calhoun: such a defense of slavery had all but erased the principle on which the country was founded.

Yet Lincoln continued to have public reverence for the Constitution. Only on occasion did he publicly allow a glimmer of the truth of the situation break through. This is in the "House Divided" speech of June 16, 1858, in which Lincoln famously cited the Gospel according to Mark to the effect that "a house divided cannot stand."[27] Yet it is unclear what exactly that division was and why one division or another might lead the house to fall. After all, the House had stood for more than eighty years. (One need hardly note, however, that one may here properly and seriously question Harry Jaffa's contention that Lincoln was challenging Douglas from an Aristotelian philosophical position.[28])

In 1858, a convention of the Republican Party of Illinois endorsed Lincoln for US Senate. This was an unprecedented move—senators were elected by the members of the state legislature. Lincoln responded to the endorsement by repeating the claim he had made previously but in a less salient context: "A house divided cannot stand." Seeking reelection as US senator was Stephen Douglas, a Democrat. The stage was set for conflict between the two men—in the end, however, who was chosen senator would be determined by the state legislature, so the conflict between Lincoln and Douglas would be decided by which party would attain a majority there. The two men agreed to a set of seven debates (though Lincoln had originally wanted fifty).

LINCOLN AND DOUGLAS

The issue of the divided basis of American citizenship is at the center of these famous debates that Lincoln had with Stephen Douglas between August 21 and October 15, 1858. The debates were exceptionally well attended (ten thou-

26. Abraham Lincoln to George Robertson, August 15, 1855, *CW*, 2:318.

27. See here Kateb, *Lincoln's Political Thought*, 125–27, 46.

28. See Harry Jaffa, *Crisis of the House Divided: An Interpretation of the Issues in the Lincoln-Douglas Debates* (Chicago: University of Chicago Press, 2012).

sand people attended the first one, in a town with a population of five thousand) and widely reported. Each side (and each partisan newspaper) made transcripts available (most often with corrected syntax and grammar for its own side only). Lincoln had them published as a book. The agreed-on format was that the first speaker had sixty minutes, followed by a ninety-minute response from the opponent and then by a thirty-minute rejoinder. Lincoln lost the election to be senator. Senators were appointed by the state legislature, where a majority of those elected were Democrats, thus supporters of Douglas. The speeches, however, made Lincoln famous and contributed strongly to his election to the presidency two years later.[29]

In the first debate and then again in the others, the basis of Douglas's initial attacks were to accuse Lincoln of being an abolitionist and of desiring to "confer upon the negro the rights and privileges of citizenship." Douglas contended that Lincoln's position will "dissolve the Union if it succeeds" (*CW*, 3:9, 12), and Douglas invoked the "House Divided" speech. Lincoln's response consisted of three positions: first, he will not interfere with the institution of slavery *where it has existed*; second, he does not wish to introduce "political and social equality between the white and black races"; and third, citing the Declaration of Independence, he holds that blacks are entitled to the rights of the Declaration as much as any other person: "In the right to eat bread, without leave of anybody else, which his own hand earns, *he is my equal and the equal of Judge Douglas, and the equal of every living man*" (*CW*, 3:16, Lincoln's emphasis). Lincoln then turns to Douglas's citation of the "House Divided" speech and argues that the house *can* stand if slavery were to be restricted to its original territories, for if its spread were arrested, slavery "*would be* in the course of ultimate extinction" (*CW*, 3:18, my emphasis). The "House Divided" speech is therefore not to be understood, as it often has been, as a claim that abolition will make war inevitable—which is how Douglas wants to read it—but as a claim that the nation will endure if, *and only if*, slavery remains restricted to the original Southern states.[30] Indeed, Lincoln even argues that Jefferson, "the most distinguished politician of our history," a "slave-holder," and the "author of the Declaration of Independence," had in 1787 originated "the policy of prohibiting slaves in new territory."[31] Lincoln is in fact explicit

---

29. The speeches of both men are collected in *CW*, 3:1–325, listed under their respective 1858 dates (August 21, 27; September 15, 18; October 7, 13, 15).

30. For a complex differing argument, see Jaffa, *Crisis of the House Divided*.

31. *CW*, 2:249, October 17, 1754.

about the primacy of the Declaration. On August 21, 1858, in a speech in Lewistown, Illinois, he entered into a long discussion of the Declaration and its origins, concluding with this statement:

> Now, my countrymen, if you have been taught doctrines conflicting with the great landmarks of the Declaration of Independence; if you have listened to suggestions which would take away from its grandeur, and mutilate the fair symmetry of its proportions; if you have been inclined to believe that all men are not created equal in those inalienable rights enumerated by our chart of liberty, let me entreat you to come back. Return to the fountain whose waters spring close by the blood of the Revolution. Think nothing of me—take no thought for the political fate of any man whomsoever—but come back to the truths that are in the Declaration of Independence. You may do anything with me you choose, if you will but heed these sacred principles. You may not only defeat me for the Senate, but you may take me and put me to death. While pretending no indifference to earthly honors, I do claim to be actuated in this contest by something higher than an anxiety for office. I charge you to drop every paltry and insignificant thought for any man's success. It is nothing; I am nothing; Judge Douglas is nothing. But do not destroy that immortal emblem of Humanity—the Declaration of American Independence. (*CW*, 2:547)

In the third debate, on September 15, 1858, Douglas, clearly aware of this speech, took what I read as the bait and, practically parroting Justice Taney, turned to the Declaration. "In my opinion," he says, "the signers of the Declaration . . . desired to express by [the phrase that "all men are created equal"] white men, men of European birth and European descent and had no reference either to the negro, the savage Indians, the Feejee, the Malay or any other inferior and degraded race, when they spoke of the equality of men" (*CW*, 3:113). In the fourth debate, held on September 18, 1858, Douglas returned to this theme. He noted that Lincoln had constantly claimed that when the Declaration says "all men," it means "the negro as well as the white man." But, he averred, the "negro is incapable of self-government." In response, Lincoln first said that he was not in favor of "negro citizenship," then said that the states could authorize it except for the *Dred Scott* decision, and then said that if they could authorize it, he would be against them doing so (*CW*, 3:177-79). He continually, however, invokes the Declaration as justifying his position.

The touchstone for Lincoln is the word *equal*. For Lincoln, even though Jefferson and the others were slaveholders, when they signed their names to the proposition that "all men are created equal," they meant *all* men. Lincoln in fact cited Jefferson's letter about God's wrath at the institution of slavery. In 1860, he stated that the increasingly widespread claim that the Declaration applies only to white men is mostly consequent to what Douglas has said—and that before his opponent's interventions, no one held such a position. Such is "a long stride towards establishing the policy of indifference"—and indifference was what Lincoln feared: that men would no longer care to exercise their self-possessed independence.[32] "Equality" means for Lincoln, and only means, that all men have a right to "Life, Liberty and the pursuit of Happiness." In Lincoln's mind, at this point at least, citizenship does not include suffrage for blacks, a position he retains until sometime after his election. Leading up to his election, his constantly repeated theme is rather that one party thinks slavery "right," while the other thinks it "wrong." *In effect, Lincoln casts equality as a moral term and not a political one.* For whites, it is the basis of virtuous citizenship, *but suffrage is not necessarily an implication of equality, of, that is, a natural status.* Equality is something all men have naturally; suffrage is not—Lincoln still retained the notion of there being necessary criteria for voting, although he did not explain those criteria in any detail at this time. The abolition of slavery is a moral necessity but need not entail suffrage. The two candidates are arguing over whether or not all men are naturally endowed with the capacities required to be a free and independent person. Lincoln holds that they are; Douglas holds that as blacks are incapable of independence, they are not. This is *not* an argument about the right to the suffrage, and indeed, Lincoln tries hard to make sure that it is not. For Lincoln, one could not be self-possessed if one was dependent on (the slave of) someone else. If one was not so dependent, then self-possession was by all men attainable—and that was the basis of citizenship. Citizenship did not, however, necessarily entail suffrage. To be independent meant that one was entitled to the fruits of one's labor.

Why does citizenship not entail suffrage? When Lincoln wrote these words, he was relying on the Constitution. The Constitution makes a clear if not explicit distinction between "persons" and "citizens." Article I, Section 9, prohibits the "importation of . . . persons" after the year 1808, referring obviously to black slaves from Africa. Article I, Section 2, in apportioning the number of representatives per state, refers to "the whole Number of free Persons" (excluding Native Americans, but including indentured servants and notoriously,

32. *CW*, 4:10—March 1860; see *CW*, 4:220.

"three-fifths of all other Persons"). Article IV, Section 2, assures that the "Citizens" of each state are entitled to their privileges and immunities *and* that any "Person" charged with and fleeing from a crime shall be returned to the locus of his or her crime. A great divide in America is papered over by this almost unnoticeable distinction. Any necessary relation between personhood, citizenship, and suffrage is not mentioned until the Fourteenth Amendment, passed only in 1868, well after Lincoln's death. There is thus at this time little contradiction between Lincoln's reading of the Declaration and that of the Constitution, except for the claim that the statement that "all men are created equal" applies to all *persons* even if it in no ways entails suffrage. This is significant for it means that Lincoln retained the sense that *criteria additional to simply being a human person are necessary to be a voting citizen* and, whether for tactical reasons or not, he tended to hold or express the position that blacks in general lack those qualities.[33]

This was a difficult position to maintain, especially as earlier understandings (church membership, property, tools) were explicitly not available to him. His two early speeches (considered earlier) had enlisted self-control and reason as necessary for a virtuous polity. The erosion of past exemplary events was, however, making it increasingly impossible for a blanket denial of all versions of these new criteria to blacks. What else would be needed? Thus, in his last public address, on April 11, 1865, Lincoln in fact recognized the logical entailment of equality in the present context; but he did not move to the *universal* attribution of citizenship as a right. Instead, he indicated that rather than attribute universal suffrage to all blacks, he "would prefer that it were now conferred on the very intelligent and on those who serve our cause as soldiers" (*CW*, 8:403).

What is significant here is that Lincoln *retains the notion that certain criteria must be met* for one to be a citizen—here (high) intelligence or military service (the latter being after all a traditional route to republican citizenship). (One might also note here that around this time, John Stuart Mill advocated a double ballot for university graduates, i.e., those of superior intelligence, presumably.) Lincoln's position is not the ancient one of jus sanguinis, that one had to be born of, for example, Athenian parents to be Athenian (a position Israel holds today), nor is it that of jus soli, which will characterize the logic bound into the Fourteenth Amendment, a clause that, as we shall see, has un-

---

33. I resist then the conclusion of Fornieri, "Lincoln on Black Citizenship," 56, that Article IV, Section 2 of the Constitution logically entitles free blacks to citizenship.

foreseen consequences.[34] I might remark, however, that a photograph of the occasion apparently shows John Wilkes Booth in the audience for this speech: it made him determined to assassinate the president on the grounds that Lincoln was granting citizenship and (limited) voting rights to blacks.

Lincoln's commitment to equality came also with a secondary but significant commitment to the American state. It is a matter of historical record that, although they never recognized the South diplomatically, England and France fairly openly supported the South's cause as its victory in the American Civil War would reduce the weight and presence of the United States on the international scene. For Lincoln, however, the preservation of the American position in the world and of the example it afforded that world made the preservation of the Union necessary. In October 1854, he declared that he hated slavery "because of the monstrous injustice . . . itself" and "because it deprives our republican example of its just influence in the world, . . . insisting that there is no right principle of action but *self-interest*."[35] The need to demonstrate virtue does not disappear: in the twentieth century, a certain amount of domestic policy supporting civil rights will be deemed necessary to meet international expectations and to counter the shaming by the Soviets and Chinese as to the status of American blacks.

Thus the standard question in the secondary literature as to whether Lincoln's primary commitment was to the Union or to the end of slavery is somewhat misleading. Consider in this matter the famous letter that Lincoln wrote to Horace Greeley on August 22, 1862. Two days before, Greeley had published a nine-point editorial in the *New York Tribune* urging Lincoln to take measures to emancipate slaves and to enforce those measures of emancipation already existent. Lincoln's response claimed that he wished only to save the Union and by any means: if that meant freeing no slaves or some slaves or all slaves, he would do what was necessary. Many scholars have used this letter to argue that Lincoln cared for nothing but the Union. This has to be to some considerable degree wrong: he had already written a preliminary draft of the Emancipation Proclamation, abolished slavery in the District of Columbia, approved a law abolishing slavery in the territories, urged on Congress a law granting freedom to any slave escaping to behind Union lines (which after

34. America retains the doctrines of both jus soli and jus sanguinis—though born in a foreign country, I am American because my parents are.

35. Lincoln, "Speech at Peoria, IL, October 16, 1854," *CW*, 2:255. See also "Address to Congress, July 4, 1861," *CW*, 4:431.

three months was itself approved), and signed the second Confiscation Act authorizing the seizure of the slaves of anyone found guilty of supporting the rebellion (*CW*, 5:388–89).[36]

Lincoln closes his letter to Greeley by distinguishing between his "official" duty and his "personal" wish. His letter is publicly published: he speaks, in other words, as "*President* Lincoln," Lincoln, that is, in his purely public constitutional capacity. In 1861 and again in 1862, Lincoln had rejected proposals to announce by executive decision a limited territorial emancipation.[37] His rejection was based on his conviction that it would be unconstitutional and on the prudential consideration that it might drive the border states, still in the Union although slave states, over to the South. Kateb suggests that Lincoln made "an almost inhuman calculation," which was to *retard* emancipation *because of military necessity*. "Perhaps," Kateb concludes, "if you take the perspective of a slave rather than that of a political leader, Lincoln's decision is impossible to vindicate at all. I suppose an observer must take both perspectives."[38]

This judgment maintained "putative Constitutional correctness" and kept favor with the loyal but slave-owning border states, but these were not the most important reasons. It also brought to the South (and the North) the continuation of the war toward a hoped-for ultimate Union victory (a wager with God, if there ever was one) and the price that would exact—the situation that he described in the Second Inaugural Address. *For the expulsion of slavery to be accepted, only the payment of a fearful price would do.* Only that will constitute what he had in the lecture on "The Future of Our Political Institutions" called "a living history" (*CW*, 1.115). And only that will properly ground citizenship. *The carnage of the war was necessary to serve as the touchstone and reground citizenship on equality—it will henceforth serve as American living history.*

It is the case that during the war Lincoln suspended portions of the Constitution out of military necessity. He was in fact quite clear that no written document can ever be adequate to all circumstances: "No organic law can ever be framed with a provision specifically applicable to every question which may in occur in practical administration" (*CW*, 4:255–56, 267). There will always be exceptions, not covered adequately by law—and there is, perhaps, in Lincoln, the inauguration of a genealogy that leads to the twentieth-century German

---

36. See Kateb, *Lincoln's Political Thought*.

37. See Abraham Lincoln to General Fremont, 2 September 1861 and 11 September 1861, *CW*, 4:507, 517.

38. Kateb, *Lincoln's Political Thought*, 174.

jurist (and Nazi) Carl Schmitt's argument about the importance of the "State of exception"—Schmitt did indeed invoke Lincoln in his brief in support of Franz von Papen's declaration of dictatorial sovereignty over Prussia in 1932.[39]

Lincoln wagered with God or Providence and could not foresee what was destined; he also believed in personal responsibility and thus held the South—*as he did the North*—responsible for the horror the country had inflicted on itself. What is striking about Lincoln is that he explicitly raised the question of whether there is a compatibility of human intent and God's purpose and that he denies that such a correspondence, should it exist, could be known. He was in what Kateb calls a "metaphysical wilderness."[40] Replying on March 15, 1865, to a letter complimenting him on the Second Inaugural Address from Thurlow Weed, the newspaper publisher and leader of the New York Whigs, Lincoln demurred slightly and wrote, "Men are not flattered by being shown that there has been a difference of purpose between the Almighty and them. To deny it, however, in this case, is to deny that there is a God governing the world" (*CW*, 8:356). The prolongation of the war may or may not accord with the designation of providence: as practiced, *Lincoln understood it as a necessary retribution for the Southern embrace of slavery and the complicity of the North*. Providentially, the preservation of the Union was purely instrumental to ending slavery: Lincoln held that the Union would recognize that it deserved to continue to be reborn and to exist only if it paid a sufficiently high price—and this was true for both the North and the South.[41]

Lincoln, in the Second Inaugural Address, is frighteningly clear about the implications and costs of human equality, and the necessity to pay those costs. At least 1.1 million people died or were wounded; another million died of disease; 25 percent of those who served never returned home. The war, as it was conducted and as it lasted, was retribution to *both* North and South, necessary to impress on them the importance and implications of human equality as the moral grounding of American society. That passage, again, from the Second Inaugural Address: "If God will, that [the war] continue, until all the wealth piled by the bond-man's two hundred and fifty years of unrequited toil shall be sunk, and until every drop of blood drawn with the lash, shall be paid by another drawn with the sword."[42] Lincoln is avenger and thereby redeemer, the

---

39. See Carl Schmitt, *The Concept of the Political*, expanded ed., trans. George Schwab (Chicago: University of Chicago Press, 2008), and my foreword to that text.

40. Kateb, *Lincoln's Political Thought*, 195.

41. I am influenced here by Kateb, *Lincoln's Political Thought*.

42. Lincoln, "Second Inaugural Address."

pharmakos of and for America: *both* the North and the South are culpable for slavery and thus the war. Once Lincoln had seen that the Kansas-Nebraska Act had made a gradual extinction of slavery (if it remained confined to the South) impossible and thus that the moral basis of citizenship could not then rest on human equality, it was clear to him that getting rid of slavery was necessary not just to saving a Union but to saving this particular Union, one grounded on human equality.

The political implications of Lincoln's argument for the grounding of nationhood on equality were not clear. As we have seen, for Lincoln, equality did not of itself entail full citizenship. This position, however, left open an unavoidable dilemma. Already in 1862, Congress had passed the Militia Act, which called for the recruitment of blacks into the army. The bill authorized the president to admit blacks to the army for "constructing intrenchments, or performing camp service or any other labor or any military or naval service for which they may be found competent."[43] Eventually, as many as 180,000 blacks had served in the Union Army, often with real distinction (nicely memorialized in the film *Glory*, in a great poem by Robert Lowell, and by a monument to them on Boston Common), and a little over 20 percent had died for the cause. Military service, especially voluntary military service, has for two thousand years been thought of as entitlement to citizenship. General William Tecumseh Sherman was clear on the matter: "When the fight is over, the hand that drops the musket cannot be denied the ballot."[44]

In 1866, thus after Lincoln's assassination, Congress passed a Civil Rights Act. It became law over the veto of President Andrew Johnson: we shall have opportunity in chapter 5 to explore this situation more fully. The act, authored by Senator Lyman Trumbull of Illinois, made all male persons "citizens." This designation was not intended, it turned out, to imply very much. As Trumbull explained when he proposed the bill in Congress, this did not mean equality "in all things civil, social and political"; nor did it mean that all citizens were entitled to vote, as the criteria for that were reserved to the states. Nor did it mean that all citizens could sit on juries or attend the same schools. Civil rights had to do, explained Trumbull, only with that which has "no relation to

---

43. See Cong. Globe, 37th Cong., 2d Sess. 597 (1862) at 599, http://legisworks.org/sal /12/stats/STATUTE-12-Pg597.pdf. See Eric Foner, *The Fiery Trial: Abraham Lincoln and American Slavery* (New York: W. W. Norton, 2010), 213–15 (Foner cites this passage from the Militia Act).

44. Cited in A. Keyssar, *Right to Vote*, 69; see the additional material in footnote 18, on his page 399. Frederick Douglass had said the same in 1861.

the establishment, support or management of government."[45] After all, white women were citizens but could not vote—and for many observers, that was still considered the natural course of things.

Trumbull is trying to moderate an increasingly vigorous demand for suffrage. Various groups, especially across the former slave states, organized and took to the streets to press the demand for full political rights. As Alexander Keyssar notes, many people in the North agreed with them. Typically, however, this demand was phrased not in terms of various criteria but mostly in terms of rights. Thus, the New York minister Henry Ward Beecher held suffrage to be among the "natural rights of men, not a privilege or prerogative, but a right. Everyman has a right to have a voice in the laws, the magistracies and the policies that take care of him. This is an inherent right; it is not a privileged conferred." His justification was that it was politically dangerous to have an "ignorant class and not have them voting." Voting would, by its practice, prepare men for "intelligent suffrage."[46] These thoughts were expressed in a talk given in Brooklyn on February 12, 1865, thus before Lincoln's death, and they express at least one possible reading of Lincoln.

Seeing citizenship as entailing suffrage and as a right, however, marks an important change in the concept, although possibly an unexpected one. It is no accident that the same Henry Ward Beecher who was a radical abolitionist, a supporter of women's rights, and an antislavery activist could also argue vigorously against the participants in the Great Railroad Strike of 1877 as follows:

It is true that the $1.00 a day was not enough to support a man and five children, if a man would insist on smoking and drinking beer. Was not a dollar a day enough to buy bread, water costs nothing. Man cannot live by bread alone but the man who cannot live on bread and water is not fit to live. A family man may live on good bread and water in the morning, bread and water at midday, and good water and bread at night.[47]

The text notes that Beecher was interrupted several times by laughter.

In 1870, the daily wage of a skilled male worker was around $2.60 and for

45. Cong. Globe, 38th Cong., 1st Sess. 1117 (March 1, 1866).

46. Beecher quoted in A. Keyssar, *Right to Vote*, 70.

47. I posted this quotation on my office door for several years. Here it is cited as the epigraph to chapter 9 in Jack Beatty, *Age of Betrayal: The Triumph of Money in America, 1865–1900* (New York: Knopf, 2007).

a nonskilled male worker around $1.50 (for women, it was less than $1.00).[48] Such unthinking casual insensitivity in Beecher's sermon is no accident (a pair of shoes cost $0.98 in 1875; one hundred pounds of wheat flour cost around $2.50; a loaf of hard bread was about $0.10 a pound). A man in the economic condition described by Beecher is certainly not independent, not "his own man." But for Beecher, he can vote. If suffrage is understood purely in terms of citizenship, and if the right to vote is an inborn "natural" right, then no criteria are necessary other than obvious nondependency, which, for Beecher, clearly did not apply to wage earners. There are no external criteria that must be met—which had not been the case with the Puritans, James Madison, nor Thomas Paine.

Paradoxically, Lincoln's salutary insistence on human equality laid the foundation for a vision of citizenship that would be thoroughly compatible with the rapidly developing industrial capitalism. Indeed, to the degree that these various movements had the effect rendering the concept of citizenship less substantive and more formal, they paved the way for the economic developments to be considered hereafter. The Fourteenth Amendment will make the new understanding clear, not realizing, I think, what a change it is effectuating. It reads: "All persons born or naturalized in the United States, and subject to the jurisdiction thereof, are citizens of the United States and of the State wherein they reside." They are entitled to all the "privileges and immunities of citizens of the United States." When coupled with the rising industrial capitalism of the post–Civil War period, a radical change in the conduct of politics and in the conception of citizenship will come about.

One might ask whether Lincoln was successful in refounding the Union on this new lived history. A full answer will have to wait, but for now, consider these words of a philosopher of America, Stanley Cavell, written during the Vietnam War but that still resonate today.

> Since America had a birth, it may die. . . . It has gone on for a long time, it is maddened now, the love it has had it has squandered too often, its young no longer naturally feel it; its past is in its streets, ungrateful for the fact that a hundred years ago it tore itself apart in order not to be divided. . . . Union is what it wanted. And it has never felt that union has been

<hr/>

48. See Clarence D. Long, "Wages by Occupational and Individual Characteristics," in *Wages and Earnings in the United States, 1860–1890* (Princeton, NJ: Princeton University Press, 1960), National Bureau of Economic Research, http://www.nber.org/chapters /c2500.pdf.

achieved. Hence its terror of dissent, which does not threaten its power but its integrity. So it is killing itself and killing another country in order not to admit its helplessness in the face of suffering, in order not to acknowledge its separateness.[49]

America tore itself apart in the 1860s in order to be a unity—the question of its success, partial or full, remains with us. Lincoln hoped that the sacrifices and horrors of the Civil War would become the living memory on which build a more perfect union. In the end, perhaps from the start, it was not fully to succeed. The nation tore itself apart again in the 1960s and 1970s and today seems to be in the process of doing so again. One may doubt as to the future of unity.

49. Stanley Cavell, *Must We Mean What We Say?* (New York: Scribners, 1969), 345.

5

CIVIL WAR, CITIZENSHIP, AND COLLECTIVITY

Politically speaking, the murder of John Brown would be an uncorrectable sin. It would create in the Union a latent fissure that would in the long run dislocate it. Brown's agony might perhaps consolidate slavery in Virginia, but it would certainly shake the whole American democracy. You save your shame, but you kill your glory. Morally speaking, it seems a part of the human light would put itself out, that the very notion of justice and injustice would hide itself in darkness, on that day where one would see the assassination of Emancipation by Liberty itself. . . . Let America know and ponder on this: there is something more frightening than Cain killing Abel, and that is Washington killing Spartacus.

VICTOR HUGO, DECEMBER 2, 1859 (DAY OF BROWN'S EXECUTION)

When ocean-clouds over inland hills
Sweep storming in late autumn brown,
And horror the sodden valley fills,
And the spire falls crashing in the town,
I muse upon my country's ills—
The tempest bursting from the waste of Time
On the world's fairest hope linked with man's foulest crime.

HERMAN MELVILLE, "MISGIVINGS," IN *BATTLE PIECES*

I do not intend to deal with the horrors of the Civil War beyond noting a few salient facts.[1] Initial enthusiasm for the war had led to large-scale voluntary enlistments. Reality soon sank in and both the North and the South were forced, for the first time in the nation's history, to institute conscription, the South in 1862, eventually for able-bodied men between the ages of seventeen and fifty, and the North in 1863 for men between twenty and forty-five. Conscription had been an available state policy for as far back as the Babylonian Empire. Modern conscription dates from the First French Republic, where more than two and a half million men were drafted between 1800 and 1813.[2] In America with the advent of the Civil War, the threat of the draft led to an increasing number of volunteers. Several possibilities for exemption arose. In the South, there were at first exemptions for those in necessary occupations; soon anyone who owned more than twenty slaves was exempt as an overseer and for the first year, the rich could hire a substitute. In the North, as the war lingered on and became increasingly bloody, those who could sought ways to avoid serving. Two routes were available: hiring of someone to take your place or simply paying three hundred dollars. All men, including those who had declared their intent to become citizens, were subject to being called up, thus making this aspect of citizenship not only *not to* require certain qualities of self but also to grant to those who did not wish to serve and could afford not to exemption based on certain nonpolitical qualities, in this case wealth. The recognition of economic standing as legitimating exemption from the duties of citizenship anticipated the privileging of inequalities that were to become dominant in the post–Civil War period. And those without such means, in both North and South, could always "lite out for the territories."[3] The existence of the available escape clauses, however, show that serving one's country, even if able-bodied, was not the only entailment of the citizenship obligations of suffrage. There were, indeed, riots over the draft law, most notably in New York City, riots that often took blacks as targets.[4]

On the other hand, free blacks and escaped slaves joined the Union Army in record numbers. Shortly after the Emancipation Proclamation, they were

1. An excellent sense can be gained from Drew Faust, *The Republic of Suffering: Death and the American Civil War* (New York: Random House, 2009). Faust has several other books on the South that repay reading.

2. See Margaret Levi, *Consent, Dissent and Patriotism* (New York: Cambridge University Press, 1997).

3. More than 150,000 people refused to turn up when drafted.

4. See, e.g., Iver Bernstein, *The New York City Draft Riots: Their Significance for American Society and Politics in the Age of the Civil War* (New York: Oxford University Press, 1990).

officially permitted to be combat soldiers and were soon in the thick of combat, repeatedly distinguishing themselves. As noted in chapter 4, more than 180,000 blacks served in the Union Army, of which about half were former slaves. A little over 20 percent were killed in action.

The Fourteenth Amendment was passed in 1868 over the strong opposition of President Andrew Johnson, as also that of white Southerners and Northern Democrats. Each chamber was at least 70 percent Republican, and most Republicans saw the collective enfranchisement of blacks as essential to their interests: it would provide them with an electoral basis in the South and allow the election of state governments sympathetic to them and the Union.[5] The enfranchisement of blacks as a consequent right to the Fourteenth Amendment, however, raised a new issue (as would a similar issue later, as we shall see, for women). Under the old criteria approach (of, among others, the Puritans, James Madison, Thomas Paine, and Abraham Lincoln) the privileges and responsibilities of citizenship, in particular suffrage, were consequent to an *individually attained* status—if one, as an individual, met *these* particular criteria, then one was entitled to be a citizen and vote. The Fourteenth Amendment established suffrage as a right inherent in all citizens. A citizen was someone born in the territorial United States or naturalized. While there were tests for naturalization, there were none for domestic birth or birth to existing citizens. Thus, in the eyes of whites and to some degree in their own, when claiming or realizing citizenship, blacks necessarily did so *not* as a matter of *individual* right. Having been excluded as a group, *they* now necessarily claimed this status *as a group*, on the basis of the irrelevancy of particular group characteristics (as women would increasingly vehemently do). The claim of the irrelevancy of precisely that which defined them as a group was held to entail they be granted citizenship as a group.

The realization of citizenship on the part of blacks is thus different from that of other groups (as it will later be for women). Whereas other immigrant groups arrived with few claims on America, blacks knew that they had for hundreds of years suffered injustice and had rendered extensive services to their masters. James Baldwin, whom I will consider more extensively in chapters 10 and 11, saw this distinction clearly: "The situation of the Irish a hundred years ago and the situation of the Negro today cannot be very usefully compared. Negroes were brought here in chains long before the Irish ever thought of leaving Ireland."[6]

5. See A. Keyssar, *Right to Vote*, 72, on which I rely here.
6. Baldwin, *Fire Next Time*, 321 (see chap. 3, n. 33).

CITIZENSHIP AND COLLECTIVITY

This distinction duly noted, the newly freed blacks could at least initially couple their collective claim with more traditional arguments. Consider the following case. When General Sherman went marching through Georgia in 1864, as many as ten thousand who-had-been slaves followed his army. Sherman was in fact a racist (he had no blacks in his troops during his march to the sea), but he hated rebels more than he hated blacks. On January 16, 1865, by Field Order Fifteen, Sherman allocated four hundred thousand acres of good land to these newly freed slaves. Taken without compensation from its white owners, it was divided up into plots and provided the basis for independent small farming, in essence a Lincolnian Free-Soil policy for blacks. Over the next several months, Sherman's order was ratified by Congress and awaited the President Johnson's signature. The land given to freed slaves could have started a biracial society based on small producers, along the lines of Lincoln's vision. However, President Johnson vetoed the bill and the land was taken back—indeed, an editorial in the *New York Times* had urged Johnson's veto, arguing that the matter of the right to property, whether in the South or the North, raised a dangerous questions as to the proper relations of labor and capital in the economy at large. President Johnson was both personally opposed to the measure[7] and was responding to pressure from Northerners as to the dangers of redistributing property. He ordered that the land be returned to its former owners. Frederick Douglass, the escaped slave and by then famous abolitionist, was present at the inaugural of Lincoln and Johnson in 1864. He wrote:

> On this inauguration day, while waiting for the opening of the ceremonies, I made a discovery in regard to the Vice-President—Andrew Johnson. There are moments in the lives of most men, when the doors of their souls are open, and unconsciously to themselves, their true character may be read by the observant eye. It was at such an instant that I caught a glimpse of the real nature of this man, which all subsequent developments proved true. I was standing in the crowd by the side of Mrs. Thomas J. Dorsey, when Lincoln touched Mr. Johnson, and pointed me out to him. The first expression that came to his face, and which I think was the true index of his heart, was one of bitter contempt and aversion. Seeing that I observed

7. See the discussion in Annette Gordon-Reed, *Andrew Johnson* (New York: Times Books, 2011).

him, he tried to assume a more friendly appearance; but it was too late; it was useless to close the door when all within had been seen. His first glance was the frown of the man, and the second was the bland and sickly smile of a demagogue. I turned to Mrs. Dorsey and said, "Whatever Andrew Johnson may be, he certainly is no friend of our race."[8]

The outcome of Johnson's veto was heartbreaking. General Oliver Otis Howard, who had lost an arm in the conflict and was known as the "Christian general," had been made head of the Freedman's Bureau and was now charged with integrating blacks into the Southern economy as workers on the plantations where they had previously been slaves; they were to be paid the wages the bureau (not the blacks) had negotiated with the white owners. He brought the news of dispossession to the black inhabitants of Edisto Island, off the coast of South Carolina. In response, in October 1865, a group of freed black slaves from Edisto Island wrote to first to the Freedmen's Bureau and General Howard. In a document that is worth quoting at length (retaining its original spelling and punctuation), they addressed him as follows.

[*Edisto Island, South Carolina, October 20 or 21, 1865*]

General It Is with painfull Hearts that we the committe address you, we Have thorougholy considered the order which you wished us to Sighn, we wish we could do so but cannot feel our rights Safe If we do so,

General we want Homestead's; we were promised Homestead's by the government, If It does not carry out the promises Its agents made to us, If the government Haveing concluded to befriend Its late enemies and to neglect to observe the principles of common faith between Its self and us Its allies In the war you said was over, now takes away from them all right to the soil they stand upon save such as they can get by again working for *your* late and thier *all time ememies*.–If the government does so we are left In a more unpleasant condition than our former lot.

we are at the mercy of those who are combined to prevent us from getting land enough to lay our Fathers bones upon. We Have property In Horses, cattle, carriages, & articles of furniture, but we are landless and Homeless, from the Homes we Have lived In In the past we can only do one of three things Step Into the public *road or the sea* or remain on them

---

8. Frederick Douglass, *The Life and Times of Frederick Douglass* (1882; repr., Start Publishing 2012), 354 (Kindle e-book).

working as In former time and subject to hire will as then. We can not resist It In any way without being driven out Homeless upon the road.

You will see this Is not the condition of really freemen.

You ask us to forgive the land owners of our Island, *You* only lost your right arm. In war and might forgive them. The man who tied me to a tree & gave me 39 lashes & who stripped and flogged my mother & my sister & who will not let me stay In His empty Hut except I will do His planting & be Satisfied with His price & who combines with others to keep away land from me well knowing I would not Have any thing to do with Him If I Had land of my own—that man, I cannot well forgive. Does It look as If He Has forgiven me, seeing How He tries to keep me In a condition of Helplessness?

General, we cannot remain Here In such condition and If the government permits them to come back we ask It to Help us to reach land where we shall not be slaves nor compelled to work for those who would treat us as such

we Have not been treacherous, we Have not for selfish motives allied to us those who suffered like us from a common enemy & then Their gained *our* purpose left our allies In their Hands There Is no rights secured to us there Is no law likely to be made which our Hands can reach. The state will make laws that we shall not be able to Hold land even If we pay for It Landless, Homeless. Voteless. We can only pray to god & Hope for *His Help, your Infuence & assistance* With consideration of esteem your Obt Servts In behalf of the people.[9]

Landless, Homeless. Voteless. General Howard responded sympathetically, but nothing came of it. The islanders then sent a letter to President Johnson:

Edisto Island S.C. Oct 28th 1865.

We the freedmen Of Edisto Island South Carolina have learned From you through Major General O O Howard commissioner of the Freedmans Bureau. with deep sorrow and Painful hearts of the possibility of goverment restoring These lands to the former owners. We are well aware Of the many perplexing and trying questions that burden Your mind. and do

9. Steven Hahn et al., eds., *Freedom: A Documentary History of Emancipation, 1861–1867*, ser. 3, vol. 1, *Land and Labor, 1865* (Chapel Hill: University of North Carolina Press, 2008), 442–43.

therefore pray to god (the preserver Of all. and who has through our Late and beloved President (Lincoln) proclamation and the war made Us A free people) that he may guide you in making Your decisions. and give you that wisdom that Cometh from above to settle these great and Important Questions for the best interests of the country and the Colored race: Here is where secession was born and Nurtured Here is where we have toiled nearly all Our lives as slaves and were treated like dumb Driven cattle, This is our home, we have made These lands what they are. we were the only true and Loyal people that were found in posession of these Lands. we have been always ready to strike for Liberty and humanity yea to fight if needs be To preserve this glorious union. Shall not we who Are freed-man and have been always true to this Union have the same rights as are enjoyed by Others? Have we broken any Law of these United States? Have we forfeited our rights of property In Land?—If not then! are not our rights as A free people and good citizens of these United States To be consid-ered before the rights of those who were Found in rebellion against this good and just Goverment (and now being conquered) come (as they Seem) with penitent hearts and beg forgiveness For past offences and also ask if thier lands Cannot be restored to them are these rebellious Spirits to be re-instated in thier *possessions* And we who have been abused and oppressed For many long years not to be allowed the Privilige of purchasing land But be subject To the will of these large Land owners? God fobid, Land mo-nopoly is injurious to the advancement of the course of freedom, and if government Does not make some provision by which we as Freedmen can obtain A Homestead, we have Not bettered our condition.

We have been encouraged by government to take up these lands in small tracts, receiving Certificates of the same—we have thus far Taken Sixteen thousand (16000) acres of Land here on This Island. We are ready to pay for this land When Government calls for it. and now after What has been done will the good and just government take from us all this right and make us Subject to the will of those who have cheated and Oppressed us for many years God Forbid! We the freedmen of this Island and of the State of South Carolina-Do therefore petition to you as the President of these United States, that some provisions be made by which Every colored man can purchase land. and Hold it as his own. We wish to have A home if It be but A few acres. without some provision is Made our future is sad to look upon. yes our Situation is dangerous. we therefore look to you In this trying hour as A true friend of the poor and Neglected race. for protection and Equal Rights. with the privilege of purchasing A Homestead–A Homestead right here in the Heart of South Carolina.

We pray that god will direct your heart in Making such provision for us as freedmen which Will tend to unite these states together stronger Than ever before—May God bless you in the Administration of your duties as the President Of these United States is the humble prayer Of us all.[10]

There was no response. These are, however, an extraordinary set of documents.[11] In the second, the islanders address the question of expropriation and even agree to pay for the lands they have been given, despite the fact that "we have made These lands what they are." Nothing, of course, came of the petition to the president, and the land was duly returned to its previous owners, thereby reducing the blacks to the status of sharecroppers. The letters do raise, however, a number of questions, most particularly *as to where the blacks learned to speak like this.* They spoke the language of the citizen, practically echoing Lincoln's argument that all men should be entitled to the enjoyment of the product of their labor.[12] They claim that there is "no freedom under the domination of another"; true freedom is seen to rest on the ability to provide for oneself, on economic independence. They find that they are entitled to this economic independence on the grounds of years of unrequited labor and on their defense of the Union in times of crisis. They had, in other words, they claim, met the criteria for virtuous citizenship and sought only the means whereby to exercise that status.

This is important: what the Civil War had settled was chattel slavery but not what kind of freedom was to prevail. One might adduce here an often-criticized passage toward the end of Mark Twain's novel *Adventures of Huckleberry Finn,* at the point at which the slave Jim has been taken into custody and

---

10. Hahn et al., *Freedom,* 443–44.

11. For others, see "Land and Labor, 1865," Freedmen and Southern Society Project, University of Maryland History Department, last revised February 19, 2018, http://www .freedmen.umd.edu/LL65pg.htm.

12. Lincoln's policies were recognized approvingly by the International Working Men's Association on January 28, 1865, in a letter written by Karl Marx. See "Address of the International Working Men's Association to Abraham Lincoln, President of the United States of America," January 28, 1865, Marx and Engels Internet Archive, 2000, https://www .marxists.org/archive/marx/iwma/documents/1864/lincoln-letter.htm. Lincoln (or the US ambassador) replied: see Robin Blackburn, *An Unfinished Revolution: Karl Marx and Abraham Lincoln* (London: Verso, 2011).

is waiting to be sold down the river. He is chained to a bed in a small hut. Tom Sawyer and Huck Finn visit and set about trying to free him. For Huck, it is an easy matter: but Tom has complex plans. As a friend, Huck feels an obligation to tell Tom that he not proceeding sensibly. Whereas Huck simply wants to pull off a plank to open a hole through which Jim could escape, Tom wants an escape that is "a little more complicated than *that*." Tom wants to saw off the leg of the bed to slip the chain loose. Huck points out that they can just lift the bed and is rebuffed with the assertion that doing so would be too "old-maidy." Tom wants to dig a moat, so they can shinny down to it; he wants to saw Jim's leg off; he wants to send him a rope ladder in a pie (the cabin is on level ground); he wants to make a pen out of an old barrel hoop rather than a goose feather, despite the fact that Jim, as a slave, was not allowed to learn to write (as dictated by an 1847 Missouri law); he wants to dig a tunnel like the prisoner in the "Chateau Deef" who came out, Tom says, in China—and it goes on for some pages. Tom has "read all the books that give any information about these things."[13]

This section has indeed been much criticized, even by none other than John Updike writing in the *New Yorker*. Twain is deemed to have lost control of his narrative. But what in fact do we find? First, Twain is lampooning our attachment to a romantic idea. Huck escapes from normal society by a kind of retreat to nature; Tom escapes into romance. Neither of these directions proves satisfactory for Twain, and each without the other is even more seriously deficient.

Second, during all these preparations, Twain does not let on to the reader nor to Huck that Tom knows that Jim was in fact freed in Miss Watson's will and was thus in fact free throughout the descent of the Mississippi. Tom's constant insistence on "the authorities" as to how a person should be set free is thus from one point of view self-indulgent. Read literally, however, as one must also always do, *it is also the insistence that to be realized in life, freedom must have authority behind it, that it must be authorized*. One cannot simply "give" someone freedom and thereby make him or her truly free. Something more is required. "The authorities" provide some analysis of what it means actually to attain freedom. Not anything will count as true freedom.

Third, however, Twain sees that the question of freedom is complex. When after the escape, the chase, the wounding of Tom, it is revealed that Jim is "as free as anyone," how are we to understand that expostulation? What *is* freedom?

With these points in mind, what we see in these chapters leading up to the

13. Mark Twain, *Adventures of Huckleberry Finn*, 863.

end of *Huckleberry Finn* is an analysis of the American post–Civil War period (the book is set in around 1844 and was published in 1884). Jim—and by extension the newly freed blacks—is in some sense "free," yet that freedom is not an adequate freedom. Tom's position manifests this complexity. At some level, he grasps the reality of the situation, even though he may not be able to admit it to himself for what it is. For what we in fact see, once we bracket the theatrics, is Tom insisting that for Jim to be *truly free* will require much effort that is complex, difficult, and long. Tom will even suggest that they could "leave Jim to our children to get out"—alas, a sad truth. In this sense, Tom is right, and the point of this burlesque is profound: *Jim is not truly free until his freedom is won rather than granted.* Winning it means acquiring the qualities of a free person. Freedom has to be achieved, and that will be hard—it cannot simply be given: a citizen earns his status and for that he must be free. What Twain reminds us of by his ending is that in 1885 African Americans were free in name but not in life. The attempts made during Reconstruction had come to an end by 1877. The attempt at impeaching President Johnson had failed in 1868 by one vote.

The Edisto Islanders are clear that simply being freed from chattel slavery is not enough: to be full members of the polity, they need independence. How does it happen that they speak this language, despite two hundred years of slavery? They are not, I think, only picking up the white point of view. A number of factors present themselves. On the one hand, one can avert to a universal desire of rural people for a desire for land and refer to various seventeenth-century popular movements in England and elsewhere.[14] Land links people together as a source of both community and experience, what Victor Magagna has called "communities of grain."[15]

Second, as Orlando Patterson has written, slavery was a "trial by death." The slave, being denied dignity, was, for precisely that reason, "afire with the knowledge" of a need for dignity. Dignity, continues Patterson, "like love, is one of those human qualities that are most intensely felt and understood when they are absent—or unrequited."[16] The possibility of being killed for what one thinks is right can be a profound source of speech. We saw this al-

14. E. J. Hobsbawm, *Primitive Rebels* (New York: Praeger, 1963); see also any of the works by Christopher Hill on the English seventeenth century.

15. Victor Magagna, *Communities of Grain: Rural Rebellion in Comparative Perspective* (Ithaca, NY: Cornell University Press, 1991).

16. Orlando Patterson, *Slavery and Social Death: A Comparative Study* (Cambridge, MA: Harvard University Press, 1982), 100. I was reminded to go back to this book by the excellent Nick Bromell, *The Time Is Always Now: Black Thought and the Transformation of US Democracy* (Oxford: Oxford University Press, 2013), from which I have learned a lot.

ready with the Puritans and at the end of the Declaration of Independence. We will see it again in some of the movements of the 1960s.

Additionally, the blacks could draw upon their own experiences. There were "legitimate" black churches, often with a required white minister, but also underground churches that provided an escape from white domination and a chance to form a sense of a collectivity. Important here is the theology of black Christianity where the emphasis was on worldly and collective deliverance. In the words of the great spiritual dating from 1853, "When Israel was in Egypt's land/ Let my people go." Additionally, blacks were aware of the attempts at collective revolt, successful in Haiti in 1791, and multiply repressed in the American South from the beginning of the nineteenth century. While their call for citizenship was individual, black former slaves necessarily came to understand from its refusal that their lot was collective.

It was not that the newly freed blacks did not try. After the Civil War, all across the South, newly freed blacks, as Steven Hahn puts it, "sought to contest the power of their owners, circulate intelligence, interpret events, and cultivate relations suitable to a world of freedom as well as in the aspirations of freed people for family and community reconstitution, local justice, meaningful authority of their own spheres of life and, increasingly, social separatism from whites."[17] These actions had in fact started with the beginning of the Civil War: on the day of Lincoln's inauguration, seventeen slaves in Virginia proclaimed that they were now free and marched off their master's property.[18] As Reconstruction developed, freedmen's conventions appeared all across the South, seeking to organize blacks politically and to express to whites that, as a Tennessee minister put it, "we are part and parcel of the American Republic." And they were clear what being part of America meant. As the Reverend James W. Hood, the president of the North Carolina convention, wrote, they sought "the right to testify in courts of justice, . . . representation in the jury box, . . . and that the black man should have the right to carry his ballot to the ballot box."[19] The purpose of these organizations was "to elevate our race, to make us better citizens . . . to educate ourselves that we may be able to vote more intelligently on questions of vital interest to our people."[20]

But to what result? The movement was not to last. Reconstruction had col-

17. Steven Hahn, *A Nation under Our Feet: Black Political Struggles in the Rural South from Slavery to the Great Migration* (Cambridge, MA: Harvard University Press, 2003), 6.

18. Hahn, *Nation under Our Feet*, 13.

19. Hahn, *Nation under Our Feet*, 122–23.

20. Hahn, *Nation under Our Feet*, 417.

lapsed under a combination of Southern white oppression and Northern in-difference and hostility.[21] And as debilitating was the vision of citizenship en-forced on whites and blacks alike. The condition of the newly free slaves after October 1865 was set out for the freedmen of Orangeburg, South Carolina, by a young army captain, Charles Soule. Again, the document is worth citing at length.

[*Orangeburg, South Carolina, June 1865*]

To the Freed People of Orangeburg District.

You have heard many stories about your condition as freemen. You do not know what to believe: you are talking too much; waiting too much; asking for too much. If you can find out the truth about this matter, you will settle down quietly to your work. Listen, then, and try to understand just how you are situated.

You are now free, but you must know that the only difference you can feel yet, between slavery and freedom, is that neither you nor your children can be bought or sold. You may have a harder time this year than you have ever had before; it will be the price you pay for your freedom. You will have to work hard, and get very little to eat, and very few clothes to wear. If you get through this year alive and well, you should be thankful. Do not ex-pect to save up anything, or to have much corn or provisions ahead at the end of the year. You must not ask for more pay than free people get at the North. There, a field hand is paid in money, but has to spend all his pay ev-ery week, in buying food and clothes for his family. and in paying rent for his house. You cannot be paid in money,–for there is no good money in the District,–nothing but Confederate paper. Then, what can you be paid with? Why, with food, with clothes, with the free use of your little houses and lots. *You do not own a cent's worth except yourselves. . . .* Now you must get something to eat and something to wear, and houses to live in. How can you get these things? By hard work–and nothing else, and it will be a good thing for you if you get them until next year, for yourselves and for your families. . . . Do not think, because you are free you can choose your own kind of work. . . . There must be a head man everywhere, and on a plan-

---

21. The literature is extensive. See, e.g., Leon Litwack, *Been in the Storm So Long* (New York: Vintage, 1980); C. Vann Woodward, *Reunion and Reaction: The Compromise of 1877 and the End of Reconstruction* (Oxford: Oxford University Press, 1966).

tation the head man, who gives all the orders, is the owner of the place. Whatever he tells you to do you must do at once, and cheerfully.... Whatever the order is, try and obey it without a word....

You do not understand why some of the white people who used to own you, do not have to work in the field. It is because they are rich. If every man were poor, and worked in his own field, there would be no big farms, and very little cotton or corn raised to sell; there would be no money, and nothing to buy. Some people must be rich, to pay the others, and they have the right to do no work except to look out after their property. It is so everywhere, and perhaps by hard work some of you may by-and-by become rich yourselves....

Never stop work on any account, for the whole crop must be raised and got in, or we shall starve. In short, do just about as the good men among you have always done.... Remember that even if you are badly off, no one can buy or sell you: remember that if you help yourselves, GOD will help you, and trust hopefully that next year and the year after will bring some new blessing to you.[22]

"You are now free, but you must know that the only difference you can feel yet, between slavery and freedom, is that neither you nor your children can be bought or sold. You may have a harder time this year than you have ever had before; it will be the price you pay for your freedom.... You do not own a cent's worth except yourselves." This is the new vision of freedom and citizenship brought by the North. It is also, albeit perhaps unwittingly, the abolitionist vision: freedom is self-ownership and self-discipline. No other criterion need be met. The practical result was to reduce the newly freed blacks at best to the status of sharecroppers and to legitimate a vision of citizenship completely compatible with the wage-labor-based economy that was becoming increasingly dominant in the North. As Marx pointed out at the same time, under capitalism, capitalist economy is based on the traffic of commodities, and the only commodity that the man at the bottom of the pile had to sell was his ability to work, what Marx called the commodity of his "labor-power" (*Arbeitskraft*). The system was "fair"—property was *not* theft, Marx argued against Proudhon—because the contract for labor was openly arrived at and agreed to by all parties. But while fair, it was exploitative.

As embodied in the Fourteenth Amendment, this combination of the new

22. Hahn et al., *Freedom*, 215–22.

vision of citizenship—that it was a right that entailed possession of suffrage (as states might severally determine it) and was not consequent to any specific quality of the (male) person—and the exploitation that it legitimated meant that those who found the system unacceptable had to find another road by which to make their claims. And that road, on the model of what had happened with blacks, was collective, not just for blacks but for exploited workers and eventually women.

These facts determine the situation of blacks in America, even and especially after Emancipation and the Fourteenth Amendment, to be different from that of all other immigrants. Between 1860 and 1910, more than thirty million persons had immigrated from Europe alone. They came to flee oppression or poverty at home and to seek a better life. The 1860 census listed almost four million black slaves, which, due to disruptions from the Civil War, likely underestimates the actual number. They were now free and claiming citizenship. The experience of slavery makes the status of the blacks radically different from that of the white immigrants. (And this is true despite discrimination against various white immigrant groups: "No Dogs and Irish" read the famous sign on a Boston tavern.)

Again, James Baldwin, reflecting on this reality in 1953, caught it very well:

> The rage of the disesteemed is personally fruitless, but it is also absolutely inevitable; this rage, so generally discounted, so little understood even among people whose daily bread it is, is one of the things that makes history. Rage can only with difficulty, and never entirely, be brought under the domination of the intelligence and is therefore not susceptible to any arguments whatsoever. . . . This is a fact which ordinary representatives of the *Herrenvolk* . . . quite fail to understand. . . . The black man insists, by whatever means he finds at his disposal, that the white man cease to regard him as an exotic rarity and recognize him as a human being. . . . There is a great deal of will power involved in the white man's naivete.[23]

This is the "veil" between the races of which W. E. B. DuBois famously wrote. It is a veil, however, through which blacks can, because of their history, partially see, whereas most whites cannot. As DuBois wrote in the same chapter of *The Souls of Black Folks*:

---

23. James Baldwin, "Stranger in the Village," in *Collected Essays*, 121–22.

One ever feels his twoness,—an American, a Negro; two souls, two thoughts, two unreconciled strivings; two warring ideals in one dark body, whose dogged strength alone keeps it from being torn asunder.

The History of the American Negro is the history of this striving—this longing to attain self-conscious manhood, to merge his double self into a better and truer self. He simply wishes to make it possible for a man to be both a Negro and an American, without being cursed and spit upon by his fellows, without having the doors of Opportunity closed roughly in his face.[24]

For the dominant white culture to deal with blacks and their history will require something other than assimilation. Indeed, Alexis de Tocqueville had written already in the 1830s, "If America undergoes great revolutions, they will be brought about by the presence of the black race on the soil of the United States—that is to say, they will owe their origin, not to the equality, but to the inequality conditions."[25] Blacks were an internal minority, not an external one like the flood of immigrants. Those coming from Europe had not (at least yet) suffered in and from America—as noted, Baldwin explicitly contrasts the lot of the Irish with that of blacks.[26]

With the demise of Reconstruction, the situation for blacks changed little in the South from that before the Civil War. As Captain Soule said, they were free, but all they owned was their ability to work. I obviously have no intent here to defend what happened as Southern whites reasserted political dominance. The combination of terrorizing tactics and the selective imposition of tests for voting rights was a reactionary attempt to retain some sense of criteria for the suffrage, *now with the purpose of excluding* rather than establishing criteria for admission. Among such criteria requirements were: the poll tax, as high as two hundred dollars in some states, a descendant of the old property requirement, which was not finally struck down until 1965 in *Harman v. Forssenius* (380 U.S. 528); literacy tests—although illiterate whites benefited from their oral response to a "reasonable interpretation" of a constitutional

24. W. E. B. DuBois, *The Souls of Black Folk*, in *Writings* (New York: Library of America, 1986), 364–65. For an excellent analysis of DuBois, his quarrels with Booker T. Washington, and the elements of contemporary black American thought, see Darryl Pinckney, "The Afro-Pessimist Temptation," *New York Review of Books*, 65, no. 10 (June 7–27, 2018): 51–55.

25. Tocqueville, *Democracy in America*, vol. 1, chap. 18. See W. E. B. DuBois, *Dusk of Dawn*, in *Writings*, especially chap. 9.

26. Baldwin, *Fire Next Time*, 321.

clause; the "grandfather" clause, which exempted from all tests those who could vote before 1866 or 1867 (not declared unconstitutional until 1914); and the white primary from which blacks were excluded, a device that remained legal until 1944. Perverse in their intention as these requirements were, it is important to see that they are an attempt to retain some sense that participating in politics required some additional criteria beyond simply being a member of the polity. They could thus be defended, and were, on grounds of supposedly reasonable precedent. And there is no doubt but that they were effective: by 1892, the percentage of blacks in Mississippi entitled to vote had fallen from more than 90 percent in the early days of Reconstruction to less than 6 percent; in Louisiana, the figure was down to less than 1.5 percent. Of those, many blacks took the prudent course and abstained. This is new: criteria for citizenship were now being used specifically to *exclude* groups rather than describe the qualities an individual should have for inclusion.

THE "GILDED AGE"

Post–Civil War America was changing, and changing rapidly. Industrialization, especially in the Northeast, grew exponentially. Over the last third of the nineteenth century, the country saw a threefold increase in the number of wage laborers. By 1879, two-thirds of those outside the agricultural sector worked for wages. Concentrations of wealth made significant social mobility increasingly less possible: the country saw the creation of unprecedented fortunes. In 1875, average earnings were about $350, down from five years earlier. At his death in 1877, the fortune of Cornelius Vanderbilt was estimated at $100 million (approximately $140–$150 billion in twenty-first-century dollars). In 1900, the average wage of a working man was $500 a year, whereas the *annual* income of Andrew Carnegie was estimated at $25 million. Until the ratification of the Sixteenth Amendment in 1913, there was no broad-based federal income tax on income and property. This is the period that Mark Twain dubbed the "Gilded Age." Widespread inequalities the like of which had not been seen before became standard.[27]

The economy was essentially unregulated; competition was thus a major

27. See the discussion of economics of the period in Thomas Piketty, *Capital in the Twentieth-First Century* (Cambridge, MA: Harvard University Press, 2012), chap. 5. See the important historical discussion in Leon Fink, *The Long Gilded Age: American Capitalism and the Lessons of a New World Order* (Philadelphia: University of Pennsylvania Press, 2015).

and unrestricted force. Au courant social Darwinist doctrines held that competition produced a natural aristocracy and that any state intervention on the side of losers would be economically dangerous and, in some sense, not moral. The major exception to this restraint was dealing with labor strikes, of which there were at least sixty major episodes between 1865 and 1900. Businesses employed private police companies to break strikes. Cutthroat competition produced monopolies—at one point, Cornelius Vanderbilt owned fourteen railroads. John D. Rockefeller's control over transport allowed him to drive competitors out of business.

These developments did not go unresisted. Aside from the political movements considered subsequently, a prominent source of criticism was manifested in a new journalism. A cartoon, "Monopolists All," from the bilingual (English and German) journal *Puck*, shows the Puck figure (whose motto is from Shakespeare: "What fools, these mortals be!") questioning the American state (Uncle Sam) as to what he is going to do about the monopolies, named severally on the scales of an immense snake that has the Capital and the government in its coils.

Corruption and bribery of public officials was extensive and nearly open. The *McClure's Magazine* journalist and radical Populist Henry Demarest Lloyd[28] wrote in 1899 that "Standard Oil has done everything to the legislature of Pennsylvania but refine it," and urged that without "industrial liberty...political and religious liberty wait for their full realization."[29] Lloyd's approach, in some sense analogous to Lincoln's, was to cite hearings and documents from the trusts at length, clear that they would produce outrage. Although Lloyd had an overly strong faith in the power of science to produce prosperity if society were only properly organized,[30] he was trying to grapple with the fact that independence now required a transformation of the economy.

The lot of wage earners was difficult. In the forty-five years between 1865 and 1910, there were approximately twenty-four years of economic recession or panic. During the same period, the population grew from thirty-five million to approximately ninety million. About half of the growth was from immigration, most of it being from Europe, of which about one-third was from

28. Lloyd wrote books with titles such as *Man the Social Creator*, *Wealth against Commonwealth*, and even *A Sovereign People: A Study of Swiss Democracy*.

29. Henry Demarest Lloyd, *Wealth against Commonwealth* (New York: Harper and Brothers, 1899), 493; see also 522.

30. See the remarks in McWilliams, *Idea of Fraternity in America*, 402–6.

Russia or Slavic countries. Foreign-born population in the Northeast and extending into the West was more than 25 percent. The population of New York City went from about 800,000 in 1860 to 3,500,000 in 1900. Those not of the elite responded in a variety of ways but almost always along the same lines. Older American groups often blamed their lot on the inpouring of immigrants, whom they saw as stealing their jobs and taking over their control of society. The rise of urban "machines," which generally ran efficient but highly corrupt organizations, became a central quality of the large cities.[31] A cartoon by Thomas Nast depicting a circle of machine bosses including Boss Tweed, each pointing to the other, is entitled "Who Stole the Money? / T'was him." But no matter what their particular policy aims, most of these groups held that their problems stemmed from the effects of unrestricted competition and that the solution lay in developing forms of cooperation. This was a new development. It has its antecedents in the women's movement and in the lot of blacks. It is cooperative and therefore collective.

WHO FIGHTS BACK?

I want here to set out briefly the characteristics of a number of these groups. They have recently been the subject of a superb book by Alex Gourevitch, *From Slavery to the Cooperative Commonwealth*, that details the history of this last part of the American nineteenth century quite brilliantly. I will then spend more time on the Populist movement of the 1890s. Who are the players? Among the nonelites, the sense that the transformations of the social and economic systems were producing radical changes in the political system and in particular the place of the average citizen was very strong. Furthermore, that sense was that these changes affected collectivities and could only be dealt with collectively and not individually. The frontier to which one could "lite out" as late as the 1860s in effect existed no more. Except for a few minor skirmishes after the turn of the twentieth century, the last serious Indian war was the Battle of Sugar Point in Minnesota, in 1898, mainly over a question of the sale of alcohol and lumber.

In response to the transformations of the economic system, these move-

---

31. See Steven Erie, *Rainbow's End: Irish-Americans and the Dilemmas of Urban Machine Politics, 1840–1985* (Los Angeles: University of California Press, 1990), for a comparative study of Irish machines.

ments, sometimes parties, were mostly organized around economic issues. Up until the Civil War, the conception of citizenship we have been tracing was carried mostly by the urban middle and working classes as well as by the land-owning classes, both North and South, albeit, as we have seen, in different ways. After the Civil War, in response to the changing economic structures, it began to be carried chiefly by the working classes—artisans, skilled workers, and former slaves—as well as middle-class women. It was becoming clear that the conception of citizenship required for maintaining a democratic republic was no longer any of the old versions: in an economy dominated by wage labor, neither church membership, nor the ownership of land or tools, nor even the unalienated right to the product of one's labor were increasingly either incompatible with or irrelevant to the development of industrial capitalism and its institutionalization of previously unknown inequalities. They were, more perversely, ineffective as recourses against the demands of competition. More and more Americans worked for wages; fewer and fewer owned the means of their livelihood: one sold one's labor and had no claim on its product. As noted, economic depressions were a regular occurrence.

It is important to see how the rise of wage labor changed the nature of society and of membership in the United States. For centuries, small farmers were their own men; slaves were part of a property. In late feudal times in Europe, each was supposed to have his or her place in a household. The rise of "masterless men," consequent to the enclosure acts that put an end to the economically necessary common land, created a social crisis that King Henry VIII of England once tried to resolve in the 1500s by hanging four thousand beggars between London and Windsor. Eventually, as E. P. Thompson has argued, this group became the basis of the new working class. Wage laborers—the working class—owned only their own labor-power (which Marx saw as their one commodity) and were bound to no one person or group. On the other side of the Atlantic in the late 1800s, "masterless men" made their appearance in postbellum America.[32] They were free to move about at will (in theory at least) and to choose their associations. As such, they were a potential threat to social order, and it is not surprising that concomitant with the rise of wage labor, one saw the vast expansion of police powers, both public and private. (The

32. See Keri Leigh Merritt, *Masterless Men: Poor Whites and Slavery in the Antebellum South* (Cambridge: Cambridge University Press, 2017). She notes that "it was nearly impossible for [these people] to rise out of the class into which they had been born" (348). Her first chapter presents a fairly sympathetic account of the young Andrew Johnson's support of the Homestead Act.

Pinkerton Detective Agency, founded in 1850, eventually became the largest private police force in the world.[33])

Given this, those who protested against these developments often spoke in the name of the "producing classes" and insisted that their political heritage was being betrayed by "moneyed" classes, those they named the "interests." At first, these protests could be found grouped under the umbrella of "anti-monopoly." Soon, however, there was a vast outpouring of social and political criticism and a wide range of groups and movements vying for power. Let us discuss three of them: the Greenbackers, the Eight-Hour Day, and the Knights of Labor.

Greenbackers

The Greenbackers, or Greenback Labor Party, held that the problems of the workers derived from a shortage in the supply of money and credit. By 1862, during the Civil War, the government had taken to printing paper money, which it nominally backed up with bonds. These bonds were printed on green paper and were churned out in great numbers. A cartoon of the members of Lincoln's Cabinet shows Samuel Chase, secretary of the treasury, cranking out the bills, on the excuse of a "great victory" proclaimed as the capture of "one soldier and one rifle." Lincoln is, as he was famous for being, reminded of a story.

With the end of the war, under the urging of the new secretary of the treasury, Hugh McCulloch, the government ceased the printing of this money and called for the withdrawal of the paper tender on a month-by-month basis. There quickly arose a shortage in the supply of money and credit; what there was, was manipulated by bankers and financiers to their own advantage. A recession in 1867 led to the demand that the paper money be maintained.

There is an irony here: the economic situation threatened independence; the solution was said to be in the federalization of the currency. The average individual thereby was freed from dependence on the powerful rich but now was dependent on the benevolence and consistency of the state. To bring about the power of the state in this area, those advocating this policy soon formed themselves into a political movement focused on executive power and by 1870 were calling for the establishment of a National Labor Reform Party

33. See S. Paul O'Hara, *Inventing the Pinkertons; or, Spies, Sleuths, Mercenaries, and Thugs* (Baltimore: Johns Hopkins University Press, 2016). England had established the first professional public police force in 1829.

that would unify workers and farmers. They demanded that the printing of money be resumed and that previously issued currency remain in circulation. They wanted the government to take control with the amount of currency printed; it was to be tied neither to the banks nor to gold, but to production on the basis of a per capita allocation. What is important here is that those in this movement did not think that the state was the enemy but rather that their problems derived from the people who controlled it. They foresaw a positive role for the state in dealing with the political situation of the average citizen, *if it could be made to serve the public good.*

The situation took a turn for the worse with the bursting of an economic bubble in 1873. Congress had made possible the completion of the first transcontinental railroad in 1869, mostly by turning vast amounts of public land over to the railroad companies at no cost. The railroads needed to sell that land to new settlers: the enthusiasm was great, but inevitably railroad companies overextended themselves and in 1873 the venture collapsed. Congress sought to pass an inflation bill that was vetoed by President Ulysses S. Grant; the next Congress moved in an opposite deflationary direction, seeking to return to gold-backed currency. N. B. Ashby, a prominent figure in the Northern Farmers Alliance, was clear as to the consequences: "The result [of railroad trusts] is that our country is honey-combed with trusts, forestallers, and trade combines, the latter of which is the controlling force in local trade."[34] Ashby here was responding, albeit without much sense of what to do about it, to the fact that local economies were now subject to control by entities who simply had no local presence.[35]

The problem of local versus absentee national ownership would persist. In *The Grapes of Wrath* (1939), John Steinbeck depicted a poor farming family about to be thrown off its land. With failing crops, they had had to borrow money and the bank had now foreclosed. A man from an agency comes to tell them that that is what the bank is going to do. The squatters ask for some charity and delay. The man from the owner responds, "The bank—the monster has to have profits all the time. It can't wait. It'll die. No, taxes go on. When the monster stops growing, it dies. It can't stay one size." The farmers respond, "Sure, . . . but it's our land. We measured it and broke it up. We were born on

34. N. B. Ashby, *The Riddle of the Sphinx* (Des Moines, IA: Industrial Publishing, 1890), 30–31.

35. A revelatory study of this development over time is John Gaventa, *Power and Powerlessness: Quiescence and Rebellion in an Appalachian Valley* (Champaign: University of Illinois Press, 1982).

it, and we got killed on it, died on it." They insist that "the bank is only made of men." Not so, is the response: "The bank is something more than men, I tell you. It's the monster. Men made it, but they can't control it." Completely frustrated, the farmer who is about to be dispossessed says he will kill this man who will deliver the dispossession orders. "No, he only takes orders. . . .—Well, then I will kill the president of the bank . . .—The president of the bank gets orders from the East. . . .—I don't aim to starve to death before I can kill the man that's starving me. Who can I shoot?" The response: "Maybe there's nobody to shoot. Maybe the thing isn't men at all. Maybe like you said, the property's doing it."[36]

"Who can I shoot?" How to become a participant citizen? A lot was at stake. As Gretchen Ritter writes, "The nature of the national economy, the power of the sections, the relations between classes, the role of government and the place of democratic citizens were all debated by the advocates of financial reform and financial orthodoxy. . . . Banks and bondsmen were regarded as a danger to American society and the national government. Attacks on them were framed as part of a larger concern with corruption and the loss of citizen virtue."[37] The monopolies controlled working conditions, which were viewed by workers as so demanding as to make independent citizenry impossible. The labor leader William Sylvis, founder of the Iron Molders International Union, contended, "Our labor occupies too large a portion of our time to enable us to read, study, reflect. A high degree of intelligence is necessary to enable up to discharge all the duties of citizens. If we were sufficiently well paid for from six to eight hours work a day, to furnish ourselves with the means of cultivation, we would do better work and be more useful men. . . . We want more time and more money; fewer hours of toil and more wages for what we do."[38]

Starting around 1873, groups began to organize around the issue of government-backed paper currency, and by 1875 they coalesced into a single organization, eventually taking the name Greenback Labor Party. In 1876, they nominated Peter Cooper, a New York–based writer on economic issues, as their candidate for US president. He said, among other things, "I have

36. John Steinbeck, *The Grapes of Wrath* (New York: Library of America, 1996), 250.

37. Gretchen Ritter, *Goldbugs and Greenbacks: The Antimonopoly Tradition and the Politics of Finance in America* (New York: Cambridge University Press, 1997), 2–3.

38. James C. Sylvis, *The Life, Speeches, Labors and Essays of William H. Sylvis* (Philadelphia: Claxton, Remsen and Haffelfinger, 1872), 113–14, https://archive.org/stream/life speecheslaboosylvgoog#page/n117/mode/2up/search/citizens. I was led to this source by Ritter, *Goldbugs and Greenbacks*.

shown from history and incontrovertible facts prove it, that the commercial and industrial prosperity of a country do not depend upon the amount of gold and silver that it has in circulation. Our prosperity must continually depend upon the industry, the enterprise, and the busy internal trade and a true independence of foreign nations, which a paper circulation, well based on credit, has always been found to promote."[39] Elsewhere, in his book *Ideas for a Science of Good Government,* Cooper refers to "that system of social science . . . that seeks to harmonize and advance the social and moral, as well as the material interests of mankind . . . and seeks by the elevation of the individual man to promote the happiness and prosperity of the nation."[40] The Greenbackers thus sought not only to have the state intervene on the behalf of the average person but conceived of that intervention as both historically and scientifically justified. Citizenship rested or was increasingly understood as resting on scientific fact.

In the late 1870s, the Greenback Labor Party elected twenty-one of its members to Congress and won a greater number of state and local seats. It expanded its platform to include support for an income tax, an eight-hour workday, and women's suffrage. It eventually declined—only seven delegates attended its convention in September 1888. Its energies, however, were generally subsumed in the Populist movement.

Eight-Hour Day

As one can see from the platform of the Greenbackers, they did not alone invent their demands. The Eight-Hour Day movement had its origins in England toward the beginning of the nineteenth century; it was then championed by the progressive industrialist Robert Owen, who came up with the slogan "eight hours labor, eight hours rest, eight hours recreation." The movement spread widely in Europe and by the time of the American Civil War had become a central demand in the United States. Congress passed an eight-hour workday bill in 1868 over the veto of President Johnson—to little avail, however, as apparently wages were then most often cut by 20 percent. Those sup-

39. Peter Cooper, *The Nomination to the Presidency of Peter Cooper and His Address to the Indianapolis Convention of the National Independent Party,* 13, Internet Archive, https://archive.org/details/nominationtopres00greerich.

40. Peter Cooper, *Ideas for a Science of Good Government* (New York: Trow's Printing and Bookbinding Company, 1883), Internet Archive, https://archive.org/stream/ideasforscience00coopbrich#page/337/mode/2up/search/prosperity.

porting the movement found political expression in a variety of groups, most particularly in the Knights of Labor.

Knights of Labor

As with the Greenbackers, what is significant with the Knights of Labor is two-fold: first is the understanding that to be a good citizen one must have time for oneself; there was, in other words, something more to the human being than the ability to sell one's labor. And this something more was something that the individual was to care for on his own, for which he required only to own his own time. When the workday was as long as sixteen hours, such time for one-self was clearly impossible. Second, however, is the acceptance of the fact that one-third of one's hours do in fact belong to whoever or whatever had purchased them. *Independence was reduced to one-third of existence*, the hours of sleep being what Hannah Arendt later would see as the biologically necessary, thus not of the realm of human freedom.[41] The Eight-Hour Day movement shares the vision of Sylvis that the average person can, if conditions permit, acquire all the qualities necessary for good citizenship, but it *reduces the time in which they may be practiced*. Their version of Owen's slogan becomes "Eight hours for the boss, eight hours for me, eight to rest."

This vision of the person as citizen derives from but differs from that found in Lincoln. For Lincoln, to be a citizen meant that one had to be able freely to enjoy the fruits of one's own labor. Here, however, for the greenbacks and Eight-Hour Day men, the fruits of one's labor belonged to the capitalist, who had, after all, bought in open market, for a mutually agreed-on price, the labor-power that had produced them. In 1847, Marx had pointed out to Pierre-Joseph Proudhon that property was *not* theft, contrary to what the Frenchman had famously claimed.[42] These movements tacitly accepted the necessity of alienated labor and demanded only that there be a portion of the day left to oneself for one's own determination. In effect, the movement separated the source of one's livelihood from one's personal development. "Eight hours for me" means that what is mine has little or no public quality, unless I should choose to give it such. *The personal is thus increasingly distinguished from the public or political.* And, as it was to appear, the satisfaction of a working-class

41. Hannah Arendt, *The Human Condition* (Chicago: University of Chicago Press, 1996), 126.

42. Karl Marx, *The Poverty of Philosophy: Answer to the "Philosophy of Poverty" by Proudhon*, in *Marx Engels Collected Works*, vol. 6 (Progress Publishers, 1976).

demand turned out to have benefits for the owners also. When Henry Ford instituted an eight-hour workday and doubled salary in 1914, absenteeism fell dramatically, turnover decreased, productivity doubled, and profits rose.

None of this effort went smoothly, however. There was real agitation and violence associated with these movements. The Noble and Holy Order of the Knights of Labor was founded, as were its sister movements, in the late 1860s, as a semisecret fraternal organization, on the model of the Freemasons, with initiation rites and membership rituals. As it moved to becoming more of a labor movement, such membership criteria were dropped. Membership increased, and the Knights of Labor were soon prominent in various labor disputes, the most signal of which was a victory against Jay Gould's Wabash Railroad in 1885. A cartoon shows several workers, each with a different occupation, joined on a pedestal, under an American flag, with the caption "Labor Vincit Omnia" (Labor Conquers All). By 1886, membership was estimated at more than seven hundred thousand, with some estimates as high as one million, comprising fifty thousand black men and women and as many as ten thousand white women. The most famous slogan of the Knights of Labor was "That is the most effective government in which an injury to one is a concern of all," which, however, is hardly a political slogan. The "prytaneum" listed on the organization's shield is the communal dining hall of the Greek polis.

Like the other movements considered here, a primary demand was for the eight-hour workday.[43] The Knights of Labor also espoused nationalization of the railroads and the telegraph and telephone systems, as well as a graduated income tax, which was to be imposed on income and not just on property. An income tax had been occasionally imposed in England since the French Revolution but then only to deal with expenses for war. It was not until after the middle of the nineteenth century that such a tax had become an ongoing part of the British economy. The basic principle, as set forth in the Knights' Declaration of Principles, was "to abolish as rapidly as possible the wage system, substituting co-operation therefore" and to "make individual and moral worth, not wealth the true standard of individual and National greatness."[44]

The Knights of Labor held the wage system to be analogous to slavery, and it was the immediate memory of slavery, and its abolition, that shaped their

43. The first country to institute an eight-hour workday was Uruguay in 1915. It was urged in the Versailles Treaty of 1919 and slowly became standard.

44. *Preamble and Declaration of Principles of the Knights of Labor of America* (1878), items XIV and I, http://iasmrmoore.weebly.com/uploads/1/3/3/5/13352475/laborunionfounding docs.pdf.

activities. As one member wrote, "While there is no doubt that the relations of employer to employe [sic] might be better than they are, it is still true that the system retains some of the spirit of master and slave. No man is at his best without the feeling of independence that he is the master of his own acts. Strive as he may, no many can take the same interest in the affairs of another that he takes in his own. . . . It is well know that wage slavery made intellectual culture next to impossible." In a cooperative system, however, "each man can feel that he is a proprietor, . . . working for himself."[45] The vision is a noble one, but it is limited to the workplace. Workers are deemed capable of self-governance, but the matter is only raised in relation to production, conceived of by this point as a cooperative enterprise. To the degree that the vision was political, it tended to be formulated as a small-scale more or less practical utopia, as in the set of small communities founded around Puget Sound around the turn of the century by Eugene V. Debs and Henry Demarest Lloyd and loosely federated as the "Brotherhood of the Cooperative Commonwealth." Edward Bellamy, to be considered later, helped start the colony Equality on Padilla Bay, just off the Seattle Coast.[46]

All of this does seek to give a role to the government in making the polity more just. Comparatively less attention is paid as to the correct relation of the citizen to that government. The presumption is that it can, in itself, be good. If it fails, that would only be because of inadequate means, means that can be compensated for. In L. Frank Baum's 1900 allegory of popular movements that is *The Wonderful Wizard of Oz*, after the dog Toto draws back the curtain to reveal the wizard, Dorothy exclaims, "I think you are a very bad man," to which the wizard replies, "Oh, no, my dear; I'm really a very good man, but I'm a very bad Wizard, I must admit."[47] We need, it appears, good wizards. The relation between a good government and the citizenry is generally only a secondary matter: "eight hours for me." For *me*, as I wish, as a private person.

The decline of the Knights of Labor had multiple sources, some of it attrib-

45. S. M. Jelley, *The Voice of Labor* (Chicago: Gehman, 1887), 260–61. Extensive portions of the book are quotes from "the voices" of other Knights.

46. On Northwest radicalism, see Tracy B. Strong and Helene Keyssar, *Right in Her Soul: The Life of Anna Louise Strong* (New York: Random House, 1985), chap. 5. See the excellent discussion in Alex Gourevitch, *From Slavery to the Cooperative Commonwealth: Labor and Republican Liberty in the Nineteenth Century* (Cambridge: Cambridge University Press, 2015), 118–32. I do not agree, however, with his sense that this approach applied easily to politics.

47. L. Frank Baum, *The Wonderful Wizard of Oz* (Oxford: Oxford University Press, 2015), 129.

utable to what Gourevitch calls "the ambiguities of cooperation itself."[48] The relation between cooperation and centralized compulsion was never satisfactorily resolved, and there was thus a natural tendency for the movement not to coalesce. Cooperation itself as a value was not called into question, but the question of the relationships among cooperation, independence, and leadership was not settled. As we will see shortly, the same problem affected the Seattle General Strike of 1919.

Another, more direct, cause of the decline was the association with the violence that accompanied some of the strikes and the consequent repression. Most salient here was the Haymarket massacre of May 4, 1886, where an initial peaceful demonstration for the eight-hour workday and in protest at the police killing of several workers the day before at a strike had turned bloody. A first flyer (in both English and German languages) calling for the demonstration had urged men to come armed: that this clause was removed in a second one indicates that more anxious or circumspect heads seem to have prevailed. The powers that be had themselves urged violence before the rally. "Load your guns. They will be needed tomorrow to Shoot Communists," was a *Chicago Times* headline in 1875.[49] The meeting turned violent when an unknown person threw a bomb that killed seven police officers and wounded many others. An exchange of gunfire followed. Eight men were arrested and eventually convicted. Most were hung, even though there was no evidence that any of them had thrown the bomb. The incident and the trial became a touchstone for the labor movement, both in America and worldwide. (To this day, on May Day, one may hear in Latin American countries the cry "Viva los martires de Chicago" ["Long live the Chicago martyrs"]). They also produced an extensive state-enforced antilabor policy around the country.

Support for the Knights of Labor and parallels groups, such as the various farmers' associations, came from the reality of economic conditions. Miners, small farmers, and railroad workers came naturally to the realization that individually they had no chance against the powers of the monopolies but that collectively they might be able to resist. And such resistance required collective action. For instance, the country was increasingly settled up to the eastern slopes of the Rocky Mountains. That land was, however, generally arid and dependent on irrigation. Irrigation was either a cooperative venture or

48. Gourevitch, *From Slavery to the Cooperative Commonwealth*, 125.
49. Cited from Alex Gourevitch, "Police Work: The Centrality of Labor Repression in American Political History," *PS* (April 2017). This article is an excellent summary of a range of material dealing with strikes in American history, and I have learned a lot from it.

was monopoly controlled. In turn, the economic viability of crops depended on access to railroad transportation, which was increasingly dominated by a few monopolies. A set of natural alliances developed that would eventually be conceptualized as the "cooperative commonwealth." It is important to note that these alliances arose not only in rural areas but also among workingmen in cities. As Robert McMath observed, "By 1887, it was possible to imagine the consolidation of urban and rural protest groups into a permanent cooperative movement and labor party."[50]

For such movements to be successful, the organizations that grew up had to be able to compete with the monopolies, mostly by acquiring from members enough produce that could then be sold profitably to their own to buyers, often overseas. In 1887, the Farmers Alliance was able, for instance, to sell its members' cotton crop to buyers in the Northeast and in England. Success here, however, depended on having enough resources to acquire sufficient crops as to make the transaction profitable for all concerned. And, as it turned out, generally speaking and certainly over time, sufficient funds were not available. (The Farmers' Alliance had estimated its membership at five hundred thousand; it asked for a voluntary two-dollar contribution from each member but succeeded in raising only twenty thousand dollars).

ECONOMY AND POLITICS

None of these are, in the end, a political vision. While the solutions to problems were conceived of on a collective level, the relation to the political power of the state was not a central concern. What were the relations between economic distress and the political realm? As noted, there was repeatedly a lot of violence associated with these developments, but it was violence in response to or aimed at the conditions of economic production. And even some of the most popular "solutions" retained only a secondary sense of the importance of the political realm. In an attempt to devise an institutional solution to the damage done by monopolistic practices, Henry George developed a proposal for a new form of taxation and published it in his six-hundred-page *Progress and Poverty*, which became a best seller in the nineteenth century, second only to the Bible. George held that the concentrations of wealth that had developed since the Civil War were a symptom of a gradual transition of Amer-

50. Robert McMath Jr., *American Populism: A Social History, 1877-1898* (New York: Hill and Wang, 1992), 83.

ica from a republic of small producers to a tyranny of the very rich—and he sought analogies with the Roman Republic. "We have traced," he wrote, "the unequal distribution of wealth which is the curse and menace of modern civilization to the institution of private property in land."[51] And if this was the evil, the solution was to remove its cause, and that meant substituting "a common ownership" for individual ownership of land. This was not, however, a demand for national ownership but for national regulation. The monopolistic control of land by nonproducers forced farmers into tenancy and ruined cities. The solution was to establish a "single tax" that was based on the value of annual rent—that is, what the land *could* produce. Confiscation would be unnecessary because in order to pay the tax, owners would either have to make their lands productive in fact or else sell them. The state would remain small—government was not to play an important role, nor to be the focus of individual political action. George's plan was widely read and discussed: some attempts at implementing it in the new territories were made. (In the next century, attempts were also made in Australia, a German protectorate in China, Denmark, and elsewhere.)

George extended the fear of slavery to private property itself: "If chattel slavery was unjust, then is private property in land unjust."[52] His argument extended the arguments against chattel slavery to the economics of distribution. Ownership in land was, in effect, ownership of men, which George referred to explicitly as "enslavement." He pointed out as proof that even though chattel slavery had been abolished, "the planters of the South find they have sustained no loss." And in fact, he noted, the newly freed were likely to be worse off.[53] This is the same vision of independence that was found in Lincoln and others: dependency was slavery and made being one's own man impossible. George quoted Victor Hugo's *Les Misérables* approvingly: "every citizen without exception may be a land owner."

The vision of citizenship remains tied here to owning: for Lincoln it was owning oneself and one's production; for George, it was property, however understood. As it was framed, the idea was not particularly political—it involved no participation and carried no conception of any duties of citizenship. George was also an ardent exponent of free trade, which put him at loggerheads with the Knights of Labor, who otherwise supported him. He did run for mayor of New York in 1886 and came close to being elected (losing, probably

51. Henry George, *Progress and Poverty* (New York: Appleton, 1881), 329.
52. George, *Progress and Poverty*, 317.
53. George, *Progress and Poverty*, 354–55.

by fraud, to the Tammany candidate but beating out, incidentally, the young Theodore Roosevelt).

UTOPIAN DREAMS

What George did accomplish was to produce a vision of what a world might be like without monopoly power. And he was not alone. During the same period, Edward Bellamy, in *Looking Backwards* (1888), set out a technocratic scientifically regulated utopia he called "Nationalism." He envisaged an "industrial army" that would produce for the public good. In his novel, the young hero falls asleep in 1877 and awakens in 2000 to find himself in an America where production is organized for the good of all, retirement happens at age forty-five, and technology makes all things easily available. At the end of the novel, he reawakens in 1877 Boston and finds that, having seen other possibilities, he is now "a stranger in his own city." "Wretched men, I was moved to cry, who because they will not learn to be helpers of one another, are doomed to be beggars of one another from the least to the greatest."[54] The problem, a "Historical Preface" to the book, dated "2000," had indicated, was that people do not realize that conditions could be other than they are at present.

The theme of imaging a society not beset with monopolistic capitalism was not unique to Bellamy. Whatever the hopes were for technology, there was from early on mostly only minimal ambivalence. In 1872, Samuel Butler had published a utopian novel, *Erewhon: or, Over the Range* ("Nowhere" more or less backwards), satirizing Victorian society. Jules Verne published *A Mysterious Island* in 1874: the island is the hideaway of Captain Nemo (thus a modern Odysseus) who has developed technologies far in advance of the rest of society. Nemo is generally beneficial to the castaways shipwrecked onto the island, but he dies and the island and its scientific achievements blow up and are lost to civilization. In Verne's earlier *20000 Leagues under the Sea* (1871), Nemo had been a more ambivalent character, expressing support for the downtrodden and hoping to use technology to make the world a better place, yet quite willing to sink passing warships. It is worth noting that these years also see the appearance of Lewis Carroll's Alice stories. In 1892, the author, designer, and socialist activist William Morris published *News from Nowhere or An Epoch of Rest, being some chapters from A Utopian Romance*, about a society without politics where ownership is in common and production is democrat-

54. Edward Bellamy, *Looking Backwards* (Boston: Ticknor and Fields, 1887), 441.

ically controlled. In the second chapter, the protagonist, new to the society, attempts to pay a ferryman and is rebuffed: "You think that I have done you a service; so you feel yourself bound to give me something which I am not to give to a neighbour, unless he has done something special for me. I have heard of this kind of thing; but pardon me for saying, that it seems to us a troublesome and roundabout custom; and we don't know how to manage it. And you see this ferrying and giving people casts about the water is my *business*, which I would do for anybody; so to take gifts in connection with it would look very queer."[55]

WHAT GOD WANTS

All of these works, and many others, turn around two themes: the awful problems of the present system and the hope for a noncoercive system in which there is enough for everyone. Most of them are cooperative; most have a positive view of science and technology. Almost none of them have a positive view of political activity. This is even true with the proponents of the Social Gospel movement, many of whom, after reading Bellamy, were led to infuse their Christianity with a social conscience. The Social Gospel movement, led by Walter Rauschenbusch, held that Christ would not return for the Final Days until humans had made the world a just place. Social Gospel adherents took seriously the words of the Lord's Prayer: "Thy Kingdom Come. Thy Will be Done, *on Earth as it is in Heaven*." Hence, it was one's duty as a Christian to strive for social justice on this earth, now.

It is worth considering the Social Gospel movement as a search for a viable conception of citizenship. Rauschenbusch was a Baptist minister who, after studying in Germany, taught at the Rochester Theological Seminary. The Social Gospel theology that he developed held that while Christianity had generally made the sources of *individual* sin clear, it had paid inadequate attention to those of institutional sin. He found antecedents in the work of the Protestant clergyman Josiah Strong. In *Our Country* (1885), Strong argued that all people could be improved by being brought to Christ, and thus he encouraged home missionary activity, particularly in the American West. Strong

---

55. William Morris, *News from Nowhere or An Epoch of Rest, being some chapters from A Utopian Romance* (Boston, 1890), chap. 2, Project Gutenberg, http://www.gutenberg.org /files/3261/3261-h/3261-h.htm.

advocated a "brotherhood of religions" that would realize Judeo-Christian doctrines in actual life. His belief in the superiority of white Protestant, and particularly American,[56] culture derives from his sense that alone a theology like theirs could form the basis of a harmonious cooperative state that would counter the competitive realities of the present. In essence, Strong sought to extend the vision of a harmonious family to the country and the world at large. He was thus led to worry at length about immigration, the growth of population, corruption, and related matters. It was a peculiar combination of nationalistic racism and compassion for one's fellow human beings. As he wrote, "When [Jesus] took God by the hand and called him 'our Father,' he democratized the conception of God. He disconnected the idea from the coercive and predatory State, and transferred it to the realm of family life, the chief social embodiment of solidarity and love."[57] Friendship and love are deemed an adequate basis for citizenship.

Strong called up both a Social Gospel vision of social justice *and* the dangers of the flood of immigrants. Repeating an argument made by Thomas Hobbes in 1651, he held that Roman Catholics, as they owed allegiance to the pope, were incompatible with American republican citizenship. Citizenship required "intelligence and virtue" and was, however, quite compatible with a strong central government. With Henry George and Henry Demarest Lloyd, Strong attacked the monopolists and capitalists: "Here is taxation without representation with a vengeance. We have developed a despotism vastly more oppressive and more exasperating than that against which the thirteen colonies rebelled."[58]

One finds much the same in Rauschenbusch, who indeed cites Strong approvingly on the first pages of *A Theology for the Social Gospel* (1917). By far the greater theologian, Rauschenbusch argued that humans must cast off the yoke of the past, for only then will the possibilities for the present become realizable. A "transformation" was needed: "While in actual life there is no case of a complete Christian transformation, . . . it takes an awakened and regenerated mind a long time to find itself intellectually and discover what life henceforth

56. He chose this quote from Emerson as epigraph: "We live in a new and exceptional age. America is another name for Opportunity. Our whole history appears like a last effort of the Divine Providence in behalf of the human race." Josiah Strong, *Our Country: Its Possible Future and Its Present Crisis* (New York: Bible House, 1885).

57. J. Strong, *Our Country*, 174–75.

58. J. Strong, *Our Country*, 106. See the discussion in Smith, *Civic Ideals*, 355–56 (see intro., n. 7), where a portion of this passage is quoted.

is to mean to him."[59] Eschatology could be and should be converted into development, Rauschenbusch argued.[60] In *Christianity and the Social Crisis* (1908), he asserted, "Western civilization is passing through a social revolution unparalleled in history for scope and power. . . . The mission of the Church is to implant the divine life in the souls of men, and from these regenerated individual forces of righteousness will silently radiate, and evil customs and institutions will melt away without any propaganda."[61] Social Gospel thus comes closer to conceiving of the problem of membership in relation to institutional structure than do most of the others we have examined. However, it ultimately falls back on a faith in history and on the belief that material and technological advances would come together to solve the problems of industrial society. One notes, however, that Rauschenbusch conceived of the problem in terms much broader than simply those of America: for him, it was "western civilization" that was in question.

Social Gospel doctrines fit nicely with the orientation of many of the Populists, including William Jennings Bryan. They thought that, as a Christian, one was obliged to strive for the conditions on earth that permitted humans to behave justly and morally toward one another. It is thus off target to claim, as does Richard Hofstadter, that theirs was a "dualistic version of social struggles."[62] Rather, the struggle for social justice was a Christian imperative, but this did not mean that the struggle would not be political.

59. Walter Rauschenbusch, *A Theology for the Social Gospel* (New York: Macmillan, 1917), 100; see also 218.

60. Rauschenbusch, *Theology*, 225.

61. Walter Rauschenbusch, *Christianity and the Social Crisis* (London: Macmillan, 1908), xi, 151.

62. Hofstadter, *Age of Reform*, 62 (see intro., n. 16).

6

POPULISM AND SOCIALISM

Election night at midnight:
Boy Bryan's defeat.
Defeat of western silver.
Defeat of the wheat.
Victory of letterfiles
And plutocrats in miles
With dollar signs upon their coats,
Diamond watchchains on their vests and spats on their feet.
Victory of custodians, Plymouth Rock,
And all that inbred landlord stock.
Victory of the neat.
VACHEL LINDSAY, "BRYAN, BRYAN, BRYAN, BRYAN"

Chapter 5 left us with the problem of the development of a vision of citizenship adequate to meet a wide and complexly interrelated set of changes: in the national economy; in the expansion of the country; in the sudden presence as more or less full members of society of more than 4,200,000 blacks; in increasing pressure from the nonenfranchised women; in problems deriving from the tyranny of wage labor; and in those consequences of the new gross inequalities of wealth. The cooperative movements had had occasional regional or local electoral successes, but the overwhelming strength of the monopolies—the "interests"—and both the weakness and the hands-off attitude of the federal government generally ensured that things would stay as they were. The recurrent recessions and depressions made life insecure for a wide span of the electorate.[1]

James Weaver, an Ohioan transplanted to Iowa, had served in the Union Army and had made his way to joining the Greenback Labor Party.[2] In that capacity, he was elected to the House of Representatives in 1878 on a Greenback-Democrat fusion ticket, earning a reputation as an eloquent congressman, although he produced few concrete results. In the meantime, the Greenback Labor Party split into two factions, Weaver remaining a member of the less radical. Consequent to an attempt at reconciliation, Weaver was nominated for president in 1880 but received just 3 percent of the vote, with his strongest support in the Great Plains and the Southwest. In the coming years, tensions between the Democrats and the Greenbackers kept recurring. In 1884, however, Weaver was reelected to the House, now as the only Greenback member. He proposed policies that would enhance the role and range of the federal government, including the establishment of a Department of Labor. By 1890, Weaver was out of Congress again; the Greenback Labor Party and the Union Labor Party that had tried to replace it were basically defunct. After some resistance, in 1892 Weaver joined with others to form a new third party, the "People's Party" or Populist Party, and was selected as their candidate for the presidency. The Populist platform was by now standard for the progressive element of American politics: a graduated income tax, a limited-hour workday, public ownership of railroads and the means of communication, the replacement of National (i.e., private) banks with a government-issued and -controlled currency,[3] and the unlimited coinage of silver—all positions common to the movements that preceded the new party.

Despite the scandal of having fathered an illegitimate child,[4] Grover Cleveland won the 1892 election (his second) on a gold standard campaign with a national majority of about four hundred thousand votes over the incumbent

---

1. For the data, see Piketty, *Capital in the Twentieth Century*, chap. 5.

2. See the discussion in Lawrence Goodwyn, *The Populist Moment: A Short History of the Agrarian Revolt in America* (New York: Galaxy Books, 1978). Frederick Haynes wrote a biography of Weaver in 1919 that I have been unable to obtain.

3. The US Constitution authorizes Congress to issue only coinage (Section 8). Thus until the National Banking Acts of 1863–64, paper money was issued by banks—approximately eight thousand institutions issued paper money, which they hoped could, supposedly, be exchanged for coinage.

4. The anti-Clevelanders chanted "Ma, Ma, where's my Pa?" which after Cleveland's election was responded to with "Sarah, Sarah, where's your Pa? Gone to the White House, ha, ha, ha."

Benjamin Harrison: his lead was 132 electoral seats. Weaver, however, carried five plains and Rocky Mountain states for a total of twenty-two electoral seats and more than one million votes. He also showed strength in the other plains states, in some of the Northwest, and in parts of the South. Harrison, a Republican, and Weaver both ran on a bimetallism platform: had their support been combined to one candidate, most assuredly the Republican, that person would have won a majority of the popular vote.

The 1892 election showed that there were real possibilities for a national movement structured along the issues that had been coming to the forefront over the previous twenty years. The necessity was for citizen organization. Small farmers in the West and the South as well as workers and miners in the Midwest and the Rocky Mountain states supported various redistributive policies and, as the Populist platform was a version of what had become mostly standard demands for reform, could find them in the new party. These groups wanted the government to control the issuing of credit on the basis of 1 percent interest determined on the best crop price; the abolition of National banks; the free coinage of silver; government ownership of railroads and telegraph service; a graduated income tax; a secret ("Australian") ballot; and the end to alien land ownership.[5] Most of these demands we have seen previously. What matters for the developing conception of citizenship at this time is the sense one makes of, first, the secret ballot, and, second, the "alien ownership" clause.

The Australian or "secret" ballot was first used in Louisville, Kentucky, in 1888 and was gradually adopted on a widespread basis over the course of the 1890s. Until its usage, ballots were most often printed by partisan newspapers listing the candidates for only "their" party; these were then used as ballots by supporters. The Australian ballot, on the other hand, listed all candidates, organized by party affiliation, and required the voter to check his preferences in secret, casting then his ballot, which remained presumably unknown to anyone else. The presumption of the nonsecret ballot system had been that, as an independent person, one was not ashamed of one's political preferences—indeed, that making them publicly known was part of citizenship. During times where most of those who voted were similarly free and independent—their own man, as the expression goes—this manifestation of one's citizenship made some sense. To this day, in the *Landsgemeinde* system of some Swiss cantons, votes are taken at a public assembly by raised hands, by (until

5. See "Populist Party Platform (1892)," W. W. Norton, http://www.wwnorton.com /college/history/eamerica/media/ch22/resources/documents/populist.htm.

recently[6]) male citizens, who each carry a sword or other weapon. In these cantons, each person is therefore expected to vote as an independent, self-sufficient citizen, capable of defending himself, the *Vaterland* (fatherland), and his *Heimat* (home). Back in the United States at the end of the nineteenth century, both the direct physical method of voting and the preprinted (newspaper) ballot permitted easy voting by the illiterate or semiliterate, thus also by foreigners in the North and former slaves in the South. (Indeed, in eighteen states, "aliens" were permitted to vote until around 1900.[7]) The adoption of the secret ballot, on the other hand, generally privileges literacy and works to the disadvantage of the less than literate. Responding to the pressure of those who made this point, nine states did allow for various kinds of help in the case of illiteracy or incapacity (e.g., blindness).

More to the point here is the fact that by the 1880s—the "Gilded Age" as dubbed by Mark Twain—many of those entitled to vote were *not* independent or self-sufficient and were often responsive to threats or bribes. With the growth of inequalities, the possibilities for pressure on the part of the "interests" and the general prevalence of corruption increasingly either made such open voting dangerous to the man who voted "the wrong way" or opened the door to corruption. The move to the secret ballot was, then, to some considerable degree prompted by a response to the economic transformations that beset America after the Civil War.[8] The secret ballot reconceptualizes the vision of citizenship from one of manifested independent self-sufficiency to one for which independence is no longer a public criterion. It is also worth noting that the urban "machines" had ways of determining how "their" people voted and rewarding or punishing them accordingly.

Who, though, is entitled to partake of the benefits of citizenship? The "alien land ownership" plank of the Populist Party platform reads as follows: "LAND.—The land, including all the natural sources of wealth, is the heritage of the people, and should not be monopolized for speculative purposes, and alien ownership of land should be prohibited. All land now held by railroads and other corporations in excess of their actual needs, and all lands now

6. In Switzerland, women could vote on national issues only after 1971. The last canton to grant women suffrage on cantonal issues was Appenzell Innere Rhoden in 1990, by decision of the Federal Court.

7. See A. Keyssar, *Right to Vote*, table A 12.

8. See the brief discussion in A. Keyssar, *Right to Vote*, 115–16, without, however, the point I am making. On Switzerland, and for a discussion of this vision of citizenship, see Benjamin R. Barber, *The Death of Communal Liberty: A History of Freedom in a Swiss Mountain Canton* (Princeton, NJ: Princeton University Press, 1974).

owned by aliens should be reclaimed by the government and held for actual settlers only." This clause has often been read as showing the problematic nativism of the Populists. That interpretation, though, is much too strong. The second clause of the platform reads: "Second.—Wealth belongs to him who creates it, and every dollar taken from industry without an equivalent is robbery. 'If any will not work, neither shall he eat.' The interests of rural and civil labor are the same; their enemies are identical."

The "any" in the quoted sentence links those Americans who control too much as incapable of being or unwilling to be concerned with the public good and those who, as aliens, are not concerned with the public good. Populists, it must be said, were not alone in excluding aliens, but their grounds are different. The Republican-sponsored Chinese Exclusion Act of 1882, renewed in 1892 and made permanent in 1902, was specifically aimed at all "skilled and unskilled laborers and Chinese employed in mining"[9] and targeted primarily the Japanese and, explicitly, the Chinese who provided cheap labor. It not only excluded all noncitizens but also made the achievement of citizenship by Asians almost impossible. Because the primary basis of the exclusion was the fear of cheap labor, if one were Asian, it proved to be very difficult to demonstrate that one was *not* a laborer. The Populist exclusion appears to be racist, but it is based on the sense that to be a citizen, one had to produce: according to the second plank of the platform, "Wealth belongs to him who creates it, and every dollar taken from industry without an equivalent is slavery." Cheap (Asian) labor tended to encourage monopoly, competition, and exploitation: such made citizen independence difficult if not impossible. White laborers on the transcontinental Central Pacific railroad (completed in 1869) were never more than 10 percent of the workforce, whereas Chinese comprised 90 percent and totaled as many as fifteen thousand laborers.[10]

Likewise, the so-called anti-Semitism often attributed to the Populists, while often expressed in terms that might seem explicit, is to a great degree

9. For the text of the act, see "Chinese Exclusion Act, May 6, 1882," sec. 15, Archives of the West, PBS, https://www.pbs.org/weta/thewest/resources/archives/seven/chinxact .htm#act. See also Erika Lee, *At America's Gates: Chinese Immigration during the Exclusion Era, 1882–1943* (Chapel Hill: University of North Carolina Press, 2003).

10. See George Kraus, "Chinese Laborers and the Construction of the Central Pacific," *Utah Historical Quarterly* 37, no. 1 (1969): 41–57. Kraus quotes Leland Stanford, president of the Central Pacific Railroad, writing to President Andrew Johnson that the Chinese are "quiet, peaceable, industrious and economical" (45). See Stephen Ambrose, *Nothing Like It in the World: The Men Who Built the Transcontinental Railroad* (New York: Simon and Schuster, 2000).

hostility toward those unseen Eastern controllers of money and credit who worked to the disadvantage of the working and farming classes: "the Shylocks of Europe" pitted against the "toilers of America." (Think here of my earlier citation from Steinbeck, in chapter 5, of the dispossessed farmer wondering whom he can shoot.) As Walter Nugent has argued, "None of the platforms bore any overt sign of nativism or anti-Semitism, unless the now customary alien land and contract labor planks, which were derived from the homestead principle and a competitive labor situation can be construed as such."[11] Michael Kazin, similarly, asserts that anti-Semitism was but "a minor element of the movement's language that stemmed more from a nationalist hatred of international bankers than from a specific antagonism towards Jews."[12] Much, although not all, of what has been taken to be Populist racism and xenophobia had, in fact, solid nonracist politico-economic bases.

Against this economic power, the Populists sought to use government to counter corruption, to help those in need, and to control the power of the monopolies and the banks—the vision of government was that it rested or should rest on the mass of independent producers, both workers and farmers. By and large, they were, with some exceptions such as alien ownership, inclusive. As the Populist congressman (and Georgite single taxer) Jeremiah "Sockless Jerry" Simpson of Kansas, put it, "We must own the railroads *or* enough of them to do the necessary carrying. . . . The government *is* the people and we *are* the people."[13]

The sentiment is admirable, but Simpson's formulation both hides and reveals a problem: the assimilation of citizenship and the citizenry to the government covers over a mass of difficulties. Who is the "we" in Simpson's exhortation? How does it come into being? What is it relation to the "non-we"? Part of the problem of conceiving of citizenship as the opposition between the "people" and the "interests" is that one never needs to determine precisely

11. See Walter Nugent, *The Tolerant Populists: Kansas Populism and Nativism*, 2nd ed. (1963; repr., Chicago: University of Chicago Press, 2013), 56. Until the 1950s, the general judgment on the Populists was that they were the forerunners of liberalism. This perspective changed when Richard Hofstadter, responding in *The Age of Reform* (1955) and in *The Paranoid Style in American Politics* (1965) to the McCarthy scare, became centrally responsible for identifying Populism with the Right, in part out of a fear derived from the experience of the 1930s. Hofstadter, as he later admitted, was "not much for sources." Hofstadter quoted in Nugent, *Tolerant Populists*, x.

12. Michael Kazin, *The Populist Persuasion: An American History* (New York: Basic Books, 1985), 39.

13. Quoted in Karel Denis Bicha, "Jerry Simpson: Populist without Principle," *Journal of American History* 54, no. 2 (September 1967): 291–306, at 297.

what makes a people. By and large, the "people" tended to be defined as that which was opposed to the "interests." Karl Marx, in his great 1852 essay on the rise of Louis Napoleon, caught the problem exactly. Referring to "the democrats," one of the party factions in midcentury France, he wrote:

> The democrat . . . imagines himself elevated above class antagonism generally. The democrats concede that a privileged class confronts them, but they, along with all the rest of the nation, form the people. What they represent is the people's rights; what interests them is the people's interests. Accordingly, when a struggle is impending they do not need to examine the interests and positions of the different classes. They do not need to weigh their own resources too critically. They have merely to give the signal and the people, with all its inexhaustible resources, will fall upon the oppressors. Now if in the performance their interests prove to be uninteresting and their potency impotence, then either the fault lies with pernicious sophists, who split the indivisible people into different hostile camps, or the army was too brutalized and blinded to comprehend that the pure aims of democracy are the best thing for it, or the whole thing has been wrecked by a detail in its execution, or else an unforeseen accident has this time spoiled the game.[14]

The same critique applies to the vision of "the people" versus "the interests." Marx points to a basic question: a central issue of citizenship concerns the composition of the "we"—the "people." In America, this "people" now included up to six million blacks, the males being legally entitled to present themselves as qualified voters. What attitude can a movement, run by whites and explicitly dedicated to social justice, take toward this new group of citizens in relation to suffrage? The white Populist attitude toward blacks was complex. To the degree that economic issues were foregrounded, many white Populists tended early on to push for a biracial polity of small producers, something like what would have been possible had land remained under the ownership of the Edisto Island blacks. Foremost here was the Georgian agrarian rebel Thomas Watson, who became the Populist Party candidate for vice president in 1896. In 1892, he had published the article "The Negro Question in the South" in the Boston-based *Arena*, a journal that carried articles by such authors as Upton Sinclair and Stephen Crane and often published writ-

---

14. Karl Marx, "The Eighteenth Brumaire of Louis Napoleon," in *Marx Engels Collected Works*, vol. 11 (London: Lawrence and Wishart, 1979), 133.

ers who supported socialism and the trade union movement. In 1896, it supported William Jennings Bryan for president.[15] Among many other topics, the issue in which Watson's article appeared also carried articles on "The Rights of Children," a symposium on which of the three political parties should elect the next president, a symposium on women's clubs, and a symposium on women's dress.

Watson noted that emancipation had changed relations between the races but was producing "mutual distrust and dislike," which was the source of potential bloody conflict. This distrust and dislike, Watson argued, had led to a situation where, because of remembered danger of Southern Democrats, the "black man [is] managed by northern Republicans." The lack of independence on the part of blacks—often nothing more than defenseless sharecroppers on the lands where they previously had been slaves—was an open door to corruption. The problem, as Watson then poses it, "is, can these two races, distinct in color, distinct in social life, and distinct as political powers, dwell together in peace and prosperity?" The solution to this problem, he averred, is a new party, hostile neither to (poor Southern) whites nor to blacks, whom he saw as remaining in the South. The same grievances, he argued, afflicted the poor Southern white farmer as the black. The solution was the "People's Party," which said to each, "You are kept apart that you may be separately fleeced of your earnings. You are made to hate each other because upon that hatred is rested the keystone of the arch of financial despotism which enslaves you both. You are deceived and blinded that you may not see how this race antagonism perpetuates a monetary system that beggars both. . . . Why should not my tenant come to regard me as his friend rather than the manufacturer who plunders us both?" This will not lead to "Negro Supremacy," he asserted, as each person was to decide for himself about social equality. Watson in effect reproduced on a biracial basis the Lincolnian vision of the citizenship of the small yeoman producer.[16] (It is also a sad fact that after 1904, distressed with the fact that blacks let themselves be manipulated by whites, he thought, and opposed to the prominence of Booker T. Washington and W. E. B. Dubois,

15. Thomas Watson, "The Negro Question in the South," *Arena 6* (October 1892): 540–50, https://archive.org/stream/ArenaMagazine-Volume06/189206-arena-volume06#page/n3/mode/2up.

16. See Hahn, *Nation under Our Feet*, chap. 8. See also C. Vann Woodward, *Tom Watson: Agrarian Rebel* (New York, 1938). For the development, see Steven Hahn, *The Roots of Southern Populism: Yeoman Farmers and the Transformation of the Georgia Upcountry, 1859–1890*, updated ed. (New York: Oxford University Press, 2006).

Watson became a racist and anti-Semite, supporting, with considerable rhetorical eloquence, black disenfranchisement).

Nor, in the early 1890s, had Watson been a solitary voice. After the organization of a Populist Party in Georgia in 1892, "the white people" of their county asked for the "cooperation of the colored people in this, our effort to free our country from its present depressed condition and put in office men who will legislate for the masses and not the classes. . . . Your race today, like ours, is groaning under the oppression of taxation and the low estimate place on labor." Their lots were cast together for "to better our condition means to better yours."[17]

That said, white Populism always maintained an uneasy relation with blacks. In the South, the problem soon arose from the Populist-Democrat alliance of 1896. White Southerners were for obvious reasons ferociously Democratic. A more natural alliance would have been Populist-Republican, and this did indeed occur on a limited basis.[18] But to the degree that alliances that included blacks had some political success, white Democrats increasingly took to paramilitary intimidation and murder. May 1896, thus a time at the height of the presidential campaign, marks the Supreme Court decision in *Plessy v. Ferguson* that established a firm constitutional basis for segregated facilities. Interestingly, the court found itself obliged to decide exactly what constituted "race," as the plaintiff Homer Plessy was physiologically indistinguishable from a white man.[19] The case is the source of the notorious "one drop" clause—contrary to all other countries in which slavery was legal, *any* black ancestry qualified the person as black.[20] Ironically, the majority decision was authored by, among others, a justice named Brown and agreed to by another named White. Six of the justices in the seven-to-one majority decision were from Union states. Justice Harlan was the sole dissenter, finding the decision

17. Hahn, *Nation under Our Feet*, 433.

18. Hahn, *Nation under Our Feet*, 438–39.

19. See Mark Golub, "*Plessy* as Passing: Judicial Responses to Ambiguously Raced Bodies in *Plessy v. Ferguson*," *Law and Society Review* 39, no. 3 (2005). See also Brian Jones, "The Social Construction of Race," *Jacobin*, June 25, 2015, https://www.jacobinmag.com/2015/06/racecraft-racism-social-origins-reparations/, which mistakenly asserts that Plessy claimed to be white.

20. Charles W. Chesnutt, a black author, wrote a novel, *The House behind the Cedars* (New York: Houghton Mifflin, 1900), in which the heroine experiences herself as white, wishes to live as a white person in white society, but is in terms of the law, black. See the discussion in Bromell, *Time Is Always Now*. Chesnutt, incidentally, could pass for white.

to be "as pernicious as the decision made by this tribunal in the *Dred Scott* case." He continued:

> If evils will result from the commingling of the two races upon public highways established for the benefit of all, they will be infinitely less than those that will surely come from state legislation regulating the enjoyment of civil rights upon the basis of race. We boast of the freedom enjoyed by our people above all other peoples. But it is difficult to reconcile that boast with a state of the law which, practically, puts the brand of servitude and degradation upon a large class of our fellow-citizens, our equals before the law. The thin disguise of "equal" accommodations for passengers in railroad coaches will not mislead any one, nor atone for the wrong this day done.[21]

In anticipatory critique, Mark Twain, who had been following the case since its inception in 1892, published in 1894 *Pudd'nhead Wilson*, a hugely complicated story about two children exchanged at birth. One is "one-sixteenth black" and indistinguishable from the white baby. The "black child" is raised as white, the "white" raised as "black" in a slave family: for Twain, nurture—and not nature or race—makes all the difference in their characters as we find out when, finally correctly identified by their fingerprints (taken before the exchange), they are returned to their birth mothers. The child now identified as "black" but brought up "white" kills a man but is spared the death penalty on the grounds that he is now "property" and can be sold "down the river" to repay various debts—which he is.[22] The "white" child, brought up "black," proves to be unable to adapt to his new race.

If Populist attitudes toward blacks were ambivalent, they also varied considerably in practice. Some writers, among them C. Vann Woodward, have found in Populism a strong concerted approval of a biracial society. Others have pointed at the wide range of racially prejudiced stances taken by the Populists.[23] Regional variations were substantial. One might, however, generalize and say that Populists tended to support biracialism where it was to their electoral advantage. After 1896, as the Democratic Party in the South came back under the complete control of whites and the North was willing to let the

---

21. Plessy v. Ferguson, 163 U.S. 537 (1896).

22. See Eric Sundquist, "Mark Twain and Homer Plessy," *Representations* 24 (Autumn 1988): 102–28. See also Tracy B. Strong, "What Can Be Learned on a Raft? Huckleberry Finn and the Price of Freedom," *Journal of Law, Philosophy and Culture* (2010).

23. This best summary of that range seems to me to be in Gerald Gaither, *Blacks and the Populist Revolt* (Tuscaloosa: University of Alabama Press, 1977), chap. 5.

white South pretty much manage its own affairs, any sympathies that blacks might have had toward the Democrat-Populist fusion melted quickly away. During the period that the Populists were a force, it seems correct to say that they supported a political alliance with blacks but not any kind of social egalitarianism. They wanted black votes but generally not much else. They thus supported a vision of citizenship that is basically limited to the ballot and not to anything that might follow from that. When President Cleveland sought to appoint a black from Birmingham consul to the town of Santos in Brazil (which had abolished slavery in 1888 and where close to half the population was mulatto or black), extensive protests were mounted by Populists, including Tom Watson.[24]

WILLIAM JENNINGS BRYAN

Still, a great experiment was under way. In 1896, the Democratic Party chose William Jennings Bryan to run against the Republican William McKinley. The Democrats had repudiated Cleveland and the gold standard. At their convention, Ben "Pitchfork" Tillman spoke first and distressed many delegates by a speech with a confusing mixture of free silver and racism. The thirty-six-year old Bryan spoke next and carried the nomination by the enthusiasm engendered by his "Cross of Gold" speech (although it did take five ballots). Arthur Sewall was named as vice presidential candidate. The Populist Party held its convention subsequently. Mindful no doubt of the consequences of divided sympathies in 1892, and desirous of national success, after considerable infighting including fisticuffs on the convention floor, they elected also to nominate Bryan but named Thomas Watson as the vice presidential candidate. Bryan left up in the air the issue of who would be vice president should he win. He chose, contrary to established practice, to campaign all around the country, whereas McKinley merely received visitors at his home, opting for the standard "front porch" campaign.

The results of 1892 had placed a heavy pressure on Populist leaders to obtain political results. Bryan's speech, to be considered in this section, followed the free silver plank almost exclusively. It is likely, however, that the desire for national success led, after considerable debate and despite the fact that free silver was not their most prominent cause, to the acceptance of a fusion with

24. Gaither, *Blacks and the Populist Revolt*, 76.

the Democrats.[25] Other attempts at third parties—the Grange, the Knights of Labor, and so forth—had failed nationally and had substantially waned over time. Over the 1890s, Populists elected eleven governors, six senators, about forty-five members of Congress, and uncounted local candidates: the most successful record of a third party in America. As it turns out, however, over time the fusion with the Democrats around the silver issue proved to be a fatal move to the prospects of Populism. Still, it was a great campaign, and important issues other than silver coinage were raised. As Vachel Lindsay put it:

> There were truths eternal in the gap and tittle-tattle.
> There were real heads broken in the fustian and the rattle.
> There were real lines drawn:
> Not the silver and the gold,
> But Nebraska's cry went eastward against the dour and old,
> The mean and cold.[26]

For the first time in American history, Bryan chose to take his campaign directly to each state and locality. He traveled over eight thousand miles and made more than six hundred speeches, but he proved unable to convert white Easterners, especially as many of the workers were explicitly threatened with loss of work should Bryan win. McKinley's campaign was masterminded by Mark Hanna, the first great unscrupulous campaign manager of American politics and the Karl Rove of his day: "bulldog . . . low-browed Hanna," as Lindsay put it.[27]

What was the vision that so overwhelmed the Democratic convention that they chose Bryan? The "Cross of Gold" speech is thought of as one of the greatest pieces of American political oratory. That it is, but it is also worth examining carefully for its conception of citizenship. It was an event that no one present ever forgot. Again, Lindsay captured some of it:

> And Bryan took the platform.
> And he was introduced.
> And he lifted his hand

25. See Norman Pollock, *The Populist Response to Industrial America* (Cambridge, MA: Harvard University Press, 1976), 103.

26. Vachel Lindsay, "Bryan, Bryan, Bryan, Bryan," PoemHunter.com, https://www.poemhunter.com/best-poems/vachel-lindsay/bryan-bryan-bryan-bryan/.

27. Lindsay quoted in Thomas Beer, *Hanna* (New York: Knopf, 1928), Internet Archive, https://archive.org/details/in.ernet.dli.2015.273233/page/n3.

And cast a new spell.
  Progressive silence fell
  In Springfield, in Illinois, around the world.
Then we heard these glacial boulders across the prairie rolled:
"The people have a right to make their own mistakes
  You shall not crucify mankind
  Upon a cross of gold."[28]

Bryan's speech is noteworthy not only for its extraordinary rhetorical power but also for the limitations of its argument. On the one hand, he framed the issues as "us against them": it is "my friends" against "they": "We defy them!" The "they" is never spelled out—it is simply a shady anonymous group of interests, and Bryan goes out of his way to say that he has no hostility to the people of the Eastern states. On the other hand, the "we" are confusingly defined as "a broader class of businessman." "When you [the "they"] come before us," he asserts, "and tell us that that shall disturb your business interests, we reply that you have disturbed our business interests by your action." And not just businessmen, as it turns out: the wage earner, the country lawyer, the small-town merchant, the farmer, the miner are all the "hearty pioneers" who have opened the country and "are as deserving of the consideration of this party."[29] The vision is that we are in business for ourselves and each of us should have the right to pursue each our own interests. The assimilation of independence to being a businessman is significant: there is little consideration of a public vision. Still, Bryan's peroration is deservedly famous: "If they dare to come out in the open field and defend the gold standard as a good thing, we shall fight them in the uttermost, having behind us the producing masses of the nation and the world. Having behind us the commercial interests and the laboring interests and the toiling masses, we shall answer their demands for a gold standard by saying to them, you shall not press down on the brow of labor this crown of thorns. You shall not crucify mankind upon a cross of gold."[30]

A great speech. But the almost exclusive focus on silver meant that the panoply of issues that had mobilized the Populist movement went almost unattended. And, indeed, Bryan campaigned almost exclusively as a Democrat focusing on the silver issue—which was *not* the issue that would bring over the

28. Lindsay, "Bryan, Bryan, Bryan, Bryan."

29. William Jennings Bryan, "Bryan's 'Cross of Gold' Speech: Mesmerizing the Masses," History Matters, http://historymatters.gmu.edu/d/5354/.

30. Bryan, "Cross of Gold."

industrial Northeast and upper Midwest. And, by not addressing the race issue directly, Bryan left the Populists open to subsequent antiblack campaigns
and thus, in North Carolina, the one state where Populists had had statewide
success in a fusion with the Republicans, the 1898 election saw a return to
power of white, overtly racist Democrats.

Bryan continued to be an important factor in American politics, running
for president (and losing) a total of three times and serving as secretary of
state for Woodrow Wilson. He is perhaps later remembered mostly as the
prosecuting attorney in the Scopes "Monkey" trial of 1925. It is worth considering that trial as it is relevant to the vision of citizenship that Bryan espoused.
In 1925, Tennessee had passed the Butler Act forbidding the teaching of evolution in the state and providing for a fine of between one hundred and five
hundred dollars for each offense. Bryan had been a driving force behind the
bill. Among his other successful accomplishments had been the strong support for the direct election of senators (1913), the progressive federal income
tax (1913), female suffrage (1920), and Prohibition (1920).

Tennessee required the teaching of a textbook by George W. Hunter called
Civic Biology, which clearly, if briefly, set out what it understood as a kind of
theory of evolution. On page 196, the text concluded its discussion of evolution by indicating that there had evolved five races of humans, to wit, the
Ethiopian, Malay, American Indian, Mongolian, and "the highest type of all,
the Caucasian, represented by the civilized white inhabitants of Europe and
America."[31] This last was the only race to whom the adjective *civilized* was applied, and the text continued by suggesting some possibilities for the improvement of the race.

A group of citizens in Dayton, Ohio, persuaded a local teacher, John Scopes,
to claim that he had, in using this textbook, taught evolution and was hence
in contravention of the Butler Act. No account was apparently made of the
fact that the text in question was state required. A trial ensued, with Bryan
the central figure in the prosecution and Clarence Darrow, fresh from having
obtained a sentence of life in prison rather than the death penalty for the confessed and brutal nineteen-year-old murderers Nathan Leopold and Richard
Loeb, the major figure for the defense.[32] The children, he successfully argued,
were products of the mercilessness of nature, hence not (fully) responsible.

---

31. George W. Hunter, *Civic Biology* (New York. American Book Co., 1914), 196.

32. Text can be found at University of Missouri–Kansas City Law School website, http://
www.law.umkc.edu/faculty/projects/ftrials/scopes/scopes.htm. In his summation for that
case, Darrow had invoked the following: "Nature is strong and she is pitiless. She works in

Bryan was an evangelical Christian who believed in the truth of the Bible. He also knew good deal about Darwin—more, in fact, than the defense did. And he certainly knew more about the Bible than did Darrow.[33] The point here is that Bryan's opposition to the teaching of evolution had to do *both* with his Christian fundamentalism *and* with the fact that the theory of evolution appeared to justify, on the one hand, the claim that human responsibility is diminished by the claim that humans are subject to nature's supposedly immutable laws and, on the other hand, the claim that some beings (or races) were superior to others, a stance that could be used, as he pointedly reminded Darrow, to mitigate responsibility for a confessed vicious murder. He also knew that during the First World War, German militarism had legitimated itself by appeals to Darwin.

Bryan had labored over a speech by which to respond to Darrow but never got to give it, for after Darrow asked for a "guilty verdict" so that the case might be appealed, the judge ruled the speech to be irrelevant. Here is part of what he would have said:

> Science is a magnificent force, but it is not a teacher of morals. It can perfect machinery, but it adds no moral restraints to protect society from the misuse of the machine. It can also build gigantic intellectual ships, but it constructs no moral rudders for the control of storm tossed human vessel. It not only fails to supply the spiritual element needed but some of its unproven hypotheses rob the ship of its compass and thus endangers its cargo. In war, science has proven itself an evil genius; it has made war more terrible than it ever was before. Man used to be content to slaughter his fellowmen on a single plane—the earth's surface. Science has taught

---

mysterious ways, and we are her victims. We have not much to do with it ourselves. Nature takes this job in hand, and we only play our parts. In the words of old Omar Khayyam, we are only 'Impotent pieces in the game He plays / Upon this checkerboard of nights and days, / Hither and thither moves, and checks, and slays, / And one by one back in the closet lays.' What had this boy had to do with it? He was not his own father; he was not his own mother. . . . All of this was handed to him. He did not surround himself with governesses and wealth. He did not make himself. And yet he is to be compelled to pay."

33. Alan Dershowitz, *America on Trial: Inside the Legal Battles That Transformed Our Nation* (2004; repr., New York: Grand Central Publishing, 2005), writes, "Nor was Bryan the know-nothing biblical literalist of *Inherit the Wind*. For the most part, he actually seems to have gotten the better of Clarence Darrow in the argument over the Bible" (265). Bryan explicitly denied that everything in the Bible was to be understood literally. See "Transcripts from *Tennessee versus John Scopes* (1925)," Hanover College Department of History, https://history.hanover.edu/courses/excerpts/111scopes.html.

him to go down into the water and shoot up from below and to go up into the clouds and shoot down from above, thus making the battlefield three times as bloody as it was before; but science does not teach brotherly love. Science has made war so hellish that civilization was about to commit suicide; and now we are told that newly discovered instruments of destruction will make the cruelties of the late war seem trivial in comparison with the cruelties of wars that may come in the future. If civilization is to be saved from the wreckage threatened by intelligence not consecrated by love, it must be saved by the moral code of the meek and lowly Nazarene. His teachings, and His teachings, alone, can solve the problems that vex heart and perplex the world.[34]

Except for the last two sentences, I imagine that many who read this book would generally agree with the rest of this statement. The point here is that there is no such thing as a "scientific truth" divorced of contexts—and the plural is important. Bryan is explicit that were one to base one's standard of virtuous politics on science and scientific knowledge—as many were trying to do—one can be led to the legitimation, whether logically or not, of terrible consequences. Bryan stood opposed to evolution, which he saw as a "doctrine destructive of civilization" and to eugenics. Another grounding is necessary—he found it in Christianity, which he saw as both a sign of the "favored position" of the white race and as a duty to carry those blessings to the "dark-skinned races."[35] Christianity, however, was, despite his efforts, increasingly proving politically inadequate. Bryan's "white man's burden" attitude is distressing in that it eliminates what could have been a possible fruitful alliance. Frederick Douglass, who did not die until 1895, was also a religious fundamentalist who denounced evolution as "scientific moonshine that would connect man with monkeys."[36] But for the lack of an interracial alliance, religious doctrine could have provided a leverage against what appeared to most whites as the "normal"—and scientifically justified—relation between the races.

Bryan's distress with making science the political authority was not his

34. "Text of the Closing Statement of William Jennings Bryan at the Trial of John Scopes, Dayton, Tennessee, 1925," California State University Dominguez Hills, http://www5.csudh.edu/oliver/smt310-handouts/wjb-last/wjb-last.htm.

35. William Jennings Bryan, "The White Man's Burden," address to the American Society of London, July 4, 1906, Social Justice Speeches, EdChange Multicultural Pavilion, http://www.edchange.org/multicultural/speeches/w_bryan_white.html.

36. Cited from H. Brotz, ed., *Negro Social and Political Thought* (New York: Basic Books, 1966), 199–200, as quoted in McWilliams, *Idea of Fraternity in America*, 582.

alone, nor did it require Christianity to support it. Contrary to those who saw a golden future time in technology, Mark Twain was one of the sharpest critics of these developments. In 1889, he published *A Connecticut Yankee in King Arthur's Court*. After a blow on the head, the novel's protagonist Hank Morgan wakes up to find himself in Arthurian times. In a parody of "Yankee ingenuity," he rises to a position of power—he sees himself as becoming "boss [of] the country inside three months." He introduces a stock market where he makes a killing, develops science and technology and industrialization. Camelot does indeed fall, but not because of an illicit love affair. Rather, the novel ends with a bloody battle because Lancelot has cornered the stock market—the affair with Guinevere is thin air. Morgan's forces, armed with machine guns, massacre the knights opposing them. Twain likely developed his ideas as a response to *Triumphant Democracy*, Andrew Carnegie's 1886 paean to technology, wherein Carnegie had argued that technological development had brought America to surpass Europe in a mere sixty years.[37] The powers of science and its supposed relation to democratic citizenship would continue to be a major theme in the American discussions, in particular as we shall see in the discussion of the Progressive movement in chapter 8. To base social policy on science is to base it on the judgements of experts, not of ordinary individuals. It is to turn politics into a professional enterprise.

The fusion ticket marked the beginning of the end of the Populist Party. What remained of that movement was to a great degree taken over by Eugene Victor Debs, who had declined to stand for nomination by the Populists in 1896. The course of Debs's life bears discussion as it exemplifies the transformations taking place in the country.

EUGENE VICTOR DEBS

Debs, born in 1855, was the son of prosperous French immigrants who ran a successful grocery business in Terre Haute, Indiana.[38] They brought him up reading the classics—an important childhood book was Victor Hugo's *Les Misérables*. Debs quit school at age fourteen to work as a locomotive paint scraper and eventually became a railroad fireman, working for an Indiana-

---

37. Andrew Carnegie, *Triumphant Democracy*, https://pdcrodas.webs.ull.es/anglo /CarnegieTriumphantDemocracy.pdf.

38. All biographical details and much information come from Nick Salvatore, *Eugene V. Debs: Citizen and Socialist* (Urbana: University of Illinois Press, 1982).

based railroad. In 1875, he joined the local Brotherhood of Locomotive Firemen, a fraternal organization dedicated to the provision of insurance and widow's benefits to its members. Especially in the early days, it was structured as a semisecret society on the model of the Freemasons. Debs later recalled the day of his initiation as follows: "A new purpose entered my life, a fresh force impelled me as I repeated the obligation to serve the 'brotherhood,' and I left that meeting with a totally different and far loftier ambition than I had ever known before."[39] The experience of communal fraternity dedicated to a purpose was to stay with him for his entire life.

In 1880, he was elected grand secretary and treasurer of the organization and became active in Democratic Party politics, being elected to the Indiana General Assembly in 1884. At this point in his life, he believed in the possibility of a harmonious relation of labor and citizen—the railroad he worked for was locally owned. He rejoiced in the expansive nature of American society and, as an assemblyman, saw himself as a spokesperson for labor urging improvements to the length of the working day and working conditions in general, all the while not wanting to bring into question the actual reality of a commonality of interests between capital and labor. The task was rather to increase the dignity of labor. Tellingly, he thought the Great Railroad Strike of 1877 against the Baltimore and Ohio line (which had cut wages for the third time in a year) to be "sheer folly," even though it was supported by about one hundred thousand workers (who were not unionized) across five states and bloodily put down by a combination of armed militias and National Guard. Debs's focus was mainly on skilled workers, those with a craft, and he had little to say about unskilled workers, blacks, immigrants, or dependents. His vision at this stage was derived from essentially a small business model: companies are local, employees are local. They know each other; they live in the same towns.

The economy, though, was changing: monopoly power was ever increasing.[40] In 1888—when Debs was thirty-three—his local railroad was sold to an Eastern corporation. A dispute and strike broke out over the scale of wages; the company refused to negotiate; the workers were divided among brotherhoods, and the company used their diverging interests as wedges to defeat the strike. Debs came away from this experience having learned that to fight corporate power, a single organization committed to the basic interests and

39. Salvatore, *Eugene V. Debs*, 26.
40. For a brilliant study of such changes over an extended period, see Gaventa, *Power and Powerlessness*.

values of the workers as workers was necessary. Such a union would have to include all workers so that the unskilled could not be set against skilled: in 1893, he became the first president of the American Railroad Union (ARU).

The following year, the ARU won a strike against the Great Northern Railroad, which had agreed to arbitration; it soon counted as many as 150,000 members. This victory was to prove its only one. In 1894, after a year of depression, the Pullman Company cut wages between one-third and one-half. Pullman's sleeping cars were made in a company town, where all workers lived in company houses and shopped in company stores. Pullman did not cut the prices it charged when it cut wages. The Pullman workers went on strike and appealed to the ARU for support, which was agreed to: a national boycott of Pullman cars was initiated. The company, however, refused to negotiate or accept arbitration (as had Great Western) and used its influence to get President Cleveland to issue an injunction based on the Sherman Antitrust Act of 1890 on the grounds that the strike disrupted US mails and restrained commerce. Federal troops, hired strikebreakers, and hired nonunion "scabs," including many blacks, were dispatched to take over strike sites. There was considerable violence, and the strike was eventually broken. Debs and six other leaders received six-month prison terms. The strike had lasted about three months—when during that period Debs had called for a general strike, he was opposed not only by Pullman and the federal government but by the skilled worker craft unions led by Samuel Gompers.[41]

The Pullman strike made their problem clear to Debs and others. The new corporations had lots of power, not only on their own but also through the backing and direct support of the federal government. The corporations had no social responsibility. Their workers were therefore inevitably dependent on them: the Pullman company town is only an extreme example. It was a form of slavery: to be a slave, wrote one of the Knights of Labor, "is to be a person consciously capable of self-government, and to be, at the same time, subject to the will of another person."[42] The solution thus appeared to Debs to be the development of a "cooperative commonwealth"—in effect, this meant abandoning hope for progress to be achieved by trade unions alone and pursuing an alternative form of political organization. In 1897, Debs embraced social-

41. On the cooperation of the American Federation of Labor, Gompers, and the corporations, see James Weinstein, *The Corporate Ideal in the Liberal State, 1900–1918* (Boston: Beacon Press, 1968).

42. Cited in Alex Gourevitch, *From Slavery to the Cooperative Commonwealth: Labor and Republican Liberty in the Nineteenth Century* (Cambridge: Cambridge University Press, 2015), 121.

ism, "for humanity," he said. In America, "socialism" was at that time a rather inchoate ideology and had remained such until, in 1901, Debs helped organize the Socialist Party of America.

The move was important for the consciousness it reflected. As with the movements of the last third of the century, in particular as with the attempt at a fusion Populist-Democrat ticket, it was becoming clear that however a polity of free and independent citizens was to come about, it could not be achieved on an individual basis. A collective movement was necessary—for, as the labor song "Solidarity Forever" put it, "no force on earth is weaker / than the feeble strength of one / but the union makes us strong."[43] It is obvious to note that the quarrel between these two visions remains with us to this day.

The new Socialist Party was as much as anything else an attempt to respond to transformed demographic and economic conditions. The Socialists and many other Americans thought the new corporations dangerous, an early (but by no means the last) anxiety over whether or not their country was developing qualities that they considered "un-American." Debs was a spellbinding orator, and under his leadership the Socialist Party established itself as a political presence across the country. In Pennsylvania, a Polish worker who spoke no English wept at a Debs speech. When queried as to how he could have understood, he replied, "He spoke to us with his hands and we understood." In 1894, in state and local elections, Socialist Party candidates received more than 40 percent of the popular vote in six states; 30 to 39 percent in six more; and 20 to 29 percent in a further seven. In 1912, voters elected 79 mayors, 1,200 municipal legislators, and 20 state legislators from the Socialist Party. Around the first decade of the twentieth century, there were more than thirty socialist newspapers in the state of Washington.[44] At the national level, however, in his five candidacies for president, Debs never received more than 6 percent of the vote, though in 1912 and 1916 his vote total number surpassed nine hundred thousand (he was in jail at the latter election).

Debs's vision was of a unified party—but it never really materialized. Among the issues it did not resolve were the distinction between native and nonnative members (many of supporters of Social Gospel were politically

43. "Solidarity Forever" was written by Ralph Chaplin in 1915 and sung to the tune of "The Battle Hymn of the Republic," available multiply but originally in the *Little Red Song Book* (repr., Chicago: Kerr Publishing, 2003).

44. See Jeffrey A. Johnson, *"They Are All Red Out Here": Socialist Politics in the Pacific Northwest* (Norman: University of Oklahoma Press, 2008), chap. 2.

sympathetic but nativist or nationalist); the distinction between craft and trade unions—as noted earlier, Gompers and the American Federation of Labor opposed the Pullman strikers; the urban-rural divide; and the race question, which he recognized but saw only as "the shriveled fruit of economic inequality."[45] It is not surprising, therefore, that their most visible successes came in the Northwest, where these issues were not so prominent. Edward Bellamy, author of *Looking Backwards*, helped Debs found the colony Equality on Padilla Bay, just off the Seattle coast. Debs and Henry Demarest Lloyd established a loosely federated group of semiutopian settlements around Puget Sound known as the Brotherhood of the Cooperative Commonwealth. The Constitution of the Brotherhood started, "Beholding the self-evident fact, patent to all the world, that the present civilization of warring interests has reached its climax of development, and that until a new social order, expressive of the central law of universal life, the brotherhood of man and the solidarity of human interests, is evolved, the course of this nation and every nation in Europe will be steadily downwards." To become a member of the commonwealth, a "good moral character" was explicitly required.[46] The language—"self-evident"—is intended to echo the Declaration of Independence: that presumption would prove not to be such, nor, contrary to those who had made the American Revolution, were Debs and his allies able to make it actual.

For all these partial successes, one can identify other problems that would beset any attempt at a third party: in particular, the presence of strong intergenerational party loyalties and in the fact that the industrial elite began to co-opt the demands of the progressive movements.[47] In 1904, for instance, Theodore Roosevelt, having inherited the presidency after McKinley's assassination, ran for reelection as a trustbuster.

Most important, America was now stretching its muscles in a new direction. In 1898, an expedition to liberate the people of Cuba from their status as a colony of Spain turned into a de facto annexation of the island after the (apparently accidental but sensationalized in Hearst's newspapers) explosion

45. Eugene V. Debs, "The Negro in the Class Struggle," *International Socialist Review* 6, no. 5 (November 1903), E. V. Debs Internet Archive, 2006, https://www.marxists.org /archive/debs/works/1903/negro.htm.

46. Brotherhood of the Co-operative Commonwealth, *Constitution* (Thomaston, ME: Secretary's Office, [ca. 1898]), University of Washington Libraries, http://digitalcollections .lib.washington.edu/cdm/ref/collection/pioneerlife/id/8882.

47. See Weinstein, *Corporate Ideal.*

of the battleship *Maine* in Havana Harbor. The imperialist fervor was soon extended to the Spanish colony of the Philippines, which was annexed in 1899.[48] For the first time, America sought to extend itself beyond the continent. Opposition was substantial, with the anti-imperialist camp comprising such diverse allies as Andrew Carnegie and William Jennings Bryan. Mark Twain, in Vienna during the Spanish-American War, after some initial enthusiasm that this might be an intervention for liberation, reacted with anger.

The question raised by the imperialist ventures reflects an unresolved quality in America's conception of itself. What is considered the idea of American citizenship is increasingly understood as existing not as an idea or standard but only in space. And the questions cannot be avoided: *Where does "America" stop? Are* there limits? The understanding of citizenship had over the course of the previous two centuries become increasingly abstract such that now it could simply mean "entitled to vote" (which still left the status of women undefined). Nevertheless, it also had remained all the while tied to the notion that America was an exceptional place designed and destined to show the world a virtuous society. Now it was perhaps to bring that society to some of the rest of the world, whether it wanted to or not. In principle, no place was not (potentially) America, with the partial exception of those lands thought to have given birth to it, in particular England. When Bryan protested to Theodore Roosevelt, a major proimperialist, about the annexation of the Philippines, Roosevelt's response was that if Bryan had not objected to the acquisition of California, he could not now object to that of the Philippines.

In most ways, Debs was without a response to these developments. Indeed, he proclaimed that "I have no country to fight for; my country is the earth; I am a citizen of the world,"[49] which effectively is no citizenship at all. Being human is centrally important, but it is not the same as being a citizen. This distinction became all the more evident with the outbreak of the First World War. Sentiment was at first strongly against participation in the war—that was the old world. Germany, however, had expanded submarine warfare against all ships of the Allies and on May 7, 1915, had sunk the British ship *Lusitania*

48. See Stephen Kinzer, *The True Flag, Theodore Roosevelt, Mark Twain and the Birth of the American Empire* (New York: Henry Holt, 2017). See the relatively sympathetic account of Taft and Theodore Roosevelt in Doris Kearns Goodwin, *The Bully Pulpit: Theodore Roosevelt, William Howard Taft and the Golden Age of Journalism* (New York: Simon and Schuster, 2013).

49. Eugene V. Debs, "When I Shall Fight," in *Appeal to Reason* (newspaper), September 11, 1915, cited in Howard Zinn, "Voice of the US Socialist Movement," *Socialist Worker*, May 21, 2004, http://socialistworker.org/2004-1/500/500_06_Zinn.shtml.

eleven miles off the coast of Ireland. The ship was carrying 128 Americans as well as many English and Canadians from New York to Liverpool; additionally, it transported some munitions, which made its exemption under the Carrier Rules dubious. (The German embassy in Washington, DC, had in fact placed newspaper advertisements warning passengers not to take the crossing.) While America remained neutrally oriented, anti-German sentiment swelled. On April 2, 1917, Germany announced a resumption of unrestricted submarine warfare; it recognized that this action would likely bring America into the war and, in what became known as the "Zimmerman telegram" of January 1917, had offered Mexico much of the Southwest in return for entering war against the United States. The telegram was intercepted and decoded, and anger spilled over against Germany.[50] On April 7, 1917, at President Woodrow Wilson's request, Congress declared war. A great reversal of opinion occurred, and many of those previously opposed to the war took up the cause of belligerence.

Debs and other socialists and their supporters remained against participation: the war was "a capitalist war for empire and markets, with workers for cannon fodder." And on June 16, Debs spoke against involvement, mentioning the war but once. He had carefully attempted to avoid breaking the law but was promptly indicted under the Espionage Act of 1912 and convicted. In his defense, he invoked the names of Thomas Paine, Thomas Jefferson, William Lloyd Garrison, and George Washington and closed with this poem by James Russell Lowell:

He's true to God who's true to man:
  Whenever wrong is done.
To the humblest and the weakest,
  'neath the all-beholding sun.
That wrong is also done to us,
  And they are slaves most base,
Whose love of right is for themselves,
  And not for all the race.[51]

Debs was sentenced to ten years in jail and nevertheless polled more than nine hundred thousand votes for president in 1920 while still incarcerated.

---

50. The literature is extensive. For a popular but still good account, see Barbara Tuchman, *The Zimmerman Telegram* (1958; repr., London: Folio Society, 2004).

51. Cited in Salvatore, *Eugene V. Debs*, 296.

He was pardoned in 1921 by President Harding, who invited him to the White House. But his health was gone, and he died in 1926 from complications of afflictions developed while in prison.

Some sense, albeit ironic, of the line of thought of which he was a legacy—and of what became of it—can be gained from this little piece of a family history. Around the turn of the twentieth century, a Polish Jewish tailor emigrated to America. He had three sons and named them Ralph Waldo Emerson Rostow, Walt Whitman Rostow, and Eugene Victor Debs Rostow. It is a matter of historical irony and of some importance to our story that despite Victor Rostow's attempt at inscribing his progeny in a progressive American genealogy, his second two sons became principal architects of the Cold War and the Vietnam War.

7

AMERICA MOVES INTO THE WIDER WORLD: THE LABOR MOVEMENT AND THE EXAMPLE OF THE USSR

And I think: Man
Has so few years
And so many problems,
It is best to UNDERSTAND each other.
WHY do we try so hard
To KEEP from understanding?
There is so little light
Each soul may offer
In the great puzzle
Of engulfing DARKNESS.
What do we seek to HIDE
That LITTLE LIGHT,
When all of them together
Flaming GOLDEN
Might make us truly
A CITY OF LIGHT
Set high on many hills.
ANNA LOUISE STRONG, "A CITY OF LIGHT,"
IN *RAGGED VERSE*

At this point in the story, it becomes necessary to separate out various elements. By the turn of the twentieth century, the overall issues confronting America concerned what response might be made to (1) the growth of radical inequalities; (2) periodic economic turmoil; (3) industrial capitalism; and (4) the change in the international sphere as represented by the response to the First World War and in particular the emergence of the Union of Soviet Socialist Republics (USSR). Race and the status of women remained perennial issues that, from the point of view of males and the white majority, simmered in the background. By the second decade of the new century, America would be, for the first time, fully immersed in global politics and confronted by another power claiming universal validity and the need to spread it.

Let me first recap where we are—what the country was before these developments required attention. I have tried to show that from the earliest days there existed languages for the legitimation of power. Over the course of the century, it mostly passed in a transformed quality from elites to claims made by and on the part of nonelites. In doing so, it became increasingly abstract and general. Those earlier languages became the grammar of contestation. Typically, when the nonelites entered the public world, they did not do so as interest groups but, as had the early elites, they attempted to speak for a vision of the public good. In great part, the voice of citizenship was originally framed in individual terms, with the important exception being the entry into the public realm of blacks, a group that had been collectively repressed. The great progressive movements of the latter part of the nineteenth century— the Grange, the Knights of Labor, Social Gospel, the Populists, and eventually the socialists—had generally understood their situation as one of a set of individuals suffering from a self-interested collective, often simply referred to as "the interests," and had worked to oppose concentrated power in the name of individual liberty. These movements were neither pluralist nor particularly liberal: theirs was a vision of the public good, framed in terms of individual independence. Over the course of the nineteenth century, the criteria for citizenship became increasingly abstract, except when they were used to exclude people (mainly blacks) from suffrage. As Alexander Keyssar has shown, the United States is the only Western country where suffrage was more restricted at the end of the nineteenth century than it was at the end of the eighteenth.[1]

There were obvious flaws in this more abstract vision. The United States entered the twentieth century unprepared for a successful way of dealing with large concentrations of private economic power; state and federal governments were weak; and there was almost no national administrative apparatus. There was no general income tax; no social security; no national banking system or regulation; no national transport system. Furthermore, there was no

1. A. Keyssar, *Right to Vote*, xxiii.

acquiescence on the part of nonelites to what one might call a "proletarian" status: the notion that one would primarily and permanently be a wage earner was neither accepted nor adequately confronted. Finally, there was no large military establishment: a professional military of any size had always been resisted. In 1890, US military forces totaled just over 38,000. By comparison, in 1900, after the Spanish-American War and with the occupation of the Philippines, that number was up to 125,000; by 1925, even after post–World War I demobilization, it was 247,000; and by 2016 it was two million, counting reserves composed of professionals and volunteers but not the state-based National Guard.[2] It was not until the 1880s that all major cities had professional municipal police forces.[3]

It is with these qualities that the United States moved into the international world, at first with the Spanish-American War.[4] This entry did not go without serious dissent. With the takeover of Cuba and the acquisition of the Philippines, there were furious debates over the question of America's imperialist ventures. An odd set of alliances evolved. William Jennings Bryan and Andrew Carnegie, for instance, found themselves in the same anti-imperialist camp, despite their disagreement on the silver question.[5] As previously noted, after his initial support of the Cuban adventure on the grounds that it was to lead to a free Cuba, Mark Twain wrote furiously against the Philippines takeover, penning several savage attacks including "The People Who Dwell in Darkness."

The proimperialism faction included, among others, Theodore Roosevelt, elected governor of New York in 1898; Senator Henry Cabot Lodge; and President William McKinley, who directed the Filipinos to accept "benevolent assimilation." The imperialists were explicit about the need for markets but also about the fact that America, in McKinley's words, was to bring the "blessings of good and stable government" to the people of the Philippines.[6] Passions ran high on both sides in America; meanwhile the Filipinos, under the lead-

2. US Department of Defense, "Department of Defense (DoD) Releases Fiscal Year 2017 President's Budget Proposal," news release no. NR-046-16, February 9, 2016, https://dod.defense.gov/News/News-Releases/News-Release-View/Article/652687/department-of-defense-dod-releases-fiscal-year-2017-presidents-budget-proposal/.

3. Samuel Walker, *The Police in America: An Introduction* (New York: McGraw-Hill, 1996).

4. There had been the Barbary wars (1801–5; 1815) where the United States and Sweden fought against state-backed North African pirates raiding merchant ships.

5. See the account of their meeting in Kinzer, *True Flag*, 98–99, 107–8.

6. Goodwin, *Bully Pulpit*, esp. chaps. 1 and 9.

ership of Emilio Aguinaldo, refused a simple acquiescence to the American takeover. The anti-imperialist Senator George Frisbie Hoar of Massachusetts, in a lengthy and eloquent address to the Senate, framed the issue as the contrast between the doctrine of buying or conquering sovereignty and that of the "Declaration of Independence."[7]

The American version of the "white man's burden" that writer Rudyard Kipling had identified as the fate of England[8] was that those peoples conquered, or rather "freed," had to be made ready for the blessings of self-determination—for an American conception of citizenship, which criteria they did not at this point meet. Indeed, contrary to the thrust of Kipling's poem, this challenge was conceived not really as a white man's—or even American—"burden" but more of a moral responsibility. Addressing Congress in 1900, Lodge practically echoed the argument of John Stuart Mill's *Considerations on Representative Government*:

The form of government natural to the Asiatic has always been a despotism. It is perhaps possible for an extremely clever and superior people like the Japanese with their unsurpassed capacity of imitation, to adopt Western forms of government, but whether the underlying conceptions— which are the only sound foundations of free institutions—can exist under such circumstances is yet to be proven, and all human experience is against the theory. Some of the inhabitants of the Philippines, who have had the benefits of Christianity and a measure of education, will, I have no doubt, under our fostering care, and with peace and order, assume at once

7. George Frisbie Hoar, "The Attempt to Subjugate a People," 5298, Internet Archive, https://archive.org/stream/attempttosubjuga00hoar#page/6/mode/2up.

8. Rudyard Kipling, "The White Man's Burden: The United States and the Philippine Islands," in http://www.kiplingsociety.co.uk/poems_burden.htm. Here is the first verse. One should note that Kipling's tone overall develops a much more complex view than a simple glorification of colonialism. Likewise, when Kipling distinguished East from West, he also said that the difference was overcome when "two strong men meet face to face."

TAKE up the White Man's burden—
Send forth the best ye breed—
Go bind your sons to exile
To serve your captives' need;
To wait in heavy harness
On fluttered folk and wild—
Your new-caught sullen peoples,
Half devil and half child.

a degree of self-government and advance constantly, with our aid, towards a still larger exercise of that inestimable privilege, but to abandon those islands is to leave them to anarchy, to short-lived military dictatorships, to the struggle of factions and in a very brief time, to their seizure by some great western power who will not be at all desirous to train them in the principles of freedom, as we are, but who will take them because the world is no longer large enough to permit some of its most valuable portions to be bare and ruined, the miserable result of foolish political experiments.[9]

This passage is completely open as to Lodge's understanding of America's role—and he was not the only one to hold such views. Several claims are made. First, the inhabitants of the Philippines will not be able to control themselves until they become the sort of persons that Americans presently (supposedly) are. The idea of being an American citizen is to be made available to those who are not yet fully capable of it, and therefore don't act like (real) Americans—this is true even of "clever" races like the Japanese. They will thus need to be educated. Second, such self-control is the defining characteristic of someone who has the virtues of American citizenship. Third, unless America shows the Philippines the way, those islands will surely fall prey to those dangers that beset the American republic in its early days—"anarchy, the struggle for power, the play of factions." Fourth, this is not precisely racism, as history both requires and makes possible that the American idea-ideal be extended to those for whom the behavior of true citizens does not exist naturally. Americans like Lodge could not accept the possibility that the American regime was not potentially universalizable: it could be, with the proper effort, extended to all: eventually *all* men can have, or can acquire, the qualities of citizens of America. It is even possible that Lodge's later opposition to the League of Nations Treaty derives from the fact that such paternalism was deemed not possible with Europe. It is not hard to see the echoes of this view still prominent in American foreign policy adventures from the late 1960s to today.

The passage is also noteworthy in that it conceives of citizenship as requiring certain qualities of personhood which, it holds, the supposedly backwards Filipinos do not (at this time) have. It thus retains the notion of criteria, but now these criteria are not necessarily available to any independent person and are denied more or less collectively to the supposedly backward races. Add evolutionary racism to Lincoln and universalization—one has Lodge: the

9. Henry Cabot Lodge, *Congressional Record*, March 7, 1900, 2621–22; see also 2618, 2627, and 2629.

science of evolution, as understood at the time, has added a new criterion for legitimacy in the political realm. Those failing to meet the criteria must be taught (and should be grateful for the lesson).

The argument of the imperialists was both old and new. It was old in that it portrayed America as particularly virtuous, the best hope for a political system of free and independent men, committed to public virtue. It was new in that it asserted both the legitimacy of extending this vision wherever the United States might choose and that most of those over whom it was to be extended were thought to be incapable of free and independent self-governing. As Roosevelt said to Bryan, "If you did not object to California, you cannot object to the Philippines."[10] Roosevelt defended American action in the Philippines as done "with sword girt on thigh, [to] preach peace, not from ignoble motives, nor from a fear of distrust of our own powers, but from a deep sense of moral obligation."[11] Expansion was a moral imperative created by the cause of peace and of being an American. American adventures in Southeast Asia and the Middle East some sixty to one hundred years later merely repeated the understanding. While other incentives are always in play, it is a serious mistake to overlook the importance of the "moral" ones.

Peoples were held to evolve and were thus at different stages of evolution. For all of the damages inflicted by the extension of Christianity,[12] this new vision lacked the Christian understanding of the equality of all people under God. Rather, the capacity for citizenship is held to be a *historically* acquired quality and, while not something for which all people are at the same stage of ability, eventually something all those capable may aspire to given sufficient evolution. As Rogers Smith put it, "Imperialists deployed liberalism, republicanism, and racism to contend that America's lucky new subjects should be tutored in enlightened civilization and self-governance."[13] The values that America was supposed to embody were to be universalized in due time, but the privileges of citizenship, such as suffrage, were, certainly for some time, to be withheld.

America had become a kind of colonial power, but one with the task of educating poor benighted souls—the "people that live in darkness," as Twain had

10. Theodore Roosevelt, *The Writings of Theodore Roosevelt*, ed. William H. Harbaugh Roosevelt (Indianapolis: Bobbs-Merrill, 1967), 47.

11. Roosevelt, *Writings of Roosevelt*, 31.

12. Herman Melville had been sharply clear about this in his first two novels, *Typee* and *Omoo*.

13. Rogers Smith, *Civic Ideals*, 429; see also 429-33 (see intro., n. 7).

savagely put it—to the supposed virtues of independence. While there was exploitation, the venture was not legitimated on that basis. Several issues have come together here. On the one hand, economic reality has radically changed. The ever-increasing dominance of wage-labor industrial capitalism and the unprecedented concentrations of wealth had placed most members of the polity in a radically insecure position, subject to the ebb and flow of the market, unable to exert any meaningful power. Second, the doctrine of "manifest destiny" that had originally served to legitimate the development of a localized virtuous polity no longer knew any bounds. Along with the Philippines, America acquired Cuba, Guam, Puerto Rico, and Hawaii.[14] (Alaska had been purchased from Russia just after the Civil War, in great part to keep Britain from acquiring it.) US military forces were actively involved in putting down the Boxer Rebellion of 1899–1901 in China, and US military garrisons remained on the Chinese mainland on a permanent basis. Third, it was becoming increasingly clear that any response to these developments, both domestic and foreign, that aimed at the achievement of any kind of political power on the part of the average citizen was going to require collective action.

WHAT WAS TO BE DONE?

Political and social movements in opposition or resistance to the changes brought about by large-scale industrialization and the concomitant inequalities of wealth and power had numerous sources, mostly homegrown. One of the most significant ones in the early part of the twentieth century was the Industrial Workers of the World—the IWW or "Wobblies." (The origin of the term "Wobblies" is unclear: for some it comes from the fact that the IWW repeatedly changed tactics; for others, it was a mispronunciation on the part of the Chinese.) The IWW was founded in Chicago in June 1905 at a convention composed of a diverse collection of socialists, anarchists, early American Marxists, and trade union activists. In effect, the IWW continued the policies of groups such as the Knights of Labor, with, however, a much stronger emphasis on a radical division of society. Where the slogan of the Knights had been "An injury to one is the concern of all," that of the IWW was "an injury

14. Hawaii had become an independent republic in 1894 and was summarily annexed by an act of Congress in 1898. The others were taken from Spain after the Spanish-American War.

to one is an injury to all." There were only two classes, one pamphlet proclaimed, a "capitalist or parasite class and a working class."[15] And, as only one
class "controls and owns the industrial necessities: to wit the means of producing the wealth of the world,"[16] it could only be opposed by one big union
of all workers. Only collectivities have significant existence: for the first time
an unbridgeable gulf is held to exist between two irreconcilable groups. In effect, the movement re-created along different lines the kind of the structural
division that the country had known with Southern theorists of chattel slavery.

Famously, in the preamble to the IWW constitution, "the working class and
the employing class have nothing in common. . . . Between these two classes
a struggle must go on until the workers of the world organize as a class, take
possession of the means of production, abolish the wage system and live in
harmony with the Earth."[17] Labor—or the ability to work—was understood
not on an individual basis but collectively. Owners were parasites—hence not
really citizens, even though they had the power. In 1915, the IWW songwriter
and organizer Ralph Chaplin wrote:

> When the Union's inspiration
> Through the worker's blood shall run
> There can be no power greater
> Anywhere beneath the sun
> *For what force on earth is weaker*
> *Than the feeble strength of one,*
> But the Union makes us strong.[18]

The individual, alone, against the forces of the elites, will lose; salvation lies
only in collective action. Chapin's 1915 lyrics for "Solidarity Forever," set to
the tune of the great civil war anthem the "Battle Hymn of the Republic," became the rallying song for the IWW. The tune itself had in turn been slightly
adapted from that of "John Brown's Body," a memorial tribute song to the
martyred radical abolitionist. It also perfectly captured for the labor movement the energy that had gone into the great struggle over slavery. What was

15. Industrial Workers of the World (IWW), *What Is the IWW? A Candid Statement of Its
Principles, Objects and Methods* (Chicago: IWW, n.d.), 3.

16. Industrial Workers of the World (IWW), *One Big Union of All the Workers* (Chicago:
IWW, n.d.), 3.

17. IWW, *What Is the IWW?*, 9.

18. Chapin, "Solidarity Forever" (see chap. 6, n. 43), my emphasis.

important was, and was only, the capacity to work. The IWW thus carried forward a vision of the individual as determined only by his (or her?) capacity to work—ironically, the same vision that Captain Charles Soule had set forth for the blacks of Edisto Island. The IWW vision in effect adopted the stance of industrial wage-labor capitalism and turned it against itself.

It is not surprising, therefore, that while the IWW proclaimed itself a "revolutionary labor union," it also insisted, in bold type, that it had *"absolutely nothing to do with political revolution or political action of any kind."*[19] Following the model of some utopian socialists, it minutely detailed the entire productive system, as illustrated in its "Structure of the Industrial System Wheel." Around the circumference are segments for each of the industries. As one moves toward the center, each industry is subdivided into its various subcomponents. What is noteworthy is that in all the elaboration of production, there is not one reference to, nor space for, anything political. "The main object" of this depiction "is to show how industries are grouped together in a scientific order."[20] The IWW takes over the "scientific" rationale for its activity. Indeed, the IWW argued, with the abolition of the wage system, it would follow that classes themselves would be abolished. An early argument as to whether the best tactics were to be centered on political action or on direct actions (e.g., strikes, boycotts) was settled in favor of the second—the winning group was led by William "Big Bill" Haywood.[21]

In the beginning of the twentieth century, the IWW had considerable success in organizing workers, especially on the West Coast of the United States.[22] Given their explicit avoidance of the political realm, much of their organizing efforts centered around fights for free speech, free speech being necessary to convince workers to join the IWW irrespective of their particular craft or trade. And, unsurprisingly, this was the venue in which they were strongly resisted by the powers they confronted. An attempt at organizing in San Diego in 1912 was broken up by the police and vigilantes with such barbarity that the report made to California governor Hiram Johnson by one Colonel Harris

19. IWW, *What Is the IWW?*, 3.

20. IWW, *One Big Union*, 9.

21. Haywood started as a socialist, campaigning with Eugene V. Debs. See Peter Carlson, *Roughneck: The Life and Times of Big Bill Haywood* (New York: W. W. Norton, 1983).

22. See the accounts in Eric Thomas Chester, *The Wobblies in Their Heyday: The Rise and Destruction of the Industrial Workers of the World during the World War I Era* (Santa Barbara, CA: Praeger, 2014), and Melvyn Dubofsky, *We Shall Be All: A History of the Industrial Workers of the World* (1969; repr., New York: Quadrangle, 1973).

Weinstock noted, "It was hard to believe that [he] was not sojourning in Russia instead of this alleged land of the free and home of the brave."[23] The May edition of the *Industrial Worker* carried a song with these lines:

> In that town called San Diego, when the workers try to talk
> The cops will smash them with a sap and tell 'em, "take a walk."
> They throw them in a bull pen, and they feed them rotten beans,
> And they call that "law and order" in that city, so it seems.[24]

Weinstock also found no violent act on the part of the IWW but nevertheless concluded that as the IWW aimed to "clog the machinery and overwhelm the city . . . such conduct cannot but merit the most extreme punishment within the law."[25] The *San Diego Tribune* pulled out all stops: "Hanging is too good for them, and they would be better off dead: for they are the waste material of creation, and should be drained off into the sewer of oblivion there to rot in cold obstruction like any other excrement."[26]

The *Tribune* clearly wanted to exclude the IWW and friends from membership in America. It is important to note here that the IWW emphasis on free speech, characteristic of all its efforts at organizing, is precisely *not* understood here as a civil liberties demand. Free speech was rather one of the criteria that made it possible to be a full active and participant member—a citizen—of America under the socioeconomic and political circumstances that had developed over the previous forty years. It was public rather than private. Today we tend to think of free speech as a right not to be interfered with by the state—a kind of negative liberty, to take up the distinction made famous by Isaiah Berlin. For the IWW, it was a positive liberty—a basic condition making possible a full citizen's activity, a precondition for attaining social justice. When later, in the 1930s and after, responding mostly to accusations of being pro-Communist, the American Civil Liberties Union (ACLU) conceived of free speech as a neutral right, hence applicable irrespective of political orientation, they were led to defend the right of the American Nazi Party to hold

23. Quoted in Jeff Smith, "The Big Noise: The Free Speech Fight of 1912, Part Eight," *San Diego Reader*, July 12, 2011, http://www.sandiegoreader.com/news/2012/jul/11/unfor gettable/#.

24. Quoted in J. Smith, "Big Noise."

25. Quoted in J. Smith, "Big Noise." Interestingly, this event appears to have been important in the radicalization of Agnes Smedley (who was there), later to be an important left-wing journalist, especially covering China.

26. Cited in Gourevitch, "Police Work" (see chap. 5, n. 49).

a march in the Illinois town of Skokie in 1977. This was a radically different, and now mainline liberal, understanding of free speech and quite at odds with the earlier position held by the IWW and others.[27]

The overall membership of the IWW is difficult to determine as turnover was very great, many workers joining at the times of strikes and then letting their membership lapse. It is noteworthy, however, how much the IWW provided initial political experiences for many people who became prominent in progressive politics in the twentieth century. These include some leaders we have already met, such as Eugene Debs, and many we will meet in the upcoming chapters of this book: Elizabeth Gurley Flynn; William Z. Foster and Earl Browder, later leaders in the American Communist Party; Roger Baldwin, founder of the ACLU; the journalist John Reed, who covered the Russian Revolution; Daniel DeLeon; Anna Louise Strong, who reported on revolutions around the globe; and many more, as well as cultural figures such as Helen Keller and Eugene O'Neill. The organization still officially exists.[28]

The response of the "establishment" was increasingly violent and widespread. Joe Hill, of whom one "dreamed [one saw] last night" as in the opening line of a famous song by Ralph Chaplin, was indicted for murder on likely trumped-up charges and executed by a firing squad in 1915.[29] Vigilante and company police forces were increasingly violent—Frank Little, a member of executive committee of the IWW, was viciously murdered in 1917 by being dragged behind a car (so violently that his kneecaps were scraped off) and then hanged. As an important organization of American labor, the IWW was effectively suppressed by 1917 under the terms of the Espionage Act. More than 160 leaders were indicted late that year, more than one hundred of whom were sentenced en masse to long prison terms in 1918. Haywood jumped bail and fled to the new USSR, where he remained until his death in 1928. It is,

27. See Laura Weinrib, *The Taming of Free Speech: America's Civil Liberties Compromise* (Cambridge, MA: Harvard University Press, 2016). See the excellent review by David Cole, in *New York Review of Books* 64, no. 5 (March 23–April 5, 2017). See the tortured attempt to criticize the ACLU on Skokie by Irving Louis Horowitz and Victoria Curtis Bramson, "Skokie, the ACLU and the Endurance of Democratic Theory," *Law and Contemporary Problems* (Spring 1979): 328–49, for a somewhat awkward argument that the Nazis should have been banned not on speech grounds but "for showing the Swastika" with all the historical baggage it carries.

28. See Wikipedia, s.v. "Category: Industrial Workers of the World Members," last modified January 19, 2016, https://en.wikipedia.org/wiki/Category:Industrial_Workers_of_the _World_members.

29. See William M. Adler, *The Man Who Never Died: The Life, Times, and Legacy of Joe Hill, American Labor Icon* (New York: Bloomsbury, 2011).

however, worth looking in a more focused fashion at one place and two events in which the IWW and its sympathizers played a key role.

The IWW and similar movements represented a change in the American conception of the criteria for citizenship. They no longer conceived of the situation on individualistic terms but in terms of a collectivity. If, in the words of the *Internationale*, the working class "has been naught," then in overthrowing that nothingness, it "shall be all." The change to a collective vision had been brewing over the course of the nineteenth century, with blacks, women, and the division of society into "haves" and "have-nots." If, however, the new vision was to gain political purpose, it would have to have some political success. Despite some early strike victories on the part of the socialists, the powers that be had mostly successfully been able to contain these tactics.[30]

WHAT WERE THE CHANCES FOR POLITICAL SUCCESS?

By the first decade of the twentieth century, Seattle, Washington, was one of the most progressive cities in America. With the defeat of populism and Western silver, it had become a focus for progressives seeking new opportunities. As noted previously, various utopian and semiutopian communities—the Brotherhood of the Cooperative Commonwealth—were established around Puget Sound.[31]

In addition to the utopians, more practical socialists of all persuasions flocked to the Northwest. The state of Washington had dozens of socialist newspapers. The 146th issue of the *Socialist* urged its readers to "Join the Party of Your Class" and carried as its cover page a bare-chested male worker swatting away the "parasites" with a hand on which was written "Your Union." Since the turn of the twentieth century, young industries and a new workforce, much of it of Scandinavian extraction, had made the West a fertile organizing ground for the IWW and other unions. The Seattle workforce was close to 100 percent unionized. On May 1, 1916, the International Shingle Weavers' Union, a member of the craft union organization, the American Federation of Labor, had called a strike throughout the Northwest. By August of that year, the strike

30. The literature is vast. See, e.g., Melvyn Dubofsky and Foster Rhea Dulles, eds., *Labor in America: A History*, 8th ed. (Chichester, UK: Wiley-Blackwell, 2010). More generally, see the website Labor History Links, http://www.laborhistorylinks.org.

31. See the excellent discussion in Gourevitch, *From Slavery to the Cooperative Commonwealth*.

had either been won or called off in almost every city except Everett, Washington, the home of the Jamison Mill. Shingle weaving was among the most dangerous of jobs: the workers had constantly to reach around the cutting blades to turn the shingles so that they were cut evenly on all sides. If the weaver did not catch cedar asthma from the dust that penetrated even the sponge tied over his mouth, it was only a matter of time until he lost a hand or even an arm to the whirling saws. On August 1, a group of thugs hired by the Jamison Mill savagely beat with ax handles the eighteen picketers walking the line. Shortly thereafter, the police in Everett began to enforce an "ordinance" passed by the city council prohibiting speechmaking downtown. As noted, since the earliest days of the labor movement, free-speech questions and the positive civil right to address groups in public had been essential issues to the unions as a practice essential to citizenly activity. The Everett ordinance was tantamount not only to shutting down union organizing but also to denying the groups an essential part of their being as citizens. With this action, the IWW joined forces with the Shingle Weavers' union.

This is the background for what became known as "Bloody Sunday," November 5, 1916, the Everett Massacre.[32] The IWW called a rally in Seattle for two in the afternoon, and the assembled crowd marched to the docks and boarded the steamer *Verona* for the thirty-mile trip up the bay to Everett. As the steamer approached the shore, the passengers could see only three men assembled on the dock. A collective vision rang out in song from the boat:

Hold the fort for we are coming.
Union men, be strong!
Side by side we battle onward;
Victory will come.

In fact, a large crowd of sympathizers and supporters had come to the docks to accompany those arriving from Seattle, but they had been kept off the dock area. One of the three men waiting for the boat was the sheriff of Everett, who forbade the arrivals from coming ashore. When the IWW men disregarded his warning and started ashore, volley after volley of rifle fire broke out from two hundred deputies hidden behind the warehouse, on an opposing dock, and in an adjoining tugboat. The IWW returned fire. Twelve Wobblies were killed or

32. Details of the event come from the Anna Louise Strong Papers and the Everett Massacre Collection, both in the Suzzallo Library, Special Collections, University of Washington.

drowned, as were two deputies; forty-seven others were wounded. All on the *Verona* were arrested and charged with conspiracy and murder. They were formally indicted on December 16, 1916. It is worth noting here that the United States has the bloodiest labor history of any industrialized nation.[33]

The trial of the first defendant, the IWW leader Thomas H. Tracy, started on March 7, 1917. Tracy was ably defended, and on May 5, after twenty hours of debate, a verdict of "not guilty" was returned. Shortly thereafter, all charges were dropped. This was a victory—most particularly for the IWW and union organizing—and more important, it seemed to signal that there were possibilities for successful progressive politics within the terms of the system.

As noted in chapter 6, on February 1, 1917, Germany had announced the resumption of unlimited submarine warfare and, after the discovery of the "Zimmerman telegram," President Woodrow Wilson appeared before Congress requesting a declaration of war. Before 1917, it was generally respectable to wish to keep America out of European wars. Indeed, most liberals, including even the mayor of Seattle, were of that persuasion. With the declaration of war, however, pacifism became illegal. Anna Louise Strong, the journalist who had been active with the IWW and had reported extensively on the Everett situation, wrote, "Nothing in my whole life, not even my mother's death, so shook the foundations of my world. . . . 'Our America' was dead. The people wanted peace; the profiteers wanted war—and got it."[34]

Strong had earned a PhD in philosophy from the University of Chicago in 1908 with a dissertation influenced by William James on "A Consideration of Prayer from the Standpoint of Social Psychology." She published several articles in academic journals. She then became active in Progressive causes such as the child welfare movement and Jane Addams's Hull House work.[35] After coming to Seattle with her Social Gospel minister father, Sydney Dix Strong, she had been elected to the school board. In 1918, consequent to her open support of the IWW and of pacifist causes, she was subjected to a suc-

33. Philip Taft and Philip Ross, "American Labor Violence: Its Causes, Character, and Outcome," in *The History of Violence in America: A Report to the National Commission on the Causes and Prevention of Violence*, ed. Hugh Davis Graham and Ted Robert Gurr (New York: Bantam, 1969).

34. Anna Louise Strong, *I Change Worlds: The Remaking of an American* (repr., Seattle: Seal Press, 1982).

35. Strong ran a series of workshops on health, sanitation, and child care, making use of interactive exhibits and film. They were apparently a great success. Her account of one of them can be found in Anna Louise Strong, *Child-Welfare Exhibits: Types and Preparation* (1915; repr., Hardcore Press, 2012).

cessful recall vote from the board. She turned to writing editorials and other material for the *Seattle Union Record*, one of the major papers in Seattle. The *Union Record* was a daily and for a time the only general-circulation newspaper owned and operated by a trade union, in this case the Seattle branch of the American Federation of Labor. The editor, Henry Ault, was a socialist and had pushed daily circulation to well over forty thousand. Anna Louise became editor of the features department, writing news analysis, detailing international developments, interviewing figures such as the suffragette Jeanette Rankin and Mikhail Grusenberg (later Borodin), a Russian colleague of V. I. Lenin, on his way back to the new USSR. The paper printed Lenin's *Soviets at Work*, his 1918 address to the Congress of Soviets. This and other pamphlets from the Russian Revolution were widely read in Seattle.[36] Strong often attended IWW meetings in the evening and, according to the informant for the Bureau of Investigation (ancestor to the FBI), she at times led the crowd in cheering for the "Bolsheviki."[37] In addition, she regularly continued to publish well-received topical poems under the pen name "Anise." One of them serves as epigraph to this chapter.[38]

There was considerable truth to her sense that the country had been turned by "the interests." A keystone of Wilson foreign policy had always been an opposition to the system of alliances he thought characterized Europe and were responsible for the Great War. It was, however, also clear to him that American commercial interests were affected by that war. Thus, in his war message of April 6, 1917, Wilson announced that "neutrality was no longer feasible or desirable where the peace of the world is involved."[39] It is important to point out that this stance did not dissociate the country from George Washington's warning about "entangling alliances" but rather asserted that American interests were being affected by the consequences of that entanglement. To preserve American independence from the world, it was thus necessary for America to reorganize the European state system such that matters like the

36. Jeremy Brecher, *Strike* (Chicago: South End Press, 1997), 120.

37. BI files on microfilm, in author's possession.

38. Anna Louise Strong, *Ragged Verse* (Seattle: Piggott Publishing, 1937). She was actually a well-published poet already. Her poetry has been the subject of analysis in a chapter of Joseph Harrington, *Poetry and the Public: The Social Form of Modern US Poetics* (Middletown, CT: Wesleyan University Press, 2002), 127–58, and discussed in Cary Nelson, *Repression and Recovery: Modern American Poetry and the Politics of Cultural Memory, 1819–1945* (Madison: University of Wisconsin Press, 1989).

39. Woodrow Wilson, *Public Papers*, 68 vols. (Princeton, NJ: Princeton University Press, 1967), 41:133.

Great War could no longer affect American commerce. In his fifth annual message to Congress, in which he recommends the extension of the state of war to Austria-Hungary, he makes clear that the aim is to renew the "possibility of free economic intercourse which must inevitably spring out of the partnership of a real peace."[40] America's move to becoming a major player in the international system is done in the name of a traditional American view of itself.[41]

The war came to an end in November 1918, and President Wilson was complexly involved in the peace conference in Paris. He urged a reorganization of the international system, a "League of Nations," such that the world be "made safe for democracy." Quietly against him were the powers of old Europe—British prime minister David Lloyd George, French prime minister Georges Clémenceau, Italian prime minister Vittorio Emanuele Orlando—all of whom hoped to retain the past state-centered balance-of-power system or at least retain control of the eventual League of Nations. A new player was also present at the table, even if not in Paris, one who oddly enough shared Wilson's vision for the need to reorganize the international system—the new USSR under the leadership of Lenin.[42] The Bolsheviks had not only managed to make a revolution in 1917 but had consolidated it and, against all predictions, put it on firm ground despite the invasion of armed forces from England and the United States, as well as a domestic civil war.

In it is in this context that an event occurred in Seattle that would be of great symbolic importance. During the First World War, the shipyard workers had accepted a no-strike agreement. As the war drew to an end, they opened negotiations. In December 1917, Charles Piez, the president of an engineering corporation, had been made manager of the Ship Board, responsible for merchant marine construction.[43] Over the course of the next year, Piez refused to engage in negotiations, realizing, no doubt, that with the end of the war, demand for ships would fall dramatically and the union's bargaining power

40. Wilson, *Public Papers*, 42:133.

41. It is thus, I think, wrong to apply European categories, such as "realist" versus "idealist" to this behavior. I resist the conclusions of George Kennan, *American Foreign Policy, 1900–1950* (Chicago: University of Chicago Press, 1951). Kennan, like Hans Morgenthau, shared much of the world view of Reinhold Niebuhr, on whom see Wilson Carey McWilliams, "Reinhold Niebuhr: New Orthodoxy for an Old Liberalism," *APSR*, December 1962, 874–85.

42. See Arno Mayer, *Wilson and Lenin: Political Origins of the New Diplomacy, 1917–1918* (New York: Meridian, 1969); see also centrally N. Gordon Levin, *Woodrow Wilson and World Politics: America's Response to War and Revolution* (New York: Oxford University Press, 1968). I am in debt here to conversations many years ago with Professor Levin.

43. See *Chicago Tribune*, December 18, 1917, page 1. This is also the day that the Eighteenth Amendment was passed by the House of Representatives to establish Prohibition.

would be greatly reduced. In December 1918, more than two-thirds of the shipbuilders' union members voted to go on strike. A telegram messenger "mistakenly" delivered a telegram from Piez intended for the Metal Trades Association (employers) to the Metal Trades Council (unions) threatening the owners with the loss of their steel allocation unless they held firm. Indignation erupted, and the workers went out on strike.

Nearly everyone among the union leadership, however, was in Chicago at a convention urging the commuting of the death sentence of Tom Mooney, an activist who had likely been framed for a bombing that he did not commit. (Pressure, both domestic and international, was such that Wilson did commute the sentence to life imprisonment; Mooney was eventually pardoned in 1934.) When word came that the Seattle workers had voted to call a general strike, the leadership rushed home and on arrival realized that they had no choice but to throw in their lot with the membership and go ahead with the strike. A general strike is a strike in which all workers participate—thus raising the question of how basic services (firefighting, medical, and other essential services) will be carried out.

Anna Louise Strong was passionately enthused and threw herself into preparations. She was certainly not responsible for the strike, but her writings informed and inspired many readers to believe that their city might lead the nation in beating the old system to dust. On February 2, 1919, a general strike committee was formed, composed of three hundred delegates from 110 unions. The strikers planned to run the city themselves: they did not want simply to stop capitalism but to supplant it. A steering committee of fifteen, among them Strong, was selected and the strike date set for February 6.

The middle and upper classes in Seattle were understandably highly apprehensive. Not only was a general strike such as this practically unprecedented in American life, but it called to mind the supposed chaos and revolution of the European countries. The *Seattle Star*, usually sympathetic toward labor issues, warned workers, "These false Bolsheviks haven't a chance to win anything for you in this country, *because this country is America—not Russia.*" Strong published a front-page editorial setting forth what the strike would accomplish.[44] For her, the workers were like pioneers, unsure of their destination but with their sights on the property and power of the upper classes rather than (supposedly) virgin land.

44. Discussion of the strike draws on T. Strong and H. Keyssar, *Right in Her Soul*, chap. 5, and the references cited there. The entire content of the editorial is reproduced there. Full disclosure: she is my great-aunt.

The editorial—"No One Knows Where"—became the most famous piece of writing to come out of the strike and remains one of the best-known documents of the American labor movement. "We are undertaking," she started, "the most tremendous move ever made by LABOR in this country, a move which will lead—NO ONE KNOWS WHERE!" Unfortunately, her pioneer enthusiasm for uncharted territory—"no one knows where"—did not help the cause of the strike. Harry Ault was supposed to have vetted the editorial only after extensive changes but let it slip through because he was overtired.

The tone of the editorial was quietly influenced by Lenin but lacked key elements. Like the editorial, Lenin had said that the future could only be thought of as a question mark and that no particular result was guaranteed in advance. He had, however, understood this in the context of a highly organized and disciplined and theoretically self-conscious party as the vanguard of the working class. No such organization existed in Seattle; if anything, the council was trying to catch up with the membership. Happily ignoring all such matters, Strong set her faith in the semiorganized "natural" instincts of the working class (who would "START it again / Bit by bit as we choose, / FIXED / In the way WE WANT IT" were lines in a poem she published the same day). Life would go on, but now the workers would be in control and, as with IWW hopes, class divisions would disappear.

The editorial had three political consequences, which together produced a devastating effect. First, it was so powerful that it impeded further discussion of the aims of the strike among the workers, the executive committee, and the labor council. Second, it served to convince the middle-class public of Settle and newspapers across the country of a "revolution" in Seattle. The issue was no longer the strike or Charles Piez's intransigence but the American system of government. Third, both the editorial and the attack from the mainstream press (and those for whom it was the press) shared the sense that the issue now was between two different historical visions: America and the USSR. It is no wonder that the 1920s saw a substantial influx of Americans to the USSR, all eager to help the cause and learn lessons for their home country.

It was thus only a short step to the conclusion that the strikers were Bolsheviks and anarchists. The *Seattle Star* ran an editorial entitled "Under Which Flag?" From early on, the reality of the USSR made it possible for those in power to categorize their opponents as foreigners: this was a new development. The IWW had divided America into two irreconcilable classes, but each remained, in some sense of the term, "American." Now those opposing the dominant forces were not simply in opposition—they were considered actual or de facto members of an enemy power. This vision of American citizenship excluded Americans on the grounds that they were "really" foreigners. The debate was reframed from one between two visions of America to one between a vision of America and of a foreign power.

In point of fact, the strike actually went wonderfully well for several days. Sixty-five thousand workers went on strike (the total population of Seattle was around 250,000). Thirty thousand meals a day were served in public dining halls; ambulances and fire engines were allocated to appropriate committees. Milk was delivered. Order was preserved and services maintained. There was no violence. The only problem was that with no need to step up or even maintain ship production now that the war was over, the government could easily afford to let things drag on. On the fifth day, the executive committee recognized this and voted, thirteen to one, to call off the strike. The general strike committee, however, turned down that recommendation and continued the strike a few more days.[45] It was then abandoned—it turned out that "no one knows where" was all too real.

For Anna Louise Strong and others like her, the defeat of the "reds" was due to the power of the dominant class interests. She also concluded that intelligence or goodwill could not be counted on to educate those who had less vision or who were scared or selfish. She thought she had lost the chance to claim America for herself simply by force of example, effort, and goodwill. It thus made sense to look for instruction to the land where revolution appeared to have succeeded. If the triumph of right and virtue—the "revolution"— had not occurred in Seattle, it must be because, as the *Star* had said, this was America and not Russia. Her writing after the strike showed a much-increased interest in the USSR. Perhaps, then, one should learn from the new Soviet Union.

It was not hard to come by news of the events in the Soviet Union. Lenin's writings were widely circulated; a Soviet ship, the *Shilka*, had arrived in port, the sailors having been instructed by Lenin himself to carry the news of the new Soviet world to the Seattle workers. Progressive reporters who had been to the new USSR drifted though Seattle on lecture tours: Raymond Robins,

---

45. Details on the Seattle strike from History Committee of the General Strike Committee, "The Seattle General Strike of 1919," Prole.Info, http://www.prole.info/texts/seattle 1919.html. This account was written by Anna Louise Strong and is deemed generally accurate if clearly sympathetic to the strikers. See also Robert Friedheim, *The Seattle General Strike* (Seattle: University of Washington Press, 1964), which draws heavily on the History Committee report. See also "Seattle General Strike Project," Seattle Civil Rights and Labor History Project, University of Washington, http://depts.washington.edu/labhist/strike /index.shtml.

Louise Bryant, Wilfred Humphries, Albert Rhys Williams, most of them sympathetic non-Communist observers of the Bolshevik Revolution. Strong spent long hours with each of them and established a Bureau of Russian Information.

The leadership of the strike was placed under arrest in April and indicted as attempting to "incite, provoke and encourage resistance to the United States . . . by presenting and purporting to advance the interests of laborers as a class and give [them] the complete control and ownership of all property . . . through the abolition of all other classes of society described as 'capitalists' [or] as the 'master class' . . . and of using the post office to distribute indecent and unmailable matters."[46] Strong posted a two-thousand-dollar bond. The indictment, however, went nowhere. As evidence came in, it became clear that not only had order been maintained—there were no deaths and no violence (as Mayor Ole Hansen himself admitted in a series of lectures on "domestic bolshevism" he gave around the country, earning thirty-eight thousand dollars[47])—but that the leadership had been a restraining force. Furthermore, the prospect of losing forty thousand labor votes from the Democratic Party to a newly formed *Union Record*-backed Farmer-Labor Party was sufficient threat for strings to be pulled, and the case was dropped in January 1920.

What was to be done now? People from around the world came through Seattle. Strong often interviewed them for the *Union Record*. The newspaper, however, was becoming increasingly dependent on advertisers who exerted a quiet and steady pressure as to editorial policy. Strong's reputation as a "red" was firmly established. At one point, people who had been her friends suggested that the paper might be better off without her. At this point, early in 1921, Lincoln Steffens revisited Seattle. After a visit to the USSR, he had written an article for the *Nation* in which he proclaimed that he had "been over into the future and it works." He was nineteen years older than Strong, and after his last Seattle visit, their names had been linked for a short while. Now they met as friends, and he spoke to her of a Soviet Union where, Steffens claimed, there was "no government and no police force . . . [and] . . . there was order."[48] Steffens told her that she had no chance of reconciling the quarreling

46. A copy is in the Anna Louise Strong archives, University of Washington.

47. See Brecher, *Strike*, 120.

48. The phrase comes from an article Steffens published in the *Nation* and is cited here from Peter Hartshorn, *I have Seen the Future: A Life of Lincoln Steffens* (Chicago: Counterpoint, 2011), 315.

factions on the *Record*. There was an alternative: she could go to the USSR as a social worker and reporter.

The suggestion brought clarity: if one could not find the solution to problems in and from the United States, then it made sense to go where they apparently been found. In May 1921, Strong wrote to her father, "The only people who can get any real fun out of life are either the frankly selfish folks who don't care what happens to the world, and the real Bolsheviks who see quite clearly that the Revolution is coming tomorrow to make all things right."[49] Then she left. On her voyage over, she picked up reporter's credentials from *Hearst's International* as well as from a few other organizations. By August 1921, she was in the USSR. There was, she noted later, "no further West to go, so I went to Moscow."[50] The image is telling: the USSR was the new American frontier—unfinished, rough, but full of hope.

For a significant portion of the progressive elements in American politics, the Soviet Union had come to represent a possible future course. The Socialist Party had not progressed; the IWW had either failed or effectively been repressed; spontaneous popular movements such as the Seattle strike had shown themselves to be without adequate organization or a clear sense of goal. Yet what the Soviets were doing seemed to work. Theirs, however, was the course of another country and one which a significant portion of the American public and most of the political elite found to be "un-American." Socialists, anarchists, syndicalists, Bolsheviks—these were all pretty much rolled into one big threat—Bureau of Investigation records make no differentiations: a threat that was furthermore perceived as dominated by foreigners. At one point, a certain amount of nativism had been associated with progressive politics—Josiah Strong and the Social Gospel movement are obvious cases in point. Now nativism became associated with a willingness to put down progressive politics, anything that smacked of "socialism, anarchism, syndicalism, Bolshevism." What has changed is that a significant portion of the political progressive movement now either identifies with or seeks instruction from another country, one that a large portion of the American population views at best with suspicion and more usually as an outright danger, as, in the phrase that would become standard, "un-American." The term "un-American" had hitherto been generally used to designate activities that were seen as contrary to the spirit and project of America. Theodore Roosevelt had said it referred

49. T. Strong and H. Keyssar, *Right in Her Soul*, 81.
50. T. Strong and H. Keyssar, *Right in Her Soul*, 81.

to "government by a plutocracy."[51] "Un-American" now becomes associated with those whose loyalty is to another country. In essence, increasingly those who opposed the dominant interests were often thought not to be citizens at all.

The American elites that were supportive neither of the more radical labor movements nor of the USSR were, however, not unaware that the United States was having serious problems integrating a whole new set of people. While these elites generally remained content to overlook any question about blacks, profiting from the fact that repression in the South seemed mostly to have that situation under control (they thought), there remained the question of women and that of the mass of new immigrants. These latter were mostly white but rarely spoke English and came from countries where they often had held progressive social views. Women did not pose an immediate problem as most of the pressure there came from groups that still showed some white, middle-class self-restraint. But the immigrants were often sympathetic to socialism and were mostly poor, often unemployed—a mass that was likely to coalesce into a radical social movement.

No one caught this concern on the part of the elites as well as Herbert Croly in *The Promise of American Life.*[52] Croly contrasted the "pioneer Democrat," who "disliked specialization" and was "essentially an all-round man . . . a person . . . expansive in feeling, who was enough of a businessman successfully to pursue his own interests, and enough of a politician to prevent an infringement or perversion of his rights. He never doubted that the desired combination of business man, politician, and good fellow constituted an excellent ideal of democratic individuality."[53] This vision of the "pioneer period," however, had been not only undermined but in fact effectively dismantled by "economic forces making for specialization and organization in all practical affairs," and then by the rise of great fortunes consequent to changes in the economic basis. Croly went on to note that "the failure of the Federal government to protect the public interest . . . has greatly accelerated the organization of American industries on a national scale, but for private and special purposes."[54] This government failure has led to the development of "political specialists," in particular the "Boss," referring here to the rise of the great urban "ma-

51. Theodore Roosevelt, "Theodore Roosevelt Quotes," AZ Quotes, https://www.az quotes.com/quote/1232809.

52. Herbert Croly, *The Promise of American Life* (1909; repr., New York: Da Capo Press, 1986).

53. Croly, *Promise of American Life*, 103.

54. Croly, *Promise of American Life*, 113.

chines," who become "rulers of the community, even though they occupy no offices and cannot be held in any way publically responsible."[55] Croly was, however, equally worried about "the most serious danger to the American democratic future which may issue from aggressive and unscrupulous unionism," which gives rise to "a profound antagonism between our existing political system and what the unionists consider to be a perfectly fair demand."[56]

America, Croly argued, confronted a "problem which the earlier national democracy had expected to avoid—the social problem."[57] This was not simply the consequence of the inequalities of wealth but rather "the problem of preventing such divisions from dissolving the society into which they enter—of keeping such a highly differentiate society fundamentally sound and whole.... [The] social problem demands the substitution of a conscious social ideal for the earlier instinctive homogeneity of the American nation."[58] The aim is not to change the system but to mitigate its problematic consequences.

The problem was the changed environment; hence the solution—"social engineering," Roscoe Pound called it—was to change the environment and to do so "scientifically." This change was to be accomplished by freeing men from their atavistic attachment to small groups, clans, and corporations. Break up the machines; eliminate monopolies and trusts; make it impossible for any one group to make comprehensive claims on the loyalty of any individual.[59] This was, as Croly wrote, "scientific management," a scientific management, I might say, joined to a kind of neo-Madisonianism. Croly took the term "scientific management" from Frederick Taylor, who used it to designate a rational and ruthlessly efficient way to organize production, such as that found in the Ford automobile factory and later parodied by Charlie Chaplin in *Modern Times*. Felix Frankfurter, then at Harvard Law School and later to become a Supreme Court justice, wrote with twelve of his colleagues, a "Report upon the Illegal Practices and the Unites States Department of Justice," attacking the *manner* in which the Palmer Raids were carried out. They did not do this so much in defense of the radicals targeted by the raids but on procedural grounds and ineffectiveness. "There is no danger of revolution so great as

55. Croly, *Promise of American Life*, 125. Interestingly, in his seminal "Politics as a Vocation," Max Weber picks up on the importance of the boss. See David Owen and Tracy B. Strong, eds., *Weber: The Vocation Lectures* (Cambridge, MA: Hackett, 1995).

56. Croly, *Promise of American Life*, 126–29.

57. Croly, *Promise of American Life*, 139.

58. Croly, *Promise of American Life*, 139.

59. I am influenced here by McWilliams, *Idea of Fraternity in America*, 489, and take the Pound citation from him.

that created by suppression, by ruthlessness and by deliberate violation of the simple rules of American law and American decency."[60] A concern for procedure replaces a concern for substance. The presumption is that the procedures supposedly guaranteed by the Constitution will be, if enforced, adequate to the new economic and social environment.

As change in the social environment was producing problems, the basic idea motivating Progressivism was that the solution came in changing the environment, consciously, by enforcing correct procedures. This is the period of the growth of settlement houses, such as those run by Jane Addams in Chicago (with whom Anna Louise Strong had worked for a while) and Lillian Wald in Henry Street in New York City. They sought to provide new immigrants, mostly women, with the knowledge and means to become a version of a white lower-middle-class American. Cleanliness, education, how to take care of children, shopping, a general concern with child welfare—these movements were often supported by rich liberals who saw in them, not unreasonably, a way to stave off demands for socialism.[61] Likewise, the craft unions of the American Federation of Labor, under the leadership of Samuel Gompers, were working out a cooperative mode with industry.[62] The basic premise was that since industrialization had produced a progressive isolation of individuals one from another, artificial means to produce social cohesion had to be developed. Such was the premise behind the education theory of, for instance, John Dewey. In *The School and Society* (1900), *The Child and the Curriculum* (1902), *Democracy and Education* (1916), and other writings, Dewey presented a vision of a school as an "embryonic perfect community" that would educate students to the requirements of democracy now that it could no longer be expected that their immediate environment would do so.

A change in the environment, however, could only result from the activity of the state rather than from individual effort. Citizenship, it now appears, *has to be taught*, at least to those new and apparently unwashed immigrants. Dewey found that developments in society had been such that they no longer made citizenship available (not an impossible conclusion); he hoped that schooling would take its place. As this notion develops, it becomes a vison of the management of industry and the political realm by qualified profession-

60. Felix Frankfurter et al., *Report upon the Illegal Practices and the Unites States Department of Justice* (repr., New York: Workers Defense Union, 1920), 8.

61. See e.g., the report of the success of one of her exhibits and films in Anna Louise Strong, *Child-Welfare Exhibits*.

62. See Weinstein, *Corporate Ideal*.

als. The period marks the beginning of the study of "public administration" as a science and a rise in the importance of universities and the study of social science. Woodrow Wilson was a political science professor before entering politics and the author of a standard text, *Congressional Government*, the first edition of which was published in 1884. By the time of the fifteenth edition in 1900, Wilson noted the vast increase in executive power and the possibilities for a different kind of leadership that it made possible.

Croly's central image of the political leader is tellingly that of the *architect*, who by the excellence of his designs will "have gradually created his own special public. He will be molding and informing the architectural taste and preference of his admirers. . . . The case of the statesman, the man of letters, the philanthropist or the reformer does not differ essentially from that of the architect."[63] Thus, a mainstream response to the problems caused by the economic and social transformations was to develop a vision of rule by the knowledgeable elite. Except for periodic elections, politics was seen as too important and, more significantly, too complex to be left to the people. The people neither needed nor had, to reverse Bryan's phrase, the right to make their own mistakes. Politics had become a *professional* sport, as it were, and this is an important change. During the nineteenth century, the average tenure of a House of Representatives member was just under two years; in the twentieth century, it quickly rose to about ten years. The Senate followed the same pattern of increasing time of service, modified by the longer election cycle.[64] In effect, active participation in politics had become a profession.

These changes came rather quickly. Citizenship was no longer a natural corollary to freedom and independence: it had to be taught. The situation for

---

63. Croly, *Promise of American Life*, 444–45.

64. See Matthew E. Glassman and Amber H. Wilhelm, *Congressional Careers: Service Tenure and Patterns of Member Service, 1789–2017* (Washington, DC: Congressional Research Service, 2017), 3: "During the 19th century, the average service of Representatives remained roughly constant, with only 12 Congresses having an average service greater than 3.0 years and just one Congress having an average service less than 1.5 years. Additionally, there appears to be little or no change over time; the average years of service was slightly higher for the first half of the century than during the second. During the 20th century, the average years of service for Representatives steadily increased, from an average of just over four years in the first two Congresses of the century to an average of approximately 10 years in the three most recent Congresses. The average years of service peaked at 10.3 years of service in the 102nd Congress (1991–1992) and was also 10.3 years of service in the 110th and 111th Congresses (2007–2008 and 2009–2010)." Incumbents are generally reelected at an 84 percent rate. As of 2017, seventy-nine members of the House had been in service for at least twenty years.

the new immigrants was similar to that thought necessary for the Filipinos under American rule, except for the fact that the immigrants were among the rest of the population and potentially formed a restless mass movement. And when citizenship has to be taught, one needs teachers—teachers who can be taught to teach a particular vision of being American. By the early twentieth century, the professionalization of American politics was well under way— amateurs should stand aside and watch. There seemed to be nothing else to do.

8

WHITHER PROGRESSIVE POLITICS?

Innumerable force of Spirits armed,
That durst dislike his reign, and, me preferring,
His utmost power with adverse power opposed
In dubious battle on the plains of Heaven
And shook his throne. What though the field be lost?
All is not lost—the unconquerable will,
And study of revenge, immortal hate,
And courage never to submit or yield:
And what is else not to be overcome?
JOHN MILTON, *PARADISE LOST*

Beasts of England, beasts of Ireland
Beast of every land and clime
Come and raise the glorious tidings
Of the golden Future Time.
GEORGE ORWELL, *ANIMAL FARM* (PARODY OF
"THE INTERNATIONALE")

With the defeat or repression of certain elements of Progressive politics and the general increasing professionalization of the dominating political class, it was not unexpected that American Progressives might look to the country where politics committed to a vision of social justice, as they thought, had actually succeeded. For all the talk of "revolution" in America, it had not come about. Revolution had triumphed, however, in the new Union of Soviet Socialist Republics (USSR). And for many observers, there appeared to be a natural

affinity between the two countries in that they both conceived of their particular pursuit of domestic virtue to be applicable on a universal scale.

In terms of the possibility of "revolution," however, the most salient major
difference between the two countries was not the development of a professional political elite but the existence in the USSR of a disciplined professional
revolutionary *party*. Professionalization of politics was taking place in America, but in the service of a modified capitalist system. In 1919 Germany, Max
Weber, in his great lecture "Politics as a Vocation," discussed politicians and
politics only in terms of professionalization. To enable the pursuit of Communism, Soviet leader V. I. Lenin had organized the Communist Party as a
professional organization: to be a Communist Party member was to have a job,
like being a doctor or a lawyer, requiring training, and, as with all vocations,
to be a Communist meant one had to fulfill certain professional requirements.
Above all, one must not be what Lenin called "a wretched amateur."[1] Such
a party was, very clearly, what had been lacking in Seattle—they were all in
some sense *amateurs*—nor had the various other movements considered here
ever managed to professionalize themselves in this manner. The consummate
"professional" in the 1896 elections was undoubtedly Mark Hanna. As we saw
in chapter 7, if the Leninist party was a party of professionals, a somewhat
parallel development was taking place in America but in service of the dominant forces. And, in both countries, professionalization easily became a claim
to authority, and the claim to authority almost always backed itself up with
power.

The elements of a professional party were worked out in detail by Lenin
(whose *Collected Works* extend to forty-five volumes). They include the idea
of a *line*—that once a particular policy had been decided on, supporting it was
required of all members. Hence, such parties were subject to *discipline*—each
member was expected or could be required to hold to the line. The line could
of course change, and disciplined concomitant change was expected of all
members. Decisions about what the line was at any particular time were to be
arrived at by *democratic centralism*—after discussion and debate and analysis.
In actual practice, members tended to defer to the most prestigious figures,
most particularly to Lenin himself. (An analogy that is helpful is to think of the
party as somewhat analogous to an industrial firm: once it has been decided
to produce a particular product, all members of the directorate are expected

1. See my detailed discussion of these matters in Tracy B. Strong, *Politics without Vision:
Thinking without a Banister in the Twentieth Century* (Chicago: University of Chicago Press,
2013), chap. 4.

to support the production and marketing of that product or to resign.[2]) A final element was that there would be times before the seizure of power during which the party was generally to function in a *covert* manner.

The announced aims were appealing. In 1903, Lenin wrote, "We want to achieve a new and better order of society: in this new and better society there must be neither rich nor poor; all will have to work. . . . The working people must enjoy the fruits of their common labor. Machines and other improvements must serve to ease the work of all and not to enable a few to grow rich at the expense of millions and tens of millions of people. This new and better society is called a *socialist* society."[3] If one was not of the elite in America, thoughts like these would be appealing and familiar. After the revolution of 1917, Communist parties were formed all around the world to provide a model for how to realize change. The Communist Party of the United States of America (CPUSA) was established in 1919 in Chicago. By 1922, most major countries had at least an embryonic Communist Party, most often actively encouraged, instigated, and advised by agents from the USSR. Even parties that were spontaneously locally formed (such as the Chinese one, in 1921) soon requested and received a delegate from Moscow (in the case of China, Mikhail Borodin [Grusenberg]). These parties in general looked to Moscow for guidance—not out of a feeling of subservience but more from the sense that the Soviet Communists had something to teach them. Max Schachtman, an early member of the CPUSA (and later a strong critic), recalled the following:

> When I first reached the border of Russia the train stopped for customs and I saw the first Red soldier I had ever seen in my life outside of a moving picture or a photograph. A young peasant in his teens, you know, parading up and down with his rifle right under the big arch that's marked in four languages "Proletarians of the World Unite." It was a shattering experience. . . . We all felt inadequate as compared with those enormous figures. . . .
>
> On the question of control from Moscow: The party had taken a decision: Then [Leon] Trotsky pressed us and the decision was reversed. This was not pressure. This wasn't something that the party membership considered as a policy imposed upon it which it was reluctant to accept. At

2. See Alfred G. Meyer, "USSR, Incorporated," *Slavic Review* 20, no. 3 (October 1961): 369–76.

3. V. I. Lenin, "To the Rural Poor," *Collected Works*, vol. 6 (New York: International Publishers, 1967), 366.

that time the authority of the Communist International, that is to say of the leaders of the CI who were the Russian comrades was inconceivably invulnerable. It was overwhelming. It was taken for granted that it would decide and that would be the correct policy. . . . Some people who have written about it look at it as a sign of docility or stupidity of the Communist Party members. The elements of ignorance were there and the elements of uncriticalness . . . but there were other elements as well. You have to bear in mind that in the earlier years of the Communist movement most of its policies proved absolutely wrong in the eyes of the membership. Authoritative attention had been called to the falsity of the American party's position by the leaders of the CI [Communist International]. They had, so to speak, straightened out the American movement and not simply by decree, but by persuasion, by argument. I have already told that at one time it was regarded by the majority of the Party as a gospel that a revolutionary part in the US must be an underground party, it can't be a legal party—this was changed around by the CI.[4]

It is clear that at least in a general way, the official *aims* of Communist parties, and of the American party in particular, were not completely incompatible with the vision of citizenship that the groups described earlier in this book had espoused. Nevertheless, in that American Communists took direction as a matter of course from the Soviet party—Moscow was commonly referred to by Communists as "Rome"—their tactics were not those of independent individualism but rather an acknowledgement of and subservience to the authority of those deemed (and proven) expert. It will thus be important to see how the Communists were, on several occasions, to attempt to take over historically validated notions of American citizenship.

As the twentieth century proceeded, there developed two standard arguments about the CPUSA in relation to "Americanness."[5] The first is that it was a subversive party, dedicated to the overthrow of the American Constitution, run by a relatively small group of leaders, and, while dangerous, never in its own name had much broader public influence. What influence it did have was generally from covertly duping groups ("fronts") disposed to foster sympa-

4. Max Schachtman, Oral History, Columbia Center for Oral History Archives, Butler Library, Columbia University.

5. The literature is immense. See Wikipedia, s.v. "Bibliography on American Communism," last modified August 14, 2017, https://en.wikipedia.org/wiki/Bibliography_on _American_Communism.

thetic causes. This was the view of J. Edgar Hoover, director of the Federal Bureau of Investigation (FBI), and the FBI spent many manpower hours in surveillance of these leaders; it eventually brought many of them to trial and blacklisted many others.[6] (It is worth noting that by 1957, some sources estimate that 50 percent of the card-carrying members of the CPUSA were agents for the FBI.[7])

The second standard argument about the CPUSA in relation to "Americanness" is that the CPUSA was always a fringe group, not really part of the American tradition and that what influence it had was limited to dupes and naive do-gooders, never a serious danger except for the FBI. Thus *Life* magazine would in 1949 publish a spread of photos of "50 dupes and fellow travelers," including Albert Einstein, Leonard Bernstein, and Katherine Hepburn.[8]

I think both of these understandings are mistaken—though neither is without some ground. I want to argue that the Communist Party of the USA was in part the inheritor of the Progressive movements we have examined and that it *was* important politically, even if its understanding of the relation between itself and the American tradition was complex, at times confused, and eventually lost. It is the case that many Communists and sympathizers had strong attachments to this tradition. Daniel DeLeon, member of the Social Labor Party and for a while of the Industrial Workers of the World (IWW), published a book, *Madison and Karl Marx*, in which he tried to link the German to the American tradition. Various Christian groups found hope for the evangelization of Protestant Christianity in the changes brought about by the Bolsheviks.[9] Other groups saw both the opportunity for helping the new USSR (where a famine hit in the mid-1920s) and making money—the Russian Reconstruction Farms was an American-incorporated company that sought to bring American agricultural techniques and machinery to the Soviet farms.

6. This is also the basic understanding of the many books by Harvey Klehr, in particular *The Heyday of American Communism: The Depression Decade* (New York: Basic Books, 1984). See also John E. Haynes and F. I. Firsov, *The Secret World of American Communism* (New Haven, CT: Yale University Press, 1995).

7. See, e.g., Branko Marcetic, "The FBI's Secret War," *Jacobin*, August 31, 2016, https://www.jacobinmag.com/2016/08/fbi-cointelpro-new-left-panthers-muslim-surveillance/; and esp. Ward Churchill and Jim Vander Wall, *Agents of Repression* (Cambridge, MA: South End Press, 2002), chap. 2.

8. In 1980, I spoke with one of them, Stephen Fritchman, pastor of the First Unitarian Church of Los Angeles (a left-leaning church, to be sure), and he had the spread framed above his fireplace.

9. See F. W. Burnham, "Report on a Visit to Russia," *Christian Evangelist*, August 1925, 1370; Karl Borders, "Modernism in Maslov Kut," *Christian Century*, January 1926, 75-77.

As Ellen Schrecker has written, "It [the CPUSA] was for a long time tied to the Soviet regime" but was also "the most dynamic organization within the American Left during the 1930s and 1940s."[10] For many Americans in search of an active Progressive politics, the Soviet Union became a kind of mecca. Men and women arrived, eager to help in the building of socialism and to take those lessons back to their homeland. Julia Mickenberg observed that "while most Americans greeted the Bolshevik Revolution with skepticism and even fear, a large swath of activists, idealists, and cultural arbiters, many feminists among them, had a very different reaction."[11]

What was the appeal? It was diverse. Vivian Gornick saw some of it:

> [There was] a larger need to which Marxism ever spoke and which the Communist Party ever embodied: the need within the human spirit to say no to the judgment of man upon man that is the politicalness of life. Nothing in the twentieth century has spoken as compellingly—with such power and moral imagination—to this need as has Communism; nothing in modern times has so joined the need with the real and the ideal to produce a university of internal experience as has communism; nothing has induced in man and women all around the world a commonly held dream of passionate proportion—one whose betrayal could never be forgiven, whose promise could never be relinquished—as has Communism.[12]

It took a while for the CPUSA to find its own path, in part because it would generally respond affirmatively to directives from Moscow. Over the period 1921–45, at least five major shifts in line occurred. From 1919 to 1922, there was merely unproductive domestic factionalism. Between 1923 and 1928, the authority of the Communist International (Comintern) took over. The ordained policy became to "bore from within"—join unions and get them to pressure the United States to recognize the USSR; amalgamate craft unions with industrial unions; organize the unorganized. From the Sixth Comintern meetings in Moscow in 1928 and until 1934, the party took a left turn on the belief that

10. Ellen Schrecker, "Soviet Espionage in America: An Oft-Told Tale," *Reviews in American History* 38, no. 2 (June 2010): 359.

11. Julia L. Mickenberg, *American Girls in Red Russia: Chasing the Soviet Dream* (Chicago: University of Chicago Press, 2017), 3. The book is an exhaustively researched study of the American women who came to the USSR, Anna Louise Strong figuring prominently among them.

12. Vivian Gornick, *The Romance of American Communism* (New York: Basic Books, 1977), 13.

capitalism was entering a crisis; it condemned socialists and entered into independent unions. With the rise of fascism, from 1934 until 1939, there was a popular front in a common struggle against fascism rather than against capitalism. The Communist Party at that point sought collective security between the United States and the USSR and entered the American Federation of Labor and the Congress of Industrial Organizations (CIO), the two most important groupings of labor unions. With, however, the 1939 Nazi-Soviet pact (about which more later), the slogan became "The Yanks Aren't Coming," and only with the German invasion of the USSR in June 1941 did it, once more, change to "Everything for Victory." Lenin said that "the locomotive of history takes many turns," and most American Communists had little trouble staying on the train. Even with the Nazi-Soviet pact of 1939, most resignations were from intellectuals. There were fifteen verses to a satirical song popular among the Trotskyite opposition, "Our Line's Been Changed Again." Among them:

We're simply Communists devout;
Our line's been changed again.
We don't know what it's all about;
Our line's been changed again.

Bourgeois tricks we'll have to use;
Our line's been changed again.
Our women must not wear flat shoes;
Our line's been changed again.[13]

The growth of the Communist Party and its most important political impact started in the 1930s, when the main organizing technique was the establishment of various "fronts." The front was an organization, not overtly Communist, dedicated to the pursuit of a progressive goal shared by a significant range of the American citizens.[14] As these fronts developed, they ran the

13. "Our Line's Been Changed Again," video, 1:51, published December 8, 2010, YouTube, https://www.youtube.com/watch?v=t4CgFRgVoVQ.

14. See Bernard K. Johnpoll, ed., *A Documentary History of the Communist Party of the United States*, 8 vols. (Westport, CT: Greenwood, 1994), esp. vol. 5. See also David Caute, *The Fellow-Travelers: A Postscript to the Enlightenment* (New York: Macmillan, 1973). For a more conservative view, see Klehr, *Heyday of American Communism*. The 1955 Attorney General's list of front organizations numbers 301, almost all left-wing. All those subject to a draft physical in the 1960s had to fill out a form where one could check off from a similar list those organizations to which one could claim membership.

gamut of Progressive causes, causes that had often been in the forefront of the politics of the Progressive movements over the last part of the American nineteenth and into the early twentieth centuries. Among them were the following:

- *The Spanish Civil War.* The Communist Party was the moving force behind the Abraham Lincoln Brigades, in which as many as four thousand Americans participated. Fifty percent were party members; of those who fought in Spain, 50 percent died and 25 percent were wounded.[15]
- *Antimilitarism and propeace.* The American League for Peace and Democracy had half a million members and was controlled by the Communist Party with the aim of keeping America out of war. It was abandoned in 1939 with the onset of World War II.[16]
- *Civil rights.* The CPUSA was centrally active in the founding of the Southern Conference for Human Welfare, a group to which President Franklin Delano Roosevelt later appealed when he needed it to counter pressure from Southern Democrats. The CPUSA sparked the campaign to put Negro History Week into schools; pressured Branch Rickey, the manager of the Brooklyn Dodgers, to hire the first black major-league baseball player, Jackie Robinson; and was active in the campaign to ban the sale of "darky dolls," such as the cigarette lighter depicting a pickaninny that one pressed to get a light. If you were actively sympathetic to civil rights, you necessarily came into contact with Communists. Mark Naison has shown that the Communist Party had significant influence in Harlem and among blacks in general.[17]
- *Women's rights.* This was more of a contested issue in the Communist Party. Elizabeth Gurley Flynn argued regularly and forcefully in the *Daily Worker* for women's rights. Gender, however, usually took a backseat to class. Mary Inman wrote a retrospective critique of the party in 1980, entitled "13 Years of CPUSA Misleadership on the Woman Question."[18]
- *Communication and the arts.* In 1936, fifty-three prominent authors, in-

15. See e.g., Arthur Landis, *The Lincoln Brigade* (New York: Citadel, 1967).

16. See Harvey Klehr et al., *The Secret World of American Communism* (New Haven, CT: Yale University Press, 1995).

17. Mark Naison, *Communists in Harlem during the Depression* (Urbana: University of Illinois Press, 1983). See also Philip S. Foner and James S. Allen, eds., *American Communism and Black Americans: A Documentary History* (Philadelphia, PA: Temple University Press, 1987).

18. It first appeared in *Theoretical Review* 19 (November–December 1980); see Mary Inman, "13 Years of CPUSA Misleadership on the Woman Question," *Encyclopedia of Anti-Revisionism On-Line*, https://www.marxists.org/history/erol/periodicals/theoretical -review/inman.htm.

cluding John Steinbeck, Thornton Wilder, Theodore Dreiser, and Ernest Hemingway indicated that they would vote for the Communist Party and urged others to do so as well. In 1937, 150 prominent intellectuals protested the investigation by the Dewey commission of the accusations made by Moscow against the exiled Trotsky on the grounds that it interfered with the judicial processes of the USSR. The Screen Actors Guild in Hollywood was for some period in effect a front, producing pro-Soviet films such as *Mission to Moscow*, staring Walter Huston as actual American ambassador and Ann Harding.[19]

- *Military.* Beyond such groups, after 1941 many CPUSA members were knowingly hired by the Office of Strategic Services (OSS), General William J. Donovan's newly formed and integrated intelligence service (superseded in 1945 by the Central Intelligence Agency, or CIA). With the coming of the Second World War, Communists, like all others, joined the armed forces. In politics, they played a sizable role, to be discussed further in this chapter.[20]

- *Labor unions.* The CPUSA had a strong union presence, in particular in the CIO, where it is estimated that one-third of the executive committee members were either CPUSA members or fellow travelers. The CIO controlled one million workers.[21]

19. President Roosevelt approved the making of the film. Other pro-Soviet films of the time include Samuel Goldwyn's *The North Star* (1943), MGM's *Song of Russia* (1944), United Artists' *Three Russian Girls* (1943), and Columbia's *The Boy from Stalingrad* (1943), and *Counter-Attack* (1945). See the discussion in Mickenberg, *American Girls in Red Russia*, chap. 7, esp. 311–14; Beth Holmgren, "Russia on Their Mind: How Hollywood Pictured the Soviet Front," in *Americans Experience Russia*, ed. C. Chatterjee and B. Holmgren (New York: Routledge, 2013); and Harlow Robinson, *Russians in Hollywood, Hollywood's Russians: Biography of an Image* (Boston: Northeastern University Press, 2007). I owe these last two references to Mickenberg.

20. For the (censored) FBI list of twenty-three suspected Communists in the OSS, see FBI, "OSS List of Suspected Communists," Internet Archive, https://archive.org/details /1944_22sep_oss_list_suspected_communists.

21. "Fellow travelers" were not party members but were sympathetic to Communist ideals and activities. The literature on Communist involvement in American labor unions is extensive. See in particular Bert Cochran, *Labor and Communism, The Conflict that Shaped American Unions* (Princeton, NJ: Princeton University Press, 1977). The government reaction can be seen in the sixty-page report from the Committee on Socialism and Communism, which understood such unions as "the "bridgeland of a foreign power" (54); see *Communists within the Labor Movement: The Facts and Countermeasures* (Washington, DC: Chamber of Commerce of the United States, 1947), Internet Archive, https://archive.org /details/CommunistsWithinTheLoborMovementTheFactsAndCountermeasures.

By 1938, the Communist Party was a significant presence in American life.[22] Its success was due not only to the hard work of its members but also to the changes in line brought about by the general secretary, Earl Browder. With Browder, we confront the question of the relation between being an American citizen and being a Communist, a question subordinate to the broader question of the relation of being an American to the world at large.

A key point here is that the activities of the Communist Party in relation to women, blacks, and the opposition to fascism (except between 1939 and 1941) were attractive to a wide range of people. Ralph Ellison, in his great novel *Invisible Man*, spends a good deal of time showing the attraction of the party (named "The Brotherhood" in the novel) to blacks. Bigger Thomas, the protagonist of Richard Wright's novel *Native Son*, is defended (unsuccessfully) in the trial for his life by a Communist lawyer. And even those who were not immediately drawn to the CPUSA found in the policies of the New Deal an alternative to the exit strategy of Marcus Garvey.[23]

EARL BROWDER AND THE ATTEMPT AT AMERICANIZING COMMUNISM

Browder was born in 1891 to a family strongly sympathetic to the Populist cause. A bookkeeper by profession, he joined the Socialist Party and then the Syndicalist League of North America. The league, under the leadership of William Z. Foster, adopted the tactic "to bore from within." Browder failed to register for the draft in 1917 and was jailed; after release in 1920, he joined the CPUSA, which in 1927 sent him to China for two years as a participant in the Trade Union International.

During the 1920s, the American party was riven by factionalism, much of it centered around the allegiance to or rejection of Trotsky, whom the Soviet Communist Party General Secretary Joseph Stalin was actively marginalizing. By 1927, Trotskyism was declared a heresy and Trotsky was expelled from the party and exiled. In 1930, Browder was nominated for general secretary of the

22. See Maurice Isserman, *Which Side Were You On? The American Communist Party during the Second World War* (1982; repr., Middletown, CT: Wesleyan University Press, 1987).

23. See, for instance, the exceptional play by Theodore Ward, *Big White Fog* (Nick Hearn Books, 2007). See the excellent analysis in H. Keyssar, *Curtain and Veil* (see chap. 5, n. 20).

CPUSA, in great part because, having been in China, he was identified with no particular faction.

The tactics of the CPUSA had in general been premised on the expectation of an impending catastrophe, at which time the workers would rise up and seize power. The 1920s did little to confirm this expectation until late 1929, when the Great Depression hit. While this economic downturn seemed to confirm the wisdom of the adopted tactics, with Roosevelt's first election as president in 1932 and the launching of the New Deal, it began to appear to Browder that capitalism was not going to necessarily self-destruct. As general secretary, he started off by abolishing those emblems by which the Communist Party had separated itself from the rest of the labor movement and the working class in general. The party had had, for instance, a policy of separate shop newspapers—these were done away with. Browder began to be concerned with the possibilities for success *in* America rather than seeing the party as yet another participant in a worldwide revolutionary movement led from Moscow. And a new danger had taken shape, first in Italy in 1922 and then in Germany in 1933.

The sense made by Browder's vision was strongly enhanced by the success of fascism in Italy and Nazism in Germany. Whatever else the Nazis were, it was clear that they held Communists to be their major enemy. Browder offered to run as Norman Thomas's vice presidential candidate in 1936 on the Socialist Party ticket but was turned down. Thus, in 1936, the Communist Party ran Browder for president under the slogan "Communism Is Americanism of the Twentieth Century" and *also* urged that one must "defeat [Republican candidate Alf] Landon at all costs," a less-than-hidden show of support for Roosevelt and at least parts of the New Deal. During the 1936 presidential campaign, the Communist Party mounted parades in places such as Des Moines, Iowa, with posters showing Karl Marx, Friedrich Engels, George Washington, and Abraham Lincoln. It ran no candidate for president in 1944. Communists were important participants in the founding and development of the progressive CIO in 1935—John L. Lewis of the United Mine Workers (UMW), for instance, knowingly used Communist organizers. Labor showed growing success: one might note the victory of the CIO, in a forty-four-day sitdown strike, over General Motors in 1937.[24]

---

24. See essay on the Flint, Michigan, strike by Michael Walzer, *Obligations: Essays on Disobedience, War and Citizenship* (Cambridge, MA: Harvard University Press, 1982), chap. 2.

By 1936, more than 50 percent of CPUSA members were US born and eager to assert their Americanness; those who were born outside the United States anglicized their names—thus Isok Granich became Mike Gold. The support base expanded significantly—major figures including the physicist Robert Oppenheimer, soon to direct the Manhattan Project building the atomic bomb, were drawn to the progressive politics associated with the Communist Party.[25]

Browder was in fact engaged in a reevaluation of American working-class experience. Before his leadership, the line had been that all that was necessary for the pieces to click together in the final revolution was to follow the dictates of the Soviets and have the Communist Party understand itself to be the real, if to-be-realized, leadership of the working class. By the latter part of the 1930s, Browder slowly became convinced that there was nothing inherently revolutionary in the American working-class experience and that class consciousness would only arise slowly through work on many fronts. Membership had indeed risen: by the early 1940s, it was around one hundred thousand, with a possible ten thousand more in the armed services. But its influence was far greater. It is difficult to estimate the number of fellow travelers, but it was substantial and important, often in influential circles. The party was helped by the disruptions caused by the Depression, by divisions inside the American elite consequent to the rise of European fascism, and thus by growing parallel interests between the United States and the USSR.

A problem for the conception of citizenship remained—that of double loyalties. Browder, it may be said, was trying to establish the Communist Party on its own, American, feet; the Chinese were doing the same at the same time for China, as was Josip Broz Tito in Yugoslavia. The events mentioned, in particular the rise of fascism, worked to Browder's advantage. The Browder line gained further support by the fact that on May 15, 1943, the Presidium of the Executive Committee of the Communist International (ECCI), made up of the leaders of numerous Communist parties but under the control of Moscow, officially dissolved Comintern. In that document the Presidium wrote:

> But long before the war it became increasingly clear that, to the extent that the internal as well as the international situation of individual countries became more complicated, the solution of the problems of the labor movement of each individual country through the medium of some international centre would meet with insuperable obstacles.

25. See Ray Monk, *Inside the Centre: Robert Oppenheimer* (London: Cape, 2012), esp. chap. 9.

The deep differences in the historical roads of development of each country of the world, the diverse character and even the contradiction in their social orders, the difference in the level and rate of their social and political development and finally the difference in the degree of consciousness and organization of the workers' conditioned also the various problems which face the working class of each individual country.[26]

Browder was as encouraged by this development as he was by the December 1943 conference of Roosevelt, Stalin, and British prime minister Winston Churchill in Teheran. The three heads of state apparently agreed on the disposition of postwar Europe. Churchill famously established a set of "zone of influence" divisions that he shared with Stalin and to which Roosevelt did not object.[27] Churchill's percentage figures essentially gave the USSR a buffer zone, left central eastern Europe pretty much jointly controlled (or divided, depending on how one looked at it), and required the Soviets to desist in Greece—which, to the distress of the Greek Communist Party, they did, and abandoned the Greek Communists to their fate, which was not a happy one.

This is not yet the Cold War. To all appearances, the Big Three powers had come to some kind of mutual coexistence. Accordingly, in May 1944, without consultation with Moscow, Browder dissolved the CPUSA and replaced it with what he called the Communist Political Association (CPA). He conceived of it as essentially a left-wing pressure group to the Roosevelt administration, what the prominent Hollywood screenwriter and Communist Party member Ring Lardner approvingly called "a sort of educational Marxist entity." The CPA Constitution is quite clear:

THE COMMUNIST POLITICAL ASSOCIATION is a non-party organization of Americans which, basing itself upon the working class, carries forward the traditions of Washington, Jefferson, Paine, Jackson, and Lincoln, under the changed conditions of modern industrial society.

It seeks effective application of democratic principles to the solution of the problems of to-day, as an advanced sector of the democratic majority of the American people.

It upholds the Declaration of Independence, the United States Consti-

26. "Dissolution of the Communist International," Marxists Internet Archive, https://www.marxists.org/history/international/comintern/dissolution.htm.

27. UK Public Record Office, PREM 3/66/7.

tution and its Bill of Rights, and the achievements of American democracy
against all the enemies of popular liberties. . . .

It adheres to the principles of scientific socialism, Marxism, the heritage of the best thought of humanity and of a hundred years' of experience
of the labor movement, principles which have proved to be indispensable
to the national existence and independence of every nation; it looks forward to a future in which, by democratic choice of the American people,
our own country will solve the problems arising out of the contradiction
between the social character of production and its private ownership, in-
corporating the lessons of the most fruitful achievements of all mankind
in a form and manner consistent with American traditions and character.[28]

This is indeed a picture of "Communism as Twentieth-Century Americanism." Browder would even say that Roosevelt was "the only political figure
in our country whose election next November would constitute a guarantee
that the policy of Teheran will guide our country for the ensuing four years."[29]

Communism offered a promise of engaged citizenship in the pursuit of social justice. John Steinbeck, who voted for Browder in 1936, caught the mood
well: "In the jail there were some Party men. They talked to me. Everything's
been a mess all my life. Their lives weren't messes. They were working towards something. I want to work toward something. I feel dead. I thought I
might get alive again."[30] In effect, Browder tried to offer a Progressive wing
of American politics meaningful participation in the political realm; he un-
derplayed any commitment to historical inevitability and tried in practice to
ignore the authority of Moscow.

It was not to last. With Roosevelt's death in April 1945, Harry Truman became president. Truman had a history, well known to the Soviets, of strong
anti-Communism and had even proposed some years before, that after Germany was defeated, the United States should continue on to attack the USSR.
Browder nevertheless issued a statement hoping that Truman would "keep
Roosevelt's legacy." Whereas the February conference in Yalta had apparently

28. See "Constitution of the Communist Political Association," in *The Path to Peace, Progress and Prosperity: Proceedings of the Constitutional Convention of the Communist Political Association, New York, May 20-22, 1944* (New York: CPA, 1944), 47–51, https://www.marxists.org/history/usa/parties/cpusa/1944/05/0522-cpa-constitution.pdf.

29. Earl Browder, "Statement by Earl Browder on the 1944 Presidential Election," Anna Louise Strong Archives, University of Washington. See also Isserman, *Which Side Were You On?*

30. John Steinbeck, *In Dubious Battle* (1936; repr., New York: Bantam, 1961), 6.

resulted in general agreement among the Allied powers, the July conference in Potsdam showed their mutual hostility. Truman had replaced Roosevelt, and Clement Attlee of the Labour Party had replaced Churchill. Truman was much more hostile toward the USSR than Roosevelt had been, viewing Soviet behavior in Eastern Europe as aggressive and contrary to the Yalta agreements. Truman mentioned to Stalin that the United States had a powerful new weapon without being more specific—though it is likely that Stalin had been informed of the progress of the physics of the Manhattan Project by spies. The USSR was not at war with Japan. Four days after the end of the conference, the United States dropped an atom bomb on Hiroshima. Some observers have argued that Truman wanted as little involvement of the USSR with Japan as possible: in any case, Stalin declared war against Japan two days later; the United States dropped a second bomb on Nagasaki on August 9. Japan surrendered officially on August 15.

THE DECLINE OF COMMUNISM IN AMERICA

Back in April 1945, shortly after Roosevelt's death, Jacques Duclos, a French Communist Party theoretician, published an article "On the Dissolution of the American Communist Party," in the French party journal *Cahiers du communisme*. The article was actually a French translation of an article written in Moscow some months earlier and kept secret by the highest Soviet Communist Party members. The article ran for ten pages, double-columned, and concluded as follows:

> The Yalta decisions thwart these plans, but the enemies of liberty will not disarm of their free will. They will only retreat before the acting coalition of all the forces of democracy and progress.
>
> And it is clear that if Comrade Earl Browder had seen, as a Marxist-Leninist, this important aspect of the problems facing liberty-loving peoples in this moment in their history, he would have arrived at a conclusion quite other than the dissolution of the Communist Party of the United States.[31]

31. Jacques Duclos, *On the Dissolution of the Communist Party of the United States*, ed. Tim Davenport (Corvallis, OR: 1000 Flowers Publishing, 2005), Marxists Internet Archive, https://www.marxists.org/history/usa/parties/cpusa/1945/04/0400-duclos-on dissolution.pdf.

Duclos argued that the United States could not hold to the Teheran agreements because America would not be able to maintain a high level of production after the war was over. Thus a seizure of power would be necessary; peaceful coexistence would be impossible. Browder was accused of transforming a diplomatic settlement into a domestic political program and of American exceptionalism.

It is unclear why the Soviets chose to launch this printed attack. It is possible that the faction anticipating negative post-Roosevelt developments had won out and convinced Stalin of that. It is certainly likely that with the Yugoslav and especially the Chinese parties acting increasingly independently of Moscow, Stalin wanted to keep the American party from going the same route. It is also the case that the French and Italian parties had achieved enormous prestige fighting the Nazis and were garnering more than 25 percent of the vote in the 1945–46 elections: they might very well thus also decide to take an independent course. In any case, it was impossible for the American party to ignore the letter. The party met on three occasions to discuss how to respond. The FBI had bugged the party headquarters and took down the discussion.[32] On May 16, there was no resolution. A letter to Duclos was drafted saying that he was right but that the American party was doing quite well. The hostility toward Browder was led by William Z. Foster, who had been at odds with Browder since the early 1930s. On May 22, Foster told Browder that he must acquiesce to Duclos's argument. Browder, somewhat to a general surprise, insisted on his position: "An American program cannot be a reflection of the Communist movement in Europe." He told Foster that he had "no intention of becoming a zombie." Foster, stunningly, asked, "What is a zombie?" to which Browder replied, "A zombie is a modern myth about a dead person who has been raised by some magical process and walks about under the control of another mind." Browder indicated that he wanted "a workable economic program short of capitulation to capitalism" and held that it may be possible for a country such as the United States "to find the way of peaceful coexistence and collaboration with the Union of Soviet Socialist Republics within one framework, within a single world of order of nations which they jointly sustain." At a third meeting, June 4, Foster carried the day and the entire Communist Party leadership somersaulted over one another to condemn Browder. He was removed from his posts and replaced by Eu-

32. Transcript in author's possession from a Freedom of Information Act request. Thanks to Peter Irons.

gene Dennis. The following year, Browder was expelled from the party; he died in 1973.

Browder also wrote a nine-page single-spaced essay "On the Question of Revisionism" that he never published but did circulate among friends.[33] It is notable for the claim that "new and unprecedented policies enforced by governmental power . . . can save America" from an economic crisis—and will, as they are in the interest of the ruling classes but will also be so for the workers.

The Communist Political Association reverted to being a party loyal to Moscow, waiting for the final crisis of the capitalist system. It never came. Instead, in 1948, the entire leadership of the CPUSA was arrested and charged with advocating the violent overthrow of the government. They were convicted, mainly on the hearsay testimony of former party members and quotations from Marx and Lenin. Their conviction was upheld in 1951 by a 6–2 margin in *Dennis v. United States*, and the eleven defendants were each sentenced to five years in jail and a ten-thousand-dollar fine.[34] Justices Black and Douglas filed stinging dissents pointing out that there was no evidence that the Communist Party members had done anything other than express opinions and that such was protected under the First Amendment. Prosecution of second-rank members then proceeded, and the party decided to go underground, thereby enhancing even further its political isolation.

THE END OF COMMUNISM AS A POLITICAL FORCE

In effect, the Dennis prosecutions mark the end of the end of the Communist Party as a significant presence in American political life. The beginning of the end had come with the Duclos letter and the decision of the leadership to capitulate to Moscow. The threat of the party, however, remained and even gained in prominence in the minds of many Americans and in particular in that of governmental officials. Crackdowns were launched against actual and imagined threats from all sides. In late November 1947, ten prominent Hollywood producers and writers, all of whom had been members of the Communist Party at one point or another, were blacklisted for their refusal to testify before the House Committee on Un-American Affairs. They would be con-

33. Copy in author's possession. Undated, probably 1946.
34. Dennis v. United States, 341 U.S. 494 (1951), Justia Legal Resources, https://supreme
.justia.com/cases/federal/us/341/494/case.html.

victed of contempt of Congress and sentenced to prison.[35] Over the next several years, more and more entertainment figures were similarly denied work.

And the purge extended far beyond Hollywood. Frank Coe, who had been a principal architect of the postwar Bretton Woods financial agreement, was blacklisted and fired (he denied under oath having been a Communist Party member, but it is likely that his brother had been). Coe had been director of the Division of Monetary Research in the Treasury Department, the technical secretary at Bretton Woods, and later secretary of the International Monetary Fund. Out of work in the United States, he was silently recruited by the Chinese in the mid-1950s to play a prominent role in their international financial affairs. After the triumph of the Chinese Communists in 1949, almost all State Department officials with any knowledge of China were cashiered for being insufficiently pro-Nationalist.[36]

And so it went. Among the consequences, two stand out. First, all government officials with any orientation toward coexistence with the Communist states were dismissed or forced to resign. Among them were John Paton Davies and John S. Service, the State Department officials with extensive knowledge of China, who had been clear that Mao and the Chinese Communists were going to win and had advocated accommodation so as to keep China from becoming subject to the USSR. Second, and as important though frequently overlooked, the effect of the Red Scare was to shrink the more or less legitimate political spectrum dramatically. No longer was the Left, or positions associated with the Left, an available stance: one risked one's livelihood if one were even suspected of sympathies with anything Progressive. And causes that were identified with the Left—civil rights in particular—were likewise under suspicion. It was to fall to the courts to make whatever progress was made in these areas *and not to action by ordinary citizens*.

The effect of the advent of the Cold War was to reduce the range of political choices that were safely available in America. Active participation for a Progressive political cause became personally dangerous: to the degree that any progress could be made for such causes, it could not be made by ordinary citizens, at least not without exposing themselves to considerable personal political and social risk. Furthermore, and as problematic, if one was sympa-

35. See, e.g., Lester Cole, *Hollywood Red: The Autobiography of Lester Cole* (Palo Alto, CA: Ramparts Press, 1981); Victor S. Navasky, *Naming Names* (New York: Viking, 1980); and Ellen Schrecker, *The Age of McCarthyism: A Brief History with Documents* (New York: Palgrave, 2002). At least four hundred Hollywood people were blacklisted.

36. In a large literature, see in particular E. J. Kahn, *The China Hands* (New York: Viking, 1975).

thetic to such causes, one increasingly tended to allow them to be pursued by those institutions that were not easily subject to harassment. Hence one stayed more or less out of the political arena. For a long time in the 1950s and 1960s, those pushing Progressive policies focused on the courts, the US Supreme Court in particular. Racial equality was furthered by the desegregation decision of *Brown v. Board of Education* in 1954, but it was a decision from on high. Collective organization on a wide scale was felt increasingly to be unnecessary and potentially dangerous: get a good case and give it to the court.[37] It is important to note that the conservative forces in America, finding themselves relatively shut out judicially during this period, turned their energy to political organizing and research such that by the 1970s they had developed both the policies and the organization to carry out their vision of the country. The policies associated with active citizenship were gradually reduced to the more conservative and elite sections of society.

The organized progressive factions of America melted away, in part from their own doing, in part from repression, in part for conflicts that the end of World War II made almost inevitable—this all happens in the context of complex and widespread changes in the American polity, society, and economy. In the next chapter, I need to take a step back, as it were, and pick up the thread in relation to the New Deal and its aftermaths.

37. While I am somewhat critical of this tactic, an attempt to defend it has been made by Justin Driver, *The Schoolhouse Gate: Public Education, the Supreme Court and the Battle for the American Mind* (New York: Pantheon, 2017). While he may be right on civil liberty issues, he is less so, it seems to me, on civil rights ones.

9

THE POLITICS OF "AT HOME" ABROAD

They realize that in thirty-four months we have built up new instruments of public power. In the hands of a people's Government this power is wholesome and proper. But in the hands of political puppets of an economic autocracy such power would provide shackles for the liberties of the people.

FRANKLIN D. ROOSEVELT, MESSAGE TO CONGRESS,
JANUARY 3, 1936

Remember, remember always that all of us, and you and I especially, are descended from immigrants and revolutionists.

FRANKLIN D. ROOSEVELT, REMARKS BEFORE THE DAR,
APRIL 21, 1938

In the future days, which we seek to make secure, we look forward to a world founded upon four essential human freedoms. The first is freedom of speech and expression everywhere in the world. The second is freedom of every person to worship God in his own way everywhere in the world. The third is freedom from want which, translated into world terms, means economic understandings which will secure to every nation a healthy peacetime life for its inhabitants everywhere in the world. The fourth is freedom from fear which, translated into world terms, means a world-wide reduction of armaments to such a point and in such a thorough fashion that no nation will be in a position to commit an act of physical aggression against any neighbor anywhere in the world.

FRANKLIN D. ROOSEVELT, STATE OF THE UNION ADDRESS, 1941

Chapters 5 through 8 have described some of the responses both to the concentrations of wealth and to America's new presence on the international scene. It was the case that, for many Americans, the understandings of the Soviet experience and experiments (often misunderstood) seemed to provide some sense of a path by which to deal with concentrated power. I looked in chapter 8 at the attempt at confronting these issues made by the Communist Party of the United States of America (CPUSA). For reasons internal to the party, as well as consequent to its relation to the Soviet Union and to suffering from domestic repression, a significant portion of progressive American political actors was suppressed—and as we shall see in this chapter, a large segment of the political spectrum disappeared along with it. One was at risk if even named "soft on Communism." What disappeared is potentially misleadingly captured by calling it the "Left." It was rather the vision of citizenship as a quality of participation and involvement of ordinary men and women, not as experts, not as professionals. Politics in that vision was, as it were, rather to be a pickup sport, not a professional one. (I noted in chapter 7 the fact that after World War I, being a member of Congress or a senator tended to become a long-term professional job, not something that one did for a shorter period. (Lincoln had indicated that he would stay in the House for a single term—and did.)

What was clear, however, is that any successful vision of active citizenship would have to both resolve the question of relations to the Union of Soviet Socialist Republics (USSR) and develop policies that curbed private power. Only the accomplishment of these dual objectives could create and respond to the link between domestic and international experiences and overcome the isolation of America in political space and in time—from a sense of the project that had been and to some degree still remained its future. The present chapter looks at these developments in what is now seen as the more "mainstream" flow of American politics. I necessarily start back at the same period with which chapter 8 started.

The early 1920s had given rise to an America in which the central government was feared (there were, for instance, almost no national data); there was a strong association of private power with independence; a mass market had more than begun to develop; there were some efforts at benevolent corporate paternalism; unions were weak (fewer than 10 percent of nonagricultural workers were union members, while in Western Europe 25 to 40 percent were); unemployment remained below 5 percent and often half of that.

WOMEN'S SUFFRAGE

Women in the United States gained the right to vote in 1920. The success in passing the Nineteenth Amendment was consequent to a long campaign that had, despite setbacks from the US Supreme Court, been slowly gaining strength over the latter part of the nineteenth century. Partial victories had been won in some states, but from around 1915, the push for female suffrage focused increasingly on the passage of a constitutional amendment. The cause of female suffrage had been resisted on the claim that women were not capable of voting independently—a reprise of arguments that, in another form, date back to the seventeenth century. (Prior to that, except in some isolated cases such as the Swiss cantons, popular voting was not usually a central part of the political system.) Women were deemed not as intelligent as men, as properly beholden to their husbands, as financially dependent, as biblically required to be subordinate to their husbands, and so forth. Interestingly, these are versions of the criteria arguments that we have been seeing through the course of American history. In other words, the denial of suffrage to women (as it had been to blacks) was on the grounds that they did not meet the criteria that defined a citizen. The suffragette movement did not reject these criteria but rather vehemently denied their accuracy as applied to women. What is important here is that the push for women's suffrage, like that for blacks, was not so much on the grounds that it was a right or that women would contribute something different to the polity, but on the grounds that women (and blacks) were mistakenly understood as not to meet the criteria that white males at that time thought necessary for citizenship.

Central to the eventual success of the push for a women's suffrage amendment were two factors: in the cities that had well-organized political machines, the bosses, who in effect offered an early form of welfare to their supporters, came to realize that support for female suffrage would if anything help their position; they thus either withdrew their opposition or openly supported the cause. Even more significant were the consequences of the First World War. With a large number of men in military service, women had come to occupy the jobs previously the domain of men, many of which were directly in support of the war effort. With this development, the only argument that women should not vote because they could not defend the country—an ability historically seen as a qualification for citizenship—fairly quickly faded away. President Woodrow Wilson himself dropped his earlier opposition to female suffrage and even proclaimed that "this war could not have been fought . . . if it had not been for the services of women."[1] Women made fighting possible.

A combination of class support from the urban machines, the effect of the war, and interparty competition put ratification of the Nineteenth Amendment over the top in Congress and obtained the necessary ratification with positive votes in the legislatures of the states of the Northeast, Midwest, and West, though not those in the South. The amendment was finally enshrined by the affirmative vote, by a margin of one, of the Tennessee Legislature in August 1920. The *political* effect of a near doubling of the electorate was minimal, however: women voted at even a lower rate that did men; it had almost no effect on the situation for blacks in the South. The long journey from Seneca Falls brought forth no great immediate political consequences.

It did, however, have a consequence conceptually. Before the Nineteenth Amendment, one of the few remaining natural criteria that had to be met in order to have the right to vote was that one be male. I am not arguing that this was an appropriate criterion—merely that it was one. With the passage of the Nineteenth Amendment (and in the context of the existing Fourteenth Amendment), even this criterion disappeared, and voting became more and more an abstract right rather than the privilege consequent to the meeting of certain standards (though hardly ones of character or achievement in the case of being male). It did bring into public life, however, a whole set of women who either had the experience of having been political organizers or were the exemplars for the following generation. Fewer middle-class white women born in the last quarter of the nineteenth century married than before or after that period. A good number of them entered active public life (e.g., Lillian Wald, Jane Addams, Francis Perkins, Julia Lathrop, Ellen Gates Starr, Anna Louise Strong[2]) and provided an exemplar of independence that would become a model (think here of the strong independent women in the films of the 1930s, women like Katherine Hepburn, the daughter of a prominent suffragette and birth control advocate). Women were increasingly looked at differently by men: their competitive competence was undeniable. In George Cukor's *Adam's Rib* (1949), starring Hepburn and Spencer Tracy as married lawyers who wind up on the opposite sides of an attempted murder case, Hep-

1. Cited from Alexander Keyssar, *The Right to Vote* (New York: Basic Books, 2000), 175. His chapter 6 provides an excellent summary analysis of the campaigns for female suffrage.

2. See Mickenberg, *American Girls in Red Russia*.

burn brings three women to the stand in defense of the wife accused of trying to kill her adulterous husband. One is a brilliant scientist, the second a
top business administrator, and the third a weight lifter—exemplifying that
women have brains, financial acumen, and strength. Hepburn wins the case.
But in terms of actual political differences in who gets elected, changes were
slower to come, if they did at all. The first woman appointed to the Cabinet
was Francis Perkins in 1933; she served as secretary of labor for twelve years.
(The next woman appointed was Carla Hills in 1975.)

THE GREAT DEPRESSION AND THE NEW DEAL

In 1929, the bottom had fallen out of the American economy. The Great Depression, however, presented progressive forces with an opportunity to rectify this situation and to do so with a highly visible and not unpopular target.
The target was this: by 1932, the two hundred largest corporations controlled
56 percent of domestic output, while real gross domestic product (GDP) had
fallen by at least 25 percent. One could no longer claim that prosperity was
around the corner, nor that the market was self-correcting.[3] Corporate effort at paternalism (e.g., Edward Filene and credit unions; Gerald Swope and
profit sharing at General Electric) had collapsed; by 1932, manufacturing output was at 54 per cent of the 1929 level. Unemployment was about 25 percent
of the labor force[4] nationwide and at least 30 percent in New York City and
close to 50 percent in Philadelphia. President Herbert Hoover waited for the
market to correct itself. ("Yes, the market corrects itself in the end," quipped
John Maynard Keynes, "and in the end we are all dead."[5]) Promising a "New
Deal," Franklin Delano Roosevelt (nicknamed "FDR") was elected president
in 1932, winning all but five states.

Roosevelt's election led to the various acts and policies of what one might
call the "First" New Deal: the Wagner Act; the National Labor Relations Act;
the National Industrial Recovery Act, which promulgated industrial codes of

3. There is a wonderful book by John K. Galbraith on the denial of the continuing reality
of the Great Depression. See J. K. Galbraith, The Great Crash: 1929 (1955; repr., New York:
Mariner Books, 2009).

4. This probably significantly underestimates the actual percentage. See Alexander
Keyssar, Out of Work: The First Century of Unemployment in Massachusetts (Cambridge:
Cambridge University Press, 1986).

5. John Maynard Keynes, A Tract on Monetary Reform, in The Collected Writings of John
Maynard Keynes, 30 vols. (Cambridge: Cambridge University Press, 1971), 4:65.

fair competition, guaranteed trade union rights, regulated working standards and the price and transportation of certain refined petroleum products; the Tennessee Valley Authority; the repeal of the poll tax; the extension of unions to the South.[6] Most of these acts sought to empower the middle and working classes or improve their living conditions.

Overall, the New Deal was an effort to bring the United States into the twentieth century without seriously reinvigorating a traditional vision of citizenship as individual and participatory, nor empowering domestic and now international Communism. It relied on socialist-type measures: governmental planning and input-output analysis as developed by the economist Wassily Leontief, who, ironically, had begun his studies in the USSR in the early 1920s. It continued the line of thought about politics that had characterized the Progressives: *experts* were now needed to manage to manage the political system. Governance become a 365/24/7 enterprise, now made possible during the stifling summer months in Washington, DC, by the development of air-conditioning consequent to the invention in 1928 of a nonflammable, (supposedly) nontoxic chlorofluorocarbon gas known as Freon.

What the New Deal barely undertook was a remedy to the racial divide. In 1933, W. E. B. DuBois noted that America had "den[ied] equality of rights, of employment and social recognition to American Negroes, has said that the Negro was so far below the average nation in social position, that he could not be recognized until he had developed further," to which DuBois pointed out that in fact as a collective, blacks had remedied any deficiencies and the "emergence and accomplishment of colored men of ability has been un doubted."[7] Nevertheless, little or no social progress has been made. Blacks were last hired, first fired. As the New Deal developed, some relief programs did benefit blacks, though Roosevelt never pushed strongly for civil rights or even an antilynching bill. Still, about 15 percent of the Works Progress Administration workers were black (of about 350,000 individuals), and by the time that the Civilian Conservation Corps was shut down in 1938, about 11 percent were black. The Public Works Administration of 1934 did include a clause for a quota of blacks based on the 1930 census. This was about all that resulted from the New Deal policies. Eleanor Roosevelt was more actively sympathetic than her husband was, and she achieved a significant symbolic effect by setting up the 1939 performance at the Lincoln Memorial by the black contralto

6. See Ira Katznelson, *Fear Itself: The New Deal and the Origins of Our Time* (New York: Liveright, 2013).

7. W. E. B. Dubois, "On Being Ashamed of Oneself," *Writings*, 1023.

Marian Anderson, who had been denied the use of the hall of the Daughters of the American Republic (DAR).[8]

Overall, the policies of the New Deal were met with resistance, often by those who found them, not completely incorrectly, "socialist."[9] The resistance generated a counter New Deal, mainly from the Supreme Court overturning various New Deal policies as unconstitutional.[10] Frustrated, Roosevelt proposed expanding the court membership, but the proposal backfired. In 1936, however, Roosevelt was reelected president by an enormous margin. The Congress of Industrial Organizations (CIO)—the most progressive of the labor organizations—made organizing gains, mostly consequent to the 1935 Wagner Act authorization of required collective bargaining between unions and management. All this activity encouraged many observers to think further planning had to come. When, in the 1937 case *West Coast Hotel v. Parrish*, Justice Roberts switched his position on economic regulation, the Supreme Court subsequently bowed reluctantly to pressure and reversed some of the earlier anti–New Deal decisions. A new Agricultural Administration Act was passed in 1938; by 1939, 30 percent of nonagricultural workers were in trade unions. While Roosevelt centralized unprecedented power in the executive branch, he was also convinced that, as he once said, the most important task of the president was the education of the populace.

THE STRUGGLE AROUND HENRY WALLACE

What happened? There was growing resistance. The domestic endgame can be understood by focusing on the figure of Henry Wallace. Wallace had been secretary of agriculture in the 1930s and at Roosevelt's insistence was vice president in 1940. (The Democratic Party bosses had initially refused to

8. See Harvard Sitkoff, *A New Deal for Blacks: The Emergence of Civil Rights as a National Issue; The Depression Decade* (1978; repr., New York: Oxford University Press, 2008). Anderson did not sing at the Metropolitan Opera until 1955, and she was the first black performer to do so.

9. See Albert Reid, *Roosevelt and His Enemies* (New York: Saint Martin's Press, 2015).

10. The best study of these cases is Peter Irons, *The New Deal Lawyers* (Princeton, NJ: Princeton University Press, 1982). The National Industrial Recovery Act was overturned in *Schechter Poultry v. United States* (1935); the Agricultural Adjustment Act was overturned in 1936 in *United States v. Butler*, which declared the act unconstitutional for levying this tax on the processors only to have it paid back to the farmers, holding that regulation of agriculture was to be a state and not a federal power. The Tennessee Valley Authority, however, was narrowly upheld in 1936 in *Ashwander v. Tennessee Valley Authority*.

nominate him. Roosevelt simply said that in that case, he would not accept the nomination. The bosses caved.) Wallace saw the need for an international aspect to the New Deal and was explicitly concerned with America's place in the coming new international order, thinking that democracy at home would require a worldwide New Deal. Colonialism was going, but the colonial powers had little or no regard for their colonies. It was therefore important, argued Wallace, to help the poor third world countries so that they could buy the surplus production of the West as the postwar situation would dramatically cut down domestic spending and it would need to be compensated for. Wallace was not naive about the often unsavory qualities of the growing number of new third world countries, and he knew there would shortly be many more. America would need to combine domestic planning at home and the development of markets abroad, a combination that would require policies of anti-imperialism, anticolonialism, and antifascism. He supported the establishment of international development banks. Open hostility or conflict with the USSR would make all of this much more difficult, if not impossible. So at home the issues became (1) planning and (2) relations to the USSR. And, by 1940, traditional elites were already highly suspicious of Roosevelt on both matters.

It was also clear to both the Progressive and conservative sides that a consequence of the New Deal and somewhat later the war was a vastly increasing power of Washington and the federal government—and that this power would persist. The question became what to do with this power.

Two answers were proposed. In February 1941, Henry Luce, editor of *Time* and *Life* magazines, wrote a long and famous editorial in *Life* that he entitled "The American Century."[11] (One learns much about the times in seeing that the cover of that issue featured a smiling Hollywood starlet—Cobina Wright Jr, "a young New Yorker of excellent family"—in décolleté, with the caption "Hollywood Party.") In his editorial, Luce wrote that while America was "the most powerful and most vital" nation, it had been "unable to accommodate itself spiritually and practically to that fact. . . . Hence [it has] failed to play [its] part as a world power." This failure has "disastrous consequences" for America and the world. What the country must rather do now, he urged, is "exert on the world the full impact of our influences for such purposes we see fit and by such means as we see fit."

The layout of the issue carried Luce's message. Much of the first thirty-two pages of that issue of *Life* were given over to various reports on the European war, all sympathetic to the British and hostile to the Germans and their French

11. Henry Luce, "The American Century," *Life*, February 17, 1941, 61-65.

quislings. Most of the rest of the issue was given over to proper behavior at college, fashion, parties, theater, consumption, and such. The contrast was startling and no doubt intended: while life continued in America in its usual pleasant manner (for whites at least), the country was ill prepared to take up a world role. Luce's editorial came in the middle of the issue and held that it was basically better that the United States become engaged in the European war (which, of course, at that time it was not), and that when and if it did, the war would be won by America. At the end of the war, the United States would have the whole world to itself: "The American Century." The United States would be the dominant power in the world and could and should act accordingly. Luce's vision was not territorial—this was not a demand for empire but a claim that the American vision of politics and citizenship (as he understood it) was universal and should apply or be applied globally. As he wrote:

> We are not in a war to defend American territory. We are in a war to defend and even to promote, encourage and incite so-called democratic principles throughout the world. As America enters dynamically onto the world scene, we need most of all to seek and bring forth a vision of America as a world power which is authentically American and which can inspire us to live and work and fight with vigor and enthusiasm. And as we come now to the great test, it may yet turn out that in all our trials and tribulations of spirit during the first part of this century we as a people have been painfully apprehending the meaning of our time and now in this moment of testing there may come at last the vision which will guide us to the authentic creation of the 20th Century—our Century.[12]

Not without consequence, perhaps, as several commentators have noted, was Luce the son of missionaries to China.[13]

What is particularly striking about the editorial is that it was written eleven months before the country went to war. Luce *called for war* as a way of bringing American ideals to the whole world. The universalism inherent in the American conception of itself was to "promote, encourage and incite" American values around the world. His understanding of being an American has its ancestors in Theodore Roosevelt and Wilson—and as we have seen, there had been many opposed voices.

12. Luce, "American Century," 61–62.
13. The best account is Alan Brinkley, *The Publisher: Henry Luce and His American Century* (New York: Alfred A. Knopf, 2010).

The war, of course, came to America on December 6, 1941, with the Japanese attack on Pearl Harbor in Hawaii, after which the United States declared war on Japan. Against the advice of most of his staff, Adolf Hitler took a strong interpretation of Germany's pact with Japan and declared war on the United States on December 11, 1941, thereby sparing Roosevelt a difficult policy decision. Whereas Luce's editorial had been written as a directional signpost, the fact that the United States was now engaged in a war on two fronts, a war that in the long term it was, despite early setbacks, likely to win, meant that immediate serious thought had to be given as to what outcome the country should aim for. And that had been the intention of Luce's editorial.

The opposing voice came from Henry A. Wallace, then vice president of the United States. He responded the next year, on May 8, 1942, with a speech that came to be known as "The People's Century," the actual title being "The Price of Free World Victory." He advocated the policies with which he was associated and was explicitly aware of the fact that many observers would use anti-Soviet feelings to oppose those policies.[14] On the other hand, after Hitler's attack on the USSR in June 1941, America and the USSR had a common enemy.[15] Wallace saw the twentieth century as "the march of freedom for the common man. Progress in education had led to progress in production had led to progress in self-government and to the degree that this progress had been realized around the world, this century was to be for all." He continued, "Some have spoken of the American Century. I say that the century on which we are entering—the century that will come out of this war—can and must be the century of the common man. Everywhere the common man must learn to build his own industries with his own hands in a practical fashion." The vision was of international regulation in the name of a global common good—"those who write the peace must think of the whole world."

He drew to a close as follows: "The people's revolution is on the march, and the devil and all his angels cannot prevail against it. They cannot prevail, for on the side of the people is the Lord." Wallace then cited a passage from

14. For complete text, see Henry A. Wallace, "The Century of the Common Man," May 8, 1942, American Rhetoric Online Speech Bank, last updated August 5, 2017, http://www.americanrhetoric.com/speeches/henrywallacefreeworldassoc.htm. Subsequent quotations in the text are taken from this source. On Wallace, see, e.g., N. D. Markowitz, *The Rise and Fall of the People's Century: Henry A. Wallace and American Liberalism* (New York: Free Press, 1973).

15. The BBC report is worth reading: "1941: Hitler Invades the Soviet Union," BBC, http://news.bbc.co.uk/onthisday/hi/dates/stories/june/22/newsid_3526000/3526691.stm.

Isaiah 40:23 about how the Lord gives strength, and he ends with, "strong in the strength of the Lord, we who fight in the people's cause will never stop until that cause is won." The great composer (and Communist Party fellow traveler) Aaron Copland was moved to write his "Fanfare for the Common Man" later that year.[16]

Before the war, a major question at stake was whether the CIO (the most left-wing large labor group) might ally itself explicitly with a major political party. Many Republicans thought it had in effect taken over the Democratic Party. Robert McCormick, publisher of the *Chicago Tribune*, wrote in 1944:

> They call it the Democratic National Convention but obviously, it is the CIO convention. Franklin D. Roosevelt is the candidate of the CIO and the Communists because they know if elected, he will continue to put the government of the United States at their service, at home and abroad. . . . The CIO is in the saddle and the Democrat donkey, under whip and spur, is meekly taking the road to communism and atheism. . . . Everybody knows that Roosevelt is the Communist candidate, but even the Communists cannot be sure where their place will be if he wins. His purpose is to overthrow the Republic for his own selfish ambitions [but] it is the duty of every American to oppose The Great Deceiver [Roosevelt].[17]

Note the easy association of Roosevelt, the CIO, and Communists. This was not an idle fear by McCormick, for the CIO was a major force in the American political scene and a significant portion of its leadership were at least not unsympathetic to many Communist Party causes. And it was an effective political force. As Robert Cantwell had observed in the *New Republic* in 1938, "the CIO . . . has made the greatest record for practical achievement in the history of American labor."[18]

A more formal alliance of labor and much of the executive branch might have had important implications. For instance, in September 1945, the Senate approved the Full Employment bill, a version of which Roosevelt had orig-

16. Aaron Copland, "Fanfare for the Common Man," recording from Coolidge Auditorium, Washington, DC, November 4, 2000, Library of Congress, sound cartridge, 3:32, https://loc.gov/item/ihas.100010429.

17. Cited in D. M. Jordan, *FDR, Dewey, and the Election of 1944* (Bloomington: University of Indiana Press, 2011), 201.

18. Robert Cantwell, "The Communists and the CIO," *New Republic*, February 22, 1938, https://newrepublic.com/article/104585/the-communists-and-the-cio.

inally set forth in his 1944 State of the Union address.[19] This second "Bill of Rights" shows what Roosevelt and one side of the New Deal had as hopes for the American polity. It also shows what was, in their estimation, lacking for Americans at that time (and, we might note, still is). In his 1944 State of the Union Address, delivered to Congress, FDR first attacked those who thought only of their self-interest:

> There are pests who swarm through the lobbies of the Congress and the cocktail bars of Washington, representing these special groups as opposed to the basic interests of the Nation as a whole. They have come to look upon the war primarily as a chance to make profits for themselves at the expense of their neighbors—profits in money or in terms of political or social preferment.
>
> Such selfish agitation can be highly dangerous in wartime. It creates confusion. It damages morale. It hampers our national effort. It muddies the waters and therefore prolongs the war.

Against these special interests he called for a wide range of policies: a "realistic tax law" on "all unreasonable profits"; a law to take undue profits out of war contracts; a food law, placing a floor under what is paid to the farmer and a ceiling on what the consumer should pay; stabilization of prices; a national service law to prevent strikes and assure production during the duration of the war. The national service proposal reflects the notion that a citizen has obligations to his (and possibly her) country and that these obligations in return give them certain privileges and powers. "National service is the most democratic way to wage a war. Like selective service for the armed forces, it rests on the obligation of each citizen to serve his nation to his utmost where he is best qualified."

Roosevelt urged that everyone had the right

1. to a useful and remunerative job in the nation's mines, industries, farms, and shops;
2. to earn enough to provide adequate food, clothing, and recreation;
3. of every farmer to raise and sell his products at a return that will give him and his family a decent living;

19. Franklin D. Roosevelt, "1944 State of the Union Address," January 11, 1944, TeachingAmericanHistory.org, http://teachingamericanhistory.org/library/document/state-of-the-union-address-3/. All text quotations of the address are from this source.

4. of every businessman, large and small, to trade in an atmosphere of freedom from unfair competition and domination by monopolies at home or
   abroad;
5. of every family to a decent home to adequate medical care and the opportunity to achieve and enjoy good health;
6. to adequate protection from the economic fears of old age, sickness, accident, and unemployment;
7. to a good education.

The first four items of this list correspond to a vision of citizenship that had
been current since the beginning of the nineteenth century. The rest are contemporary additions, made necessary by the changing political, economic,
and social circumstances. What is significant in particular is the fact that Roosevelt and his allies recognized that these qualities had to now be guaranteed
by the state, that in the present economic and political system, they were not
and could be considered qualities attainable by independent individuals. The
national service requirement derives from the sense that in order to be a citizen, one has to make concrete one's membership in the state—that citizenship
is not a free ride. To have served one's country in some manner is thus the objective correlative of a legitimating criterion. It is also of political democratic
import. All-volunteer armies are much less likely to resist and to generate resistance to bad policies than ones that each citizen has a potential obligation to
be in or have been part of. (This was one of the reasons that President Richard
Nixon did away with the draft in 1973.)

Domestically, there was considerable support. Unionization had reached
more than 30 percent of the nonagricultural workforce. The Wagner Act of
1935 had authorized and required collective bargaining. Lines were clearly
drawn. These issues—domestic democratic planning and relations with the
USSR and the less-developed countries of the world—were the major ones that
confronted the United States as the war came to an end. There were important ancillary factors. Domestic politics brought a new scope to union power.
There had been a no-strike pledge during the war (overly enthusiastically supported by the CPUSA after 1941). An effect of this pledge was that there was
not much practical experience with what exactly collective bargaining would
entail. At the end of the war, there occurred a set of major strikes, which the
CPUSA helped organize. In November 1945, labor and business met. Labor
refused to list *any* functions that would belong exclusively to management.
Among the demands at the United Auto Workers (UAW) strike at General

Motors (GM) were a 30 percent rise in wages with no rise in prices and, most important, comanagement of all the decisions involving production, product development, pricing, and distribution. This last set of demands manifested the desire by the workers to have some say not only over their pay but also over production itself—the emblem of independence. Comanagement is now understood *as an essential part of* what it means to be able to sell one's labor-power. Charlie Wilson, head of GM and later secretary of the treasury under President Dwight D. Eisenhower, responded by saying that this was "an idea from east of the Rhine." It was not the first time, and would not be the last, that association with Communism was used as a reason for denying a demand. I do not think this association was ad hoc: those who raised the threat of Communism were authentically convinced that it was a threat, and many people in the CIO were Communist Party members or sympathizers.

In effect, what the UAW was demanding and what Roosevelt was proposing in his 1944 State of the Union Address was that citizenship entail certain qualities of life, qualities that would be manifest by serving in the military or as a participant in some national service system, by a substantial safety net guaranteeing fairness, and by having some control over what one produced. The effect of this legislation, had it become reality, would have been to undercut the basically abstract and automatic conception of citizenship that had been inserted into the national consciousness by the Fourteenth Amendment.

Roosevelt's 1944 proposals were, however, strongly opposed as paternalistic, socialistic, and Communistic by much of the House of Representatives and by business—and because they would cut into profits. It does not stretch matters too far to suggest that FDR had adopted the position of John Winthrop and that his opposition adhered more to that of Roger Williams—the past lives on as the present. Roosevelt put forth a Full Employment bill (a kind of planned expansion), which, after his death, passed the Senate by a vote of 71-10. The Democrats had a majority of thirteen in the House, but sixty of those seats were from the Deep South. In conjunction with the chamber of commerce, the House thus rewrote the bill to advocate tax cuts rather than planning and reduced the emphasis on government spending. It took out the claim in the original bill that employment was a right; it replaced "full employment" with "maximum employment"; specific public works proposals were replaced by urging the use of "all practical means." At stake was the role of the government in the establishment of citizenship qualifications. Any emphasis on government spending and planning was reduced or eliminated, and there was no emphasis on reducing inequality.

WHO WILL SUCCEED ROOSEVELT?

Even if they specifically materialized later, all of these issues were part of the political climate when Roosevelt came up for reelection in July 1944. His failing health was obvious to both parties: the most important question was thus as to who would be vice president. Labor and the Old New Deal wanted Wallace to remain as vice president. Southern Democrats and the urban machines wanted someone else. Racial questions were also centrally important: the urban machine bosses worried that Wallace's support for racial equality would lead the Southern Democrats to split off and that this would in turn weaken the machines and possibly defeat Roosevelt.[20] The CPUSA, astonishingly, was noncommittal, even saying that "a less controversial candidate [than Wallace] might help unify the country."[21] Roosevelt was approached by various Democratic Party leaders opposed to Wallace and told that his nomination would split the party. Roosevelt was publicly silent, and this silence was taken as lack of support for Wallace. The president wrote a letter that was leaked in which he indicated that he would accept Senator Harry S. Truman or Supreme Court Justice William O. Douglas. Truman, it must be said, was the junior senator from Missouri and as such the product of the Pendergast machine, which controlled, in particular, Jackson County, site of Missouri's largest city, Kansas City.[22] When Truman first ran for the Senate, in 1934, Jackson County announced its totals in the primary only after all the other counties had registered their votes. Truman was at that point 96,000 votes behind. Jackson came in at 137,000 for Truman and 1,500 opposed. Democrats carried the actual election easily and Truman became senator.

After 1942, the Democrats retained majorities, albeit somewhat smaller ones in the House and the Senate, but as a substantial bloc were Southerners, those sympathetic to the New Deal were no longer a majority. The Southern Democrats eliminated the Farm Security Administration and the Civilian Conservation Corps in 1942-43. The anti-New Dealers and most of the Northern urban machines were hostile to Wallace. In addition to reelection

20. See again Katznelson, *Fear Itself.*

21. See Thomas W. Devine, *Henry Wallace's 1948 Presidential Campaign and the Future of Postwar Liberalism* (Chapel Hill: University of North Carolina Press, 2013).

22. See the marvelous movie about such machine politics by Robert Altman, *Kansas City* (1996).

fears, Roosevelt probably was mindful of the need of the support of Southern Democrats for the coming United Nations proposal.

Wallace, as vice president, seconded the nomination of Roosevelt at the July 1944 convention with an uncompromising social and economic justice speech. He was almost swept in by acclamation.[23] The Wallace forces knew this was their one chance and tried to stampede the nomination. Edwin Pauley, treasurer of the Democratic National Committee and the head of the anti-Wallace Democrats, actually ordered the power leads to the organ cut with a fire ax so as to stop the twenty-five-minute-plus pro-Wallace demonstration. The initial vote was 429.5 to 319.5 in favor of Wallace. This result lacked 159.5 votes for a majority, those votes going to favorite sons. Pauley (with the help of Clark Clifford, a top Truman aide) called for an adjournment and gaveled it as "passed," despite a manifest lack of support from the floor and just seconds before Senator Claude Pepper was able to approach the rostrum to make a motion to nominate Wallace by acclamation. The Truman forces regrouped. The next vote on the morrow was 475.5 to 473, still for Wallace, but then realignments and shifts were announced and Truman won, 1,031 to 105, going on to win the presidential election. Wallace was made secretary of commerce, and Congress promptly removed the Reconstruction Finance Corporation[24] from his control. War plants were sold off to private industry. Roosevelt died on April 12, 1945. Had he died several months earlier, Wallace would have become president.

Wallace was centrally concerned with the place of America in the coming new international order, hence his reply to Luce. He argued that democracy at home—hence the possibility of a democratic citizenry—was now dependent on how America dealt with the developments that were sure to come out of the Second World War. Colonialism, he saw, was on its way out. The countries that had had colonies manifested little or no concern with their colonies after liberation. Only four countries in Africa were self-governed in 1945; over the course of the twentieth century around the world, forty-five more countries gained independence from Britain alone. Wallace proposed that the rich Western countries help the poor countries develop so that they could become

---

23. See R. H. Ferrell, *Choosing Truman: The Democratic Convention of 1944* (Columbia: University of Missouri Press, 1994). See David McCullough, *Truman* (New York: Simon and Schuster, 1992).

24. Its powers had been expanded during World War II, and it had merged with the Federal Deposit Insurance Corporation. During the war, it established eight new corporations and purchased an existing one.

markets for the surplus production in the rich countries. As noted, he was aware the third world countries were often corrupt and their use of aid and frequently dictatorial: what was unusual was that whereas most either only saw a need for planning at home or rejected planning at all in favor of open markets, Wallace wanted to combine democratic planning at home with planning abroad.

This sort of combination would have entailed a foreign policy that was not only antifascist but also anti-imperialist and anticolonial. He proposed the reestablishment of International Development Banks. For these policies to work, however, it was essential that America avoid a confrontational interaction with the USSR—partnership at home and abroad was necessary. The coexistence agreements at the Tehran conference thus seemed to have moved in the right direction.

As noted, while Wallace was not alone in these policies, he was also strongly opposed. In 1941, the then Senator Truman famously had said that "if we see that Germany is winning we ought to help Russia, and if Russia is winning we ought to help Germany, and that way let them kill as many as possible although I don't want to see Hitler victorious under any circumstances."[25] In 1941, the Joint Chiefs of Staff were quite prepared to give Asia to the Japanese and Europe, except for the United Kingdom, to the Germans. By 1940, additionally, traditional American elites were increasingly suspicious of Roosevelt on both planning and the matter of relations with the USSR.

The preceding account has sketched out the domestic factors that shape the context in which the Cold War was to develop and the concomitant gradual reduction of a role for an active citizenry. I need now to turn to the interplay of these factors with the international situation. More than ever before, what transpired internationally came to shape the American idea of citizenship.

THE POLICY OF THE USSR

During World War II, the United States, Great Britain, and the Soviet Union— the three major Allies—had agreed on joint three-power military occupation of all the conquered territories. Although there were multiple nonobservances of agreements, the United States was the first to break the agreement during the war by allowing the USSR no role in the military occupation of Italy. Despite this serious breach of agreement, Soviet premier Joseph Stalin generally

25. As quoted in the *New York Times*, June 24, 1941.

displayed a consistent preference for the conservative interests of the Russian-led nation-state as opposed to pushing a revolutionary ideology—in particular, he repeatedly betrayed or curbed indigenous Communist movements.

Apparently to preserve peaceful relations between the USSR and the West, Stalin consistently tried to hold back the success of certain Communist movements. He was successful in France and Italy, where Communist partisan groups profiting from the legitimacy of a major role in the Resistance might have tried to seize power in the wake of the German military retreat; Stalin ordered them not to do so and instead persuaded them to join coalition regimes headed by anti-Communist parties. In both countries, the Communists were soon ousted from the coalition. In Greece, where the Communist partisans almost *did* seize power, Stalin irretrievably weakened them by abandoning them and urging them to turn over power to newly invading British troops. The conservative forces in Greece massacred most of the Communists.

In other countries, particularly ones where indigenous Communist partisan groups were strong, the communists flatly refused Stalin's requests. In Yugoslavia, the victorious Josip Broz Tito refused Stalin's demand that Tito subordinate himself to the anti-Communist General Draza Mihailovich in a governing coalition. And in China, Mao Zedong refused a similar Stalin demand that he refrain from finally defeating the Chinese Nationalist Party leader Chiang Kai-shek: Stalin had urged that the Communist army's advance stop at the Yangtze River. Lu Ding Yi, the head of the Central Propaganda Department of the Chinese Communist Party (CCP) in Yen'an and a top Central Committee figure, told me in 1980 that the CCP had received no military support from the USSR and, with a smile, noted that at key times when the CCP was making decisions of import, the radio contact between Moscow and Yen'an would mysteriously go bad. He was still angry at the Soviets. There is no doubt that these rejections were the beginning of the later, extraordinarily important schisms within the world Communist movement. Truman openly expressed the widely shared attitude, however, that all Communist parties and countries took their orders from Moscow. (There has always been an unanswerable question as to what could have been done in those times between the United States and Yugoslavia and China and Vietnam—places with successful and indigenous communist movements?)

The USSR, therefore, governed Eastern Europe as military occupier after winning a war launched against it through those countries. The USSR's initial primary goal was probably not so much to communize Eastern Europe on the back of the Soviet Army but to establish the reality that Eastern Europe could not be the broad highway for another future assault on Russia—such had been the case three times in a century and a half, the last time in a war in which more than twenty million Russians had been slaughtered. This policy also required a Western Europe that was basically neutral. It is worth noting that the Soviets were suspicious that the West had worked out an agreement with the Germans such that Western forces would occupy most of Germany. During the last stages of the war, German resistance in the East to the advancing Soviet troops was much surprisingly stronger than it was in the West to the Western Allies, something Stalin pointed out in a letter to Roosevelt on April 7, 1945.[26] (On the other hand, Germans may have simply been more receptive to the Western allies than to the Soviets.)

It is also the case that as the war was coming to an end, some elements in the USSR leadership seemed open to some kind of coexistent relations with the United States. In 1945, Soviet foreign minister V. I. Molotov indicated to the American ambassador William Harriman that the USSR was willing to order six million dollars' worth of American goods when the war ended. He explained that with the end of war production, the United States would need new markets (sounding remarkably like Wallace). In August 1945, an article in a party paper (*Bolshevik*) indicated that "war was not irreversible under present conditions": Stalin endorsed this view the following month (and apparently the US Joint Chiefs of Staff then shared this position). I leave aside here the importance and constraint of the now generally recognized facts of the devastation of the USSR and of a Soviet military demobilization parallel to that of the United States. It is important to note, however, that in 1946 the Soviet Air Force was elevated to the status of the other armed forces.[27] None of this activity implies close friendship or even trust: it does make the situation potentially quite fluid.

In the meantime, there was a great deal of debate in the press (especially in Great Britain) about Soviet intentions. The British were especially strong on

26. For example, Stalin writes, "It is hard to agree that the absence of German resistance on the Western Front is due solely to the fact that they have been beaten. The Germans have 147 divisions on the Eastern Front. They could safely withdraw from 15 to 20 divisions from the Eastern Front to aid their forces on the Western Front. Yet they have not done so, nor are they doing so. They are fighting desperately against the Russians for Zemlenice, an obscure station in Czechoslovakia, which they need just as much as a dead man needs a poultice, but they surrender without any resistance such important towns in the heart of Germany as Osnabrück, Mannheim and Kassel. You will admit that this behavior on the part of the Germans is more than strange and unaccountable." Joseph Stalin to Franklin D. Roosevelt, 7 April 1945, "Correspondence with Franklin D. Roosevelt and Harry Truman, 1945," *Revolutionary Democracy*, http://www.revolutionarydemocracy.org/Stalin/corrv2_1945.htm.

27. See Caroline Kennedy-Pipe, *Stalin's Cold War: Soviet Strategies in Europe, 1943–1956* (Manchester, UK: Manchester University Press, 1995), 84–86.

pushing the claim that the USSR had wide ambitions, a position that became the general theme of Churchill's famous "iron curtain" speech on March 5, 1946, in Fulton, Missouri, which drew headlines in the United States as "A Lesson for America."[28]

Thus, in the immediate aftermath of the war, opinion in the United States was divided. To some considerable degree, the progressive elements had tended to insulate themselves or were insulated from the rest of the political spectrum. The situation in Europe was not clear. The USSR was busy installing pro-Soviet governments in Romania and Bulgaria as allowed under the terms of the Teheran agreement; Moscow betrayed the Greek Communists who were supported by Tito, as it did the Iranian Communists. Charles Bohlen, a senior foreign policy advisor, noted that the American diplomat George Kennan in fact suggested forgoing the United Nations Organization and simply accepting the division of Europe into spheres of influence.[29] The USSR was very anxious to remain the "Rome" for the Communist movement. Mao came to Moscow and after an initial meeting or two was kept waiting six weeks for any kind of agreement.[30]

At this point, there were coalition governments in Hungary and Czechoslovakia; elections were indeed held in which the Communists got less than

28. Churchill said, among other things, "The United States stands at this time at the pinnacle of world power. It is a solemn moment for the American Democracy. For with primacy in power is also joined an awe-inspiring accountability to the future.... Opportunity is here now, clear and shining for both our countries. To reject it or ignore it or fritter it away will bring upon us all the long reproaches of the after-time.... Before we cast away the solid assurances of national armaments for self-preservation we must be certain that our temple is built, not upon shifting sands or quagmires, but upon the rock." He went on to say that the dangers are war and tyranny. The United States' sole possession of atomic weapons made war unlikely, and such would not be the case if the USSR had them. To deal with tyranny, he called for a "fraternal association of the English-speaking peoples" explicitly to be military, without which the "dark ages may return, the Stone Age may return on the gleaming wings of science." He argued that "it is my duty however, for I am sure you would wish me to state the facts as I see them to you, to place before you certain facts about the present position in Europe. From Stettin in the Baltic to Trieste in the Adriatic, *an iron curtain has descended across the Continent* ... I do not believe that Soviet Russia desires war. What they desire is the fruits of war and the indefinite expansion of their power and doctrines" (my emphasis). Full text can be found in several places online.

29. C. E. Bohlen, *Witness to History, 1929–1969* (New York: Norton, 1973), 176 (thanks to Kennedy-Pipe). Bohlen was generally more in favor of accommodation with the USSR than was Kennan.

30. See the discussion in D. Halberstam, *The Coldest Winter: America and the Korean War* (New York: Hyperion, 2007), 352–54. See the text of Mao's telegrams to the Central Committee of the Chinese Communist Party in "Mao's Moscow Visit, December 1949–February 1950," Temple University, http://astro.temple.edu/~rimmerma/Mao%27s_Moscow_visit.htm.

20 percent of the vote. Poland was a particular question in that the prewar government had fled to London (the so-called London Poles) while the Soviets had backed a resistance group centered around Lublin.[31] Poland was where the test for the future of West-East relations unfolded. As Stalin noted in an April 7, 1945, telegram to Roosevelt, "The Polish question has indeed reached an impasse."[32] Stanisław Mikołajczyk, the leader of the London Poles, returned to Poland. In a 1946 referendum, less than a third of the electorate supported Communist-backed policies of land reforms and nationalization of industry. Mikołajczyk insisted on continuing to organize a political group outside the Lublin party. Great conflicts arose, including the arrest and terrorizing of members of Mikołajczyk's People's Party. But in the January 1947 elections, the official result gave 80 percent to the Communist-led Democratic Bloc (BD, comprising the Polish Workers Party, PPR, i.e., the Communists; the Polish Socialist Party; the People's Party, SL; the Democratic Party, SD; and various unaligned groups[33]). There is strong evidence, however, that the pressure and violence imposed by the occupying Soviet forces (along with a good deal of fraud) were instrumental in producing this result. It was reported to Stalin that at most 50 percent voted for the BD. Mikołajczyk got 10 percent (28 seats to the BD's 394). Effectively these results imposed a one-party state. (Interestingly, in 1948, Władysław Gomułka, deputy prime minister and longtime member of the leadership of the Polish Communist Party, was imprisoned as harboring a "nationalist tendency" contra Stalin.) Mikołajczyk fled to England in April, where those Poles left in London accused him of being a traitor for having cooperated with Communists; he then emigrated to the United States.

HOW TO MAKE SENSE OF ALL THIS

What to make of this? How is one to make something of all this? What policy should be pursued? This detailing of history is necessary as it makes clear that

31. See D. Curp, *A Clean Sweep? The Politics of Ethnic Cleansing in Western Poland* (Rochester, NY: University of Rochester Press, 2006).

32. See "Personal and Secret from Premier J. V. Stalin to the President, Mr. F. Roosevelt," April 7, 1945, in "Correspondence between the Chairman of the Council of Ministers of the USSR and the Presidents of the USA and the Prime Ministers of Great Britain during the Great Patriotic War of 1941–1945," Document 418, Marxists Internet Archive, http://www.marxists.org/reference/archive/stalin/works/correspondence/01/45.htm.

33. Abbreviations in the parenthetical description correspond to the groups' names in Polish.

one was now in the realm of contingencies. What there was not was clarity. For instance, Averell Harrimans, who had just stepped down as American ambassador to the USSR. wrote to the US secretary of state in April 1946, "It may be difficult for us to believe but it still may be true that Stalin and Molotov considered at Yalta that by our willingness to accept a general wording of the declaration on Poland and liberated Europe, by our own recognition of the need for the Red Army for security behind its lines and of the predominant interest of Russia and Poland as a friendly neighbor and as a corridor to Germany, we understood and were ready to accept Soviet policies already known to us."[34]

Here I must ask you to put yourself in the position of an assistant or deputy assistant secretary of state for East European affairs in the American government at this time (or in the British equivalent). An agreement had been reached with the Soviets at Teheran and Yalta. Elections had been held in the westernmost of the East European countries. There was a lot of pressure and indeed violence from the Soviets, in particular in Poland. It was known that Truman was much more hostile to the Soviets than Roosevelt had been. The Soviet ambassador to the United States, Nikolai Novikov, sent a telegram to Stalin on Truman's accession to the presidency saying that he considered Truman "politically unstable . . . with certain conservative tendencies" and saw in the appointment of James Byrnes as US secretary of state a "strengthening of the . . . most reactionary circles of the Democratic Party."[35] Wallace was not only not president but was increasingly clearly marginalized. A split in the Democratic Party over the long run undercut the impact of the progressive group. Henry Stimson, a Republican and still secretary of war, had, for instance, proposed in the Truman cabinet in September 1945 that America simply share what it knew about atomic weapons with the Soviets, failing which there would be an arms race.[36] He had written twice to Truman saying that the United States should approach the USSR and "invite them into a partnership." He predicted that in any case the USSR would develop an atomic bomb within four to twenty years. Stimson warned, "Unless the Soviets are

34. "The Ambassador in the Soviet Union (Harriman) to the Secretary of State," no. 711.61/4-645: Telegram, in Foreign Relations of the United States, vol. 5, Diplomatic Papers, 1945, Europe, document 624, Office of the Historian, US Department of State, https://history.state.gov/historicaldocuments/frus1945v05/d624.

35. See "The Novikov Telegram, 27 September 1946," Brooklyn College, http://academic.brooklyn.cuny.edu/history/johnson/novikov.htm.

36. See Michael D. Gordin, Red Cloud at Dawn: Truman, Stalin and the End of the Atomic Monopoly (New York: Farrar, Straus and Giroux, 2009). The bomb will be discussed further later in this chapter.

voluntarily invited into the partnership upon a basis of cooperation and trust, we are going to maintain the Anglo-Saxon bloc over against the Soviet in the possession of this weapon. Such a condition will almost certainly stimulate feverish activity on the part of the Soviet toward the development of this bomb in what will in effect be a secret armament race of a rather desperate character."[37] On September 21, the proposal to share US knowledge of atomic weapons with the USSR was placed before the Cabinet. Wallace, Stimson, Secretary of State Dean Acheson, presidential adviser Abe Fortas, and Secretary of the Interior Harold Ickes all voted for it; nine others voted against it. Secretary of the Navy James Forrestal subsequently leaked a story that Wallace wanted to give the atomic bomb to the Russians.

Suppose that all this information is known to you as a deputy assistant secretary of state. What does the world look like to you? The Soviets appeared to have kept their promise in Greece; it was hard to care about what they were doing to their portion of Germany (indeed, the United States was doing much the same to the Western occupied zones: this was the Morgenthau plan, not officially abandoned until September 1946). The US elite is divided. Western Europe is economically unstable. Communists get more than 25 per cent of the vote in France and are in the government. They receive close to the same vote percentage in Italy in 1946. Colonial empires are collapsing. The progress of the Red Army appears increasingly unstoppable in China, Mao having ignored Stalin's request not to go south of the Yangtze River. (When the Nationalists moved their capital one last time to Guangdong in August 1949, the *only* power that went with them was the USSR.) The United States is demobilizing rapidly. I present this information chaotically on purpose to emphasize that the situation was chaotic. (The question of whether or not the USSR was also confused I must leave aside, but it is clear that were multiple dissenting voices.)

Put yourself into the American foreign policy bureaucracy. Your boss comes to you and asks something like, "What am I going to tell the president?" You ask for time to figure it out. It is at this point (February 22, 1946) that George Kennan sent the eight-thousand-word "Long Telegram" from Moscow. It identified what Kennan called the "Kremlin's neurotic view of world affairs" and the "traditional and instinctive Russian sense of insecurity." He was explicitly responding to a February 13 request from the State Department for an

37. See "Memorandum by the Secretary of War (Stimson) to President Truman," September 11, 1945, Office of the Historian, US Department of State, https://history.state.gov /historicaldocuments/frus1945v02/d13.

analysis of the situation. For Kennan, Marxism was a "fig-leaf" which led the Kremlin to view the outside world as hostile. He also referred to the Soviets' "disrespect for objective truth—indeed their disbelief in its existence." They will want to "disrupt the internal harmony" of American society, destroy our "traditional way of life," break the "international authority of our state," Kennan claimed.[38] Only in the 1947 *Foreign Affairs* "Mr X" article, but not explicitly in the "Long Telegram" as best I can determine, does Kennan explicitly advocate a policy of *containment* (to be "long-term, patient but firm and vigilant" that could take place by the "adroit and vigilant application of a counterforce at a series of constantly shifting geographical and political points").[39] There is some debate about how much military force Kennan was willing to countenance; the message though was clear—we can outlast the Soviets if we just keep them contained (thus in the "Long Telegram" he differentiated the USSR from Hitler, who worked "by fixed plans"[40]). Most of those in authority on either side did not think that a war was inevitable.

The telegram, however, must have been a godsend to officials in the various departments.[41] It made sense of everything that was going on. And it also—I do not mean to be flip—allowed you to have something to say to your boss that made sense (*a* sense) of everything. It also had consequences: Kennan did not stop with "containment" but also spoke of "an overwhelming threat to our way of life"[42]: the American government was instructed to educate the American people. It was easy to point at the possible leftish sympathies of government employees as well as to the left-wing tendencies of trade unions and political reform organizations as key Soviet tactics. And these repressive mechanisms came slowly into place. The issue was not facts: military intelligence reports from this period indicate that the Soviets were weak and potentially reasonable. But a process was started.

My point is that Kennan's telegram *was* a godsend to the bureaucrats—it

38. George Kennan, Moscow Embassy Telegram no. 511, in Office of the Historian, *Foreign Relations of the United States: 1946*, 11 vols. (Washington, DC: Government Printing Office, 1947), 6:686-709, https://nsarchive2.gwu.edu//coldwar/documents/episode-1/kennan.htm. See also George Kennan, *Memoirs, 1925-1950* (Boston: Little, Brown, 1967), 292-95.

39. "Mr. X," *Foreign Affairs* 25, no. 4 (July, 1947): 566-82.

40. Kennan, Moscow Embassy Telegram no. 511, 61.

41. See in particular Hugh Mehan, C. E. Nathanson, and J. M. Skelly, "Nuclear Discourse in the 1980s: The Unraveling Conventions of the Cold War," *Discourse and Society* 1, no. 2 (1990): 133-65.

42. Kennan, Moscow Embassy Telegram no. 511, 61.

made sense of the whole confusing and confused situation and gave a direction and a plan, even if, as Kennan later held, that as implemented, it was not always done so in a manner completely consonant with his intentions.

Kennan's telegram—or at least various understandings of it—soon became the dominant discourse for the makers of American foreign policy. On July 23, 1946, Wallace sent a memo long letter to Truman essentially questioning the Kennan telegram and raising the question of how American actions appeared to the Soviets. He urged that America "should ascertain from a fresh point of view what Russia believes to be essential to her own security as a prerequisite to the writing of the peace." He pointed out that atomic weapons were cheap and that some members of the administration were urging their use before the Russians developed theirs. Such an action, he said, would be "disastrous."[43] In September of that year, Wallace, still secretary of agriculture, gave a speech in Madison Square Garden to a rally organized by National Citizens Political Action Committee (NCPAC) and the Independent Citizens Committee of the Arts, Sciences, and Professions, called "the Way to Peace."[44] The "price of peace," said Wallace, was to give "up prejudice, hatred, fear and ignorance," by which he meant mainly of the USSR. He urged that America come to understand the "Russian character" and several times asserted that just as the Russians had no business in Latin America, so the United States had none in Eastern Europe, even when America may disapprove of what the Russians

---

43. Henry A. Wallace to Harry S. Truman, 23 July 1946, reproduced in "'Achieving an Atmosphere of Mutual Trust and Confidence': Henry A. Wallace Offers an Alternative to Cold War Containment," History Matters, http://historymatters.gmu.edu/d/6906/. For a photocopy of the actual letter, see Henry A. Wallace Correspondence, April 1956–March 1958, reel 51, Iowa Digital Library, University of Iowa Libraries, http://digital.lib.uiowa.edu/cdm/ref/collection/wallace/id/48499.

44. Quotations from the September speech in this paragraph are from *Selected Works of Henry A. Wallace*, Internet Archive, https://web.archive.org/web/20071219100614/http:/newdeal.feri.org:80/wallace/haw28.htm. The NCPAC was a progressive organization dedicated to backing the candidacies that supported the FDR New Deal; it had strong ties with the CIO. It allowed Communist participation in a kind of "united front" policy. The willingness to have Communists participate drew extensive attention from the House Committee on Un-American Affairs and eventually led to a rift inside NCPAC. The Independent Citizens Committee of the Arts, Sciences, and Professions was a CPUSA front dedicated to working in the electoral process and with wide non-CPUSA support. For its founding document with a list of the Board of Directors, see Independent Citizens Committee of the Arts, Sciences, and Professions, *January 1946–June 1946: The History of the First Eighteen Months of the Independent Citizens Committee of the Arts, Sciences, and Professions*, June 1946, University of Massachusetts Library, http://credo.library.umass.edu/view/pageturn/mums312-b110-i301/#page/3/mode/1up.

might be doing there. Over time, he argued, the two countries would come to see more eye to eye: "The Russians will be forced to grant more personal freedoms; and we shall be more and more absorbed with the problems of socio-economic justice." He said that "a large segment of our press is propagandizing our people for war in hope of scaring Russia" and called this "criminal foolishness" and urged that the control of atomic weapons be taken out of the hands of the military. He referred to "the hysteria of anti-Communism. I hear the world crying out for peace. The President is less concerned with the need of the Greek people for food than the need of the military for arms." This speech occurred in the context of the increasingly dominant vision of the USSR that had been drawn by policy makers from the "Long Telegram" and the revised version in *Foreign Affairs* early in 1947. Whether or not Kennan was read correctly (he later argued that he was not), the text certainly permitted those readings and the consequent policies.

Secretary of State Jimmy Byrnes had just given a hard-line speech known as the "Restatement of Policy" on Germany in Stuttgart, in which he made it US policy to repudiate the Morgenthau plan, which had forbidden the rearmament and heavy industrialization of Germany. He stated that the US intention was to keep troops in Europe indefinitely and expressed American approval of the territorial annexation of 29 percent of prewar Germany, but he did not condone further claims. Truman stated in a memo of September 14, 1947, that he respected Wallace's right to give the speech but that it did not constitute in any way the foreign policy of America. Wallace responded that he stood by the speech and noted that the Right had booed him on peace and the Left on his criticisms of the USSR. In any case, Truman would not stand for the public controversy and fired Wallace.

With this dismissal, no Old New Deal appointees remained in the Cabinet. Questions of foreign policy and of one's attitude toward that policy became central in the definition of American citizenship at this point. The perception of the inevitable and unrelenting hostility of the USSR to America did not lead to a relaxed attitude—the USSR not only was supposedly the enemy but also wished to wipe America and what it supposedly stood for off the face of the earth. This is the Cold War—and it is important to remember that in a war, be it hot or cold, toleration of differing points of view on matters relating to the enemy are rapidly deemed inadmissible. (We saw something similar after the outbreak of World War I.) The essential criterion defining citizenship became expressed hostility toward the USSR and Communism, domestic and foreign.

In retrospect, most commentators have tended to claim that Wallace was very naive about Soviet Communism—that he was "soft." I have cited earlier some of the debates that were going on inside the USSR about relations with the United States. We know that Communists in Vietnam, China, Yugoslavia, and elsewhere in the immediate aftermath of the war reached out to the United States, only to be rebuffed. On February 28, 1946, precisely at the time of the Kennan telegram, Vietnamese Communist leader Ho Chi Minh sent a telegram to President Truman requesting American support for Vietnamese independence in their struggle and negotiations with the French colonial rule.[45] Whether Truman ever saw it or not, it went without an answer. And the same happened with the Soviets: when the Marshall Plan was announced, Maurice Thorez, the head of the French Communist Party, was in Moscow and expressed delight with it, only to be slapped down hard.

AND THERE WAS THE BOMB

Wallace had asserted that as long as the United States continued to produce atomic weapons, it would be seen as a world bully. Expectations as to when the Soviets might develop their own atomic weapons ranged up to twenty years (by General Groves, who had been in charge of the Manhattan Project). When, however, the Soviets did explode their first bomb, in August 1949, American reaction was to authorize the development of a hydrogen-based weapon. What is most important, however, about the bomb was how it tied into the development of the political culture. During the war, the US Army Air Force (which became a separate branch of the military only in 1947) had developed plans for a system of bases, without knowing about the bomb. The Yalta conference came and went, resulting in the division of Europe. Stalin knew of the program to develop the bomb. With Roosevelt's death in April 1945, many scientists were unclear as to what to do about the bomb, especially after the surrender of Germany.[46] Truman, as we know, had no such doubts and retained no regrets for the double bombing of Japan.

There was thus a new weapon. With the end of the war, the military budget was frozen at thirteen billion dollars. The air force (still under the army) was worried about its future role. It realized that its future was assured if American foreign policy focused on containing the Soviets. Given the reduction in

45. See Ho Chi Minh to Harry S. Truman, February 28, 1946, National Archives, https://www.archives.gov/historical-docs/todays-doc/?dod-date=228.
46. See the excellent discussion in Monk, *Inside the Centre*.

defense spending, the cheapest way to have an anti-Soviet foreign policy was with atomic weapons: atom bombs are much cheaper than divisions. Only an air force, however, can deliver large atomic weapons. Bureaucratic survival coincided with the developing policy of containment.

There was an interservice rivalry concerning funds.[47] The air force, however, had a global strategy (which it could justify with Kennan) and wanted three hundred A-bombs to implement it (General Curtis LeMay, a man who never knew of an enemy target that he did not want to bomb, is here an important figure). Given the range of delivery airplanes, the United States needed additionally to construct bases close enough to the USSR for a containment strategy to be viable. (The B-29, the mainstay of the air force bomber fleet until the development of the B-47 in 1951, had a maximum range of 3,250 miles, round-trip. The B-52, introduced in the late 1950s, had a range of 8,000 miles.) *Time* magazine of November 4, 1962, noted that the United States *necessarily* maintains many military installations overseas—2,230 of them, according to a Pentagon count.[48] Chalmers Johnson in *Sorrows of Empire* notes that the United States in 2005 still had eight hundred bases.[49] The Novikov telegram to Stalin of September 27, 1946 (discussed earlier in this chapter) was clearly written to urge a USSR counter to Kennan and went to some length to detail the number of bases planned in 1946 by the United States and their distance from the Soviet mainland.[50]

The timing of the first use of the bomb had been distressing to the USSR. At Yalta, the quid pro quo for postwar agreements was that the USSR would enter the war against Japan a few months after the defeat of Germany. After August 6, 1945, Stalin declared, "Hiroshima has shaken the whole world.

47. See J. Neufeld, *The Development of Ballistic Missiles in the United States Air Force, 1945-1960* (Washington, DC: Office of Air Force History, United States Air Force, 1989). The short-range Redstone missile project was assigned to the US Army Ordnance Corps in 1948. The USSR successfully tested an ICBM (the R-7) in August 1957; the United States had success with the Atlas in November 1958.

48. These bases were already of concern in Novikov's 1946 telegram, where he noted that as some of the bases are "1000-1200 km distant from the US there is no doubt as to their aggressive intent."

49. Chalmers Johnson, *The Sorrows of Empire, Militarism, Secrecy and the End of the Republic* (New York: Metropolitan Books, 2005), chap. 6.

50. In 1949, the United States had 258 bases in Europe, Canada, and the North Atlantic. By 1957 it had 566, and in 1967, 673; in the Pacific and South East Asia, it had 235 in 1949 and 256 by 1957. See J. R. Blaker, *United States Overseas Basing* (New York: Praeger, 1990), table 1.2.

The balance has been broken. Build the Bomb—it will remove the great danger from us."[51] Subsequent Soviet premier Nikita Khrushchev later recalled, "What if Japan capitulated before we entered the war? The Americans might say, we don't owe you anything."[52] David Holloway sees this as evidence that Stalin feared that the United States and Great Britain would "renege on Yalta."[53] Furthermore, the bomb demonstrated that the United States had the capacity to attack the USSR. Stalin—who now seemed persuaded by Malenkov and on-the-ground realities—appears to have once hoped for a kind of return to isolationism by the United States.

It was thus important to the USSR that the ring of US bases at least be kept as far away as possible, hence the need for dependable buffers. And that was how the world seemed to them at that point. The Novikov telegram (probably heavily drafted and certainly annotated by Molotov) said that "the US has abandoned its post-war tradition of isolationism and is now driven by the desire for world domination."[54] At the Cominform conference of September 1946 in Poland, the Soviets strengthened their control over East European Communist parties and by 1948 had imposed a set of bilateral treaties on East European countries (except for Yugoslavia).[55] Their worry appears to have been an American sponsored German resurgence.[56]

THE PIECES ARE IN PLACE

Thus, by the fall of 1946, the Cold War had been launched internationally. The elections of 1946 resulted in the first Republican-controlled House and Senate in thirty years. What did this Congress give the country?

It transformed the relation of the government to the citizenry in manifold

51. D. Holloway, "Entering the Nuclear Arms Race: The Soviet Decision to Build the Atomic Bomb, 1939–1945," *Social Studies of Science* 11, no. 2 (1981): 159–97, and D. Holloway, *Stalin and the Bomb: The Soviet Union and Atomic Energy, 1939–1956* (New Haven, CT: Yale University Press, 1996). See also Gordin, *Red Cloud at Dawn.*

52. Quoted in William Taubman, *Khrushchev: The Man and His Era* (New York: Norton, 2004).

53. Holloway, "Entering the Nuclear Arms Race," 185.

54. "Novikov Telegram"; see also G. K. Zhukov, *The Memoirs of Marshal Zhukov* (London: Cape, 1971), 102.

55. The Soviet pressure on Tito to come back in line with Moscow failed. See W. O. McCagg Jr., "Domestic Politics and Soviet Foreign Policy at the Cominform Conference in 1947," *Slavic and Soviet Series* 2, no. 1 (Spring 1977): 3–31.

56. See Kennedy-Pipe, *Stalin's Cold War,* 121–22.

ways. Space does not allow a detailed analysis, but one must note the following developments:

- The government engaged in searching out possible spies in government and other groups.
- A Loyalty Board was established in April 1947. Its role was to inquire into political beliefs of all employees. Seth Richardson, head of the board, stated, "Government entitled to discharge any employees for reason that seem reasonable with no hearing. Any suspicion may suffice."[57] FBI documents recorded testimony about supposedly pro-Communist sympathies from "Confidential informants stated to be reliable," and this testimony was enough to indict or dismiss. These efforts continued to escalate, to the point where, as noted in chapter 8, *Life* magazine published a list and pictures of fifty "dupes and fellow travelers" on April 4, 1949.[58]
- The Taft Hartley act of 1947 forbade any union that did not certify that none of its leadership at any level had Communist affiliation or sympathies from engaging in collective bargaining. A substantial proportion of the CIO leadership fell into this blacklisted category. The CIO caved in, thereby reducing the pressure from the labor movement and leading eventually to its amalgamation with the American Federation of Labor, always a more conservative movement, into the AFL-CIO that still exists today.
- A peacetime draft—the Elston Act—was instituted in 1948.
- In April 1948, Wallace launched his bid for president with the newly founded Progressive Party on a "Peace Plan" and met with little success—indeed, several times he faced rock-throwing protesters. In July, just before the Progressive Party convention, the FBI, using in part the bugged transcripts described in chapter 8, arrested the top leadership of the CPUSA under the Smith Act. In the November election, Wallace (one of *Life* magazine's "dupes," of course) garnered just 2.6 percent of the vote (40 percent of which came from New York City).

57. See "Truman Orders Loyalty Checks of Federal Employees," March 22, 1947, History.com, https://www.history.com/this-day-in-history/truman-orders-loyalty-checks-of-federal-employees. See Alan D. Harper, *The Politics of Loyalty: The White House and the Communist Issue, 1946-1952* (New York: Greenwood, 1969). Richardson lays out the rationale in Seth Richardson, "The Federal Employee Loyalty Program," *Columbia Law Review* 51, no. 5 (May 1951): 546-63.

58. For the list, see "Dupes and Fellow Travelers Dress Up Communist Fronts," *Life* 26, no. 14 (April 4, 1949), 42-43, Astronauticsnow.com, http://astronauticsnow.com/history/dupes/index.html.

- There was a fairly systematic repression of all who were thought to support a line not hostile to the USSR. For instance, in 1952, with a group of others, W. E. B. DuBois was put on trial (his detention lasted nine months) as the chair of the Peace Information Committee; he and the others were accused of being agents of a foreign power (the USSR). Eventually, the prosecution case was so weak that the judge directed a judgment of acquittal.[59]

There were also consequences internationally, as American foreign policy supported these positions in the following ways:

- The Central Intelligence Agency (CIA) poured in money to France and Italy in order to undercut, with some success, the 1946 electoral achievements of the Communists in those countries.
- The Truman Doctrine used the Kennan telegram to assert, in March 1947, the right of United States to "support free peoples who are resisting takeovers from armed minorities or outside pressure."[60] Wallace proclaimed it "futile" in his Madison Square Garden speech. I have already noted what happened to the Greek Communists.
- In July 1947, Truman scrapped JCS 1067, a 1945 directive to the Joint Chiefs of Staff which had decreed that one "take no steps looking toward the economic rehabilitation of Germany [or] designed to maintain or strengthen the German economy" (this is part of the Morgenthau Plan) and supplanted it with JCS 1779, which decreed that "an orderly and prosperous Europe requires the economic contributions of a stable and productive Germany."[61]
- The Marshall Plan was put into place from early 1947 on. As the United States had anticipated and in all likelihood wanted, the USSR refused participation. The policy was to rebuild Europe along capitalist lines and to

59. W. E. B. DuBois, "The Trial," and "The Acquittal," in *Writings* (New York: Library of America, 1986), 1071–1109. In concluding, DuBois thanked blacks and whites "who have risen above race prejudice not by philanthropy but by brotherly and sympathetic sharing of the Negro's burdens and identification with it as part of their own." Disturbingly, one of the main witnesses against DuBois was John Rogge, who had been for most of his life strongly associated with left-wing causes and was clearly turned by the prosecution.

60. Harry S. Truman, "President Harry S. Truman's Address Before a Joint Session of Congress, March 12, 1947," Avalon Project, Yale Law School, http://avalon.law.yale.edu/20th_century/trudoc.asp.

61. See "Revised Plan for Level of Industry in the Anglo-American Zones (August 29, 1947)," German History in Documents and Images, http://germanhistorydocs.ghi-dc.org/pdf/eng/Econ%20WZFR%206%20ENG.pdf.

rearm and rebuild West Germany (the USSR had wanted a united neutral Germany; Ambassador Novikov referred with distress to the "monopolistic associations of German industrialists on which German fascism depended"[62]). In partial response, the USSR clamped down in Hungary, on Czechoslovakia, and on East Berlin. In February 1948, the Soviets advised Western powers that they had learned that the West intended to call a three-power meeting in London to consider policies in the Western zones. The note asserted that given the absence of the (uninvited) USSR, this constituted a violation of the Potsdam agreements.[63] The West went ahead with the meeting. On March 20, 1948, Marshall Sokolovsky, the head of the Soviet Military Administration in Germany, walked out of the Allied Control Council in protest. In June, against agreements with the USSR, the West engaged in currency reform in the West: upon being officially informed of this action, the USSR closed access to Berlin. This Soviet closure of access to the city led to the Berlin crisis of 1948–49. To some degree in response, the North Atlantic Treaty Organization (NATO) was established, with a nuclear guarantee whereby an attack on any one member would generate a response by all—Novikov had worried about such an official military alliance between the United States and Great Britain in his telegram of 1946.

- The US defense budget was nine billion dollars in 1948; it rose to reach fifty-three billion dollars in 1953. It dropped slightly but remained in the high forty-billion-dollar range for the next several years, rising eventually to and staying well over one hundred billion dollars during the Vietnam War and after.[64]

- The Communists triumphed in China in 1949; this victory led to the completion of the ongoing purge in the US State Department of any officer with China expertise.[65]

With all these developments, and the effect of the Kennan telegram, it is unsurprising that in 1949 the United States formulated the principles of its

62. "Novikov Telegram."

63. See H. Adomeit, *Soviet Risk-Taking and Crisis Behavior* (London: Allen and Unwin, 1982), 80. I owe this reference to Kennedy-Pipe.

64. See United States Office of Management and Budget and United States Bureau of the Budget, *Budget of the United States Government Series*, accessed October 11, 2015, https://fraser.stlouisfed.org/series/4527. These are adjusted figures.

65. See Kahn, *China Hands*. Prominent among the purged were Oliver Edmund Clubb, John Paton Davies Jr., Everett F. Drumright, Fulton Freeman, Raymond P. Ludden, James K. Penfield, Edward E. Rice, Arthur R. Ringwalt, John Stewart Service, Phillip P. Sprouse, and John Carter Vincent.

foreign policy in the National Security Council's "NSC 68" memo, mainly authored by Paul Nitze.[66] The document became the basis for American foreign policy for the next several decades and, contrary to the multipronged approach advocated by Kennan, was much more militarily focused. It argued that (1) American free society was confronted by a threat to basic values; (2) the integrity of the American polity would not be jeopardized by anything that the United States might do against the USSR; (3) the US defense budget should be tripled. With the start of the Korean War,[67] the American military budget went from thirteen billion to forty-eight billion dollars (one sees the military uses of Keynesianism) and has remained high ever since. It thus legitimated as national policy all of the elements domestically and internationally as shown in the foregoing bulleted list.

With the Cold War, the substance of American politics accomplished a change that had been in the making since the Civil War. The supposed reality of the Soviet threat and the consequent damming accusation of being "soft on Communism" effectively drastically narrowed the political spectrum, especially on the Left. Gone was the proposal for, let alone the realization of, policies such as those sketched out in Roosevelt's 1944 State of the Union message. The existence of atomic weapons meant that they were there for potential use. General Douglas MacArthur urged their use in Korea; Vice President Richard Nixon and Admiral Arthur Radford, chairman of the Joint Chiefs of Staff, urged acceptance of the French proposal to use three atomic weapons against the Viet Minh as they threatened to overrun the French stronghold at Dien Bien Phu (and eventually did). President Eisenhower kept the option on the table, only turning it down after the British refused to go along.[68]

---

66. See N. Thompson, *The Hawk and the Dove: Paul Nitze, George Kennan, and the History of the Cold War* (New York: Henry Holt, 2009). For the text of NSC 68, see "NSC 68: United States Objectives and Programs for National Security (April 14, 1950)," Federation of American Scientists, http://fas.org/irp/offdocs/nsc-hst/nsc-68.htm.

67. The history of the origins of the Korean War is complex. It does appear, however, that after some resistance, Stalin and later Mao gave into the demands of North Korean President Kim to receive permission to invade South Korea on the latter's belief that the United States would not seriously defend it (Secretary Acheson had given a speech that appeared to leave South Korea outside the US defense perimeter). US forces were in fact so unprepared that the initial push of the North Korean Army made it almost to the south coast. See Bruce Cummings, *Origins of the Korean War* (Princeton, NJ: Princeton University Press, 1981); and Halberstam, *Coldest Winter*.

68. This consideration of an atomic option was revealed in the Pentagon Papers. See Don Kasprzak, "French Request to US: Drop 3 Atomic Bombs at Dien Bien Phu," *Don Kasprzak* (blog), January 31, 2013, http://donkasprzak.com/drop-3-atomic-bombs-at-dien-bien-phu/.

Corporations acquired increased power and influence. Charles Wilson, who had been CEO of General Motors and became secretary of defense under Eisenhower, was famous for claiming that "What was good for our country was good for General Motors and vice versa."[69] Corporations acquired a moral and political identity that have continued and intensified to the present. There was no attempt to extend democracy to the economy and little or no industrial planning or policy except in the military. Any attempt at overcoming the legacy of slavery and racism would be accomplished, to the degree that it was at all, by the courts—which over the long run would prove disastrous for Progressive forces as they would increasingly tend to rely on the courts rather than political organizing to carry out their policies. The public sector—infrastructure, mass transit, housing, the environment—would be pretty much left to its own means, except for the interstate highway system, which Eisenhower, who had been impressed by the German *Autobahnen*, pushed through on the grounds of military necessity.

Internationally, the Cold War led to a general support for third-world capitalism and a support for those regimes that were on "our side" in the Cold War, even if they were at times highly authoritarian and repressive (Augusto Pinochet in Chile; the shah in Iran). Counterfactuals are always historically suspect, but the conviction of the monolithic nature of Communism led to a disregard for the exploitation of possible fissures between Communist countries. America tended to pick up the pieces of the colonial empires and tried to enlist them against the USSR.

CONCLUSION

Understanding a historical event must not only be multicausal but also leave open space for accident and contingency. In this chapter, I have tried to sketch the factors that went into the development of the Cold War. They were domestic; they were international; they were bureaucratic; they were technical; they were matters of historical accident. It is not at all clear to me that the Cold War was inevitable, though it was perhaps in the end overdetermined, to use a structuralist term. What is clear is that the period from 1940 until sometime in 1946 was a period in which the dynamics in American society were complex

69. Usually remembered as "What is good for General Motors is good for America." See Justin Hyde, "GM's 'Engine Charlie' Wilson Learned to Live with a Misquote," *Detroit Free Press*, September 14, 2008, from Wikipedia article on Wilson.

and varied enough to have made possible other outcomes. What is also clear is that whatever made apparently reasonable sense of a confusing concatenation of events was likely to determine the course the policy would take. In this sense, Kennan made sense of a Cold War although he did not cause it.

The Cold War left little space for an active citizenry: to the degree that activity was possible, the participant had to pass a test of not being "soft" on Communism. And that test eliminated much of what had passed for legitimate politics over the previous 150 years. It drastically narrowed the available political spectrum for any kind of Progressive understanding of being a citizen. It dramatically enhanced the surveillance powers and practices of the state. It thinned out the range of available opinion in the executive branch. Alger Hiss, for instance, who had been director of the Bureau of Special Political Affairs and a central adviser to Roosevelt for the Yalta conference, was accused in August 1946 by Whittaker Chambers, himself an ex-Communist, of being a member of the Communist Party. (Chambers, then working as an editor at *Time* magazine, had written an editorial violently denouncing the Yalta agreement.) Hollywood turned to making anti-Communist films, among them subtle ones such as Alfred Hitchcock's *North by Northwest* and somewhat more explicit ones such as John Frankenheimer's *The Manchurian Candidate*, as well as blatant propaganda films including Gordon Douglas's *I Was a Communist for the FBI*, Alfred E. Green's *Invasion U.S.A.*, and Robert Stevenson's *The Woman on Pier 13* (originally titled *I Married a Communist*).

Teachers who would not swear that they were not Communist were fired; anyone thought susceptible to blackmail (e.g., homosexuals) was at risk of losing their job; civil rights organizations purged themselves of Communists and fellow travelers. One hundred and sixty-one Hollywood actors were blacklisted on the basis of having been named in a right-wing pamphlet. The repression only increased after the USSR exploded an atomic weapon in 1949—it led to the execution of Julius and Ethel Rosenberg, who were accused of passing secrets on the bomb to the USSR.[70] Eisenhower, then president of Columbia University, once responded to a member of his faculty who was extolling the excellence of the Columbia faculty: "Dammit, what good are exceptional physicists, exceptional anything, unless they are exceptional Americans?"[71]

70. See generally James T. Patterson, *Grand Expectations: The United States, 1945-1974* (New York: Oxford University Press, 1996), 85-206, esp. 165-206.

71. Stephen Ambrose, *Eisenhower: Soldier and President* (New York: Simon and Schuster, 1991), 241.

That which was deemed "exceptional" was significantly narrower than it had been fifteen years earlier. That said, events consequent to contingencies have more or less necessary consequences, especially as they become reality. In essence, the Cold War consolidated political power in Washington, DC, without any gestures toward active citizenship such as those set forth in Roosevelt's 1944 State of the Union Address.

10

WHERE DO ALL THESE STORIES GO? THE 1960S, THE NEW LEFT, AND BEYOND

I woke up this morning with my mind
Stayed on Jesus . . .
Hallelu, hallelu, hallelujah.
Won't you walk and talk with your mind,
Stayed on Jesus? . . .
Hallelu, hallelu, hallelujah
Hallelujah.
OLD GOSPEL SONG

The mainspring of popular government in peacetime is virtue, amid revolution it is at once *virtue* and *terror*: virtue, without which terror is fatal; terror, without which virtue is impotent. Terror is nothing but prompt, severe, inflexible justice; it is therefore an emanation of virtue. It is less a special principle than a consequence of the general principle of democracy applied to the country's most pressing needs.
ROBESPIERRE, MAY 2, 1794

In the early 1960s, while spending time in jail, the Reverend Osby changed one word in the old gospel song that serves as epigraph above: he replaced "Jesus" with "freedom." The song went on to become an anthem of the American civil rights movement. I first heard it as a freshman at Oberlin College, when Chuck McDew and other civil rights activists visited the campus and started singing it in the lobby of Dascomb Hall—music then new even to that generally progressive campus. A few years later, P. F. Sloan wrote a song entitled "On the Eve of Destruction," where one heard that human respect was disintegrating, for "the whole crazy world is just too frustrating." As later covered by many artists, in particular Barry McGuire, it too became an expression of the age. What was happening?

With the Cold War and the decline of what one might somewhat misleadingly call "the Left," progressive multi-issue politics were generally increasingly discredited. During the 1950s, whatever advances in civil and voting rights were made were due mostly to decisions of the US Supreme Court rather than political or legislative action, and even with those, progress was very slow. The economy was generally strong as America was one of the few industrial countries not ravaged by war. New markets in former colonies and expanded ones in many of the wartime allies opened up. With the GI Bill, a much larger portion of the population partook of postsecondary education. Unions became generally less militant: throughout the 1950s, there were only twelve strikes of note; those that threatened to go on at length were often curtailed by the invocation of the Taft-Hartley Act. Living habits changed as suburbs developed rapidly, thereby often placing a commuting distance between living space and workplace. With the separation of work and commercial institutions from living places, neighborhoods tended to become less varied culturally and more homogenous ethnically, especially in the new suburbs. Automobiles and television became necessities.

The increasing ubiquity of the automobile as a mode of transformation tended to homogenize the country. Now that one could travel three to four hundred miles in a day, how was one to determine in a strange place where might be a good place to eat, or to stay for a night? The answer, in brief, was exemplified by Howard Johnson. The fried clam roll in his chain of namesake restaurants was predictably and comfortably the same whether one was in Pennsylvania or Iowa. By 1954, there were four hundred "HoJo" restaurants in thirty-two states; with the Federal Aid Highway Act of 1956, they were increasingly located along these major thoroughfares.[1] This proliferation of right-off-the-highway eateries did lead to some unpredicted consequences, as the very presence of these establishments raised mostly unforeseen issues. Many public eating places and restaurants were (if not de jure, then de facto) segregated because they were in communities dominated by one race. The new network of highways, however, meant that blacks could come to a wide range of restaurants, including those in white communities, often far removed from

---

1. Wikipedia, s.v. "Howard Johnson's," last modified November 28, 2018, https://en .wikipedia.org/wiki/Howard_Johnson%27s; see also the bibliography cited there.

their place of residence. A series of incidents and lawsuits in the late 1950s and early 1960s effectively led to a degree of integration outside of the South.

Slowly, but steadily, America was becoming more of one piece—not in the sense of the parts becoming the same or integrating into a whole, but in the sense that the parts were interacting much more than they had before. The first national television news broadcast came in 1950. The first broadcast to feature live reports from both coasts was Edward R. Murrow's *See It Now* on CBS in 1951. In 1963, the major networks moved from a fifteen-minute evening news report to a thirty-minute one. Also in 1963, the introduction of numerical postal zip codes (the "zip" in the name derived from "zone improvement plan") meant that various areas of the country were now differentiated bureaucratically only by a set of five digits. It also meant, as national magazines were quick to realize, that advertisements and even content of mailed material could be modified depending on the demography of a given zip code. More homogeneity ironically sometimes meant more differentiation. With the introduction of area codes and the switch to numerals only, telephone exchanges lost their site specificity (e.g., "BUTterfield 8," as in the Elizabeth Taylor movie, would be replaced by "212-2888"). All sorts of things were changing in America, and their interrelation was poorly understood. On local levels, as living and working places became substantially distinct, collective experience tended to diminish; on the national level, it tended to increase but in an abstract manner. To a great extent, the federal government and certainly most of the state governments were happy not to intervene. It is in this context that a new set of participants entered the political realm, participants who in many ways were not like earlier ones.

The particular medium of television is important. Today at least two-thirds of Americans get most of their news from TV or online, and more than half get *all* their news that way.[2] Particularly here, the medium exists in an economic system that demands profit, and profit is gained by increasing the number of viewers. Two solutions to this demand are prevalent: the first is a reliance on voyeurism, epitomized as "if it bleeds, it leads." The second solution is more insidious: the cutting down of the attention time needed for any issue, such that something "new" is always appearing. Dan Hallin has shown that the average length of a clip in which the president spoke on national news shows went from 43 seconds a night to 254 in 1972 to 9 in 1988.[3] If major network

2. Amy Mitchell et al., "Pathways to News," Pew Research Center, http://www.journalism.org/2016/07/07/pathways-to-news/.
3. Dan Hallin, *We Keep America on Top of the World* (New York: Routledge, 1994). For information on time, see Jeff Hahn, "Hail King Hallin—Confirming the Length of a

news programs went from fifteen to thirty minutes in 1963, it is in that context that everything within them was shorter. This is not an argument that more time leads to truth but that less time does not lead to thought.

A further factor exacerbates these tendencies. Whereas coast-to-coast live television was not possible before 1951 and not standard until the 1960s, today almost all broadcasts emanating from chains with enough resources to have extensive staff are national. This means that their broadcasts are now oriented toward no audience in particular and must try to offend the least number of viewers possible. As a result, almost no news that is politically relevant locally gets broadcast nationally. John Gaventa, then of the Highlander Center, found that two different communities of miners in two different Tennessee valleys both got their news from Nashville and had no knowledge of the similarity of their problems.[4] The consequence of the second and third factors is that very few people have TV access to issues that affect them directly.

WHAT IS NEW?

In this general context, five more or less synchronous developments contributed to a transformation of the American political landscape: (1) rock and roll; (2) the civil rights movement; (3) a shift in Cold War attitudes following the decline of Communism in the United States; (4) expansion of enrollments at universities; and (5) a new generational divide. We will examine each in turn.

ROCK AND ROLL

In the realm of popular culture, as white musicians came to draw on black music sources, the development of rock and roll transformed the national cultural scene. Rock was music performed by white musicians who often integrated country music with the gospel, boogie-woogie, jazz, and rhythm-and-blues strains of black musicians. The development of the electric guitar and constantly improving amplifying sound systems meant that relatively few musicians could make a lot of loud music. The development of the vinyl 45 RPM record meant that individual songs could be sold separately and cheaply (less

Sound Bite," *Insight* (blog), July 16, 2015, https://hahnpublic.com/blog/the-end-of-media-relations-part-4-2/.

4. John Gaventa, interview with the author, La Jolla, CA, April 1985.

than a dollar).[5] The introduction of the microgroove 33⅓ RPM disk gave rise to the "record album" and became the industry standard format by the late 1950s. Songs were being produced that sounded "black" but were performed by whites and would thus be played on white radio stations. The release of "Rock Around the Clock" by Bill Haley and the Comets in 1954 and its use the following year in the movie *Blackboard Jungle* (with the young Sidney Poitier as the leader of a group of black students) can be taken effectively to mark the start of rock and roll and a national cultural phenomenon.[6] In effect, rock brought black culture with together white youth culture in dreams of rebellion. When Elvis Presley finally got onto the *Ed Sullivan Show* in 1956—the sign of having "made it"—the audience was full of screaming teenage girls, although, for the TV audience, the camera remained firmly above his twitching pelvis.

The integration of white and black youth audiences for rock and roll performances provoked strong racist reactions widely across the country, precisely at the time that the US Supreme Court was cautiously moving toward declaring school segregation illegal, as it ultimately did in its landmark decision *Brown v. Board of Education of Topeka* (37 U.S. 483 [1954]). In 1957, President Eisenhower was compelled to send federal troops to Arkansas to enforce integration of a high school.

CIVIL RIGHTS

The second development that led to the transformation of the American political landscape was the civil rights movement that began to take shape in the 1950s, with young people at the forefront. The movement was, in some complex manner, intermixed with the aforementioned developments in popular

5. Rare issues now sell for as much as twenty thousand dollars. See "What's It Worth? 45 RPM Records Price Guide Listing," iGuide, https://www.iguide.net/price-guide/records/45rpm/list.aspx.

6. There are lots of histories. Among the best is, I think, James Miller, *Flowers in the Dustbin: The Rise of Rock and Roll, 1947–1977* (New York: Simon and Shuster, 1996). See also James Henke et al., eds., *The Rolling Stone Illustrated History of Rock and Roll: The Definitive History of the Most Important Artists and Their Music* (New York: Random House, 1992); the review article by Jackson Lears of several books on the 1960s in *New York Review of Books* 65, no. 14 (September 27–October 8, 2018): 8–16; and the Keith Richards film *Hail! Hail! Rock and Roll*, which focuses on the genre's seminal musician Chuck Berry (and in which John Lennon said that if rock and roll were to be renamed, it would be called "Chuck Berry").

culture, though certainly with a history and kinetic energy of its own. Youth was slowly forming as a new group in America, a group defined by its own culture and interests. This group was marginal to the normal political process, as most teenagers could not vote even after the 26th amendment lowered the voting age from 21 to 18 in 1971 (some states had lowered it at the state and local level earlier).

Blacks had always pushed for racial and social justice, but this effort had manifested itself primarily in legal actions or in violence. On February 1, 1960, four black freshman students from the black North Carolina Agricultural and Technical State University, wearing coats and ties, sat in at a segregated lunch counter in a Woolworth drug store in Greensboro, North Carolina. In accordance with store policy, they were refused service (by the blacks employed by Woolworth under orders from the white owner); the young men in this historic "sit-in" refused to leave and stayed until the store closed.[7] Twenty-five black students came the next day, and one hundred the day after. Matters rapidly turned ugly, yet the students, inspired by Dr. Martin Luther King Jr. (who in turn had been inspired by India's Mohandas K. Gandhi[8]), remained resolutely nonviolent. The event quickly drew local and then national media attention, attention that technology had recently made possible. Within a week, the sit-in movement spread widely across the South. In some spots, violence did break out. In Greensboro, the loss of revenue was so pronounced that the store owner allowed his black staff to serve food to blacks and effectively integrated his lunch counter.[9]

The Supreme Court's *Brown* decision of 1954 had abandoned the "separate but equal" clause from the *Plessy v. Ferguson* decision of 1896 (described in chapter 6). But little had actually happened. The movement to direct action with the sit-ins (in effect, a form of trespass) was important as it constituted not so much a claim of the "right" to sit at a lunch counter (though it was that) as the assertion that one of the qualities of being American was that all people were entitled *as American citizens* to eat where they pleased in public places. The civil rights movement is best properly considered not first as a rights issue but rather as a claim to realize what had not been realized in what it means to be American. The sit-ins were a gesture of active citizenship, a call with rela-

7. William Henry Chafe, *Civilities and Civil Rights: Greensboro, North Carolina and the Black Struggle for Freedom* (New York: Oxford University Press, 1981).

8. See Lori Meek Schuldt, *Martin Luther King, Jr., with Profiles of Mohandas K. Gandhi and Nelson Mandela*, Biographical Connections (Chicago: World Book, 2007).

9. See, e.g., Michael Walzer, "A Cup of Coffee and a Seat," *Dissent* 7 (Spring 1960): 111–20.

tive clarity about what is involved in being an American citizen: they sought to show, to demonstrate, to those who did not have as full a sense, why they were mistaken. Direct action was necessary because only in this manner could one *demonstrate*—hence there developed *demonstrations*—to a racist lunch counter owner that *as an American* (that is, if he was to be what he was), he was required to serve blacks as well as whites. As a tactic, nonviolent action left the decision of what to do up to the other side and raised the possibility that someone engaging in violence could be led to reflect on why he or she had done so. The sit-ins were, in effect, an attempt at political education as to what it meant to be an American citizen. Nonviolent action *showed* something: putting one's body on the line—as many of us did—was meant to get the racists to reflect on what being a member of the same country meant in terms of a supposed commitment to democracy. (Thomas Jefferson had seen this but was unable or unwilling to find the words to express it, let alone do anything about it.) It is important to note that for something to be demonstrated or be manifest (Lincoln's "Living history"), the link between the act and the claim has to be visible. It is one thing to sit in at a segregated lunch counter and quite another to blockade the Fourteenth Street bridge in Washington, DC, in protest of the Vietnam War. (The late, murdered Allard Lowenstein spent a lot of time trying to teach others this difference.[10])

As such, the tactic only had a chance for success if as much pressure as possible could be brought to bear, which required that the news of the event be delocalized—and that was something that the nationalization of media was increasingly making possible. To be effective locally, these confrontations had to be seen by a wide audience of people who were not directly involved in them. Thus, sensing this need for wider exposure, during the most intense confrontations against the Vietnam War or at the Democratic Party 1968 Chicago convention, the chant at demonstrations that "the whole world is watching" would often go up.[11] And with the development of national and, via satellite, simultaneous international media, increasingly the whole world *was* watching. In the context of Greensboro, the spread of the movement and the consequent economic and political costs at times led the segregationists to reconsider—and at times it did not. The students who sat in were not asking for white racists to undergo a conversion of a "road to Damascus" type—but

10. See Richard Cummings, *The Pied Piper: Allard K. Lowenstein and the Liberal Dream* (New York: Grove Press, 1985).

11. See Todd Gitlin, *The Whole World Is Watching: Mass Media in the Making and Unmaking of the New Left* (Berkeley: University of California Press, 1981).

they were convinced that once the practice of desegregation was achieved, the wider necessary supporting understandings would eventually mature. If the reality of Southern segregation were made manifest to the entire country, then change might, just possibly might, come. Lincoln's hostility to slavery, I noted in chapter 4, had a great deal to do with what he, as a young man, had *seen* in the South. The movement relied on the *visual* appeal to an often unacknowledged sense of what it meant actually to be an American. And this required national media: with that, it could not be ignored.

Organizations promoting these approaches developed quickly. The Congress of Racial Equality (CORE), which had been around since the 1940s, joined in. The Student Non-Violent Coordinating Committee (SNCC, called "Snick" by one and all) soon developed and recruited white students from sympathetic Northern campuses to come to the South and help in the struggle. King's campaigns, working with the National Association for the Advancement of Colored People (NAACP) and with the capital achieved through the publicity over the Montgomery, Alabama, bus desegregation (achieved after a yearlong boycott by black riders beginning in December 1955), took on increasing vigor. None of these efforts would have succeeded without the national media coverage, which allowed the rest of the nation to *see* what had been allowed for a long time to pass unremarked in the South. Additionally, the Nation of Islam, which had been founded in 1930, grew exponentially in the late 1950s and early 1960s due mostly to the rhetorical and media skill and intelligence of Malcolm X.

The spark, however, generally came from nonviolent, non–centrally organized direct action. This starting point provided both strength and eventually weakness. (One is reminded of the difficulties incurred at the Seattle General Strike of 1919, described in chapter 7.) The basic belief was that nonviolence and "love" would turn racists and haters around, by showing them aspects of being an American that they had forgone acknowledging. The founding document of SNCC states, "Nonviolence, as it grows from the Judeo-Christian tradition, seeks a social order of justice permeated by love. Integration of human endeavor represents the crucial first step towards such a society. Through nonviolence, courage displaces fear. Love transcends hate. Acceptance dissipates prejudice; hope ends despair. Faith reconciles doubt. Peace dominates war. Mutual regards cancel enmity. Justice for all overthrows injustice. The redemptive community supersedes immoral social systems."[12]

12. SNCC Manifesto, University of Virginia website, http://www2.iath.virginia.edu /sixties/HTML_docs/Resources/Primary/Manifesto/SNCC_founding.html.

We have seen this language before: America had strayed from the paths of righteousness and was doing evil: it was to be *redeemed* from the error of its ways—the theme is as old as the country. Note that these demonstrations are not conceived of as an attempt to impose a new moral order. Rather, they are a claim that the country has forgotten or has avoided acknowledgement of who it is, and, much as with Lincoln's appeal to the Declaration of Independence, needs to be recalled to its true self.

The initial focus on interpersonal relations (or lack thereof) as foundational to racism often led to an overlooking of the fact that racism was not only interpersonal but also structural and institutional. It was thus the case, as Levitsky and Ziblatt argue in their recent book *How Democracies Die*, that the relative peace and prosperity and lack of conflict that white America enjoyed (albeit with some important interruptions) between the end of Reconstruction and the 1960s was to a considerable extent due to the acceptance by Northern Whites of a one-party Jim Crow–based rule in the former Confederate states.[13] So long as the race question was not institutionally raised, cooperation between white Democrats (North and South) and white Republicans (North and West) was sustainable. Once the *institutional* race question was raised, after the passage of the Civil Rights Act in 1964 and the Voting Rights Act in 1965, tolerance by neglect of historical racist practices was rapidly eroded.

What happened in response to these new, often youth-centered movements, was that the institutional question *was* raised, and raised in a manner that could not be avoided. And this of necessity produced tensions. King moved from conceiving of the race problem as resolvable by integration to one more deeply shaped by the economic, social, and political patterns dominant in the country. King said, "This may sound rather shocking. But I confess that I am not afraid of the word tension. I have earnestly worked and preached against violent tension, but there is a type of constructive non-violent tension that is necessary for growth."[14] The Black Panther Party took it upon itself to try to remedy economic and social deprivation in black neighborhoods. And, increasingly, all these groups came to hold the position that blacks could not be "expected to endure injustice submissively."[15] As Malcolm X put it when criticized for supposedly telling blacks to arm themselves, "I'm not advo-

13. See Steven Levitsky and Daniel Ziblatt, *How Democracies Die* (New York: Crown, 2018).

14. From James M. Washington, ed., *A Testament of Hope: The Essential Writings of Martin Luther King, Jr.* (New York: Harper Collins, 1991), 291. Also cited in Bromell, *Time Is Always Now*.

15. Pauli Murray, quoted in Bromell, *Time Is Always Now*, 121.

cating the breaking of any law. . . . But I say that our people will never be re-spected as human beings until we react as other intelligent human beings do. This doesn't mean that we should buy rifles and go out and initiate attacks indiscriminately against whites. . . . But it does mean that we should get what-ever is necessary to protect ourselves."[16] James Baldwin had been explicit: it would be "the fire next time."[17] What is important is that those involved in civil rights came to understand that the achievement of full citizenship across the race line would involve something other than the second-generational in-tegration achieved by white immigrant groups. Mark Twain, in the last section of *Huckleberry Finn*, had already intuited this (as we saw in chapter 5).

ANTI-ANTICOMMUNISM

Contemporary to these developments, in a third development that led to the transformation of the American political landscape, the growing irrelevance of the Communist Party in American politics led many people—young white people in particular—actively to question the Cold War focus on the Soviet Union and the semiparanoia over the dangers of domestic Communism. The House Committee on Un-American Activities (known as HUAC, for its vari-ant name House Un-American Activities Committee) was holding meetings around the country investigating purported Communist infiltration and influ-ence. The committee was itself the descendant of a set of committees inves-tigating supposed domestic subversion, some of which dated back to the im-mediate post–World War I period. Among many of the young and in particular students, a questioning, at times hostile, of the role and purpose of HUAC had developed in parts of the country. On May 13, 1960, the committee held hear-ings in San Francisco. A group of students, mostly white, from the University of California at Berkeley, Stanford University, and other academic institutions insisted on their right to attend the meetings in the city hall, pretty clearly not intending simply to sit and listen. They were denied entry, and when they at-tempted to force the issue, police with firehoses and clubs forcibly removed them, injuring some seriously. HUAC's reaction was to produce a film, *Op-eration Abolition*, arguing that the Communist Party had used "their stan-

16. Malcolm X, "Interview with Les Crane, 1964," in *The Last Speeches*, ed. Bruce Perry (New York: Pathfinder Press, 1989), 83–85. Also cited in Bromell, *The Time Is Always Now*, 173.

17. Baldwin, *Fire Next Time*.

dard tactics. They have well-trained Communist operatives incite naïve non-Communist Americans to interfere with American governmental process.... You will see these shocking scenes."[18] While there were certainly Communist Party members active in the Bay Area, and while being uncooperative to a summons by HUAC could easily cost an individual his or her job, for most of the young participants, Communism and thus anti-Communism was not a very salient issue. Not having an economic position, they had little to lose.

THE GROWTH OF UNIVERSITIES

That the new civil rights movement and the anti-anti-Communist movement were dominated by students was not a coincidence. In a fourth development that led to the transformation of the American political landscape, the postwar period saw a great expansion of the universities, first with the GI Bill and then, after the successful launch by the USSR of the first earth satellite ("Sputnik") in October 1957, an acceleration with the dramatic expansion of federal funding for higher education with the National Defense Education Act of 1958.[19] The act provided for more than one billion dollars over the next four years and dramatically increased the percentage of Americans pursuing and undergraduate and graduate degrees (albeit until 1962 with a clause that any recipient of funds had to sign a non-Communist affidavit). Universities expanded exponentially: between 1958 and 1965, the University of California added seven new campuses. These schools were becoming, however, increasingly large, with little sense of community, and often with no collective sense of their purpose. As Clark Kerr, then president of the University of California system, remarked, "The modern university is a multi-university, a group of highly intelligent individuals held together by a common concern for park-

18. House Committee on Un-American Activities, *Operation Abolition*, 1960, video, 41:48, American Civil Liberties Union Records Audiovisual Materials (MC001.02.06), published September 21, 2010, YouTube, https://www.youtube.com/watch?v=MeiW63M 3bcI.

19. By 1956 close to eight million veterans had benefited from the GI Bill, more than two million of whom had attended institutions of higher education. By 1960, more than 3.5 million additional students were enrolled in such institutions, a number that would more than double by 1970. See, e.g., Keith Olson, "The GI Bill and Higher Education: Success and Surprise," *American Quarterly* 25, no. 5 (December 1973): 596–610; and John Thelin, *A History of American Higher Education* (Baltimore: Johns Hopkins University Press, 2004).

ing."[20] In 1939, universities and colleges across the United States had awarded 122,500 BA degrees, 15,000 MAs and 2,300 PhDs. By 1950, those numbers had quadrupled; 2009 saw the awarding of 1,600,000 BAs, 657,000, MAs, and 67,000 PhDs.[21] Appointment to most academic positions usually required a PhD.

If there was little community in higher education, there was also much freedom. The right of universities to act in loco parentis was swiftly undermined; dorms became coed. And as these students did not hold a job, they were much less susceptible to the opprobrium that came from being targeted by various government agencies. Most of those pursuing graduate degrees were most often in fact funded by their institution and were well into their twenties or beyond—in essence, a new kind of group had come into being: adults with no enforceable social responsibilities.

Thus a new political cohort appeared on the American political scene, independent, financially relatively solvent, and to a considerable degree not part of the normal everyday life of most Americans. It was self-sufficient, without established social responsibilities, and culturally and soon politically often found in opposition to the generation of its parents. "Something's happening / And you don't know what it is, / Do you, Mr. Jones?," sang Bob Dylan in his 1965 "Ballad of a Thin Man" as he became the troubadour for his generation.

SEX

A fifth development that led to the transformation of the American political landscape was consequent to a myriad of factors that encouraged the establishment of a dividing line between generations. In a set of US Supreme Court decisions, the prohibition on the sale of contraception aids was declared unconstitutional. In 1964, the first oral contraceptive, Enovid, went on the market (it had previously been quietly available in some states to regulate menstrual irregularity), and its sale was shortly legitimated to the nonmarried. Sex suddenly became apparently safer—the risk of pregnancy, unwanted relationships, and a need for illegal abortion was gone (abortion would be declared le-

---

20. Clark Kerr, *The Uses of the University* (Cambridge, MA: Harvard University Press, 2001).

21. Bureau of the Census, *Historical Statistics of the United States, Colonial Times to 1970* (1976), series H, 752, 757, 761; *Statistical Abstract: 2012 (2011)*, table 300.

gal, with certain restrictions, in 1973). Sexual relations no longer needed to be thought as the basis of a commitment—contraception meant that they had no necessary consequences. And many young people took advantage of this new freedom. It was not that the older generation had not engaged in sexual activity. It had assuredly done so, but if there had ensued consequences, one was expected to deal with them or be punished or shamed. In Grace Metalious's racy (for the time) novel *Peyton Place* (1956), all the characters who engage in premarital sex wind up banished or dead. With the new freedom, it seemed that there need be no consequences: "if it feels good, do it" became a popular slogan. In effect, what became known as the sexual revolution divided the country into two parts: those who could suffer guilt and the guiltless.[22] The division was only intensified with the growing ubiquity of white middle-class drugs (mainly marijuana) by the mid-to-late 1960s.[23] The satirist H. L. Mencken had defined the American puritanical strain as "the haunting fear that someone, somewhere, may be happy."[24] Now, for many Americans, that slogan was thrown to the wind. (As I write this, the death of *Playboy* founder Hugh Hefner has been announced, and the media are replaying all the old arguments about his worth or danger.)

STUDENTS FOR A DEMOCRATIC SOCIETY

What vision of politics accompanied these developments? The youth "counter" culture, as it become known, knew pretty much what it did not want; its ideas about what it *did* want were vague. Efforts were made at defining a political program, the most important of which was the founding and development of the Students for a Democratic Society (SDS).[25] The organization

22. See David Shaw, *The Pleasure Police: How Bluenose Busybodies and Lily-Livered Alarmists Are Taking All the Fun Out of Life* (New York: Doubleday, 1996).

23. On drugs, see the discussion in Matthew Levin, *Cold War University: Madison and the New Left in the Sixties* (Madison: University of Wisconsin Press, 2013), 142–44.

24. H. L. Mencken, "Sententiæ: The Citizen and the State," in *The Vintage Mencken* (New York: Alfred A. Knopf, 1955), 624, https://archive.org/stream/mencken017105mbp /mencken017105mbp_djvu.txt.

25. Much of this information is taken from personal experience. See also Kirkpatrick Sale, *SDS: Ten Years towards a Revolution* (New York: Random House, 1973); Kenneth Keniston, *The Uncommitted: Alienated Youth in American Society* (New York: Harcourt, Brace and World, 1965); Jonathan Eisen, ed., *The New Student Left* (New York: Pantheon, 1966); James Miller, *Democracy Is in the Streets: Port Huron to the Siege of Chicago* (New York: Simon and Schuster, 1987); Tom Hayden, *Reunion: A Memoir* (New York: Random House, 1988); Todd Gitlin, *The Sixties: Years of Hope, Days of Rage* (New York: Bantam, 1993).

started with a proposal by Alan Haber to hold a conference on the theme: "has the older generation anything to say?" Haber was the son of a progressive, politically involved family and was a member of the Student League for Industrial Democracy (SLID), which had renamed itself Students for a Democratic Society (SDS) in 1960. SLID had been the youth organization of the League for Industrial Democracy (LID), a socialist organization founded in 1905. (Apologies, but we enter the age of acronyms, not only on the Left.) LID was anti-Communist because of Stalinism and the repression in Hungary in 1956 and strongly pro-labor union. It was also wary of Haber's planned conference as it did not want students (notoriously undisciplined) taking a dominant role. In 1960, Haber was elected the first president of SDS, which was mainly concentrated at that time at the University of Michigan campus.

In June 1962, Haber's conference took place anyhow at an old labor center in Port Huron, Michigan. It started with three days of nonstop talking. Early on, a young seventeen-year-old, James Hawley, showed up and asked to be seated. He was a member of and represented the Progressive Youth Organizing Committee, which was a Communist front. Communism was not an issue to the younger Left, but the members of the Old Left at the conference were strongly opposed. Younger participants thought the issue silly. Older men, among them Michael Harrington (author of *The Other America*, a book about domestic poverty that was to influence John F. Kennedy) and Thomas Kahn (a civil rights activist, a leader of the Socialist Party and later an organizer of the 1963 March on Washington), were opposed to having anything to do with an acceptance of Communists or to seeing students as the leaders of anything. Eventually the young people went their own way.

Tom Hayden, the editor of the University of Michigan *Daily* newspaper, was charged with writing a manifesto for the conference—it became known as the Port Huron Statement.[26] The document is more notable for what it omits than what it asserts. It projects a picture of unhappy men (the text refers only to "men"), living in a world devoid of community, and wanting passionately to achieve some kind of personal and collective meaning: "The very isolation of the individual—from power and community and ability to aspire—means

---

26. For the final, published statement, see "Port Huron Statement," copyright 1993, Sixties Project, http://www2.iath.virginia.edu/sixties/HTML_docs/Resources/Primary/Manifestos/SDS_Port_Huron.html. For the original 1962 draft, as distributed by Alan Haber to attendees at the SDS Northeast Regional Conference, April 23, 2006, see "Port Huron Statement Draft," SDS, http://www.sds-1960s.org/PortHuronStatement-draft.htm. For a retrospective set of revaluations, see Richard Flacks and Nelson Lichtenstein, eds., *The Port Huron Statement* (Philadelphia: University of Pennsylvanian Press, 2015).

the rise of a democracy without publics."[27] America is a country where "lone-liness, estrangement, isolation describe the vast distance between man and man today." Its focus is what will be called the New Student Left, or in short, just the New Left. The tone is set by its opening line: "We are the people of this generation, bred in at least modest comfort, housed now in universities, look-ing uncomfortably towards the world we inherit." The text then instantiates the struggle against racism and the fear of nuclear war. It calls up the mem-ory of an American dream of justice that, it finds, has now faded into shadow. The dullness of a racist and Cold War everyday is said to be accepted by most of the population with the sense that there is no alternative. "People . . . fear change itself." *There is almost no sense in the document* that there is *anything* to be learned from the American past—a past that I have been trying to set out in this book.[28] The document continues, "The decline of utopia and hope is in fact one of the defining features of society today."

According to the Port Huron Statement, the problem is values, not poli-cies: "Perhaps matured by the past, we have no formulas, no closed theories." In other words, the past of American experience provides no guidelines or help. What is then to be done? Men must develop human relations with each other: "Human relations involve fraternity and honesty . . . human brother-hood must be willed." Will is a way to make a future, but not to learn from the past. The manifesto calls upon men (and women, though not explicitly) to unite the fragmented parts of personal histories: "Men have unrealized po-tential for self-cultivation, self-direction, self-understanding, and creativity. It is this potential we regard as crucial and to which we appeal." And there is no apparent limit to what is possible: "We regard men as infinitely precious and possessed of unfulfilled capacities for reason, freedom and love. . . . The goal of man and society should be human independence: a concern not with image of popularity, but with finding meaning in life that is personally authentic." The focus is on students, for students are found to be to some degree not yet fully incorporated by the system. The solution is a democratic society, where democracy means that all are capable of participating equally in ongoing de-cisions on an ongoing basis.

The original draft was much longer than the final document. Its analysis of the then current (and still present today) American situation was detailed

27. "Port Huron Statement," 6.
28. A recent book interestingly details the entanglement of the idea of an "American Dream" with right-wing movements. See Sarah Churchwell, *Behold, America: The Entan-gled History of "America First" and "The American Dream"* (New York: Basic Books, 2017).

and often insightful. Three issues dominate (as they do in the final document): racism, the Cold War, and the threat of nuclear destruction. All three are seen as contributing to a general feeling of alienation. From the point of view of the older Left, what is not there is a central attack on totalitarianism (i.e., Soviet Communism). Even more tellingly, however, *no* American figure, past or present, is named favorably. *It is as if the entire history of the ongoing contestations over citizenship, as recounted in this book, simply does not exist.* In a real sense, the authors of the Port Huron Statement have bought precisely the vision of America that those they opposed supported, bought it so as to resist it but not to call the reality into empirical and historical question.

This is all the more troubling in that their vision of politics often remarkably and problematically resembles that of some past movements in the United States. Politics is to be carried out by "public groupings"; it is the "art of collectively creating an acceptable pattern of social relations"; it "brings people out of isolation and into community"; channels should be "commonly available to relate men to knowledge and to power so that private problems . . . are formulated as general issues." But whereas in the past these ideas were held to be possible to everyone, the focus in the statement is not ordinary citizens but the universities and students. Why so? Universities, the statement asserts, are "located in a permanent position of social influence"; they are the "central institution for organizing, evaluating and transmitting knowledge"; they "demonstrate the unchangeable reliance of men of power on the men and storehouses of knowledge"; they are "the only mainstream institutions that are open to participation of individuals of nearly any viewpoint."[29]

The proposed solution was "participatory democracy." Participatory democracy required that all people participate. Leadership was thus seen as problematically threatening and undemocratic. Endless meetings were taken up with discussion by all present—one is reminded of Roger Williams's endless holy discussion sessions. Hayden once made a group of about thirty attendees sit in a circle so that he would not have to address them as a "leader." (Barney Frank, later a Congressman from the Massachusetts Fourth Congressional District, was present and quipped, "Tom—you are so grass roots I don't know whether to debate you or water you."[30]) There were some successes in community organizing, but the negative attitude toward leadership hampered effective action and, more important, meant that decisions often were ultimately made by those who stayed the longest—and those with the most

29. Quotations in this paragraph from "Port Huron Statement."
30. Author's personal recollection.

Sitzfleisch (staying power) were very often the most ideological and often more prone to violence than not (though it should be said that, in my experience, proposals to move to violent action often also came from FBI provocateurs, whom one recognized as such because their chinos had creases). Somewhat as with the 1919 Seattle strike, there was a general sense that the problem lay with elites themselves rather than with what gave rise to the particular set of elites that dominated the country. Though it tried to expand into local communities, SDS was often an intellectual project. Indeed, initially more members were graduate students than from any other group.

There was a strong tendency in SDS to think that the cure for the problems of liberal American democracy—problems that were real—lay in more democracy. But if that democracy were conceived of as simply local and participatory, it only could be maintained on the basis of a continuing crisis. And in such a situation, no institutions can be designed to maintain the necessary intensity required to support them. This was the problem that Lincoln confronted in his "Young Man's Lyceum" speech, and it returned with the failures of the New Student Left. The difficulty here is to determine which issues are susceptible to solution at a participatory level and to distinguish them from those that are not. The late Benjamin R. Barber, in his *If Mayors Ruled the World*, attempted to confront this issue, arguing that at the level of a city the demand for responsibility on the part of leaders is much more readily salient and productive of democratic participation ("Mme Mayor, why is my f.king street not plowed?").[31] But such possibilities never bothered SDS for very long.[32]

A MOVEMENT TAKES SHAPE

And to an important degree, too much was happening too quickly for such reflections to come to the front. The year 1964 saw the Freedom Summer, an

31. Benjamin R. Barber, *If Mayors Ruled the World: Dysfunctional Nations, Rising Cities* (New Haven, CT: Yale University Press, 2013). The question about snowplowing is my invention but in line with Barber's argument.

32. The apostrophe to the mayor is my construction. A partial exception to the occasional distraction of SDS is the Education Research and Action Project (ERAP), the best of which was probably in Newark. The projects often ran into trouble because of the contradiction between leadership and the desire to let "the people (who were the local poor) decide." For a good short analysis, see Richard Rothstein, "A Short History of ERAP," 2011, Calisphere, http://content.cdlib.org/view?docId=kt4k4003k7. See Tom Hayden, *Rebellion in Newark: Official Violence and Ghetto Response* (New York: Vintage, 1967).

ambitious project to train white students in nonviolence tactics and send them to the South to register blacks. While blacks had the right to vote, the criteria for voting were, according to the Constitution, set by the states, which permitted a lot of control on the part of whites. The exam for previously unregistered voters wanting to join the roll in Mississippi required answers to twenty-one questions on any part of the 285 sections of the state constitution, answers that had to satisfy white registrars. Not many blacks succeeded in passing the exam. The Freedom Summer registration project focused on Mississippi and lasted for ten weeks. After three weeks of training in nonviolence, volunteers went to Mississippi. (It must be said that the organizers were quite aware that there would be violence and did not hide it from the participants. More than one thousand volunteers and locals were arrested; eighty of those from the North were beaten; close to eighty black churches and homes were burned.[33]) Success in registration was small, but it laid the groundwork for extensive registration after a set of US Supreme Court decisions and passage of the Voting Rights Acts of 1964 and 1965.

Sadly, the greatest impact of that summer came with the murder in Mississippi of Andrew Goodman, Michael Schwerner, and James Chaney. Goodman and Schwerner were white; Chaney, who was black, had been tortured before being killed. Black men had been killed in the South for a long time, so Chaney's murder might easily have gone unremarked; however, the national news of the death of two white students pursuing a legitimate goal caused a national uproar and forced President Lyndon B. Johnson to call for an FBI investigation. The state refused to indict on murder charges (which fall under local jurisdiction), but seven defendants were convicted in federal court of violating the students' civil rights (which is a federal crime). They received relatively minor sentences.

The outrage, however, was instrumental to the passage of the Voting Rights Acts of 1964 and 1965.[34] "Something was happening . . ." On the West Coast, at the UC Berkeley campus, the Free Speech Movement—founded to demand the right, as had the Industrial Workers of the World (IWW, discussed in chapter 7), to express opinions in public—degenerated into the "Filthy Speech Movement."[35] Vowing the "clean up the mess in Berkeley," Governor Ronald

33. See Doug McAdam, *Freedom Summer* (New York: Oxford University Press, 1988); Sally Belfrage, *Freedom Summer* (Charlottesville: University Press of Virginia, 1965).

34. See the discussion in Robert Caro, *The Years of Lyndon Johnson*, vol. 4, *The Passage of Power* (New York: Knopf, 2012).

35. See Sheldon S. Wolin and Jack H. Schaar, *The Berkeley Student Rebellion and Beyond* (New York: New York Review of Books, 1974.)

Reagan targeted the movements in what became the kickstart for his presidential aspirations, a sign of how the "culture wars" were increasingly to divide the country.[36] The war in Vietnam expanded rapidly, and the draft began to pull in middle-class white men. In 1969, all deferments were abolished, and a lottery was instituted. Back in 1965, after much internal debate, CBS had broadcast Morley Safer's recording of the destruction of the Vietnamese village of Cam Ne, from his film apparently populated only by women, children, and old men. The mission was undertaken not in response to any hostile fire but, as one soldier put it, "to punish" the village. One infantryman explained, "We had to destroy the village in order to save it."[37] Massive organized protests broke out in what was called the "Vietnam Summer" of 1967. With the massacre of close to five hundred apparently unhostile villagers in My Lai in 1968, the moral issues of the war became heavily salient.

The United States, and indeed the world, seemed to come apart in 1968. President Johnson withdrew from a campaign for a second term after the North Vietnamese and Vietcong mounted a completely surprising and, for a while, effective attack all across South Vietnam during the Tet holidays. Martin Luther King Jr. was assassinated in April 1968. Six weeks later, Democrat Robert Kennedy, running for president as an antiwar candidate and ahead in the polls, was also murdered. The Democratic National Convention that August in Chicago saw huge demonstrations, which were brutally put down by an unrestrained Chicago Police force. Inside the convention hall, Senator Abraham Ribicoff referred from the rostrum to the "Gestapo tactics of the police" only to have Chicago Mayor Richard J. Daley shout at him from the floor, "Fuck off, you kike"—and have his words captured on national television. On CBS, Walter Cronkite excoriated the "goons" beating up students on the streets. Seven so-called leaders of the demonstration were arrested and charged with collusion to riot, even though they had never been in the same room together before their arrest.[38] Abroad, Paris and much of France became

36. See Lou Cannon, *Governor Reagan: His Rise to Power* (New York. Public Affairs, 2005).

37. Morley Safer, *CBS Evening News*, August 1965, video, 4:48, published April 18, 2009, YouTube, https://www.bing.com/videos/search?q=youtube+safer+cam+ne&view=detail &mid=95E95FA1B060A412AC6695E95FA1B060A412AC66&FORM=VIRE. For Safer's account, see Morley Safer, "The Burning at Cam Ne," PBS, 2003, http://www.pbs.org/weta /reportingamericaatwar/reporters/safer/camne.html.

38. Tom Hayden, Ron Sossi, and Frank Condon, *Voices of the Chicago 8: A Generation on Trial* (Chicago: City Lights, 2008). The trial of black activist Bobby Seale was separated from that of the other seven (white) defendants. The Ribicoff and Daley quotes are taken from the YouTube clip on the convention.

a battleground between students, workers, and the forces of order. Extended student revolts took place around the world, even in places far from Europe and America such as Sri Lanka. In August 1968, the USSR invaded Czechoslovakia to keep it from turning to the West. China apparently dissolved into the chaos of the Great Proletarian Cultural Revolution.

Back at home in the United States, with no sense of a past to draw on, the antiwar movement became increasingly anti-American, with chants for Ho Chi Minh and of "Hey, hey, LBJ, How many kids have you killed today?" The rock-folk performer Country Joe sang his "Fixing to Die" rag, which included the line, "Be the first one on your block/ to have your boy come home in a box." A brief glimmer of that peace for which people had hoped occurred with the Woodstock music festival in August 1969 (an event free of violence, although Jimi Hendrix had to quiet boos when he performed his astonishing solo-guitar version of the "Star Spangled Banner"). That glow faded later that year, however, with the killing of a spectator, several other deaths, and numerous acts of violence at a Rolling Stones concert in Altamont, CA (the Stones had allegedly hired bikers from the Hells Angels as keepers of order).[39] "Rock and Roll's all-time worst day, December 6th, a day when everything went perfectly wrong," editorialized *Rolling Stone*.

Things not only seemed to have fallen apart; to a great degree, they had. By the late 1960s, the New Left had produced no credible opposition. For much of it, "America" had become a dirty word. Most notably, it manifested no historical analysis and betrayed almost no sense that there was a tradition that it could draw on. In this sense, it accepted the middle-of-the-road and standard claim that America was and had always been an individualistic, self-centered, and corrupt society. (The Port Huron Statement has several paragraphs insisting that the SDS position is not "individualism.") To be blunt, the lack of any sense of the complexities of the American past meant that the movement increasingly lacked any strong sense of being American.

TO WHAT DID ALL THESE DEVELOPMENTS LEAD?

In this context, those who retained some hope for political action often turned to terroristic violence. The most important of these groups, the Weather Underground, grew out of a radical faction of SDS. Taking its name from a line in Dylan's "Subterranean Homesick Blues" ("You don't need a weather-

39. See the discussion in J. Miller, *Flowers in the Dustbin*.

man to know which way the wind blows"), the group explicitly declared war on America.[40] Attempts to recruit working-class (nonuniversity) youth (thus in opposition to the focus of the early SDS) sometimes took the form of going to a working-class beach, picking a fight, and then trying to have a "rectification" of the working-class opinions afterward. Weather People, as the group's members called themselves, sought to "smash monogamy" and to "prove we are not hippie faggots associated with SDS. . . . We will show them we can fight."[41] In 1969, a group of Weather People took over a high school auditorium, padlocked the doors, and proceeded to harangue the students (with little apparent success). In October of that year, in memory of the 1919 riots, another group planted a bomb at the foot of a statue of a policeman in Haymarket Square. This action was followed by the "Days of Rage," a set of violent demonstrations, again in Chicago.[42] The Weather Underground's model was to create a mass movement like the one they thought was taking place in China with the Red Guards.[43] At least forty separate incidences of violence instigated by the Underground occurred in 1969 and 1970, and further episodes continued sporadically through the rest of the 1970s and into the early 1980s.

The move to a terrorist form of violence had come easily. In 1970, three Weather People were killed in a Greenwich Village townhouse when a nail bomb they were building went off prematurely. In 1981, in conjunction with some members of the Black Liberation Army, several members of the Underground tried to rob a Brinks armored car. A gun battle broke out and a guard was killed, another wounded. When the escape vehicle was stopped, the arresting officers were tricked into thinking that the only person in the truck was a white woman (Kathy Boudin). When others of the gang leapt from the back of the truck and started shooting, two more policemen were killed.[44] Needless to say, no mass movement materialized.

40. "The goal is the destruction of US imperialism and the achievement of a classless world: world communism." See the twenty-eight-page founding manifesto, Karin Ashley et al., You Don't Need a Weatherman to Know Which Way the Wind Blows, June 18, 1969, Internet Archive, https://archive.org/stream/YouDontNeedAWeathermanToKnowWhich WayTheWindBlows_925#page/n0/mode/2up.

41. Susan Braudy, Family Circle: The Boudins and the Aristocracy of the Left (New York: Anchor Books, 2004). The book is an excellent overall account of the Weather Underground. See also Ron Jacobs, The Way the Wind Blew: A History of the Weather Underground (London: Verso, 1997).

42. Braudy, Family Circle, 183–84.

43. The "rectification of names" is a disciplinary device associated with, among other things, Chinese Communism.

44. See again Braudy, Family Circle.

At the same time that all the Weather Underground activity was happening, the Black Power movement, and the Black Panther Party (originally the Black Panther Party for Self-Defense) in particular, explicitly foreswore non-violence.[45] When a group of black students took over a building at Cornell University, they emerged carrying rifles. J. Edgar Hoover at the FBI declared the Black Panthers to be "the greatest threat to the internal security of the country."[46] A substantial number of Panthers were killed in gunfights, as were several policemen. Eventually, because of internal conflicts and police repression, the Black Panther Party faded.

The result of this failure on the part of the Weather Underground and the Black Panthers is that for the first time, there was no credible opposition to the dominant powers—there was no apparent way to challenge coherently those who held otherwise. Academics often seemed not to mind. The sociologist Daniel Bell wrote a book entitled *The End of Ideology*, celebrating the arrival of a time when decisions were made rationally, democratically, and not "ideologically."[47] Robert Lane, a Yale University political scientist, wrote the book *Political Ideology*, in which he proclaimed that "a touch of anomie" was necessary for a democratic society to work—people really should not care too much—and were they to care too much, Lane heard the sound of the jackboots coming.[48] At Harvard University, Samuel Huntington, the developer of the "forced-draft urbanization" solution to the Vietnam War (which entailed bombing the peasants out of the countryside into the cities, where they could be controlled with the assumption that all who remain in the countryside are enemies), argued that there had been too much democracy during the 1960s.[49] The generation old enough to remember the 1930s thought it was coming again; those not old enough knew not where to turn.

By the 1980s, what "being American" meant for most Americans had been largely defined by the Cold War: it meant to be opposed to the USSR.

45. The literature is extensive, but see William L. Van DeBurgh, *New Day in Babylon: The Black Power Movement and American Culture, 1965–1975* (Chicago: University of Chicago Press, 1992).

46. This statement of June 15, 1969 was widely reported. See "Hoover and the F.B.I.," PBS, 2002, https://www.pbs.org/hueypnewton/people/people_hoover.html.

47. Daniel Bell, *The End of Ideology: On the Exhaustion of Political Ideas in the Fifties* (New York: Free Press, 1960). The book was updated in 2000 with a new essay by Bell, "The Resumption of History in the New Century."

48. Robert Lane, *Political Ideology: Why the American Common Man Believes What He Does* (New York: Free Press, 1967), 249.

49. Samuel P. Huntington, "The Bases of Accommodation," *Foreign Affairs* 46, no. 4 (July 1968): 642–56.

The saliency of this opposition varied greatly, but there was little of a positive conception. Those who did not accept this opposition as defining increasingly found the political system corrupt and withdrew from politics, abandoning any sense that being a citizen meant anything other than a passport or, as in the case of the Weather Underground and Black Panthers, turned to terrorism, modeled either on the Algerian National Liberation Front against the French or the Chinese Great Proletarian Cultural Revolution.

Still, some attempts of citizenly involvement persisted. The most significant attempt at an enhanced notion of citizenship probably came with President Johnson's Great Society plan, which clearly drew on his memory of President Franklin Delano Roosevelt's 1944 "Second Bill of Rights." The Great Society consisted in a series of programs designed to address civil rights, education, health (Medicare), welfare, arts and culture (Public Broadcasting System; National Endowment for the Humanities; National Endowment for the Arts), transportation, consumer protection, the environment, and labor, matters left incomplete or not dealt with by the New Deal. Notably, much like many programs in the early New Deal, it sought to implement these programs on a local level, bypassing the traditional control of governors and senators. Johnson's skill as a president led to the passage of a large number of bills spanning an enormous range of social issues. In announcing the Great Society on May 22, 1964, Johnson said:

> For a century we labored to settle and to subdue a continent. For half a century we called upon unbounded invention and untiring industry to create an order of plenty for all of our people.
>
> The challenge of the next half century is whether we have the wisdom to use that wealth to enrich and elevate our national life, and to advance the quality of our American civilization.
>
> Your imagination, your initiative, and your indignation will determine whether we build a society where progress is the servant of our needs, or a society where old values and new visions are buried under unbridled growth. For in your time we have the opportunity to move not only toward the rich society and the powerful society, but upward to the Great Society.
>
> The Great Society rests on abundance and liberty for all. It demands an end to poverty and racial injustice, to which we are totally committed in our time. But that is just the beginning.[50]

50. "President Lyndon B. Johnson's speech at the University of Michigan, May 24, 1964," Lyndon Baines Johnson Library and Museum, National Archives and Records Ad-

It was a noble vision, to some degree retracing the outlines of this book, to some degree a call for a renewed vision of citizenship: *"Your imagination, your initiative, and your indignation will determine whether we build a society where progress is the servant of our needs."* Eventually, however, resistance from the state and congressional powers that were bypassed by the programs, and mounting expenditures and time devoted to the War in Vietnam, coupled with the election of a less Progressive Congress in 1966, led to the effective demise of most of the program.[51]

It is hard to underestimate the costs of the Cold War. The federal budget for 1985 was $794 billion (note this is after the end of the Vietnam War, which was mainly paid for in still-existing debt). Of that amount, $294 billion was tied up by Social Security. Of the remaining $500 billion, $286 billion went for defense and another $12 billion for arms shipments to allies; $9 billion was for the Department of Energy development of nuclear weapons and $27 billion for veterans' benefits. Take away the $142 billion paid as interest on loans and at most $25 billion was left for domestic programs, hardly enough to meet maintenance and with nothing for new developments.[52] As the infrastructure of schools, highways, and most public goods crumbles, it is not surprising that the government is increasingly resented for taking money and producing no obvious benefits.

The consequence of all these developments is a progressive erosion of the value of the status of citizen, an erosion that, as Hemingway wrote, starts slowly and then is all of a sudden catastrophic. For those not part of the dominant mainstream, America itself became the enemy—*in effect, they accepted the understanding of America held by the mainstream.* The consequences of this are, however, general. With this, the government is increasingly perceived not as responsible for (at least some idea of) the public good, but as a faction—it is not surprising that as I write this sentence in mid-2018, the approval rating of Congress stands at 11 percent. In the increasing absence of public space, Con-

---

ministration, Internet Archive, updated February 17, 2002, https://web.archive.org/web/20020602041420/http://www.lbjlib.utexas.edu/johnson/archives.hom/speeches.hom/640522.asp.

51. See Caro, *Passage of Power*; Alan Brinkley, *Liberalism and Its Discontents* (Cambridge, MA: Harvard University Press, 2012). See also Sidney M. Milkis and Jerome M. Mileur, eds., *The Great Society and The High Tide of Liberalism* (Amherst: University of Massachusetts Press, 2005).

52. United States Office of Management and Budget, *Historical Tables, Budget of the United States Government*, 1985–2018, https://fraser.stlouisfed.org/title/383.

gress should be the body that represents one's citizenly hopes—something that James Madison knew a faction never could. In such circumstances, it is also not surprising that any residual hope for public virtue will tend to be focused on the chief executive, who since 2016 has increasingly not been a person of public orientation.

11

AT HOME ALONE: THE PROBLEMS OF CITIZENSHIP IN OUR AGE

If men are to remain civilized, or to become so, they must develop and perfect the art of associating to the same degree that the equality of conditions is among them.

ALEXIS DE TOCQUEVILLE, *DEMOCRACY IN AMERICA*

I have said more or less that the Declaration of Independence is the very ring-bolt to the chain of your nation's destiny.... The principles contained in that instrument are saving principles.

FREDERICK DOUGLASS, "WHAT IS THE SLAVE TO THE FOURTH OF JULY?"

To become ... enfranchised ..., and now, impediments removed, to stand and start without humiliation and equal to the rest; to commence, or have the road clear'd to commence, the grand experiment of development, whose end (perhaps requiring several generations) may be the forming of a full-grown man or woman—that is something.

WALT WHITMAN, *DEMOCRATIC VISTAS*

Some say the world will end in fire,
Some say in ice.
From what I've tasted of desire
I hold with those who favor fire.
But if it had to perish twice,
I think I know enough of hate
To say that for destruction ice
Is also great
And would suffice.

ROBERT FROST, "FIRE AND ICE"

I give a set of epigraphs here that are arranged chronologically and in some sense retrace part of the argument of this book. The last one, from Robert Frost, pertains mostly to the present chapter. As this last chapter is about that which is still happening or might happen, it is necessarily speculative in ways that preceding chapters were not. It starts from the sense that in the end, very little is now left of political importance of the developments described in chapter 10. This includes both the cultural and overtly political (e.g., the Great Society) aspects. The frantic creativity of the 1960s popular culture has to a considerable degree been appropriated by large companies. In the 2016 election for Congress, it was estimated that 402 seats out of 450 were "safe" in the sense that victory was won by a margin of at least 10 percentage points.[1] Much of this predictability is consequent to the shameless gerrymandering of congressional districts, mostly by Republican-dominated state legislatures. A slew of books bewailing present-day American politics continues to grow, with titles like *How Democracies Die* (by Steven Levitsky and Daniel Ziblatt), *Against Elections: The Case for Democracy* (by David Van Reybrouck), and *The People vs. Democracy: Why Our Freedom Is in Danger and How to Save It* (by Yascha Mounck).

It is not that no one has noticed that something is happening: even Mr. Jones may have. But it is unclear whether these books provide much of a realistic path to an alternate future. Yascha Mounck writes, "To save democracy, we need . . . to unite citizens around a common conception of their nation; to give them real hope for their economic future; and to make them more resistant to the lies and the hate they encounter on social media each and every day."[2] True, but not only is this more easily said than done, the sentiment is expressed from the height of someone who has no sense of being affected by the problems he often interestingly identifies (Mounck is a Harvard professor): *who* is the "we" that "needs" to unite citizens?

There are two developments since the early 1990s that dramatically affect the possibilities for citizenship. Though they have emerged more or less separately, they do to a great degree enhance each other. These developments are, on the one hand, the growing ubiquity of social media, and, on the other, the rise of non-state-based terrorism. Given these developments, what hap-

---

1. The figure comes from Joseph Califano, *Our Damaged Democracy: We the People Must Act* (New York: Touchstone, 2018).

2. Yascha Mounck, *The People vs. Democracy: Why Our Freedom Is in Danger and How to Save It* (Cambridge, MA: Harvard University Press, 2018), 194.

pens to any hopes for, to any possibilities of, citizenship? My discussion will of necessity be less historical and more conceptual than in the chapters that preceded this one.

SOCIAL MEDIA

The very idea of representation has changed. In the introduction, I cited Jane Mansbridge as pointing out that something has changed when I can, as a resident of California, be asked and be expected to support a congressional candidate in Wisconsin and find myself contributing.[3] How so? And what difference does it make?

A preliminary element: in the 1960s, in the initial decade of the growth of what came to be a youth—to some degree counter—culture, if one listened to rock and roll on the radio, there were relatively few stations to tune in to because there were not that many FM stations. Thus, when a record such as the Beatles' *Rubber Soul* first came out in 1965, basically everyone interested in rock and roll knew about it and all fans heard the same record. (I heard it first in my Volkswagen over WTRY, Radio Albany, 98.3 FM. They played it over and over again.) It was a subject of conversation, of argument; pro and con groups were formed. A kind of minipublic materialized.

Today, however, the FM band has a separate station for every conceivable type of popular music (and with online sources like Spotify, for every conceivable type of music, period). This means that one can listen to—and if one wants, *only* to—a particular type of music. The proliferation of possibilities has contributed the increasing isolation of each into predefined groups. My television subscription gives me on the order of a few hundred channels, yet not everyone will watch every available channel: for example, recent polls show that people with right-wing views get most of their news only from Fox News.

In the preceding chapter I spoke about the importance of national news media in making visible local developments. As Todd Gitlin put it, in some important sense the whole world *was* watching.[4] In the 1960s events, a collec-

---

3. Mansbridge, *Beyond Adversary Democracy*; Mansbridge, "Clarifying Political Representation" (see intro., n. 3).
4. Gitlin, *Whole World Is Watching*.

tive of some kind was generated when, sitting in front of the TV in Hamilton, New York (for instance), one became part of those distressed at the sight of police dogs and firehoses in Selma, Alabama. I am not concerned here, however, with the twentieth-century developments in radio and television, which were, to some degree, covered in chapter 10. I am concerned in this chapter with the impact of twenty-first-century social media: the internet, Facebook, video games, the proliferation of channels with expanded bandwidth, and such.

The first thing to notice is that all these media are owned. This is inevitable, not necessarily bad in itself in terms of content (for a Fox News, there is an MSNBC), but it does mean that they all respond to some similar criteria, in particular the financial necessity to break even and the desire to do as much better as possible than that. The fact that they are owned, however, may lead one to overlook an important aspect of these new media. Yascha Mounck usefully distinguishes between "one-to-many" media and "many-to-many" media.[5] Until sometime in the 1990s, the basic mode of media was one-to-many. The combination of constraints from technology and from cost meant that there were a limited number of information sources, each reaching out to a large number of listeners. What has happened since then with platforms like Facebook and Twitter and the existence of the World Wide Web (as of 1991) is that messages are broadcast by a wide range of users to a wide range of users, the many-to-many model.[6] In effect, this development meant that the power of any gatekeeper was drastically reduced, even in countries where the state sought to censor content. The fact that these media are owned means that any effectuated conditioning of public opinion has its origins in the private realm and to generally inaccessible decisions, hence built into such opinion is always a sense that there may be something behind it, some unknown and kept secret. (In this sense, it is different from the penny press of the nineteenth century, where the orientation of the particular newspaper was worn, so to speak, on the sleeve.) Therefore,

---

5. Mounck, *People vs. Democracy*, 139.

6. A number of technological developments had to occur for this many-to-many approach to be possible, specifically the setting up of a system of unique identifiers (uniform resource locators, or URLs), a publishing language (hypertext markup language, or HTML), and a transfer protocol (hypertext transfer protocol, or HTTP). The addition of a graphical browser in 1993 further extended capability. See Tim Berners-Lee, "The World Wide Web: Past, Present and Future," August 1996, World Wide Web Consortium (W3C), https://www.w3.org/People/Berners-Lee/1996/ppf.html.

private formed opinion will come to dominate the public through the existence of publicity.[7]

Scholars have responded to these ever-growing extensions of such media in two ways, one positive and one negative. A first response was one of welcome. Larry Diamond, a Stanford political scientist, saw a potential empowerment of the average citizen. Now ordinary people could "report news, expose wrongdoings, express opinions, mobilize protest, monitor elections, scrutinize governments, deepen participation and expand the horizons of freedom. . . . Liberation technology is any form of information and communication technology that can expand political, social and economic freedom . . . essentially . . . the computer, the internet, the mobile phone [and] 'new social media' such as Facebook and Twitter."[8] James Fishkin has used media to try to raise the level of knowledge that citizens have about particular issues and thus participate more knowingly in deliberation.[9] Such deliberation, however, takes place in circumstances separate from everyday life and pressures. The initial enthusiasm for "digital democracy" has come under criticism, basically along lines that held that even many-to-many communication would tend to consolidate beliefs in like-minded groups. Cass Sunstein, a law professor now at Harvard University, spoke of the development of "echo chambers."[10] It is much the same argument.

THE QUESTION OF "FACT"

Both the optimist's and the pessimist's take on media are able to provide cases that illustrate their claims. It seems to me that the problem lies somewhat deeper than the existence of empirically differing facts. By and large, the

7. See Eva Horn, "Logics of Political Secrecy," *Theory Culture Society* 28 (2011), 104. I owe this reference to Andrew Poe, "Politics without Secrets" (unpublished manuscript, 2018), and have profited from reading his article. For a defense of journalism's possibilities, see Michael Schudson, *Why Journalism Still Matters* (Cambridge: Polity, 2018).

8. Larry Diamond, "Liberation Technology," *Journal of Democracy* 21, no. 3 (2010): 70, http://www.journalofdemocracy.org/articles-files/gratis/Diamond-21-3.pdf. I was prompted by Mounck's book to look this up. Mounck does note that Diamond is also conscious of the dangers of such technology.

9. See e.g. James Fishkin, *Democracy and Deliberation: New Directions for Democratic Reform* (New Haven, CT: Yale University Press, 1991).

10. Cass Sunstein, *Republic.com 2.0* (Princeton, NJ: Princeton University Press, 2009). See also Siva Vaidhyanathan, *Antisocial Media: How Facebook Disconnects Us and Undermines Democracy* (Oxford: Oxford University Press, 2017).

claims made on social media are claims about facts. The news is filled these days with discussion of "post-truth," "alternate facts," "lies," "misleading statements," and much more. "News" itself is called into question—there is "fake news." Many observers worry that a significant portion of the US population (and in particular much of its present administration) rejects the validity of science and any objective determination of what are "facts."

Some scholars might call this problem a consequence of (at least part of) postmodernism—and some have. And there appears to be a certain amount of credible evidence that during the 1970s, the US Central Intelligence Agency (CIA) actively promoted interest in European postmodernism (as espoused by Jacques Derrida, Roland Barthes, Michel Foucault, Gilles Deleuze and Félix Guattari, and others) to undercut the authority of more Marxist-oriented thinkers (such as Louis Althusser, Jean-Paul Sartre, Maurice Merleau-Ponty, and Simone de Beauvoir).[11]

In the face of all this, and having spent much of my professional career in an attempt to understand and make the thought of Friedrich Nietzsche and others available, what am I to say? As he is for some scholars the originator of postmodernism, Nietzsche does appear explicit: "Against that positivism which stops before phenomena, saying 'there are only facts,' I should say: no, it is precisely facts that do not exist, only interpretations."[12] Elsewhere he asserts that "there are no things in themselves, that the very notion of a 'thing' is itself a construction."[13] Not only are there no facts, but Nietzsche will push the point further. In an entry entitled "The Researcher," he writes, "There are many kinds of eyes. Even the sphinx has eyes—and consequently there are many kinds of 'truths' and consequently there is no truth."[14] Nietzsche's point, however, is not to provide support for the Trump administration press secretaries.

Nietzsche's point is not that truths are many—a kind of becoming prag-

---

11. See Gabriel Rockhill, "The CIA Reads French Theory: On the Intellectual Labor of Dismantling the Cultural Left," *Los Angeles Review of Books*, February 28, 2017. In the late 1960s and early 1970s, several of my friends in graduate school wrote dissertations on Marx—good ones—only to find that three years later, no one seemed interested. Indeed, some decades ago, I wrote a basically sympathetic review of Herbert Dreyfus and Paul Rabinow's book on Foucault, only to ask at the end why the name of Marx was not mentioned.

12. Friedrich Nietzsche, *The Will to Power*, ed. Walter Kaufmann (New York: Random House, 1968, para. 481.

13. Friedrich Nietzsche, *Kritische Studien Ausgabe*, 15 vols. (Berlin: De Gruyter, 1990), 12:141 (hereafter cited as *KSA*). Translations from this work are mine.

14. Nietzsche, *KSA*, 11:598.

matic pluralism—but that anything that can be designated as true necessarily contains multiplicities and contradictions: "All truth is simple—is that not a double (*zweifach*) lie?"[15] That aphorism from *Twilight of the Idols* is a short version of the more extended *Nachlass* entry: "All truth is simple: that is a double lie (*zweifach*). Everything that is simply is plain imaginary, it is not 'true.' However what is real, what is true, is neither single (*Eins*) nor indeed ultimately reducible to singularity."[16] What is at stake is rather the concept of what a "fact" is.[17] If one understands the rationalism associated with Immanuel Kant and his inheritors as attempting to ground our knowledge of the world, in "Schopenhauer as Educator," Nietzsche foresaw problematic consequences: "This danger of the despair of truth attends every thinker who sets out from the Kantian philosophy providing he is a vigorous and whole man in suffering and desire and not a mere clattering thought—and calculating—machine.... As seen, however, as Kant might start to exercise a popular influence we shall be aware of it in the form of a gnawing and disintegrating relativism and skepticism.... We cannot decide whether what we call truth is really truth or rather it only appears to us to be such."[18] Nietzsche does seem to me to describe, al-

---

15. Friedrich Nietzsche, "Maxims and Arrows," in *Twilight of the Idols*, 4, repr. in Nittzsche, *KSA*, 6:59.

16. Nietzsche, *KSA*, 13:478-79. I am assisted in the passage by Babette E. Babich, *Nietzsche's Philosophy of Science: Reflecting Science on the Ground of Art and Life* (Albany: State University of New York Press, 1994), 112-13.

17. Philosophically, the matter *is* more complex and has its origins in the impact that the publication of the *Critique of Pure Reason* had on the world. Its author, Immanuel Kant, had shown that in fact we never perceive the world as it is (*an sich*) but only that which our senses make available to us. His achievement in the *First Critique* was to have shown the following line of reasoning: first, all experience is experience of and only of appearances; second, whatever it is that appearances are of is something that cannot be the object of experience; third, we can know only how it is that we have experiences; and fourth, it is in reflecting on how it is that we have experience and knowledge of experience that we can ground reason. Kant's presentation was immediately recognized as the source of a radical new conception of philosophy, one that admitted the full force of skepticism but did not remain mired in it. It was also recognized has having released what in 1792 Jacob Oberreit called a "gigantic horror" on the world. The replacement, as it were, of God with the noumenal (that about which nothing is knowable) changed the human position in the world.

18. Friedrich Nietzsche, "Schopenhauer als Erzieher," 3, in *Werke Kritische Gesamtausgabe*, 3-1 (Berlin: De Gruyter, 1970,) 346-47, my translation. One might compare the account of Kant in the preceding note to contemporary bloodless interpretations of the *First Critique*. See also Babette E. Babich, "Ex aliquod nihil.: Nietzsche on Science, Anarchy and Democratic Nihilism," *American Catholic Philosophical Quarterly* 84, no. 2 (Spring 2010): 231-56, to which I owe the quote from Oberreit, a Swiss doctor and philosopher, partly responsible or the recovery of the Nibelungen sagas.

ready in 1874, pretty much the situation that concerns us today, now not only in the rarefied air of epistemology but in everyday political life.

WHAT ARE "FACTS" POLITICALLY?

The point, then, is that anything that is seen as a "fact" is as such suscept-ible to being called into question. Hannah Arendt pointed out that it was no longer so certain that everyone will say that World War I started when Ger-many invaded Belgium, or that Trotsky played an important part in the Soviet Revolution. What is at stake here is how properly to understand what a fact is. And the existence of any political community rests on what its members share as facts. In effect, the proclamation by President Trump of "fake news" and "alternate facts" is an attempt to split apart the public or prevent any col-lective opposition from coalescing. This tactic is not new—it took a long time for understanding and experience to coalesce around the "facts" of the Viet-nam War. When I was canvassing during the "Vietnam Summer" of 1967, in house after house, I would be told that "we are against the war but no one else around here is"—which makes impossible a shared vision of the place of the citizen.

To accomplish this fragmentation requires that *both* the splitter and the au-dience conceive of facts along lines of a positivistic understanding of "fact" and "truth," which mistake paradoxically permits one then to question them. The positivistic understanding presumes three claims. The first is that there is a clear-cut conceptual separation between facts and values and that, in con-sequence, values are subjective, not of the world, and could and should be kept apart from one's analysis of social reality. This claim was not a denial that values were "important," but it was a denial that values were objects of knowl-edge.[19] In essence, contemporary claims about alternate truths hold that facts are of the same status as how positivism sees values.

There is a variant on this claim that we find in thinkers such as V. I. Lenin. For Lenin, truth was something to be realized historically. Therefore, what counted as truth was any claim that advanced the cause of Communism and, he thought, human freedom. This meant that what was true at any given time

19. See James Conant, "Must We Show What We Cannot Say," in *The Senses of Stanley Cavell*, ed. Richard Fleming and Michael Payne (Philadelphia: Bucknell University Press, 1989), esp. 252–53.

was not necessarily what had been true earlier.[20] It is no accident that Steven Bannon, at that time chief strategist in the Trump administration, proclaimed himself, quite correctly, to be a "Leninist."

The second claim of positivistic understanding is parent to the first. It is a claim that propositions about the world could and should be made to speak for themselves—thus that propositions about the world should have a validity independent of the person who advanced them. One could and should clearly separate the speaker from the spoken, for if one did one's work right, not just empirical claims about the world but concepts themselves would stand independently of the speaker. In its simplest form, the claim is that a statement such as "mass equals force times acceleration" was true independently of who said it and of when, where, and what it was said and that anything claiming to be a fact should have this quality.[21] Inside a Newtonian framework, however, there is no way sensibly to question $f = ma$. Since one can question the origins of the First World War, no claim will meet this test.

The third claim of positivistic understanding derives from the first two. It holds that certain forms of discourse (claims to knowledge) are responsible and responsive to the real world in ways that other forms (one might think of them as emotive, or expressive) are not.[22] In the first form, honesty toward the world requires something of the thinker; in the second, anything (apparently) goes. It followed from this that should a statement about the world not be "true," over time the world would provide the means of rejecting it. Yet to the degree that communication develops "echo chambers," no matter what kind, this kind of correction will not come about. Nor will the provision of "information" about a topic be of service, as information is a claim about facts. Contrary to the standard view, a claim to factual truth depends centrally on the quality of character of the person who makes it, of what he or she is able and willing to acknowledge. Simply "knowing" something to be the case is never sufficient in the human world.[23]

These rejections commit me to the position that the validity of a statement—its truth value—cannot be ascertained, at least in politics, by its

20. See my discussion in Strong, *Politics without Vision*, chap. 5.

21. To some degree, certain developments in philosophy of science have called this claim into question also. I think of the work of Thomas Kuhn, Stephen Toulmin, Ludwig Fleck, and others.

22. See the discussion in Stanley Cavell, *Themes Out of School: Effects and Causes* (Chicago: University of Chicago Press, 1984), 36.

23. See the discussion in Stanley Cavell, "Knowing and Acknowledging," in Cavell, *Must We Mean What We Say?*, 238–66 (see chap. 4, n. 47).

correspondence to the world, nor by its subservience to a set of rules. In politics, truth claims are made on the basis of "how the world appears to me." As Linda Zerilli has pointed out, the proper emphasis in that sentence falls not on the "me" but on the "appears," which, inevitably, means that truth claims in politics are expressed in speech.[24] Appearance is not "subjective," for anything that is expressed in speech is necessarily expressed in a manner common to more than one person. This is what Hans-Georg Gadamer calls "hermeneutics": "a shared and comprehensible reference to the things in themselves."[25]

Thus, to make a claim with reference to a "fact" is to place oneself in a space that is necessarily common. All those who are in this space—users of speech—will of necessity be speaking of the world as it appears. However, as the space is common, it requires of them that they enter into a dialogue with anyone else in that space. The question in relation to "fake news" and "alternate facts," then, becomes one of the actuality of dialogue between the speakers. It is of note that both Abraham Lincoln and Franklin Delano Roosevelt surrounded themselves with men of forcefully different opinions—and listened and responded. To the degree that one party refuses dialogue (that can happen also if either party insists that its opinion is *the* truth), that party is what one might call "soul-blind."[26] That person is, in an important sense, not (fully) human, certainly not a co-citizen, and the matter cannot be resolved by appealing to so-called objective "facts." As Stanley Cavell has written, "It is sometimes imperative to say that women or children or black people or criminals are human beings. This is a call for justice. For justice to be done, a change of perception, a modification of seeing, may be called for. But does it follow that those whose perceptions, or whose natural reactions, must suffer change have until that time been seeing women or children or black people or criminals as something other than human beings?"[27] The answer is, I think, that it is not that they have been seeing the others as something other than human beings so much as it is that they have been missing something about themselves. For a truth of a matter to become apparent to them requires what Zerilli calls "an exchange of plural opinions about what

24. See the discussion in Linda Zerilli, "Truth and Politics," in *Truth and Democracy*, ed. Jeremey Elkins and Andrew Norris (Philadelphia: University of Pennsylvania Press, 2010), 65.

25. Hans-Georg Gadamer, "The Problems of Historical Consciousness," in *Interpretive Social Science: A Second Look*, ed. Paul Rabinow and William Sullivan (Berkeley: University of California Press, 1987), 135. Also cited by Zerilli, "Truth and Politics."

26. See Jonathan Havercroft and David Owen, "Soul-Blindness, Police Orders and Black Lives Matter: Wittgenstein, Cavell and Rancière," *Political Theory* (forthcoming).

27. Stanley Cavell, *The Claim of Reason* (New York: Oxford University Press, 1999), 372.

might be."[28] The failure to do this makes one less aware of one's own humanity. And here one might refer back to my various citations of James Baldwin.[29]

This is one aspect, one might say the epistemological aspect or macroaspect, of what the proliferation of media makes possible. I now wish to turn to a medium level. The political realm has in the second decade of the twenty-first century seen the increased use of "big data." Cambridge Analytica, a firm that was active in the 2016 Trump campaign, had collected, mainly from Facebook, approximately five thousand data points on 250 million Americans.[30] These data could be aggregated into groups in terms of what appeals, if any, might be likely to sway the vote toward Donald Trump (e.g., single mothers worried about day care). Accordingly, the campaign issued messages aimed specifically at these groups composed of like-minded folk. Jamie Barlett recounted how he was able to feed his two hundred Facebook "friends" into a similar computer, only to have it spit out a detailed and accurate description of him, his interests, his education, his concerns, and so forth.[31]

The point here is that the increasing use of big data in politics contributes to the formation of echo chambers that can be used by candidates. The combination goes along with, and no doubt contributes to, the growing demise of political parties. Classically the function of a party was the bring together people with different agendas and interests and unify them around a mutual acceptable candidate. The party was the means by which to retain pluralism and make it work. The use of big data, on the other hand, works to increase separation. It undercuts any necessity for dialogue.[32] As Barlett says, "Big data . . . points to a more personalized model: work out who people are, find the one thing they care about, and zero in on that."[33] Alexis de Tocqueville had written in the nineteenth century that civic and private associations were a

28. Zerilli, "Truth and Politics," 66. See Jill Abramson, *Merchants of Truth: The Business of News and the Fight for Facts* (New York: Simon and Schuster, 2019).

29. Most of these citations refer to Baldwin, *Collected Essays* (see chap. 2, n. 4).

30. Much of the factual information in this section comes from the important Jamie Bartlett, *The People vs. Tech: How the Internet Is Killing Democracy (and How to Save It)* (London: Ebury Press, 2018), esp. 72–101. Bartlett is director of the Centre for the Analysis of Social Media at the think tank Demos.

31. Bartlett, *People vs Tech*, 22.

32. I do not want the invocation of dialogue to link my thought with that of Jürgen Habermas. In a different context, Chantal Mouffe put the point well. What political parties accomplished was "*Einstimmung,* a fusion of voices made possible by a common form of life [being a Democrat, for instance], not *Einverstand,*—product of reason, like Habermas." Chantal Mouffe, *The Democratic Paradox* (London: Verso, 2007), 70.

33. Bartlett, *People vs Tech*, 84.

necessity for democracies to thrive. If in the past tyrants sought to dismantle them, technology may be doing the same on its own.

The development of increasingly sophisticated media technology has and will increasingly have other consequences: the availability of unbreakable encryption will ensure that no one can know with whom they are "communicating"; the extension of cryptocurrencies such as Bitcoin will undercut the state's ability to tax; a breakdown of the state as an independent political form; growing inequality; and the development of a "barbell" society.

I now wish to turn to a microlevel, for I find some of the same dynamics in the addiction that many people have to their cyborg extensions—smartphones, video games, texting, and other online activity. The thrust of the preceding discussion was to depict a society increasingly structured along the lines of an echo chamber where like-minded talk only to like-minded. The pluralism of perspectives that Arendt found so necessary for human thriving tends simply to disappear. I considered this first conceptually and then as consequent to technological developments. On the individual level, the same developments take place. Sherry Turkle, in her book *At Home, Together: Why We Expect More from Technology and Less from Each Other* details her research into the effect of the internet and smartphones on late adolescents.[34] She writes in conclusion, "The ties we form through the Internet are not, in the end, the ties that bind. But they are the ties that preoccupy."[35] Later she continues, "At the extreme, we are so enmeshed in our [internet] connections that we neglect each other."[36] In *The Second Self*, she notes that originally relations to one's computer were "almost always one-on-one, a person alone with a machine. . . . [Later] this is no longer the case. . . . [The] computer had become a portal that enabled people to lead parallel lives in virtual worlds."[37] And with the development of mobile devices, such connectivity is with us 24/7.

My strong claim here is that all three of these developments—alternate facts, big data, and the internet—function is the same manner, albeit on different levels, to encourage "echo chambers" and a like-minded isolation. *This is a gradual disappearance of a public realm where people of different minds come together and without becoming the same come to collectively accepted conclusions, thereby constituting themselves a people.* If we all agree on the same thing, there

34. Sherry Turkle, *At Home, Together: Why We Expect More from Technology and Less from Each Other* (New York: Basic Books). See also Sherry Turkle, *The Second Self: Computers and the Human Spirit* (Cambridge, MA: MIT Press, 2005).

35. Turkle, *At Home, Together*, 280.

36. Turkle, *At Home*, 294.

37. Turkle, *Second Self*, 119 (Kindle edition).

is no citizenship. And, as I shall argue in the following section, the matter is made worse by recent worldwide political developments.

TERRORISM AND PUBLIC SPACE

In 1985, Georgi Arbatov, a member of the USSR Presidium, made a speech in the United States in which he announced "We are going to do a terrible thing to you. We are going to take away your enemy." And indeed, in 1989, the Berlin Wall came down; Soviet control over Eastern Europe loosened and disappeared; the USSR broke up—and Communism as America had known it came to an end. The Nixon-Kissinger overtures to China radically changed the form of world politics. For the first time since the late 1940s America was left without an enemy to define itself against.

In the preceding chapters, I have in effect argued that since the First World War, the answer to what being an American came increasingly to be more and more shaped by opposition to what one was not. This dialectic is the very thing that the philosopher Nietzsche meant by *ressentiment*: I know who I am because I am *not* you. I do not mean that this was all there was—much was done to give American citizenship positive content. But the danger of *ressentiment* is that, to the degree that one relies on it, one *requires* an enemy. It is in fact in one's interest, as it were, to make sure that there is an enemy in order to secure one's sense of self. I do not claim here, as some scholars have, that the perception of the USSR as enemy was only a self-protecting illusion. It is rather that one can have real problems that overlap with, and are enhanced by, reality problems. (And as I suggested in chapter 9, similar syndromes were likely at play in Moscow).

In his *On the Genealogy of Morals*, Nietzsche analyzes the logic of the development of *ressentiment*. In *ressentiment*, one defines one's identity with reference to what one is *not*, a threat. One requires the continuing existence of an enemy. Should an external enemy disappear, he points out, maintaining one's identity will require that one find a substitute. In the realm of morality, Nietzsche argues that this *ressentiment* led to the Christian doctrine of original sin. We are here concerned not so much with morality as we are with politics. The Cold War was a godsend in that it provided an enemy. Politically, for the United States and to a considerable degree much of the "West," since the end of the Cold War the new enemy was found in "terrorism," first minimally but not inconsequentially from domestic experiences such as those described in chapter 10 but soon from the world at large. In the United States, an initial experience of terrorism had come from groups such as the Weather Underground and the Black Panthers; in Europe, it came from groups such as the Red Brigades in Germany. These groups, however, were repressed either through arrest and conviction or often, as with the Black Panthers, with execution.

With the end of the Cold War, America found itself preeminent and alone as a world power. To the degree that its conception of itself had come to be defined in great part as the negation of Soviet Communism, it lacked the dynamic that had informed it since the late 1940s. Arbatov's warning had a cutting edge to it. Just in time, as it were, the outside world provided a new enemy, often from groups that the United States had been instrumental in setting up in other contexts. Again: it is not that I doubt the actuality of terrorist acts. What I am concerned with is what has been made of them and what the fear of them does to our notions of citizenship. It was one thing to fight Nazi Germany—that enemy had a generally concrete reality. It was another to fight a "war on terrorism."[38] There is no possible to end to such a war because there is no way that the "enemy" will ever (be able to) surrender. (If one followed out Nietzsche's development of *ressentiment*, we have arrived at the invention of political equivalent to the doctrine of original sin—a continuing problem with a source about which one can do nothing.) Hence a country pursuing such an "enemy" will find it necessary more and more to institute domestic measures of control. I do not need to rehearse here what these are—anyone who has taken an airplane flight recently knows. And it is hard to formulate a coherent protest against these measures (cf. Steinbeck's farmer: "Well, who can I kill?") as the surveillance discipline is justified on the grounds that it is for our own good.

On the crude surface of it, terrorism should not seem to be something to worry about. Statistically, one is more likely to be killed by falling furniture than by terrorist attack; the economist-psychologist Daniel Kahneman notes that even in Israel, the number of terrorist casualties almost never equals the number killed in traffic accidents. The difference comes, as Kahneman says, in that terrorism gives "an extremely vivid image of death and damage."[39] We are dealing with the fear of a possibility, not a totally imaginary one but not one that has existence in a defined time and space. What are the effects of this fear? The most pernicious thing about the war on terrorism is that the

38. See Zerilli, "Truth and Politics."

39. See the discussion in Daniel Kahneman, *Thinking Fast, Thinking Slow* (New York: Farrer, Straus and Giroux, 2011).

perceived remedy (surveillance and control) simply enhances the basic aim of the terrorists, which is to destroy public space, thus any grounding for legitimacy, and thus the possibility of citizenship. It strikes me that the desired effect of contemporary terrorist attacks is to attempt to transform any public space into a space where one's only concern is for oneself. It is a negation of the possibility of public space and thus the negation of the possibility of a viable citizenship.

Let us look briefly at the most salient example of terrorism—the attack on the Twin Towers in New York City on September 11, 2001. The event has acquired a symbolic importance, an importance dimly but clearly reflecting the fascination for disaster movies (recent films portray apocalyptic threats from cybercatastrophe; from apparently unstoppable plagues; from nanobots taking over humans; from invasion from other planets; from collision with asteroids). It reflects the fact that America had, after 1989, acquired and consolidated unchallenged world power and that that acquisition of necessity generated the conditions for retaliation. To the degree that any system forms a hegemonic single network, it becomes overall vulnerable to an attack at a single point.[40] Think of the damage caused by the release of a single virus on the internet. Such an attack introduces a nonassimilable element in a system that depends on coordination.

In this matter, to associate what happened at 9/11 with an ideological or political motivation risks missing an important point. Hegemony itself generates this reaction. Hence we are not here in the realm of Samuel Huntington's "clash of civilizations"—the fact that those who flew the planes were Muslims is, in an important sense, irrelevant. The effect that the operation had—enhanced by the apparently unexpected collapse of both towers—is not consequent to the use of force. The response of those so attacked is with force—as the adventures in Iraq and Afghanistan and elsewhere show—and such a response proves only the importance of conventional means of power against the enemy that *that power has itself generated*.[41]

What enables the terrorists to throw a monkey wrench into the works, as it were? The answer is simple: it is lack of fear of death. In general, no one wants to die before his or her own time—or at least this is what Thomas Hobbes was

40. I am influenced here by Jean Baudrillard, *The Spirit of Terrorism* (London: Verso, 2003).

41. See the discussion in Stephen Holmes, "Al-Qaeda, September 11, 2001," in *Making Sense of Suicide Missions*, ed. Diego Gambetta (Oxford: Oxford University Press, 2006), 131–72.

at pains to persuade his fellow citizens at the beginning of our era, the one we call the Enlightenment. The terrorist, however, is in a different situation: he (occasionally she) knows that it is his time to die. It is the terrorist's lack of fear of death that accounts for our apparent fixation on these acts—as much with 9/11 as with self-immolation.[42]

What difference does that make? I take a short detour here for a discussion of the various kinds of spaces in which humans live and have expectations.[43] As humans, we live in different kinds of spaces, each having their criteria for admission and construction. These spaces may be shaped by human criteria or by nonhuman ones; they may be open or owned (hence entry requires the meeting of criteria). This gives us the following four kinds of space:

1. *Sacred*. This kind of space is divine and owned. In Medieval England, in addition to churches, there were at least twenty-two other sites recognized as sanctuaries.[44] Similarly, in the ancient Greek tragedy *Oedipus at Colonnus* by Sophocles, Antigone designates where she is at the beginning of the play as *hieros* (sacred). Such space is increasingly reduced and not likely to be observed in our world, although some cities and institutions have declared themselves sanctuaries in response to the Trump administration's ruling on immigrants. The future of such claims is in doubt.

2. *Common*. Common land is not established by humans and is open to all—its boundaries are not subject to human modification. We no longer have much common land in the West (although vestiges survive in New England towns and parts of the United Kingdom), and it is worth reflecting on that fact. The "Tragedy of the Commons" may be a loss with far more consequences than the making of the English working class.

3. *Private*. As framed here, *private* space is space that is owned and established by human beings; it simply means that one must meet certain criteria for entering such a space. The seventeenth-century philosopher John Locke's attempt to establish an understanding of property is in effect an attempt to set up the private. Private space remains strong and is, in fact,

42. On self-immolation and politically oriented suicide in general, see Andrew Poe, "Suicide Protest and the Human/Inhuman" (unpublished manuscript, 2018).

43. A full discussion would involve discussing each in terms of Kahneman's System One (fast thinking) and System Two (slow thinking); see Kahneman, *Thinking Fast, Thinking Slow*.

44. See T. B. Lambert, "The Evolution of Sanctuary in Medieval England," in *Legalism: Anthropology and History*, ed. Paul Dresch and Hannah Skoda (Oxford: Oxford University Press, 2012), 115–44.

encouraged by our society. The proliferation of social media encourages the privatization of space.

4. *Public*. Unlike the first three types, public space is significant in terms of citizenship: it is humanly constructed and open to all; it is not owned in the sense of being controlled. In ancient Greece, the public space was the agora. It was the space of politics and the necessary attendant thought. Public space is shaped by and shapes debate and discussion: it makes possible the achievement of what one might call *Einstimmung*—the "attunement" of one to another, what Stanley Cavell has called "acknowledgement."

My basic claim here is that in our world, sacred and common space are increasingly unavailable. We are left with private space, itself increasingly subject to surveillance, whether governmental or through the media, and public space. The destruction of public space, however, is, whether consciously or not, at the root of the ever-growing fixation on terrorism.

TERRORISM AND CITIZENSHIP

In chapter 10, I noted the rise of domestic turns toward terrorism, on the part of groups such as the Weather Underground and the Black Panthers. I could have also mentioned groups such as Aryan Nation, itself a kind of radicalization of a form of evangelical Christianity; the North Florida Survival Group; and many others—such groups are increasingly right-wing and fall into three categories (or a combination of them): racist; antifederalist (who hold that they are bound by no federal, state, or local laws—note here a parallel with what Bartlett calls the "crypto-anarchists"), and fundamentalist. Antiabortion groups are offshoots of the fundamentalists.

I shall consider domestic terrorism with international terrorism, such as it has arisen since the beginning of the twenty-first century, aimed mostly at Western countries. Much of this terrorism appears to have its origins in radical offshoots of Islam. I repeat, however, that this is a historical fact that is simply consequent to the contours of history. Were Islam the hegemonic power, it too would generate a terrorist countergroup. I shall consider it first and then turn to its relation to domestic terrorism and consider the problem that both pose for citizenship.

Contemporary terrorism, both domestic and international, has as its effect and its goal the destruction of public space, thus of political relations; it reinforces the privatization of all aspects of human life. It generates increasing demands for surveillance and state control. It is important to note that for these effects to take place, it is essential in contemporary terrorism that the terrorist be willing to die. One should not confuse contemporary terrorism with terror as used by a state, as in, for instance, revolutionary France, Nazi Germany, or the USSR.[45] Nor should it be confused with terrorism used by a group against a power in order to establish a state, as with the National Liberation Front (or FLN, for its name in French, Front de Libération Nationale) in Algeria, even when the target became no longer limited focused politically but simply on whomever: when the FLN started bombing cafés in Algeria, the victims were mostly white French people, along with a waiter or two. The French government responded with torture and surveillance, and the result was a stalemate in the use of the means of violence; the collapse of the legitimacy of the French Fourth Republic; the deus ex machina rescue of the country by Charles de Gaulle, who then betrayed those who had supported him and gave Algeria its independence; and a new French constitution concentrating power in the chief executive. Over time a consequence of the use of terror has always been the development and legitimation of vastly enhanced central executive power on the part of those who were the targets of terror. (DeGaulle had, however, enough of the republican Cincinnatus in him to resign some years later when a referendum went against his wishes.)

Comparisons of the present incidents of terrorism (a truck in Nice, guns in the Bataclan nightclub, planes on 9/11) to the FLN and such terrorisms are therefore potentially misleading. Contemporary terrorists do not have in mind the takeover of the French or American state, nor the establishment of a state of their own on that soil. These contemporary terrorist attacks are only

---

45. What do I mean by "contemporary terrorism"? It strikes me that contemporary terrorism (since the mid-2010s) is both different from what came before but also adds an element to the privatization I have just adduced. George Armstrong Kelly distinguishes four uses of the word *terror* that the French revolutionaries could look to when they forged their understanding of the term: "the terror of helplessness (dates from 14th century), the terror of eternity (before God, also old), the terror of arbitrary government (Montesquieu, Malesherbes), and the terror of aesthetic witness (Burke on the sublime). See George Armstrong Kelly, "Conceptual Sources of Terror," *Eighteenth-Century Studies* 14 (1980): 21. As a *state political tool*, terrorism was established by the French Revolution and designates the capacity to reshape thought processes and behavior. As Jean-Paul Marat said, "It is these mutinies which subdued the aristocratic faction of the Estates General, which the arms of philosophy and authority of monarchy failed to impress; it is they who were reminded, by terror, of the duty to reunite themselves with the patriotic party and together save the states." Jean-Paul Marat, *Oeuvres: L'ami du peuple* (1869; repr., Kessinger Publishing, 2010), 78, my translation.

comparable to the previous ones in that they do extend the logic of those attacked of being unable or only minimally able to identify their enemy.

There are two consequences to this despecification of the enemy: a privatization of public space through surveillance and an increase in perceived necessary executive power on the part of the target. Since September 11, 2001, more than $790 billion has been spent in the United States alone on homeland security. The video surveillance market in 2015 was estimated at $35.4 billion. New York City counts more than four thousand cameras in public places.[46] Accomplishment of this additional surveillance has required the passage of laws that essentially give the executive branch and its newly formed agencies power to implement policies, largely without recourse.

As had been the case with the various movements considered in chapter 10, all this counterterrorism effort required publicity, in the sense of being announced. (One cannot stand for more than fifteen minutes in a train station without being reminded to inform the authorities if one sees "something suspicious.") Publicity goes two ways. The initial tactics of Al Qaeda were to make use of media: message after message from leader Osama bin Laden circulated throughout various channels. At first, this use of messages was coupled with attacks that were generally on political elements of the enemy. Hence, there were the 1998 embassy bombings in Tanzania and Kenya, supposedly in retaliation for the extradition and probable torture of four members of the Egyptian Islamic Jihad. Additionally, one can cite the attack on the US destroyer *Cole*. But these were not mainly *symbolic enemies* but rather the instruments of power of a force that was deemed oppressive.[47]

There is in 9/11 an echo of an identified enemy (American commerce, the Pentagon) but it has become very faint. None of those organizing or carrying out 9/11 can possibly coherently have thought that success would be a victory over the United States, even in the way that the battle of Gettysburg was one for the Union. Nor was 9/11 obviously revenge in the way that the embassy bombings or the *Cole* attack were. A consequence of 9/11, however, was vastly to enhance domestic support for the claims of executive power: as many flags flew in New York as might have been seen in Nuremberg in 1935.[48] As one can-

46. See Keith Proctor, "The Great Surveillance Boom," *Fortune*, April 27, 2013, http://fortune.com/2013/04/26/the-great-surveillance-boom/.

47. It is worth noting that in 1989, bin Laden offered the services of his mujahideen to Saudi Arabia to defend it against the Iraqi invasion of Kuwait and was turned down in favor of American troops, which apparently resulted in the split of bin Laden from the Saudis. Eventually, however, this led to 9/11.

48. I owe this remark to Professor Babette Babich.

not know who or where the enemy is, universal surveillance becomes necessary. Given this increase in surveillance, it is unsurprising that a significant number of people have apparently concluded that 9/11 was a US government–organized effort.

Of the more than six hundred terrorist groups the research institute RAND identified in 2008, more than half have ceased to exist; of these, 43 percent moved to adopt nonviolent techniques, and 40 percent have been defeated. Less than 10 percent have declared victory. However, the same study indicates that it is those groups with a religious basis for their action that are less likely to disappear or fade.[49] They are, however, less likely to achieve their objectives. The fact that these (e.g., Brussels, San Bernardino, Fort Hood, Nice) are religion based is potentially misleading.

The basis for their persistence is in the end not essentially religious: it is rather the willingness to die.[50] When Thomas Hobbes set out in the middle of the seventeenth century to reform political organization in England, the most important thing he could do was to persuade people that they were in fact afraid of dying. (For Hobbes, even your soul died: there was nothing at all until the Second Coming, which was clearly not imminent[51].) What was clear to Hobbes was what he deemed the disastrous consequence of people *not* being afraid to die—a courage that the English civil war had clearly demonstrated. If I am willing to die over whether or not the blood and body of Jesus is transubstantially present in the Communion wafer, there is not much I will not do.

One has to take seriously the fact that most, if not nearly all, terrorists appear not to be afraid of dying. There are relatively few cases of someone deciding not to explode a suicide vest. I would include here the people who shoot down children at a school before taking their own lives—it seems clear that they expected to end their attack by killing themselves. It is worth noting that for such terrorism, much as in Jonathan Edwards, *your death is not yours.* Islam, in fact, gives little theological support to the willingness to die as an act of one's own will. Surah 3.145 of the Qur'an says that "Nor can a soul die except by Allah's leave. The term being fixed as by writing." At the Day of Final Judg-

49. See "RAND Database of Worldwide Terror Incidents," 1968–2009, Empirical Studies of Conflict, Princeton University, https://esoc.princeton.edu/files/rand-database -worldwide-terrorism-incidents.

50. See Roxanne Euben, "Understanding Suicide Terror," *Perspectives on Politics* 5, no. 1 (March 2007): 129–33; Roxanne Euben, "Killing (for) Politics: Jihad, Martyrdom and Political Action," *Political Theory* 30, no. 1 (February 2002): 4–35.

51. The reason for this Christian mortalism is that Protestantism cannot accept the in-between state of purgatory.

ment, God will raise all the dead and punish and reward accordingly. The difference with Edwards comes from the belief that after a martyr's death there will be eternal reward, whereas Edwards urged the recognition that one might very well be dropped into the fire. The theological grounding of the promise of salvation in Islam, however, is tenuous. There is apparently but one verse in the Qur'an indicating—and this not unequivocally—that those who die in jihad will go to paradise (Surah 4.9: "To those who believe and do deeds of righteousness hath Allah promised a great reward"). There is much promise of paradise, however, in the *hadith* ("traditions": the collection of sayings attributed to Muhammad but not part of the Qur'an). And the whole matter is complicated by the Qur'anic prohibition on suicide.[52] The title *shahid* (which usually means "witness") was until the twenty-first century given mostly to those who died in battle for Islam. There is only one passage (Surah 3.141) in the Qur'an where it means "martyr" (incidentally, the Greek *martyrus* means "witness"). And 9/11 was not a battle.

What this means is that to the degree that motivations for terrorism remain centered around the act of death, terrorists seek to destroy the hegemon symbolically rather than to accept it by remaining alive. I can think of two ways to approach this matter.

The first would be to say that in order to curb those inclined to terrorist violence, one could use a Hobbes or the equivalent of a Protestant Reformation to make people afraid of dying. This approach is not entirely silly, for the fear of death is a powerful motivator to civic peace. Hobbes needed to convince those who had died over the question of the physical presence of Christ in the Eucharist that instead they should have been more afraid of dying. The "General Confession" in the *Book of Common Prayer* calls on the Lord to deliver us "from the fear of violent death." It was to instill the *fear* of death in compensation for the unpredictability of an angry God, as we saw, that Edwards preached of the "Sinner in the Hand of an Angry God." This path, however, seems unlikely to materialize.

The other approach would be to recover as far as possible the importance of public space. Much about contemporary Western society makes this recovery difficult. Many suburbs differ from bidonvilles only by virtue of their lawns (often mowed by those who do not live there). The question here has to do

---

52. David Cook, "The Implications of 'Martyrdom Operations' for Contemporary Islam," *Journal of Religious Ethics* 32, no. 1 (2004): 129–51. Hence we do not quite feel toward suicides like 9/11 or self-immolation as we do toward standard anomic (Émile Durkheim's term) suicides. See Poe, "Suicide Protest."

with the relation between death and the destruction of public space. *Public space and thus the possibility of citizenship requires that one not be afraid of dying*, or rather that one hold public matters to be more important than private ones. Many often problematic consequences flow from the liberal bifurcation of the self into public and private. Machiavelli preferring the salvation of his city to that of his soul and such preferences have remained behind the sense that if you fought or served for your country, it became yours and you should acquire citizenship. Machiavelli's preference for militia over mercenaries comes from the fact that as the militia man fights so as not to die, so also is he in that same fight fighting for his patria. But in the present context, and not just in the West, resisting state supervision of space will require a relaxation of state control— *the state wants one to be afraid of dying,* and every time you walk through the security checkpoint at an airport, you are reminded of that and quietly prodded to be thankful to the state for keeping you safe. The media in fact enhance all of our fears.

A relaxation of state control and an enhancement of the willingness to die likely means a willingness to allow incidents of terrorist attacks, which would, in effect, place everyone in something like the position of those who practiced civil disobedience: the good that one pursues collectively entails risking oneself. The more we are afraid of being with each other in common enterprise, the more the terrorists and the state will have triumphed—which is not to say that they have won, for victory is not, in the end, their goal. But "we" will have lost. The more we are afraid of being with each other in common enterprise, or cannot see a way or reason to do so, the less important will be our citizenship. If, however, we overcome the fear of death, then, as James Baldwin wrote, "if one is continually surviving the worst that life can bring, one eventually ceases to be controlled by a fear of what life can bring."[53] Malcolm X had said much the same:

> I don't mean go out and get violent, but at the same time you should never be nonviolent unless you run into some nonviolence. I'm nonviolent with those who are nonviolent with me. But when you drop your violence on me, then you've made me go insane, and I'm not responsible for what I do. And that's the way every Negro should get. Any time you know you're within the law, within your legal rights, within your moral rights, in accord

53. James Baldwin, "Down at the Cross," in Baldwin, *Fire Next Time,* 343.

with justice, then die for what you believe in. But don't die alone. Let your dying be reciprocal. This is what is meant by equality.[54]

There is an echo here to John Winthrop's "Speech to the General Court": "This sacred liberty we must defend in all circumstances and if necessary risk our life for it."[55] And there is an echo of the end of the Declaration of Independence—*the signers pledged* "to each other *our Lives*, our Fortunes and our sacred Honor" (my emphasis).

Yet the problems facing an achievement of a strong and more individual sense of citizenship remain grave. As Ralph Ellison noted in an interview, "The nature of our society is that we are prevented from knowing who we are."[56] Nick Bromell, in his *The Time Is Always Now*, helpfully details four major impediments to such an achievement.[57] Each, however, has a reverse side.

The first is anger, which Bromell sees mostly as deriving directly from Nietzschean dynamics of *ressentiment*. Yet anger is also a correct response to oppression and soul blindness. Can it be channeled into a productive manifestation? The protagonist of Ellison's *Invisible Man*, when accidentally mistreated by a white man, turns on him in fury, ready to kill, until he realizes that the white man did not really *see him*. And this realization makes possible a form of democratic indignation that the rest of the novel shows us as developing. Quoting Baldwin again: "The rage of the dispossessed is personally fruitless, but it is absolutely inevitable." He goes on to say that only with difficulty can it at times be brought under the control of the intelligence and, more important, that in America whites have never felt this particular rage, and that thus the relations between the races are not reciprocal.[58]

A second albeit related and derivative problem derives from the increasing diversity of the American polity. Individual or even group insistence on diversity in the absence of a common set of values can feel and at times be threatening to those espousing other cultural values. Here the response cannot be to deny the importance of these differences by relegating them to a "private sphere." Utz McKnight has shown the limitations of the work of John Rawls

54. Malcolm X, "The Ballot or the Bullet," in *Malcom X Speaks* (repr., New York: Pathfinder, 1989), 34–35. I owe this citation to Bromell, *Time Is Always Now*.

55. Winthrop, "Speech to the General Court" (see chap. 2, n. 14).

56. Ralph Ellison, *Shadow and Act* (New York: Vintage, 1995), 177.

57. Bromell, *Time Is Always Now*, 5–12. I give his four categories, but most of the examples are mine.

58. Baldwin, "Stranger in the Village" (see chap. 5, n. 23).

in relation to race in that he [Rawls] essentially removes race from the public discourse of justice.[59] That differences exist and can be and often are the source of anger is a fact that one must not deny. Baldwin makes the point well: "People who shut their eyes to reality simply invite their own destruction, and anyone who insists on remaining in a state of innocence long after that innocence is dead turns himself into a monster."[60]

The third of the challenges noted by Bromell, he calls "globalization." An early version of something analogous was discussed in chapter 5 in relation to Northern working-class opposition to abolitionism, an opposition based on the grounds that blacks were coming to take their jobs away. And here we find a tension of America's sense of itself. The Declaration of Independence holds that all men are "created equal." Winthrop's sermon saw America (as it was then) as a "city on the hill," an exemplar to provoke or call out others. Theodore Roosevelt, in his exchange with William Jennings Bryan, saw no problem is extending his vision of America across the Pacific to the Philippines. The Iraq War was fought to install "democracy" in Iraq. The city on the hill cast itself as an exemplar, but not imperially; the Declaration was open to all who are of the "we" who "hold these truths to be self-evident." Theodore Roosevelt, however, and, among too many others including the proponents of the Iraq war, sought to impose Americanness on others as an offer that that could not be refused. Globalization raises the question of what can count as an exemplar for citizenship. One can only be a citizen of some polity—hence the exemplar will to a considerable extent be parochial. Lincoln had hoped that the carnage of the Civil War would stand as the touchstone for the importance of unity. He appears to have been at best only partially correct. Exemplary beings are able to make political events (say, the Vietnam War) part of a political education—but there is not much sign that this has happened.

The fourth impediment that Bromell adduces derives from the tendency by both the Left and the Right to assert a radical gulf between faith and politics. Liberals often assume that faith is or should be purely a private matter and all that is politically important is that it be kept that way by toleration. Indeed, Rawls, in *A Theory of Justice*, argued that the achievement of religious toleration was a prerequisite for the existence of just liberal society. Many evan-

59. Utz McKnight, *Political Liberalism and the Politics of Race* (Lund, Sweden: Lund University Press, 1996), chap. 1.

60. Baldwin, "Stranger in the Village," 129. Here "remaining in a state of innocence" means wanting differences not to be actual.

gelical Christians claim the same gulf from the other side, finding that their religious truths trump the Constitution and the rule of law.

Both of these positions (Rawls and the evangelicals) seem to me wrong, and wrong in particular about religious truth. Faith is not simply a matter of holding an absolute belief and asserting its superiority. Faith deals with the tension between actuality and the unachieved. Thus in Hebrews 11, we find (verses 1–3): "Now faith is the assurance of things hoped for, the evidence of things not seen. For by it the elders obtained a good report. Through faith we understand that the worlds were framed by the word of God, so things that are seen are not made of things that do appear."[61] Faith, in this understanding, is that which permits one to hold on to a picture of what one might be despite the reality of the actuality that one is not that ("things that are seen are not made of things that do appear"). This faith was, as Bromell notes, central to the ability of black Americans to hold on to a picture of full citizenship while living under the conditions of more or less disguised Jim Crow.[62] I am not here urging a return to the or a church, merely the importance of holding on to a picture of what America might be even in the throes of what it presently is. As Martin Luther King Jr. said in his last speech, "All we say to America, is be true to what you say on paper."[63]

AND NOW WHAT?

I began this book by referring to America as a project—always requiring one more step on the staircase on which Ralph Waldo Emerson told us we might

61. Heb. 11:1–3 (AV).

62. See, e.g., William E. Connolly, *Why I Am Not a Secularist* (Minneapolis: University of Minnesota Press, 2000). The position of some evangelicals is closer to the one I am advancing here that most nonevangelicals believe. See Tanya Luhrmann, *When God Talks Back: Understanding the American Evangelical Relationship with God* (New York: Vintage, 2012).

63. Martin Luther King Jr., "'I've Been to the Mountaintop': Address Delivered at Bishop Charles Mason Temple," April 3, 1968, Martin Luther King Jr. Research and Education Institute, Stanford University, https://kinginstitute.stanford.edu/king-papers /documents/ive-been-mountaintop-address-delivered-bishop-charles-mason-temple. This is the "I have a dream" speech. Several books have recently appeared on King. Most important in terms of political theory and thus the themes of this book is probably Tommie Shelby and Brandon Terry, eds., *The Shape a New World: Essays on the Political Philosophy of Martin Luther King, Jr.* (Cambridge, MA: Belknap Press of Harvard University Press, 2017).

find ourselves. This view means, first of all, that America will not exist until it has been discovered and founded. And there are several elements to this process. It is clear that those who arrived in 1630 as well as those who eventually fought the American Revolution had come to settle in a new world and found a new social order. It means, second, that, in the words of the Declaration of Independence, they intended that order to be one of collective and individual freedom where each might pursue "life, liberty and happiness," to which, as noted, the Founders mutually pledged their lives, their fortunes, and their sacred honor.[64] These virtues were to be pursued and realized in the new land. These virtues are in fact held to be constitutive of what finding and founding America would consist in. I do not ignore that many crimes were committed in misbegotten versions of this pursuit. And finally, it is clear from the anxiety portrayed in my citations, there is a concomitant realization that America has not yet been realized.

This last point is relevant today. We hear chants of "make America great again," of "America First." That America is God's plan on earth. That America is Eden or a new Israel, God's chosen land. We have heard this rhetoric so much that we appear to be unable either to ignore it or deal with it. Those who chant these phrases have a sense that something is amiss with America, as do I. Those who thus express themselves privilege, one might say, the aspects of their citizenship rather than what would be the experience of that citizenship.[65] Their rhetoric seeks to take over the words of the early would-be founders. Yet, one must say, those who voice those words now no longer seem to know what their meaning is, despite the rote appeal to "the intentions of the founders." Indeed, it may seem to many of us that those who rehearse the old words cannot— do not—actually mean what they say.[66] This book is an attempt to show what it would mean actually to mean—as many people did—these words: to be honest and responsible to them. In an important sense, the failure of American voices to take up the words and language offered to it by many of those considered in this book, as well as the almost willful evisceration of their thought's power, is part of this failure. These fail-

64. See the discussion of this passage in Allen, *Our Declaration* (see chap. 2, n. 34).

65. See analogous remarks in Andrew Poe, "Unrepresented Fanaticism" (unpublished manuscript, 2018).

66. I am not surprised to find similar thoughts in James Conant, "The Rediscovery of Greece and the Discovery of America," in *Reading Cavell*, ed. Alice Crary and Sanford Shieh (London: Routledge, 2006).

ing voices are, as Stanley Cavell put it, "trying again to buy and bully [their] way into heaven."[67]

In the introduction, I differentiated between the criteria for citizenship that are natural (such as being male, until the Nineteenth Amendment) and those that are acquired, that require some willful action on the part of the individual. Among these latter criteria were church membership, ownership of property or tools, and self-possession. Over the course of the developments traced in this book, the "natural" criteria have pretty much disappeared. It seems relatively clear that, despite the quarrels over immigration that befog our understanding these days, America is not going to return to positing natural criteria, beyond those of being born of American parents or naturalization (which has been made more difficult since 2016). Any recovery of public space under conditions as they stand in the late 2010s will of a necessity *require of each person some public gesture*, of which voting alone is an inadequate solution. In 1944, Franklin Roosevelt proposed some form of national service: say, for example, that the right to vote required from each American one to two years of public service in some remunerated capacity. Broadly considered, this would be a start. It need not be national—even if one thinks globally, one can only act locally. Maybe actual government could start it. Maybe.

As Robert Frost put it in "The Black Cottage":

> For, dear me, why abandon a belief
> Merely because it ceases to be true.
> Cling to it long enough, and not a doubt
> It will turn true again, for so it goes.
> Most of the change we think we see in life
> Is due to truths being in and out of favour.[68]

That is as hopeful as I can get.

67. Stanley Cavell, *The Senses of Walden*, expanded ed. (Chicago: University of Chicago Press, 1992), 58.

68. Robert Frost, "The Black Cottage," in *Collected Poetry, Prose and Plays* (New York: Library of America, 1995), 61.

INDEX

316   INDEX

Babich, Babette, 293n16, 293n18, 305n48
Bailyn, Bernard, 6, 46n24, 56, 56n46
Baldwin, James, 38, 78, 126, 126n6, 137, 138, 138n26, 271, 297; do not fear death, 308, 309, 310
Balkin, Jack M., and Sanford Levinson, 82n45, 83, 83n49
Bannon, Steven, 295
Barber, Benjamin R., 160n8, 278
Barker, Deanna, 17n7
Barlett, Jamie, 297
Baudrillard, Jean, 301n40
Baum, L. Frank, The Wonderful Wizard of Oz, 179
Beatles, 289
Beecher, Henry Ward, 121-22
Begriffsgeschichte, 12
Bell, Daniel, The End of Ideology, 283
Bellamy, Edward, 155
Berlin, Isaiah, 21
Bernasconi, Robert, 16n4
Berners-Lee, Tim, 290n6
Bernstein, Iver, 125n4
Bernstein, Leonard. See Life magazine, "50 Dupes and Fellow Travelers"
Bicha, Karel Denis, 161n13
big data, 297
bin Laden, Osama, 305
Blackburn, Robin, 131n12
blacklists in 1940s, 223-25
Black Panther Party, 270; Black Power and Cornell University event, 283
blacks, 49, 59; letter to Andrew Johnson, 128-31; newly freed, 128-30; recruitment into Union Army, 120, 125-26. See also Baldwin, James; Douglass, Frederick; Dubois, W. E. B.; Freedman's Bureau (Edisto Island); Hughes, Langston
Blaker, J. R., 253n50
"Bleeding Kansas," 75, 85
Bohlen, C. E., 245n29
bonfire of the vanities, 66

Borders, Karl, 211n9
Borodin (Grusenberg), Mikhail, 195, 209
boycott (civil rights), Alabama, 269
Braudy, Susan, 282n41
Brecher, Jeremy, 195n36, 200n47
Brinkley, Alan, 234n13
Bromell, Nick, 133n16, 165n20, 270n14, 270n15, 309-11
Brook Farm, 96
Browder, Earl, 216-23; becomes general secretary, 217; seeks to Americanize the Communist Party, 217-19. See also Duclos, Jacques (letter)
Brown, John, 89. See also abolitionism; Emerson, Ralph Waldo
Brown v. Board of Education, 225, 266, 267
Bryan, William Jennings, 6, 156, 164, 167-73; "Cross of Gold," 167-70 (see also Scopes trial); and eugenics, 172; opposed to imperialism, 178, 183; to Roosevelt on expansion, 186, 205, 310; and science, 171-82; and white race, 172
Bryant, Louise, 200
Buell, Lawrence, 89
Bureau of Investigation, 201
Burnham, F. W., 211n9
Butler Act, 155. See also Scopes trial
Byrnes, Jimmy, "Restatement of Policy," 251

Calhoun, John C., 78-79, 84, 97
Califano, Joseph, 288n1
Calvin, John, 20, 33
Campanella, Richard, 106n12
Cantwell, Robert, 236
capitalism, and citizenship, 122
Carnegie, Andrew, 139, 173; opposed to imperialism, 178, 183
Caro, Robert, 279, 285
Carp, Benjamin L., 45n22
Carter, Jimmy, 25